Road Trips, Broken Hearts & Other Debris of Growing Up

Road Trips, Broken Hearts & Other Debris of Growing Up

Melissa Schad

2007

Road Trips, Broken Hearts &
Other Debris of Growing Up

TABLE OF CONTENTS

Salt in the Wounds of Love. *1*

Aargh Matey! *9*

A Ranger in a Bear Suit. *17*

Arizona Rob *25*

Singing the Blues *37*

The Scam-o-Rama of Canada *53*

The Hitcher. *61*

3 States in 3 Days *71*

Uncle Upchuck. *81*

Vegas Goes Awry. *91*

Pigs in the Trailer Park *99*

Road Sodas *115*

The Poseidon Adventure. *123*

Trapped on the Freedom Trail *131*

A Moose Intervenes *145*

The Princess Bride *155*

He Never Gave the Signal. *167*

A Double Double and a Strawberry Shake. *175*

What the Hell is the Sugar Bowl? *185*

The Boston Massacre Wedding *203*

Don't Bother Me, I'm Crabby *215*

You Can't Go Home Again *223*

Too Po to Travel? Use Your Credit Card! *233*

Everything Happens at Irish Bank *251*

They Can Eat at Fuddrucker's. *261*

Honeymooning in Muumuus *277*

Jack Daniel's Distillery: A House of Worship. *289*

Someone Else's Naked Husband. *297*

Canada with the Jordan Bear *307*

A Wicked Good Time *315*

The Ruler *327*

Wild Boars *343*

Nowhere to Eat at Pike's Market *359*
Brendan is Your Friendan to the Endan *367*
The Goat Tent *385*
The Gang's All Here *397*

If you've ever

...fallen in love eleventy million times...
...used Magic 8 ball to plot your course of action
...watched your best friend kiss your crush
...hooked up on Spring Break, ideally in Palm Springs or Mexico
...prayed that your parents wouldn't find out about 90% of your life
...stayed in a sketchy motel, a rickety tent, or a creepy B & B
...dated a co-worker (or so you thought)
...had a camp romance
...had your best friend move away for college
...broken an engagement in the eleventh hour
...been cheated on...constantly
...moved away from your hometown or home state
...thrown up or undressed publicly while drunk
...been a little bitter at a friend's wedding
...gained 10 pounds on a cruise...in one week
...gone on a really fun (or really terrible) road trip
...met the love of your life online
...kept friends for 10, 15, 20, or 25-plus years

You're welcome to pull up the barstool next to me and tell me your story. Here's mine.

This book is dedicated to everyone who's in it-

Thank you all so much for all the fun times and fiascos!

Most especially for Matthew, with all my love

Salt in the Wounds of Love

Death Valley, CA
April 1983

I had two hopes for my class trip: Scott Steinberg, my fourth-grade crush (and one of two Jewish boys in my class), would fall madly in love with me, and my best friend Courtney and I would get assigned to the same tent. When you're 10 years old, these are life-death scenarios. Neither of these things happened. In fact, the best I can say is I didn't get a third-degree sunburn.

Suggested Soundtrack: *"Rock the Casbah"-The Clash, "Mickey"-Toni Basil, "Eye of the Tiger"-Survivor, "Come On Eileen"-Dexie's Midnight Runners, "Don't Stop Believin'"-Journey, listened to on the bus radio*

- Our 5th grade class has a trip to Death Valley for four days, with a bunch of 6th graders as "chaperones" — Courtney and I are so excited! We cross our fingers we'll get a tent together! We both wear glasses, so we know all about groping around blind in the mornings, and can help each other out.

- When we see the tent assignments, our hopes for the trip are dashed. "Separated, as usual," I groan. Courtney flips her long blond braids (that I'd give anything to have instead of my dark curly hair), remarking, "Well, at least you got a good tent. My people are all weird."

- Me, Kat, Ginny, and Christine end up in a four-person tent, immediately naming our tent The Pink Ladies, even though I look horrible in pink. Currently, our obsession with *Grease* knows no bounds. Courtney gets placed in a tent with Betsy and Keiko. "This tent won't stay up!" she calls to our teachers during our tent-raising practice session, but none of them care.

- The bus ride to Death Valley involves a lot of singing to pass the time. Only now, as an adult, do I realize we sang Bible camp songs and we wouldn't be permitted to sing them on a public school trip at this point.

- Our class arrives in Death Valley in basically a tornado, and we all have to pitch our own tents. Fifth grade girls from Orange County, CA, may be the worst candidates for this job in America. All the parts look the same and we give up immediately. "We practiced this, girls," Mr. Sorenson, our math teacher rebukes, helping us put up our tent. Ten years later, I repay this favor by making out on his living room couch with his oldest son.

- The first day of the trip, we head for a swimming pool. The scene goes into slow motion as our classmate, Will, appears dressed in a **one piece girls**' bathing suit.

- He realizes One of These Kids is Not Like the Others, turns and lumbers back to his tent, not to re-emerge for the rest of the trip. He may have died of embarrassment in there. The other boys, overwhelmed by the enormity of his mistake, are too awed by the horror to even make fun of him—yet.

- The teachers vote Will's mother The Worst Mother Ever. How could she have let this happen? I feel bad for him, and Courtney agrees, "He may as well change schools now. The stigma will follow him forever." I wish I could befriend him out of pity, but I'm already friends with this one weird girl and I don't think I can take on another case.

- Everyone (except this Vietnamese kid, Lu, and I) gets enormously sunburned at the pool that day. The camp reeks of Noxzema that night as the winds pick up. All the girls in my tent are bright pink and can barely move. Courtney's feet are blistered into sandal patterns, but in her stoic Dutch way, she barely complains.

- We trek off to Old Town Death Valley the next day. I blow all my money on sticks of molasses candy, like Laura ate in *Little House on the Prairie*. It tastes <u>sick</u>. We are totally disillusioned with the simple life offered on the Prairie. Courtney buys "fool's gold" rocks, thinking they're real, but they're not.

- Getting off the bus to go to Devil's Golf Course, I fall down the steps, tear my hands and knees open, and have to wear gauze pads on them the rest of the trip. The worst part: not that my wounds might be infected and I might die out here, but that Scott Steinberg exited right behind me, and he <u>laughed</u>.

- He will never love me back at this rate. Especially not with my bad hair. My mom, who worked as a hairdresser in the olden days, still thinks her license is valid and insists on cutting my hair. Mom leaves my sister Rachel's gorgeous hair alone, so it's down to her waist and perfect. I'm so jealous as I run my bloody hands through my fluffy Afro.

- We learn Devil's Golf Course is a salt crust over a twenty-foot deep pool of mud, and under no circumstances are we to disturb the crust and sink into the mud to our doom. Especially now that I've probably cracked the crust open when I landed on it, **literally** driving salt into the wounds. Our new sneakers are all muddy and salty when we return to the bus. The driver, horrified he has to scrape dried salty mud off the floors of the bus, hates us and our muddy shoes and speeds back to our campsite.

- Commotion at 5 a.m. in a boys' tent: Mitch Austin discovered a scorpion nestled in his sleeping bag. Pandemonium spreads, and no one will get in another sleeping bag. The "chaperones" begin sleeping on the bus.

- Ms. Hillary, our English teacher, captures the scorpion in a Wonder Bread bag and releases it into a riverbed nearby. Courtney and I can't sleep for fear the scorpion has some sort of homing device and will scamper straight back to our campsite and kill us both. No one's fears are assuaged when Peter Ono points out that, "He probably wasn't the only scorpion in this area, you know."

- Since we're all awake, we decide to eat breakfast. Our prep list required metal cups and plates, procured from local camping stores. They make all our food taste like aluminum. Not that oatmeal already doesn't taste like throw-up. Would it have been so difficult to just bring fifty boxes of Trix cereal, Ms. Hillary?

- The windstorm returns. "Do not leave your tents!" Mr. Sorenson booms, "The tents will blow away without your bodies as ballast." A shriek escapes Mrs. Thornton. "The food is blowing away!" A mixed blessing, as the food was gross, but now this may turn into a Death Valley Donner Party trip!

- We eventually take down our tents, but leave our duffels in them to hold them down, as we search the nearby area for ballast rocks. None of us can get into our duffel bags now as they are trapped inside the deflated little tents. I'd love to change into a cuter outfit; Scott Steinberg is near our tent!

- He yells, "Hey! Where are we sleeping if all the tents are down?" Answer: the dirt ground, where I am terrified of being covered in a posse of scorpions. No one can breathe, since we have to keep our heads in our sleeping bags to stay out of the wind, dirt and pebbles blowing around.

- The entire campground has been deserted, except for us, due to the windstorm, which should give our teachers a clue: Leave now! The teachers worriedly discuss when the bus will return. Courtney whispers that since the bus driver hates us and our muddy shoes, he probably won't come back, ever.

- The Pink Lady tent (plus Courtney) has nothing to do but sit in our deflated tent and play Magic 8 ball, getting so desperate to entertain ourselves that we'll even ask it about grades and other lame things like that. "Will Scott Steinberg will ever like me?" I ask it nervously. I shake the window, where "Not likely," appears instantly. Magic 8 ball has psychic powers. It will not be until the year after we graduate high school that Scott will try to kiss me.

- Maybe it takes him that long to forget about my awkward fall? And the hideous granny glasses I have to wear "because that's what the insurance covers." Will the insurance cover my emotional scars, Mom and Dad? My therapy???

- The next day, dirty but trapped, we are carted off to Bad Water, a leech pond. We park next to a dead mule with a sign on it reading, "This mule tried to drink the water! Don't do that, trailhands! It's Bad Water!" Betsy starts crying until she finds out the mule isn't real. Stupid bimbo. The sign also informs us we're in the lowest point below sea level on earth. Kat asks our science teacher, Mrs. Thornton, "If we're below the sea, how come we're not underwater?" Perhaps all blondes really *are* stupid. In her defense, all we've done this year in science involved breeding rats, which occasionally escape, so none of us understand sea level. I can't even go near the rat breeding area, thanks to my mother threatening me with "rabies shots...*in your stomach.*"

- The nearby thermometer reads 121 degrees, and also has a sign, this one letting us know that "You are standing in the 2nd hottest spot on earth!" Jeff Staricynski asks, "Is this the second hottest because hell is hottest, Mrs. Thornton?" Did Courtney and I accidentally get on the short bus here? We're supposed to be in a GATE class (Gifted and Talented Education, thank you very much), but despite our supposed intellectual superiority everyone but us seems a little slow. Oh, and Peter Ono and Scott Steinberg, of course.

- We all drink aluminum flavored water from our canteens, except Kat, who bought one of those water pouches in Old Ghost Town. Her water tastes like leather. Keiko asks Courtney to share her water after Keiko's canteen springs a leak. Covering the top of her canteen, Courtney warns her, "It's survival of the fittest, Keiko! You're dead!" Mrs. Thornton applauds her knowledge of science but looks aghast at her selfish attitude. Courtney, an only child, has never had to share, nor do her parents encourage her to do so. Courtney's mom takes inventory of her clothes and accessories regularly to dissuade Courtney from borrowing things, so you see where she gets it. Her mom also eats all the Halloween candy herself and then turns off the porch light at 6 p.m., disappointing hundreds of trick-or-treaters every year.

- Next stop: giant crater hike. I go on the hike so I can stay with Scott Steinberg's group. Courtney stays on the bus, possibly stuck to the vinyl seats. She eats Red Hots and Lemon Heads with Ginny and Christine, which make them all terribly thirsty.

- Later that night, Magic 8 ball gives Courtney some hope for Dan Wolf ("Try again later") but keeps telling me "Not Likely" and "No Way" in my vain quest for Scott. Sigh. I am the ugly friend. Nothing good will happen to me until I get rid of the glasses, grow waist-length blond hair, and find my mom's tweezers to take care of the threat of a monobrow once and for all! My mom doesn't care that I inherited my dad's Yeti gene, and refuses to let me shave, wax, or Nair any part of my body. She claims, "It will all grow back thicker," as though I may eventually end up with a full pelt, but for the glorious hair-free meantime, it seems worth it.

- The last day of our trip we trek off to Scotty's Castle, and as the food all blew away, we have lunch in the castle café, Scotty's Smorgasbord. Kids who were stupid enough to eat tuna or bologna in the desert begin throwing up left and right. Those of us who aren't vomiting can tour the castle with Mr. Sorenson. Scotty's Castle smells like lemon Pledge and was apparently built as part of a gold mine scam, according to the little signs Ms. Hillary reads aloud to us.

- Mitch Austin wants to know if it's ok to lie to people to get money from them, like Scotty did, as he seems heroic and has a Castle. Mr. Sorenson answers squarely on the side of ethics: "Absolutely not! You should NOT lie to people to swindle them, Mitch. Only bad people do that." They trail off, Mitch whining, "But I want my own castle, too..." as we troop back to the bus to go home.

- The bus doesn't have a bathroom, and someone gets diarrhea, tacking three extra hours onto the trip home for frequent stops. "Why did they eat tuna?" Peter Ono mutters angrily. Two hours into the ride, one of the buses breaks down. Three buses of kids have to be crammed onto two buses, so we have to sit three or four to a seat. Courtney tries to spread out on our seat, but Keiko jams herself in anyway. We are so sweaty we stick to our seatmates, and are thrown about like eggs in a carton due to a lack of seatbelt laws.

- My parents come to pick us up. My mom wants to know if there were any showers there, but then looks closely and ascertains there weren't. I can see Mom eyeing Courtney on the drive to her house, hoping her cracked and sunburned skin won't peel on the car seats, leaving remains behind like a molting anaconda.

- What a great educational experience this trip was! What I learned:
  - Eating bologna and tuna in the desert: dumb idea
  - People with money and castles are thieves
  - Molasses candy tastes gross, Laura Ingalls!
  - I am not the pretty sister, or the pretty friend, and I am doomed a series of embarrassing moments masquerading as a life

- Not as embarrassing as Will and his one-piece bathing suit, though. Nothing could be that bad...could it?

Aargh Matey!

Dana Point, CA
March 1985

Our 7th grade class has an overnight on the Brig Pilgrim, an authentic ship anchored in Dana Point Harbor. The point of this trip: to show us how spoiled rotten we all are, or how horrid the lives of sailors were in the last century. I just want to hang around with my friends and get Scott Steinberg to ask me to go steady. Big goals for a 12 year old.

Suggested Soundtrack: *Disneyland's Pirates of the Caribbean soundtrack*

- For our 7th grade trip, we're spending the night on the Brig Pilgrim, in Dana Point Harbor. "Do our teachers Rock Scissors Paper for our destinations?" I wonder aloud, cracking Courtney up.

- To prepare, we must actually read Richard Henry Dana's *Two Years Before the Mast*, the dullest of all required reading books. I love reading, but even I can't get interested in this horrid book. "It is so very, incredibly boring," Courtney moans. She cheats off me during our daily pop quizzes on the book. Sample quiz question: "Which sailor found the cow hide in Chapter 29?"

- We are arbitrarily sorted into "crews," all of whom will have various responsibilities. Our teachers rarely take our social preferences into account, and I lose interest in the boatswain's crew when I discover Scott Steinberg wasn't assigned to it. Courtney's disappointed as well: they assigned Dan Wolf to the galley crew with Keiko. "Why do I have to be stuck on your crew?" she whines to me.

- Scott Steinberg will be on the hide gathering crew with Jonathan, my new best friend (besides Courtney) this year. Jonathan's funny and easy to talk to, but can get neurotic over odd things. "I would prefer to hold it all day than use the school bathrooms," he shudders.

- Our bus arrives in Dana Point and we board the ship, sorry, "brig." None of the crew even has a peg leg, a parrot, or an eye patch. Courtney whispers, "I thought they'd be cute sailors, like the ones that work at the Pirates of the Caribbean ride at Disneyland. Where'd they get these ones?"

- The captain berates the entire group of us for not dressing like sailors, and shouts, "Just what on earth are you wearing?" Jeans and t-shirts mostly, except for Bobby MacAfee. He's wearing chinos and a striped navy long-sleeve T-shirt and looks slightly nautical. He gets praised as a model sailor. I hate him; he pushed me off the fort in 4th grade and kicked a soccer ball in Courtney's face.

- Our sleeping bags are also inspected for "contraband." A big box of Fiddle Faddle falls out of a bag and the crew goes silent. The bag's owner, Agatha Rich, starts crying; she will be punished later. The snacks are taken back to shore on a motorboat. We are so incredibly doomed. I hate Agatha, so I'm glad she's the one who got in trouble. But sadly, I think Scott likes her.

- Jonathan has a tiny package of Sweet Tarts in his pocket. He shoves the entire package into his mouth, and sidles up to the railing to drop the wrapper overboard. He sulks that his Gap outfit did not elicit the captain's praise. "Bobby can barely match his clothes! His belt and shoes don't even go!" Jonathan argues.

- Mr. Sorenson cautions, "Now this isn't some Pirates of the Caribbean ride, kids. You actually have to work here." Why? Aren't we paying for this?

- The hide gatherer crew takes off in a leaky rowboat to find cow hides the crew stashed along the coastline. I hear Betsy ask a crewmember, "They aren't real animal skins, are they?" He responds with a scornful, toothless laugh. Jonathan and Scott both suck at rowing. I can't believe how silly they look. What is the point of P.E. every day if it doesn't help in real life?

- The galley crew goes off to make our food, Keiko already bossing them. Gary Whaler mouths off to a crewmember. His punishment: eat a *whole raw onion.* Can they really do this to us? Gary starts crying, and the captain laughs, har-har, assuring him, "Well, man, now you won't get scurvy at least!" Keiko moans, "We needed that onion for the stew! Now it's ruined!"

- Boatswains (pronounced bo-sun in some sailor language) do nothing but go up among the rigging in an uncomfortable little wooden swing, I guess to check knots or sails or something. I concentrate on not falling off the swing, thirty feet above the deck, with no net or other safety precautions.

- I want to tell the crew guy that Mom doesn't even let me stand on a chair to get something off the top of the refrigerator, like the cookie tin, because, "You want to fall and kill yourself?" He'll just laugh at me. I wonder if my mother will sense danger and come fetch me. But she doesn't drive the freeway, so she's not a possible rescuer. Suddenly I'm bitter that her lifelong warnings have made me a paranoid and tentative person.

  - I have food guilt issues because she and my grandmother would say things like, "Oh, you haven't finished your eggs yet? (Sigh). The chickens will be *very* sad to hear that." The cow was also very sad if you didn't drink all your milk. Then my mother would cock her head, and say breathlessly, "You hear that? That sad mooing? You don't hear the cow crying?" Then she and my grandmother would pretend-cry, and I would end up cleaning my plate out of guilt, possibly crying myself.

- Every time my father gets home late from work, Mom tells him, "I thought you were dead! I was sure you had been in a horrible accident and were dead on the road." He always points out there's always traffic so she should assume he'll be late, but I learn early that late=dead.

- I also want to ask them what I'm supposed to be checking up here, as the brig doesn't actually **sail** anywhere, so what does it matter if the knots are a little loose? But they will surely keelhaul me.

- Mr. Coleman and the Captain enjoy torturing whoever sits in the swing by telling the crew to pull them this way and that, trying to hit a mark. The mark Courtney hits while in the swing is ON THE RAILING, and she fears we'll dump her into the harbor. The harbor water will turn her blond hair green, and then she might as well be dead. Dan Wolf definitely won't like her with green hair.

- We also get to polish brass, with some stinky ointment that ruins my nail polish. The brass, already pretty shiny, doesn't seem to need it. Plus, from what we read in the boring book, the sailors themselves don't actually *bathe*, so their concern for brass cleanliness makes no sense. Finally, the hide gatherers return with four or five hides. Betsy cries because yes, they are real cowhides. FYI, they smell rank. Jonathan calls them all Bessie, as in: "Bessie better not have fleas."

- The galley crew, looking harried, serves our dinner into our little tin mess kits from Death Valley. They taint our food with a tinny metallic aftertaste. This may be a blessing in disguise, as it appears that we are eating vomit for dinner. Later in life, when I throw up from drinking, I remember the Brig Pilgrim.

- I look at my vomit stew disbelievingly. Watery flour and potato chunks and no onion (Gary ate it) and a gob of uncooked dough masquerading as a dumpling float aimlessly across our tin bowls. We later find out our teachers are dining with the captain and officers and eating roast chicken while we freeze our butts off on deck eating vomit. Oh, and delicious water. In a tin cup. How much are we paying again?

- The crew sings some sea shanty songs after dinner, most of which revolve around drinking, drowning, torturing other crew members by keelhauling them, and leaving women at home to rot for years while they gallivant around in ports'o'call. We are invited to make up choruses to the shanty, "What shall we do with a drunken sailor?" Bobby MacAfee suggests, "Shave his belly with a rusty razor!" Now everyone sings, "Shave his belly with a rusty ra-zor early in the mor-ning!" Trust Bobby to come up with a violent option.

- The Fiddle Faddle infractioner, Agatha Rich, merits the punishment of being locked in a small closet the entire time we sing shanties. Yes!

- We sleep "below decks." Sleeping options: wooden floor or benches for two people to sleep head to foot. The Bessie hides are stretched on the benches, presumably acting as blankets. Also, the cushions on these benches look very familiar (stolen from the local Bob's Big Boy). They are red plastic, with rips and sticky sections. I get one of the benches, thanks to Peter Ono, our boatswain master, and feel very lucky, until I notice the hides are full of fleas. Oh my God, I'm covered in bites! It proves impossible to sleep with fleabites, hides that smell like a backed-up toilet, and Gary Whaler, who wafts the stench of onions all through "below decks."

- Jonathan flips out. "I want my own hammock, like in the movies." I didn't even think of that, but what an improvement that would be! We can't sleep, so we just whisper and complain to each other most of the night. Jonathan's main complaints are that other people are touching him, breathing on him, breathing *near* him, he's cold, he can't sleep in his clothes, his new sweater from The Gap might be getting dirty, and dinner tasted like ass. His mother, Marie, will get an earful tomorrow for sending him on this trip.

- Scott sleeps fitfully clear across the deck, so there's no chance of him accidentally brushing up against me. What is the point of life? Jonathan snorts as he sees me gazing wistfully at Scott. "Dream on," he remarks cruelly, rolling over.

- Our crew has the 4 a.m. "watch" and we hang around on deck in the freezing cold sea air, looking at nothing. We log a teenage couple making out in a car at 4:32 a.m. The windows are all fogged up and we peer avidly, trying to see what they're doing. I'm especially curious, as I've never been kissed. Do you just instinctively know what to do when it happens? If it *ever* happens, in my case.

- Suddenly, we hear a churning, gurgling sound at 5 a.m. About ten feet from the brig, something rises up out of the water like the Great Pumpkin! I quickly log, "5:01 a.m.— Sea monster rears ugly head." I wonder if the captain even reads these. I bet not, but I still make an effort to entertain him. "It's just the anchor," Peter calls. But the legend spreads anyway. I refuse to alter the log entry. "The captain probably doesn't read them anyway."

- We push and shove each other to get off the boat in the morning. My parents have never seen me so ravaged by a school trip: the sleep deprivation, the fleabites, and to my mother's horror, the terrible food. I describe the vomit stew vividly and she retorts, "I told you to bring snacks! I told you!" Then I reveal the fate of Agatha Rich. "A closet? They really locked her up?" Dad asks incredulously.

• What a waste of my time. There was no gazing over the railing into the starlight with Scott, no spooning together for warmth with Jonathan (my backup crush). Sometimes anticipating turns out better than the reality. My 7th grade trip was crap, but there's always Yosemite next year! It's got to be better than having your belly shaved with a rusty razor, doesn't it?

A Ranger in a Bear Suit

Yosemite, CA
April 1986

We spend a significant amount of time before our Yosemite trip learning about conservation, pollution, and the genius of John Muir. We just want to get out of school for a week and possibly kiss in the cabins. Once we get there, the glorious beauty of the park overwhelms us, until we figure out how hard hiking can be.

Suggested Soundtrack: *Flashdance soundtrack, Pretty in Pink soundtrack, Depeche Mode's Black Celebration*

- My parents are unenthusiastic about getting up at 5 a.m. to take me to school for the 6 a.m. bus (which won't actually leave till 8 a.m.). My solution? Let me spend the night at Courtney's and her parents can drive us! Mom's solution: We'll spend the night "as a family" in our motorhome in the school parking lot so everyone will be "fresh and rested."

- I argue they can save the money on the trip, as I will <u>die of embarrassment</u> if I have to emerge from a motorhome in front of everyone (but most specifically, Scott Steinberg, Brian McCarran or Jonathan). As usual, they could care less if I die of embarrassment. It turns out embarrassment is not fatal after all, as Will found out in 5th grade after The Girls' Swimsuit Incident of Death Valley.

- I board the bus with a smaller but cuter backpack than everyone else. My mother reminds me I could have taken my Snoopy backpack from 4th grade, but no, I had to have the "ritzy schnitzy" new backpack, which barely holds anything.

- On the bus ride, Courtney and I listen to the soundtrack to *Flashdance* over and over and over. We're not clear on some of the concepts, but we love the idea of being professional dancers even though we're clumsy as hippos. Jonathan sits behind us and listens to Depeche Mode tapes on his Walkman, occasionally singing a line aloud and off-key.

- Keiko, Betsy, Courtney and I get our own cabin, and fantasize about the boys we'd like to kiss in our cabin. Courtney's father, Pete, signed up as a chaperone on our trip, so a private cabin will do us no good. He'll probably lurk around the whole time watching us. Jonathan, instead of the private cabin he longs for, ends up with Peter Ono and Brian McCarran, my 3rd backup crush. I pressure Jonathan to "find out if he likes me."

- The first day, Courtney, Jonathan and I are scheduled for the hike to the top of Eagle Peak. Courtney and I both agree Jonathan's our backup crush, so we're pleased to have him along on our hike. Mr. Coleman, our social studies teacher, gives a speech about this hike, describing it as "grueling," "almost entirely switchbacks," and "very, very steep." Courtney and I smile knowingly at each other, as we have been riding our bikes one mile each day (four times around the block) to get in shape for hiking.

- We start up the hill, and immediately our quads begin burning like mad. "This hill seems steep," I mention, wondering if I'm just very weak. Courtney can't talk; she's gasping for air already. My leg feels like the muscles might snap and roll up like a window shade if I continue to hike. How much farther could it be? Our plans of chatting the whole way up are foiled, as Courtney, who has asthma, can only wheeze and cough. She sounds consumptive.

- Jonathan complains, "Oww, my butt hurts. A lot." He begins bitterly complaining about the complete lack of physical benefits of P.E. since he can't even walk up a hill. Courtney wheezes, "Well, if you didn't take P.E., you'd probably be even more out of shape." Courtney, always one for uncomfortable truths, ignores his scowl. "I'm not out of shape for home," he points out.

- I'm suddenly occupied with my own problem: I'm pretty sure my period just (unexpectedly) started. I have an entire roll of toilet paper taking up 90% of the space in my tiny backpack, so I head off into the trees to improvise. My favorite turquoise and hot pink shorts, the ones with the matching strapless bustier top, may be ruined. (My mother: "You have to be more careful with your things! I don't spend all this money for you to just ruin things, you know.") It turns out the bustier top, which I'm also wearing, is **not** the ideal hiking ensemble. It chafes unmercifully, and I may be bleeding up top, too.

- Our English teacher, <u>Mrs.</u> Coleman, points out the Yosemite chapel in the valley floor where she and Mr. Coleman tied the knot last summer. Courtney asks hopefully, "Is the chapel air conditioned?" Jonathan whispers, "Eww, I bet they have sex." He shudders occasionally as if he's still picturing our teachers having sex. Admittedly, this would not be a pretty sight.

- Keiko sets off into the woods to take a "View Break" (bathroom stop), only to discover she didn't go far enough, and all the hikers in our group can see her bare bottom. Someone takes a picture and she falls over into the dirt. Mrs. Coleman has to step in to block the paparazzi.

- Courtney and I find that our biking has not produced the tip-top physical condition required for this hike. I hope a fire pole appears somewhere so we can slide back down to the bottom and escape. Agatha Rich asks Mr. Coleman if there's an escalator or a towrope, which makes us feel better, since she's on the track team. He stares at her for a moment, and then shakes his head no. We are literally trapped on a death march.

- Nearing the top of Eagle Peak, we discover there are still patches of snow, and the air temperature drops fifteen degrees. This does nothing to improve the chafing situation in my bustier. "I'm pretty sure my boobs are bleeding," I whisper desperately to Courtney. "At least you have boobs," she snaps mercilessly. Yes, along with the Yeti gene, I got the Big Boob gene too. It's a wash. I pray the bleeding up top does not spread and hike with my butt cheeks clenched together to prevent the stain on my shorts from showing. I try to remain optimistic that clenching my butt will tone and tighten it for summer.

- The only thing keeping us going is that we'll get to sign the book at the top of Eagle Peak, to show we'd been there and accomplished something. Mr. Coleman cautions us about our footing in the snow, right before he falls into an air pocket up to his armpits and flails around, trying to escape. Mrs. Coleman starts screaming, "Rick, Rick—are you ok? Oh my God, how will we get you out of there?" like we're on *Rescue 911*. He levers himself out using a log, and Peter Ono, our boatswain master from last year, helps pull him out. I wish I had a crush on Peter instead of Scott. But I am a slave to love.

- We wander around looking for the sign-in book for about twenty minutes. Mr. Coleman, disoriented from the late snow and his fall, can't find the book. He shrugs and turns back. "Oh well, you guys know you were here, right?" We all feel cheated out of signing the Eagle Peak book, and are gloomy on the way back.

- I try to walk in the back of the group. I will fall all the way down the mountain if I keep trying to walk with my butt clenched. Jonathan keeps peering over and reporting whether he can see the stain or not. "No, I can't see...oh, wait, gross!" Finally, I get back to our cabin, change, and then rinse out my clothes. Courtney and I wander over to the gift shop to reactively buy tampons and a sweatshirt.

- I'll have to hide the tampons from my mom when I get home, as she insists that if you use tampons, you're not a virgin anymore. We're still in the year 1906 in my house, gynecologically speaking. She can relax. I probably will be a virgin *forever*. I've broadened my interest to <u>three</u> boys, and still none of them wants anything to do with me except as friends. How many things are wrong with me?

- At dinner, Courtney's dad, Pete, joins us and tells us about all the squirrels he saw on the Muir Walk hike he signed up for. We've barely seen him so far. Courtney feels offended that he seems to be ditching her. "He didn't come to spend time with me...he just came because he wanted to go to Yosemite!" Why aren't we as smart as Pete? Squirrels and flat ground sound like the best hike ever. Pete proves to be extremely popular! Courtney prays that points with the boys (especially Dan Wolf) or her teachers will pay off for her. Sadly, it will not.

- We slide our trays along the cafeteria counter, picking out whatever we want for dinner, mostly pizza. Jonathan announces his opinion of all the food: "The pudding looks like poo. Mmmm, pizza. Sick, who would eat burritos? I hope no one in my cabin! Fruit: why bother?" He puts a pudding on his tray anyway, along with pizza. Courtney's exhaustion from all the hiking leads her to try her first cup of coffee on this trip—the start of a twenty-plus year addiction.

- All of us put on our new Yosemite sweatshirts for the campfire after dinner. My blue one has little bear paw prints on it. So cute! Halfway through the ranger's talk about ecology, Brian McCarran yells, "Hey! There's a ranger dressed in a bear suit!" and points about ten feet behind Ranger Tom.

- Ranger Tom freezes, because he knows **for sure** that the Yosemite rangers **DO NOT** dress up in bear suits. We suddenly realize he thinks it's a real bear, and freeze as well.

I can't believe no one panics or cries (Betsy). Amazing. The bear hangs around for a while, listening to the ranger drone on about moss, but then gets bored, growls, and lopes off into the woods. None of us want to walk back to our cabins after the talk, fearing our dim flashlight beams will reveal packs of bears, waiting to maul us to death behind every tree. I consider calling my mom and telling her we saw a bear, just to worry her, but decide against that, as I'll probably blurt out the tampon fiasco news as well.

• In the morning, I look around the cafeteria and determine I am definitely the <u>only</u> person who does not have a Swatch. Without a colorful Swatch watch, I may as well be dead. Courtney's parents, who love her, bought her a yellow, green and red one. She doesn't mean to flaunt it, but I am so jealous of her (again).

• I have asked for a Swatch for every holiday (including Yom Kippur) and my birthday, but to no avail. My dad refuses, on grounds that watches with no numbers are the most stupid things he's ever heard of. "You can barely tell time now!" he accuses. I explain repeatedly that I wouldn't use it to <u>tell time</u>, silly, it's just for show. This just aggravates him further. "Not practical!" he grumps. Jonathan has two Swatches, one he wheedled Marie into giving him and one Courtney and I got him for his birthday. Maybe I should have kept it...

• Today's hike: Hetch Hetchy Dam, where there is a perpetual rainbow. On the way, Jonathan gossips that he rifled Brian McCarran's bag last night, and Brian did not bring any deodorant with him. "And that's why he smells like my butt, Melissa." But does he like me??? "He doesn't know if he likes you." So no, then.

• At Hetch Hetchy, you can slide down a long natural rock slide and rip your shorts to shreds, or you can swim in the lake area and have boys try to ogle you through your wet t-shirt. If only Scott would ogle me, but he doesn't. He ogles Agatha Rich. Hate her! Everyone opts for the lake swimming after Dan Wolf and Jeff Staricynski slide down the slide, get turned around, almost drown and end up with tons of bruises and cuts. We swim all afternoon and rejoice that we're not hiking.

- At dinner, we also rejoice in the cafeteria, where your dirty dishes magically roll away on a conveyor belt and you can eat what you feel like. Pizza again!

- The campfire that night is painful, as all the cute couples hold hands by the fire. Courtney dies a little death every time Dan Wolf puts his arm around Agatha Rich. She considers joining the track team, except she hates running. "Scott isn't even with anyone. He just sits there alone when he could be with me. Why is being alone better than being with me?" I despair to Courtney.

- The third day of the trip we hike up to Bridal Veil Falls, which feels like walking around the mall after the death march up Eagle Peak. Agatha Rich gets bitten by a squirrel and has to be returned to the ranger station immediately by Mrs. Coleman for rabies shots in her stomach. God has answered Courtney and my prayers! We hate Agatha Rich! "Maybe Dan will dump her if she has rabies!" Courtney hopes.

- Recklessly, I lean over the railing too far, and my glasses almost fall into the Falls, which would leave me groping around like Velma in the *Scooby Doo* cartoons. My mother sent me off with the old-lady glasses holder string, but of course I removed that and shoved it into my tiny backpack immediately. I can't even imagine what preposterous lies I would have to tell her to explain how my glasses fell off, even <u>with</u> the protector string. "But she'd still have to get you new ones," Jonathan coaxes evilly.

- Our last night at Yosemite becomes totally maudlin, everyone hugging people they would never talk to back home in the normal social chain. We all promise to be friends back home.

• Off to one side, I see Jonathan gesture Courtney away from the campfire. He looks embarrassed. She starts smiling, her braces glinting in the firelight...and they kiss. Oh my God. I feel like throwing up. I can't believe this. I know we both had him as backup crush, but how could he like her over me? How could this happen? How can I pretend I'm fine with this? How do they know how to kiss?

• Courtney apologizes later, but she's pragmatic, as usual. She feels bad for me, but since Jonathan doesn't like me anyway, there's no reason for her not to go steady with him. Dan Wolf clearly likes Agatha, and so does Scott.

• I take my parents to Yosemite several years later. My mother mumbles, "John Muir never heard of elevators?" every time she has to walk anywhere, even to the gift shop, her favorite place on any trip. She and Dad reminisce about picking my sister Rachel up here the year she came and had to be airlifted out of the park after collapsing. She confessed she had eaten only sugar packets all week.

• I'm left with my own thoughts about how glorious natural beauty does not get properly appreciated. And how 8th grade boys are the stupidest people in the world.

Author's Note: At our 8th grade graduation dance, Brian McCarran finally asks me to dance. I'm so thrilled it takes me a few minutes to realize he smells so horrifically bad I might choke. He truly does smell like Jonathan's butt. I barely make it through the song, my crush evaporating like a Pig-Pen cloud of stench.

Meanwhile, I am over Jonathan and Courtney going out, but still feel totally vindicated when they both call me the second week of summer to get my advice on how to dump each other. I am so ready to go to high school! Maybe now my life will get exciting!

Arizona Rob

Palm Springs, CA
April 1989

*Some girls get a normal first boyfriend, one who holds hands in between classes, goes over to her house to study, and automatically assumes you'll go to school dances together. I got Darren, one of my closest friends my junior year, who gave me my first real kiss. After months of daily phone calls, meeting between classes and lots of making out at parties, I had completely fallen for him. He was "confused." It would seem he was **most** confused by how to get me to continue hooking up with him without making any firm commitments. I wanted to wear his big, ugly class ring so bad I could taste it!*

I'm 16 and still waiting for my first boyfriend, so don't judge me too harshly here.

Listen To: "Pretty in Pink"-Psychedelic Furs, "Theme from St. Elmo's Fire"-David Foster, "Erotic City"-Prince, "One More Night"-Phil Collins, "If You Leave"-OMD

- High school theatre and choir have been my saving grace, as things have gotten more frustrating at home over the past two years. My mom doesn't want to let go yet, and we fight all the time about my friends, going out, boys and pretty much everything. Her life is over—why can't she just let me live mine? My dad just hides at work and putters around in his garage so he doesn't have to get involved.

- Jonathan, Courtney and I have also made a lot of new friends in high school, and we tend to hang out as a group, so me, Jonathan, Penelope and Charlie are hanging out at our friend Glynis' house watching *St. Elmos' Fire* when Chad stops by.

- Glynis adores Chad, who's one of my best friends. Unfortunately, he's behaving rather like Darren about his relationship with her. Jonathan keeps telling her, "That's all there is with him, Glynis," but she's sure she can get more. Somehow.

- I defend her, and Jonathan rounds on me. "Please, Melissa, Darren's even worse than Chad. Especially since he got his hair frosted—could he look more like a Harbor Snob? He's a spoiled rich kid, and you...aren't." I know what he's trying to say. Darren and his family are the ultimate WASPs, complete with the blond hair, blue eyes and whitened teeth. I know, as does Jonathan, that Darren would be embarrassed to bring me home. Especially now that I'm going through a vintage clothing phase and still have unresolved hair issues.

- Chad invites us to party in Palm Springs for Spring Break with him. "You can stay at Jamie and Janelle's dad's condo for free," he adds, tempting us. "I'm in," I respond immediately. Maybe my mom will appreciate me more if I'm gone for a few days, without telling her where I'm going or when I'll be back.

- Jonathan, Penelope and Charlie decline, as they all have to work. Glynis, turning her big brown doe eyes on Chad, says huskily, "I'd love to go. Let me tell my parents." She pas de bourres out of the room, using her dancer's moves to her greatest advantage. Sometimes it gets a little dramatic, but it's her.

- Tragedy! Glynis' parents won't allow her to go. Now she's bitter I'm going. She may as well be dead. Her doe eyes well up with tears, as she's an emotional girl and can melt down quickly under duress. "Can I borrow some clothes? I can't go home before we leave or my parents won't let me go either," I ask tentatively. Glynis dolefully lends me the three items of hers that fit me: a pair of harem pants, a denim jacket and some denim shorts. Two tops barely fit, but I throw them in the bag anyway. No bikini of hers has a prayer of fitting me in this life or the next. The tops I can squeeze into look obscene. Chad's philosophy: "Show off your breasts and get us free drinks!" Glynis looks even more morose.

• Chad and I head immediately for Vegas, where being half-naked is the norm. I don't really care where we go, as long as it's away. I have to figure out how to stop caring about Darren and hooking up with him. At this rate, I'll be losing my virginity to him by Prom, which he probably won't even take me to. Chad spends the day gambling, while I try to entertain myself with no money, sustaining myself with free drinks and peanuts. Chad loves Vegas, and goes at any opportunity.

• Back in the car, headed to Palm Springs, I remind Chad, "Glynis will hear about whatever you do on this trip. You know how fast the grapevine goes." They've been hooking up for months, yet he refuses to be her boyfriend. He retorts, "So will Darren, if you do anything." Considering my last conversation with Darren was a *Pretty in Pink* rip-off, ending with me yelling, "You're ashamed to be seen with me! You're ashamed to go out with me!" I can't imagine he'll care about anything I do. It's basically our life, except I wear more hats than Molly Ringwald does in the film, and I don't have a cute pink car. I would like one, but fat chance. I barely got contact lenses when I finally "lost" my granny glasses sophomore year.

• Chad insists, "Mel, Darren **will** care. Guys want all the friends-with-benefits stuff, no commitments, but that doesn't mean we don't care." I wish I could record all this for Glynis' benefit. Neither she nor I have a clue how to navigate these quasi-relationships we seem to be stuck in. How do we <u>make</u> them be our boyfriends? If we stop making out and stuff, they'll just find someone else. It's like for them, girls are interchangeable. Maybe I'm so ugly I'll never have a real boyfriend, ever? Darren said our friendship was "too important" to risk dating, yet all the hooking up wasn't risky? All the fighting about being boyfriend/girlfriend ruined the friendship anyway. He's such an idiot. With highlights.

- We drive on toward Palm Springs, where Chad's friends from school, the Tyler twins, are spending Spring Break. We listen to the *Pretty in Pink* soundtrack, i.e. the story of my life, until Chad yells at me that if I'm going to sing along, "You can't sing everything opera! Who sings Echo and the Bunnymen opera?" I turn it down. "I'm in choir! We **do** sing everything opera!"

- Chad and I arrive to a scene of total chaos. Chad loves it! Since he usually throws the parties, it's nice to see someone else's house getting trashed for a change. Lance Linder punched a hole in the door while he was drunk and, although he offered to pay for it, the twins, Jamie and Janelle could not imagine how to keep this information from their dad. Dr. Tyler is an orthodontist, but since he has "doctor" in his title, we all assume Jamie and Janelle know all about medical emergencies. Every time someone gets hurt in a party-related accident, we turn to them and shout, "Well, your dad's a doctor, should we take him to the hospital or let him sleep it off?" They hate it.

- It turned out he already knew, as the nosy neighbor next door had called Dr. Tyler to have a conversation beginning with, "Do you know what your daughters are doing right now?" This struck fear into my heart, because my own father had been on the receiving end of *that* phone call more than once.

- I borrow a bikini from one of the twins. I need a size 34DD, not a 2, and the top literally hangs on by a thread. I have no other options, and wear the porn bikini all weekend, tying it so tight I can barely breathe. It's nearly as bad as Glynis'.

- Chad, our social ambassador, makes friends with a bunch of guys here from Tucson, Arizona and we all start drinking beer in the Jacuzzi of the condo complex. This girl Nora, a friend of the twins', spots Chad and gets in with us. I quietly caution Chad about blatantly hitting on Nora. He blows me off, reassuring me, "She's just a friend. She knows I'm just messing around."

- Why do boys think girls know when they're just messing around? I don't think Nora knows, based on how she's all over him. He knows how emotional Glynis is. She might be crying right now for all we know, doing sad little pliés.

- I drink a lot to assuage the sadness of being attractive enough to hook up with, but not important enough to introduce to someone's parents. Such as Darren's. The Arizona boys don't seem to notice I am drinking to assuage sadness, or Nora's molesting Chad. They are friendly and fun and...cute.

- Bev and Annette, friends of Lance Linder, show up in thong bikinis, which no one at school dares to wear. Perhaps because we're 16 years old and not *hookers*? The best-looking Arizona boy, Rob, who looks just like Ricky Schroeder, moves over, ostensibly to make room for Bev and Annette, but darts away from them to sit next to me. Smiling, he stretches his arm out behind me. The scent of Drakkar wafts over from him, and I am putty in his hands. All cute boys wear Drakkar Noir cologne, and it's like a bell to Pavlov's dog.

- He starts chatting me up, asking a lot of questions about drama and choir, since that's how I spend the vast majority of my day. He confesses he's not much of an academic, either. I'm actually very academic, but after a mishap in Honors Science and complete lack of interest in Honors Geography (which will only be relevant if I'm hiking somewhere and need to identify my location based on topography and main exports), I hang on by a thread to my brainiac status. Chad keeps trying to lure me to the dark side of Beans and Toothpicks Math, while Jonathan insists I should join Academic Decathlon with him.

- After a couple more beers, Rob asks me if I want to take a walk. "To where? There's really nowhere to go, but round and round the complex," I say, looking around, puzzled. "Just a walk," he replies, "so we can talk some more." All right, whatever. I clamber out of the hot tub, Chad shooting me a warning look.

- I hope Rob doesn't notice I'm keeping my arms locked to my sides, like a wooden soldier, in a vain effort to keep my bikini top from sliding off. We walk around in circles for a while, until he reaches over and takes my hand. He can take me on a forced march anywhere, as long as he keeps holding my hand! I can't believe someone wants to hold my hand *in public*! And he's cute! He's way cuter than Darren! Who cares if my top falls off?

- Chad starts shouting from somewhere, "We're going out to dinner, get out of the bushes," so I tell Rob we'll be back later, and head back to put on the denim shorts and denim jacket over my teeny-bikini top. I feel a little like one of those paper dolls that never come with enough outfits. I'm reeling from a cute boy wanting to hold my hand in public. Perhaps I'm not Quasimodo after all?

- Eric, Janelle's boyfriend, slings an arm around Chad's shoulders and announces he will pay for everyone's dinner with his new credit card. Yay for Eric and easy credit! And that he wants to impress Janelle! We head to the main street, where everyone has motorcycles and convertibles. Girls wearing bathing suits that make Bev and Annette's look modest whisk by on the backs of motorcycles. The whole main street of Palm Springs has been taken over by Spring Break traffic. It's a party scene, with people hopping in and out of strangers' convertibles, girls getting on the backs of anyone's motorcycle, and everyone wearing bikinis and swim trunks to dinner. Most everyone looks hot, too. It's the sort of place my mother fears, where I'm three beers away from drunken debauchery.

- Cruising up and down the street and chatting and inviting people to parties is a totally viable activity, as we see the same cars driving up and back all through dinner. Chad has no patience to drive his own car that slow, but loves talking with the passing groups. He's probably the most social person I know. He's also super cute, dark and handsome, and has the sort of charisma people envy. He can get just about anyone to do just about anything. Hence Glynis' obsession.

- We all pile into a booth at a Mexican restaurant but they won't take our fake IDs, so we make do with iced tea and soda. The fake ID thing irritates Chad. He heard somewhere that you could get a check-cashing card with a photo and birth date from a butcher shop in the barrio in Santa Ana. We all got them, but almost no liquor store will take them, citing (correctly) that they aren't real ID; they're just check cashing cards. Chad feels duped, but they do work occasionally, so we hold onto them.

- Bev and Annette flank Chad at dinner. Nora looks hostile, seated further down the row from him. I still don't think she knows he's "just messing around." Eric yells at Lance that he's going to have to pay for the door he punched in. Lance yells back that he knows, and can everyone just shut it? Jamie and Janelle shout that it doesn't matter. They are doomed when they get home. Their dad might even take their car away! (License plate: FOXYTWN). Mexican food rocks! Considering all I ate yesterday was peanuts and booze, I am making the most of Eric's credit card generosity. We leave the restaurant and pass by tons of clubs that we're too young to get into. Luckily, people seem eager to buy liquor for us, especially with my porn bikini top!

- Rob and his friends are still in the Jacuzzi when we get back. Rob seems perfectly fine holding my hand *and* kissing me in front of *his* friends. Clearly, the problem cannot be me; the problem must be Darren. I wonder if someone will call him tonight or tomorrow to report me kissing Rob?

- Chad has retreated to that drunken place where he just observes, occasionally laughing at something no one else can see. It's impossible to engage him in this state. His laughter infects everyone, and we all start laughing whenever Chad does. He loves Rob and smiles approvingly at me. Getting drunk with my friends could not be more fun!

- I hear Nora and Chad giggling, and when I look over, he's kissing her. Glynis will <u>flip it</u> when she hears about this dee-saster. She cries easily, but then she gets pissed and plots major revenge. I predict ugliness at home. She probably will hook up with Darren, if she hears about me and Chad kissing other people in the same call. I'll beat her with her tap shoes if she does that!

- I ask Rob if he wants to take a walk again, as I definitely can't afford to be a party to Chad's infidelity. Rob replies, "I'd rather go inside, if that's cool with you..." Why wouldn't it be? Oh, because he means "inside the *bedroom*," which throws me into all kinds of dilemmas. Someone has probably already speed-dialed Darren. Would he even care though? I doubt it. Do I even care? Kind of...considering I've only ever done anything with Darren, this seems fast.

- We get kicked out of the bedroom immediately by Eric and Janelle. Rob pulls me across the hall to the bathroom, which has a lock on the door. He starts kissing me immediately, which drives most of my misgivings far, far into the back of my mind. The scent of Drakkar drugs me like laughing gas. Rob makes it pretty clear after making out for a while that he'd like things to go further...but doesn't have a condom, and obviously neither do I. I mean, I've gone farther than making out with Darren...but not *that* much farther.

- Cons to losing my virginity to a boy I don't know on Spring Break in the bathroom: He could be a serial killer, a gonorrhea carrier, everyone will know I DID IT, someone will tell Darren before I get back and have a chance to explain, I could hit my head on the toilet and become paralyzed, I could get pregnant and have to tell my parents that some boy I don't even know knocked me up on the bathroom floor, and it will make a monumentally tacky "losing-my-virginity" story my whole life.

- Pros: Rob's super cute, it will make Darren jealous, I might never have another chance to have sex because I am too ugly to be a girlfriend, if I lose my virginity to Darren, I'll never be able to get over him, Rob will probably already know what to do, and it will make a great "losing my virginity" story since he's a hot blonde stranger and it's Spring Break. My buzz definitely increases both my spontaneity and my ability to make snap decisions.

- I decide the pros outweigh the cons while Rob kisses my neck, but decide he doesn't need to know it's my first time. He assures me he doesn't have any diseases and will pull out. Whatever that means.

- Rob is *amazing*! I love having sex!

- Outside in the party, I hear Chad turn up Prince's "Erotic City" and then Phil Collins' "One More Night" comes on— amen! I also hear a loud crash, which sounds like someone dancing on a table that fell over, and in the distance, a police siren. We hear Janelle screaming, "Jamie, how stupid are you to <u>dance</u> on a glass table?" Eric and Lance are both injured from glass cuts, and want Janelle to treat them because "your dad's a doctor."

- Eventually, Rob and I are forced to exit the bathroom, due to pleas from the twins that if any more people pee outside, the neighbors will call the cops again. I somehow emerge from the bathroom wearing Rob's underwear due to our hasty exit. It's apparently a rather old pair that has been to some sort of camp, because his name was sewn into them. Probably a sports camp. He must be going commando; I brought no underwear on the trip to swap him.

- His middle name is Lyndon???

- We watch TV on the sofa bed pulled out in the living room. Chad climbs up next to us, giving me knowing looks. I feel like everyone knows! I just had sex!!! And I liked it!!! Rob spends the night with me on the sofa bed, and stretches regretfully when his friends show up the next morning to drive home to Arizona. As I'm kissing him goodbye, I can hear someone on the phone, murmuring, "No, I think she had sex with him...I don't know...yeah, he's really cute..."

- I spend most of the day laying out and hoping I'm not pregnant. I will make any bargain God wants, as long as I'm not pregnant. And I don't have a disease. That has to be part of the bargain, too.

- Chad and I leave for home the next day in a swirl of rumors. He hits me up immediately for details about Rob, but refuses to share any information about his own sex life with Glynis. Since Glynis and Chad lost their virginity to each other, I wonder if their stories will match. Glynis was mortified that she didn't know what to do, and was so tense Chad had to liquor her up to have sex with her. According to Glynis, it got a lot easier after several games of quarters.

- I'm glad Rob <u>clearly</u> knew what to do, and that my first time was a good time. He seemed really surprised in the morning to hear it had been my first time. **Really** surprised. It's so much easier making decisions about guys when your feelings aren't involved. But then, your feelings aren't involved...

Author's Note: I just Googled Rob. He lives in Nebraska and he's a lawyer. Based on his bio photo, he's still cute. And he has his email address posted. But...best to leave this a good memory.

Singing the Blues

Lake Arrowhead, CA
August 1989

I was definitely feeling ready to branch out, meet some new friends, and hopefully find a nice normal guy. Choir camp seemed like a great opportunity, but with a safety net of having Penelope and Charlie around. Oh, and another friend from choir, Jeri, who my mother describes thus: "If Jeri didn't have bad luck, she'd have no luck at all."

__Suggested Soundtrack__: "I've Had the Time of My Life"-Bill Medley and Jennifer Warnes, "She's Like the Wind"-Patrick Swayze, "Hungry Eyes"-Eric Carmen, any Bach piece, any madrigal, and any barbershop quartet music you might have on hand.

- Our school awarded scholarships to attend a two-week choir camp over the summer to my friends Charlie, Penelope, Jeri and I! Two weeks away in the mountains sounds like fun to me. Plus, winning a scholarship boosts my confidence and makes me feel like I'm good at *something*. Charlie's parents offer to take me on their camping trip with them, and then drop us both off at camp. My parents say yes, a miracle because Charlie's parents are the most irresponsible parents of them all. Dad: "Great news! I'll only have to drive the motorhome to the mountains once!"

- The day before we leave, my mother attempts to cut my hair. The haircut she gives me has to be a <u>deliberate</u> attempt to settle a score; a chimp could have done a better job. "Why do you keep lying and saying you know what you're doing?" I scream at her, running off to my room, where I'm in tears all night. I'll **never** leave the house again, except if I get abducted to a planet where they all have bad hair. I may as well be dead (again). Mom, possibly wracked with guilt, gets me an early appointment at her beauty parlor (notice she doesn't cut her *own* hair), and the lady does her best to fix the damage, which involves cutting most of my hair completely off. With a straightening iron, I still have a little bit of bangs.

- I complain, "My hair looks like Paul Reiser when he had the fluffy mullet," but Charlie assures me it looks great. We hang out in the backseat, lounging around and eating snacks. I try to keep my breasts under wraps and away from his dad's prying eyes, no easy task during the full week of camping. Charlie and I spend most of our time discussing his relationship with Jeanine, who we all met through choir as well. He keeps encouraging me to call Darren, but what's the point? He was angry and embarrassed about Arizona Rob, as Chad predicted, and we operate under the pretense of being friends since we have mostly the same friends.

- Charlie changes his tack. "Well, you're gorgeous and fun and smart. Maybe you'll meet someone else at camp." I laugh. "Charlie, you're so optimistic. Look at me! I'm not gorgeous and never have been. That's why my life goes like this. Jeanine's the gorgeous one." Charlie smiles sweetly. "Yeah, she is."

- Charlie and I arrive at camp and find Penelope, surly because she had to ride up with Jeri. "Do the Mormons have rules about going five miles under the speed limit, or does Mr. West just drive slowly?" Then she takes a deep breath. "Be grateful for the ride," she chants to herself, a calming ritual. She leads Charlie and I into the outdoor rehearsal pavilion. "I met cool people from another school in Diamond Bar. Mel and Charlie, this is Gloria, Chip and Jacob."

- Jeri immediately becomes fascinated with Chip, an edgy boy wearing a long black trench coat, a black Depeche Mode T-shirt, black shorts, and Doc Marten boots. He's very pale, but unusually animated and friendly for a Depeche Mode fan. "How do you get your hair like that?" Jeri asks, reaching out a hand. Chip backs away. "A lot of Aqua Net and a blow dryer," he tells her, sizing her up. Jeri has strict Mormon parents, and she's fit in well with their conservative mold. She's currently sporting a permed bob the color of golden retriever fur, a bright yellow T-shirt, and jean shorts. All of her clothes are varying shades of green, peach and yellow because "I'm an autumn." Penelope looks at Jeri and Chip talking and cracks up. "This should be good."

- Gloria likes Charlie, tossing her long feathered hair around at him, but he's dating Jeanine back home, so I hope he doesn't do anything requiring me to cover up for him, like with Chad and Nora in Palm Springs. Gloria seems very possessive of Jacob, a tall guy with dark hair and eyes and glowers at me as he chats me up. Jacob's very funny and entertaining, which makes him cuter, sort of like Scott Steinberg. Who still doesn't like me. But he's also no Arizona Rob.

- Penelope and I end up bunking with Gloria, Jeri, this other girl, Heather, and a counselor, India, who trains lions "off-season" and promises to show us how to use her bullwhip. She tells us, "It's so empowering, you can't even imagine." We choose the rickety outside cabin, with no door, no windowpanes and tons of graffiti. It's still better than the orphanage-style main dorm, where they may as well be singing, "Food Glorious Food," from *Oliver!* Jeri flings her bag onto a top bunk, and begins unpacking. "I get dibs on Chip," she announces, carefully placing her brush on the shelf. "He's so...different than the boys at our school." I predict, "Your parents will totally flip," and she looks smug. "I know." Heather volunteers that a cute boy, Jackson, helped her with her bag. Penelope takes her under her wing. "That's nice. Maybe he likes you?" Heather looks all flustered.

- In the dining hall at dinner, the five of us pile onto a bench, joined by Chip, Jacob and their friend Cade. Penelope yells from the serving line, "They have ham or grilled cheese!

I'm getting you a grilled cheese, OK?" She returns to the table, telling everyone I'm Jewish and don't eat ham. Jacob pipes up, "So am I! My mother will be thrilled!" He realizes he said it out loud, and the specter of his mother haunts us already. I understand; my parents always ask if any boy I like is Jewish. The answer has always been, "No, except for Scott." I could definitely like Jacob, but I notice how he's always looking around when he's talking, like he's already looking for someone else. I don't need someone else who doesn't think I'm good enough for him!

• As we leave the dining hall, Penelope flouts the rules and takes her teacup with her, ending up with a rash of stolen teacups in our cabin. Possibly this leads to the ant infestation in our cabin. Penelope's a sassy, take-charge friend, and I just let her do whatever she wants. "What are you wearing to the dance tonight?" Heather asks us. Jeri launches into a description of an outfit that I tune out right after she says, "Electric salmon..." Penelope and Gloria are going with jeans. I'll wear my black off-the-shoulder bodysuit and striped pants with my knee-high black boots. Penelope nods. "Those pants make you look super skinny."

• Later that night, we have a big dance on the volleyball court. It's pitch dark, so they use floodlights and we feel like we're dancing in a co-ed prison. Jacob immediately asks me to dance. Maybe my hair doesn't look as bad as I think. "I think they're just letting the whole *Dirty Dancing* soundtrack run through," he notices, pulling me closer as the music changes to a ballad. Well, he's definitely into me at this moment, and maybe that's the best it gets. We talk and joke, and it's nice not having someone singing off-key into my ear, like Jonathan does when we've danced together. Gloria glumly dances by with Cade, as Charlie has already begun dancing with Heather. Heather's a lot prettier than Gloria.

• Penelope dances with this cute boy Cameron, whose sister looks a little upset. Penelope whispers, "So THAT'S how it is in their family..." I notice that every so often, as Chip dances with Jeri, he sprays Binaca into his mouth. "How fresh can his breath get?" I ask Jacob. He explains that Chip has an addiction to Binaca, and the longer you hang around him, the less you notice it. Later, back in our cabin, Gloria tells Jeri that Chip really likes her. Jeri digs her brush out of her purse and begins giggling that "at least he has fresh breath in case we get" (here she extends her hands and makes squeezing motions), "touchy-feely!" I make hand motions like I'm clawing out my own eyes at the idea of Chip and Jeri getting touchy-feely, but behind her so she doesn't see me. All the brushing makes Jeri's perm look poodle-fluffy, but I've told her that before to no avail. Penelope says flippantly, "Well, Jacob's off the table too," and looks significantly at me. I shake my head. "I don't think so. I think he thinks he's a player." Gloria agrees, relieved that I get him right from the start. Penelope scoffs. "He's not cute enough to be a player." I raise my finger. "I didn't say that. I said he *thinks* he is." I repeat my stance on someone who thinks they can do better while quasi-dating me. "No more."

• The next morning we have breakfast and Penelope pilfers another teacup. Jacob sits by me at breakfast and we all discuss what vocal section we're likely to get sent to after breakfast. I'm sent to the soprano section with Jeri, while Penelope becomes an alto with Gloria. A totally hot counselor shows up late to rehearsal. "I'm Art," he introduces himself to me, slipping into the pavilion. "I just got in from Mississippi." But you look like you're from Arizona and related to Rob. I wonder if I'll get close enough to find out if he wears Drakkar? Our director announces auditions for Chamber Singers, the elite group, and Jacob mouths, "Don't audition if you want any free time!" We spend the morning beginning our music selections. Heather, a trained opera singer, blows us all away, and Jackson definitely looks impressed. Jeri keeps motioning and waving to Chip, resplendent in a black fedora and turquoise shirt. He does turn to spray Binaca frequently, and Jacob raises his eyebrows significantly. Cade elbows him and whispers something. Cade, a tall, athletic looking guy with dirty blonde hair and dimples, is much cuter than Jacob, but he's too quiet for me. Too bad.

- Jeri and Heather make Chamber Singers, but on my recommendation, Penelope and I elect to have our afternoons free. On my first free afternoon, Jacob invites me to "take a walk," which, after Arizona Rob, I now recognize as code for "make out". We make out for like an hour in a band pavilion overlooking a grove of pine trees and mountains. It's so pretty up here, and the air smells so much better. Suddenly, I feel a soggy wet spot? Did he just *wet his pants?* He backs away, embarrassed, and I realize what happened. "I forgot, I'm meeting Gloria and Penelope, so I'll see you later," I tell him quickly, scampering down the path in my boots. I go join my friends, who are watching Art and some other people play volleyball. Gloria, already giving up on Charlie, roots for this guy Martin, even though he seems like a complete idiot. He also resembles a rodent, and Penelope and I call him Mighty Mouse in private. We hear the Chamber Singers slaving away in the pavilion and grin at our freedom. Chip and Cade join us. "Where's Jacob?" Cade asks me. I just shrug.

- Penelope and I decide to shower while the group showers are empty. Our school doesn't have group showers and we're not overly relaxed being in a scene out of *Porky's.* We debate whether to borrow Jeri's hair products without asking, not only because we are technically stealing, but mainly because they make Jeri resemble a wet golden retriever. We decide to freely use Jeri's expensive shampoo and conditioner while she's trapped in Chamber Singers, but use our own razors. Penelope reasons, "It's her poor styling techniques that result in the bad hair." Not that I can really talk about hair issues.

- That night we have a campfire out on the rocks, where everyone lays on the ground in a chain. Then the first person laughs, and it goes along the whole chain. "Who thinks of these stupid games?" Gloria wonders. I allow Penelope to put her head on my stomach, as I know she has Salon Selective-fresh hair, while laying my own head on Jacob's stomach. I think about how Penelope and I privately laughed at Jacob's wet spot earlier today, and it makes me laugh again, so I begin the laughing chain. I hear Chip asking Jeri, "Is your hair still wet?" as she's apparently gotten his T-shirt all soggy. Then the unmistakable sound of Binaca, which makes me laugh even more. Then we just have a regular campfire and sing folk songs. I love the mountains and camp! Even though it's only about twenty feet, boys walk their camp girlfriends to their cabin, which Jacob does, although he's still mortified from the Wet Spot Incident. Jackson drops Heather off, and we hear Jeri giggling outside at something Chip said. Then Jeri screams, "Yuck, a slug just crawled on me!" and a spritz of Binaca. Penelope and I crack up, because "Only Jeri would have a slug crawl on her while she's making out," I howl. Penelope predicts, "I'm going to win on this one. I think Jacob totally likes you." I start changing for bed. "We'll see. I hope you're right."

• The next day at mail call, I'm sitting next to Jacob when I get a letter from Jonathan. Jonathan was supposed to come to camp, but his grandmother died instead. He's annoyed about not coming with us, although he would obviously have been prohibitive to any new adventures. On the outside of the envelope he has written, "I am Melissa's big scary jealous boyfriend, and if you touch her, I will kick your ass!" Jacob seems jealous and scared, which I use to my advantage. I've noticed him checking out this too-tall stick-thin girl, Nancy, during breakfast. If Jacob defects, I'm going to make Art mine, bad hair and all, I decide after I run into Art on the stairs while going to read my note in private. Penelope reports Jacob *has* been talking to Nancy when I consult her later, so I must convince Art that: a) my hair will grow out and b) it <u>so</u> doesn't matter that I'm not eighteen yet. I tell her, "Whatever. Nancy's out of his league. But I'm still mad on principle. "

- We practice our operetta, which I think we might have read in English class, or at least *The Aeneid*. I could pick up a trick or two from Dido, an expert manipulator who gets Aeneas to stay with her, only to send him off anyway and kill herself. I see Jacob eyeing my red bandeau top from the tenor section. I lean over, pretending to pick up music. Twig-Girl doesn't have *these*, does she, Jacob? Occasionally we hear Chip's Binaca through the music, and see Jeri snapping her head around toward him. Charlie sits next to Chip and has basically ignored all of us so far. He writes to Jeanine every day, and just hangs out practicing his gymnastics. He doesn't like Jacob. "He's going to hurt your feelings, I think."

- After lunch, Jonathan unexpectedly shows up and flips out. Specifically, he buttons up my shirt, covering my cute bandeau top and chastises me for looking "loose." Penelope gets yelled at for making new friends "we don't even know." Predictably, he hates everyone, especially Jacob. "I can't believe you kissed him already! How could you?" Jonathan wails, bemoaning my "loose" attitude. I have no idea why; I've been waiting for Jonathan to kiss me since 7th grade and it still hasn't happened. Penelope and I keep the Wet Spot Incident between us. Gloria observes, "For just a friend, he seems pretty protective." I neglect to tell her my life story so far is all "just friends," with a memorable one-night stand. Sigh.

- Penelope, driving salt in the wounds, tells Jonathan she's become obsessed at breakfast with a tall blue-eyed brunette named Rob. I love that name! I love him already, but it throws Jonathan even more into despair. He means well, but he's so overprotective and suspicious of new people. "It's only been two days! How could this have happened?" he moans to Charlie.

- Charlie, free of Jonathan's lecture series, does a back flip off the stage right on the side of the hill, and though Jonathan yells at him that he'll break his neck, he lands perfectly.

Charlie starts to swagger away, trips over his own giant feet and sprains his wrist. Jonathan, relieved, tells us, "This will stop him from hopping around all the time." Charlie shrugs. "I'm just energetic." He's also adorably cute and gets away with anything he wants. But he does act like Tigger on crack.

- After Jonathan leaves, with his predictions of "this all ending in tears," I spend the afternoon hanging out with Jacob and Cade. Cade's way cuter than Jacob, but whittles and wants to be a park ranger. I almost say, "Like at Jellystone?" because that's how realistic I think that career choice is, but he does later become a park ranger and smokes pot out of his whittled pipes. Not exactly the white-collar champion I'm looking for. I sit with Penelope, Charlie, Nancy and Rob at dinner, figuring I'll keep my eye on the twiggy little slut. Rob would be perfect for Penelope! Jeri and Chip nuzzle in a corner of the dining hall, and he pushes his fedora back to kiss her. He seems unfazed by her turtle-green t-shirt and electric salmon shorts. Jacob and Cade ignore them at their table.

- We have a volleyball tournament that night, and Art's bare torso looks amazing by moonlight, like Michelangelo's *David*. I'm watching Art adoringly when Jacob comes up and takes my hand. He leads me under the canteen. "I missed you at dinner," he says questioningly. How do I pretend to just be independent instead of mad? "Well, I don't need to be by your side every second. You have other friends here, too," I finally answer. He clearly doesn't realize I'm jealous of Nancy, so I'm not going to bring it up. We make out aggressively in the dark. "I love these boots," he whispers, running his hands over them as I sit on his lap. I've decided to be a bad-hair vixen, and hopefully he'll stay interested.

- Penelope gets to play the cowbell in one of our songs the next day, and threatens to clock Gloria in the head with it if she doesn't stop whining about Mighty Mouse. "Quit whining! I swear, you just need to find someone who's not a loser, Gloria! I'll tell you who they are, OK? Just come to me first!" Not Mighty Mouse, who looks like an escaped hamster. She shushes Gloria in favor of hearing my hot hook-up stories. "Jacob isn't the cutest one here, but I really like him. And he's going to totally blow me off," I conclude. "Maybe the boots will lure him when we get back home," Penelope replies encouragingly. Heather leans over. "Jackson kissed me last night. It was my first French kiss!" We all high-five her.

- I spend my free afternoon time in the pool, wearing the cutest purple bikini ever. The Chamber Singers wail away in the background. Penelope whispers, "Everyone is looking at your boobs! Even Art!" Jacob now becomes possessive, spreading my towel next to his. He may as well be peeing around me in a circle. Nancy may as well not exist. Why does he only want me when other guys do too? "So are you guys already in the talent show?" Chip asks us. Penelope and I crack up. We hate talent shows. Jacob admits he and Gloria are singing together, and Chip, Cade and some other guys are writing an Aeneas rap song. "Do you want to be backup dancers with Jeri?" Chip persists to Penelope and I, and we both rebuff the opportunity. Nancy pipes up that she and Rob are singing a song together, and Jacob sits up attentively. I notice Art has left; no wonder Jacob feels cocky again. I get up too; may as well leave him to it.

- "I'm taking a shower," I tell Penelope. She's busy listening to Rob hum the song he's singing. "Don't take too much conditioner or Jeri will flip!" I find Charlie after the shower and go out to the band pavilion to talk to him about all the developments. He shakes his head. "I'm so glad to be out of all that drama," he tells me. He's only flirted a little so far, so he's still in the clear with Jeanine. Charlie's a serious musician and uses his free time wisely. Jacob looks sharply at me when he sees Charlie and I coming back from our make out pavilion. Charlie notices and hugs me goodbye. "Forget about him," he says as he leaves to change for dinner. After evening rehearsal, India shows us the fine art of using a bullwhip. I love this whip! I want to hit something with it, like maybe Nancy, still twigging along, and definitely Jacob if he keeps ogling her in front of me.

- That night we all go back out to the rocks for a campfire. We have to tell the people around us things we like about them, and Jacob murmurs, "Is there anything I *don't* like about you?" Probably his trademark line that he says to everyone. Apparently you don't like that I have more than a skeleton body, Jacob! Where's my new whip to beat you to a bloody pulp? "Why don't we have a campfire time to tell people the things we *don't* like about them?" I whisper to Penelope on my other side. "Like how I don't like when Jacob ogles some girl *right in front of me,* or how Gloria's throwing herself at Mighty Mouse just smacks of desperate? How much I hate Jeri's perm? How Art's avoidance of jailbait irks me?" She squeezes my hand sympathetically. "I would tell Rob I hate that he just likes me as a friend," she whispers back sadly. I squeeze her hand back.

- I walk back to my cabin with Penelope. Jeri reports when she gets there after making out with Chip. "Jacob's outside! He wants you to come out." She waits by the door till I relent. We kiss in the moonlight and I send him back to his bunk before another Wet Spot Incident occurs. Jeri wants to hear everything. And tell everything. "I don't think Chip could feel anything when he felt me up; I'm wearing a Cross-Your-Heart bra..." Eeek.

- During free afternoon time the next day, Chip invites us to go to the store. "No Chamber Singers today, so Jeri can come," he remarks, putting his arm around her. She's gotten tanner up here and that makes a big difference. Jacob and I walk out to the parking lot with them. "You neglected to mention your car is tiny! Jacob and I will have to fold ourselves into luggage to ride in the hatch! The good news is I won't be able to see as the car plunges over a cliff to our doom." The car ride, permeated with Chicago's "You're the Inspiration," seems long with Jeri hitting the back window and whining, "What are you guys dooooing back there??? Huh?" There's barely enough room to make out, but we manage. I cruelly grind up against Jacob, ensuring another Wet Spot, then get out, leaving him to expose his stained shorts in front of everyone at the store.

- We get Popsicles and other treats and hang out on the hood of Chip's brown 280ZX. He asks if I want to drive it. "No, I don't have my license yet," I back away nervously. "I can teach you in five minutes," Chip brags, handing his Popsicle to Jacob. We start off down the road, but I can't quite get the hang of not using both feet, and after I accelerate dangerously close to the edge of the mountain, he grabs the steering wheel. "OK," he tells me calmly, with a spritz of Binaca for good measure, "that was bad. But you'll get better." He allows Jeri to drive back after she pulls her giant glasses, worse than my granny glasses ever were, out of her purse. She brushes her hair for good measure, and Jacob laughs silently, as I've told him about Jeri's hair issues and bad luck. He nearly falls over laughing when a swarm of bees comes literally out of nowhere and flock to Jeri, leaving the rest of us alone. "Aiiiigghh!" she swats at them, dropping her glasses into the dirt.

- Upon our return, we distribute the popsicles. Penelope eats hers rather lasciviously in an effort to seduce Rob, which I think she read in Cosmo. Jacob goes off to change and never comes back. On my way into dinner with Penelope, Heather and Jackson, I see him on the volleyball court, sitting and talking to Nancy. I sigh. "So guess what she told me? Nancy, I mean," Penelope says slowly, reluctant to confide. I motion her to continue. "Nancy said she hit on Charlie, and Charlie lied and told her he had a huge crush on you. I guess she really likes him. Nancy doesn't know Charlie would just say that because he's mad at Jacob. But she <u>really</u> doesn't like you now."

- The "talent show" turns out exactly as painful as every "talent" show is. Jacob can't sing at all. He's really not good. What is he doing in choir anyway? The rap song does not benefit from our backup dancing in the least (Chip finally persuaded us, and even though we were sober, we said yes anyway), and overall I think the evening could have been better spent making out under the canteen. The next morning, we take breakfast-in-bed to the boys' cabin. They're supposed to reciprocate, but never do. Surprise, surprise.

• Why do boy places always smell like six hundred pet mice have gotten loose? Or maybe just Mighty Mouse? "Thanks, Jeri," Chip tells her. He even wears black T-shirts in bed. He's so nice. He's exactly the sort of person I would pick to be friends with, while dating the guy who rips out my heart. Maybe I need therapy. I'd also discuss the granny glasses and bad hair issues.

• Later that day we all go into Lake Arrowhead for lunch and shopping. The townspeople probably want to drown themselves in the Lake as their town runneth over with choir dorks singing their way through lunch. Jeri drags Chip off to a bench to make out, and we don't see them the rest of the day.

• There is no point at all to life if the boy you have been making out with all week actually *moves his chair* over to sit by twiggy Nancy "so he can hear what she's saying." Relationships are much easier if: a) they are only for one night and b) the person isn't as dumb as a box of rocks. Oh Arizona Rob, where art thou? Ranger Cade, a brilliant genius, urges Jacob to follow me as I storm out of the restaurant, but Jacob seems utterly baffled by this turn of events. Cade shrugs and follows me himself. How can Jacob **not** know why I'm mad? Can he not see Nancy smirking, itching to get bludgeoned by the handle of the bullwhip? "The worst part of it," I rail to Cade as we drink our sodas and walk around the Lake, "is that she doesn't even like him. She's only being nice to him to jerk my chain." Cade begins to protest, but I repeat what Penelope told me and he falls silent. As usual.

- Cade distracts me and we have a fun time shopping and chatting together. Back on the bus, Jacob finds me and sits next to me. "I'm really sorry," he begins, and then stops. I look at him. "What are you sorry for?" I prompt. He doesn't know. "I just don't want you to be mad at me," he implores. I stare at him. "I just don't want you hitting on Nancy right in front of me," I challenge. He sits back with a guilty look on his face. My stomach hurts. Luckily he's not smart enough to realize I have been flirting with Art and Ranger Cade all week, but since it didn't hurt his feelings, it doesn't count.

- Later on, back in camp, we have a big sing-a-long after dinner for our last night. Tearjerkers like "The Circle Game," "You've Got a Friend" and other such songs get everyone crying, and even Penelope and I are hugging each other and crying, though we're riding home together. Sadness makes me relent and I let Jacob hug and kiss me. I'm positive I'll never see him again anyways. He apologizes again and promises to call. Yeah, we'll see.

- Art finds me and hugs me goodbye. "I wish you hadn't been here as a student," he tells me earnestly, resting his hand on my waist. "Maybe next summer I won't be," I tell him pertly. He smiles and says, "Well, I guess we'll see."

- The next morning, Charlie rides home with Jeri, whose parents may suffer heart attacks when they see her kissing Chip. Chip couldn't be more polite to her parents, but as predicted, the trench coat, Docs and Binaca fetish send them over the edge. "I'll call you as soon as we get home!" Chip promises Jeri, and he's probably not lying. He drives off with Cade, and Gloria and Jacob leave together.

- My father comes to pick us up in the motorhome. Penelope and I survive the "Suicide Death Ride of '89" by lying on the couch and not watching Dad take the hairpin turns on mountain roads at top speed. She's sad over Rob and I'm sad over Jacob (and Art and even Ranger Cade, who turned out to be great, but that seems slutty, so I only say Jacob but Penelope knows better). We agree that we'll live together forever and eschew boys to avoid the pain and sorrow they cause, even Mighty Mouse. Dad's not sympathetic to our nun plight, saying, "This will all seem **so** stupid when you're older. Either they'll call or they won't. That's that." Yeah, and I didn't *need* a Swatch in 8th grade either, Dad.

- It does all seem pretty stupid years later. But when you're 16 and in love, you have a lot to learn about perspective. And boys. Chip does call Jeri. He dates her for a few months, and then palms her off on his friend Aaron. I see Jacob a couple of times, when Chip drives down with him to see Jeri and I. But that's it. He's not even dating anyone else but can't be bothered to date me either, until Penelope invites him to my surprise birthday party late that year. Somehow that changes things, and we become friends. And then after the Fiasco of Prom, we finally start dating for real right before graduation. But during the drive home, all seems lost.

- The only consolation: Once I turn 18, I can always track Art down...and my hair will have grown out by then.

The Scam-o-Rama of Canada

March 1990
Vancouver, Canada

It's my senior year in high school. I'm sexy and 17. Darren, Jacob and everyone else are yesterday's news (most of the time). Jonathan and I are inseparable friends. Will this be the year where he finally likes me back? Or will I be forced to meet some loooooooser (as Courtney's dad, Pete, calls all our dates) yet again?

Suggested Soundtrack: *"King of Wishful Thinking"-Go West, "Wild Wild West"-Escape Club, "Red Red Wine"-UB40, "Right Here Waiting"-Richard Marx, "Vogue"-Madonna,*

- As Choir President senior year, I decide, "Our choir should get to go somewhere to sing in a festival. I choose the Hyack Festival in Vancouver, Canada." Jonathan (as vice president) seconds. "That's better than other festivals in cities we can't go wild in, like Salt Lake City where we'd be thrown in Mormon jail." Jeri gives him a sour look. I'm suddenly inspired. "Plus, Canadians might be less suspicious of our fake ID/check cashing cards and let us drink! It'll be awesome!"

- Courtney, Jeri, our friend Kelly and I sign up to share a room. Amanda, our choir director, agrees that we can share the room "as long as we don't get in trouble." I wish Penelope and Glynis were coming, but Glynis captains the dance team, and Penelope has to work. Since Chad doesn't sing, Glynis doesn't care about being on the trip. Courtney and I scheme in advance to pilfer Jeri's hair products while she's out of the room, as that worked out well last summer at music camp.

- Jonathan wants his own room, but that dream ends quickly. He has to share with Charlie and Matt, the only other guys he knows on the tour. He also wants to sit separately from the rest of us on the plane, as we are an embarrassing assortment of choir geeks, singing snatches of *Phantom of the Opera* at the drop of a hat.

- Upon arriving at the hotel in Vancouver, Courtney and I realize there are tons of other choirs from other states, and we immediately head for the pool to scope out the guys. We both have contact lenses now, so we have to be careful at the pool, lest we lose one and have to go around seeing out of one eye all week.

- Yes! Potential for a Scam-o-Rama! Scam-o-Ramas can happen anywhere there are large numbers of cute boys who are trapped in a place for a set period of time, like camps, festivals, spring breaks, fraternity parties, etc. "Who knew there were all these cute guys in other choirs?" Courtney marvels. "Jonathan's cute," I volunteer, but she gives me a withering look. "Don't worry," I reassure her, "I'm here to have fun." With that, I exchange soulful glances with cute (but mute) guy, whose friends call him Adam. His friends tell us they are from some town, Aberdeen. Courtney tells the Aberdeenies we're in room 1301, just in case. I notice I tend to home in on one guy, while Courtney prefers to keep her options open. Being a tall blonde, she can do that.

- Amanda hustles us out to Stanley Park to see the totem poles on our first of many tours that afternoon. Our bus driver, Parker, keeps saying, "Eh?" Jonathan wants to know if we'll see moose in the park. Parker says, "Eh?" Jonathan patiently explains he has read up on Vancouver, but Parker doesn't care. It turns out there are mostly Canada geese in the park, as well as elaborately carved totem poles made by Native Americans. Charlie asks, "Oh is that why Canadian geese are called that? Because they're from Canada?" Parker says, "Eh?" Matt wants to know how there were Native Americans here if we're not in America. Parker thinks we're all idiots, and points out that we're in Canada, "in North America. America, get it, eh?"

- Jonathan, Kelly, Courtney and I pose for photos by the totem poles, looking somber like the Native Americans who were driven out. Kelly, a sophomore, lets Jonathan spend his life bossing her around. Chad also bosses her around, but since she's in love with him, she doesn't mind as much.

- Parker despairingly tries to get us all back on the bus at the same time, but it proves impossible. Matt refuses to leave the gift shop. We clue Parker that if he had *treats* on the bus, like Ding Dongs, we might come back. He relents and takes us to McDonald's, where we order Poulet McCroquettes (Chicken McNuggets, but with joie de vivre!) They have beer at this McDonald's but won't take our check cashing cards here either. "Damn it, Chad!" Jonathan curses.

- Our next stop: the Capilano Suspension Bridge, destined to break as soon as I step foot on it, plummeting to my death hundreds of feet below like in *Indiana Jones and the Temple of Doom*. Hilarious Jonathan shakes the bridge while we're on it until he looks down and realizes the bridge has not aged well, and there are probably not personal injury laws like there are in regular America. He quells his taste for adventure by stealing a hat from the gift shop. His upper middle class upbringing has not provided much in the way of adventure yet. I wonder, "Will we get deported if you're caught?"

- His mother, Marie, has come as a chaperone on the trip and eyes the hat suspiciously, as if remembering Jonathan never asked her for money for it. Jonathan and his two older sisters mercilessly harass Marie for money and gifts, which she hides from their father, Eduardo. Eduardo despairs over Jonathan, who he feels should be interested in things besides shopping, cooking and reading history books. Jonathan ignores Eduardo for the most part and refuses to work on any of the junk cars Eduardo brings home. Marie's attention gets diverted by Parker flirting shamelessly with Amanda in the front of the bus.

- Eventually, we return to the hotel to rehearse. Our selections:
  - *The Belly of the Whale*, where Charlie gets to sing the part of Jonah and complain to the Lord from the whale's belly.
  - *One Lonely Candle*, a standard about how if you're wandering around in the snow and wind and you see a candle in the window somewhere, you're not alone. Except you may still be cold and hungry, as the owner of the candle does not offer any Ding Dongs or Poulet McCroquettes in the song.
  - *Gloria in Excelsis*, pronounced Egg-shell-sees.

- Courtney and I are late to rehearsal due to Adam, the mutie cutie boy, calling our room. He's smart enough to have 1) remembered our room number and 2) dialed a telephone successfully, so he's already a winner! Or shall I say, Adamth, as his lisp became immediately noticeable as soon as he talked, and my attraction to him waned instantly. So much for the Scam-o-Rama, unless I can convince Adamth, as I'll call him now, to just mime at me.

- After rehearsal we go to dinner. Jonathan and I get our own table so we can talk about everyone else. Topics of conversation include:
  - Why Jeri always goes around with wet dog hair and clutching a Le Sportsac purse under her armpit like a grandma, "but yet always seems to have a boyfriend," I point out. Jonathan sighs. "Is she still dating that friend of Chip's?" I nod. "Yeah, and you know what she told me? His wiener has a bend in it!" Jonathan insists

I not use that word, but I protest, "But Jeanine says it all the time." He doesn't like that either.

- Whether Kelly will ever get over Chad or not, and whether she and Glynis will become physically violent at some point (I think maybe).

- Whether Amanda and Parker will hook up on the bus while we're supposed to be sightseeing. "My mom will flip," he predicts.

- Jonathan avoids the topic of why he refuses to go out with me after five years and I am forced to find boys with speech impediments, because **that** is what's out there.

- The next day, we take the aerial tram up Grouse Mountain. The tram, suspended high above the ground from tiny wires, meets the definition of what my mom calls "a death trap" with flying colors. On top of Grouse Mountain, snow has fallen in droves. None of us has dressed for snow, but we merrily disregard Amanda's pleas to stay out of the snow and not get sick (as she evidently subscribes to my mother's theories of "going outside with a wet head"). Instead, we have snowball fights and then have to ride the tram back in wet cold jeans.

- Kelly, Charlie and Jeanine elect to stay in the warm hut at the top where you can buy hot chocolate and not be wet and cold. They're not seniors though, and don't feel the sense of impending mortality and doom that Jonathan, Courtney and I do.

- Courtney buys a giant moose hat at the gift shop, looking pointedly at Jonathan as she actually pays for hers. Jeri flips out in the gift shop, realizing she left her Le Sportsac purse on the tram. Jonathan yells, "It's a miracle!" She punches him in the arm. "Why do these things always happen to me?" she grouses.

- We play poker and toilet paper the rooms that night—until we are caught by Amanda. Courtney defends us with, "The other choir with hot boys went out touring, so there's absolutely nothing to do." Besides, how would I even hook up with Adamth with Jeri, Kelly, Courtney and usually Jonathan clogging up the room? Unless he's an exhibitionist...but the bathroom has no carpet, a definite problem for any hooking up in privacy. Not that Jonathan wouldn't pound on the door the whole time and yell, "What are you doing?"

- I think Amanda feels that as long as no one gets pregnant on this trip, she will be successful. She may be right, as Charlie has blocked the door to the guys' room and barricaded himself and Jeanine in there. Meanwhile, we eat candy and gossip in our room. "How can you go out with someone who has a crooked penis?" Courtney demands of Jeri. "Well, at least Aaron wants to do something with it!" Jeri defends herself, not noticing her Hot Tamales are melting and dribbling onto her yellow pants. "Chip never wanted to sleep with me." She pauses significantly. "He told Aaron he broke up with me because...he likes Mel!" Courtney looks at me appraisingly as I reel from this news. "If you go out with Chip, get Cade to go out with me." I shake my head distractedly. "Um, considering I may or may not have slept with Cade on New Year's Eve when I had alcohol poisoning, I cannot ask him for any favors." Jeri stares at me. "Why didn't I know about this? You didn't tell me when I came back to town?"

- Yeah, and I didn't tell Jonathan either, which could account for the horror stricken look on his face. I distract him by putting the pressure on Jeri. "Jeri, pull it together! Chip was the person that claimed that it happened in the first place, OK? So you can ask him, or Aaron. I am just going to pretend you never said anything. Chip and I are friends. I've never thought about him as anything more." Courtney, probably still salivating at the thought of Cade, points out, "Chip is the nicest guy we know. You might try dating someone who's not a total ass for a change." Jonathan decides it's time for us all to go to bed and leaves. Jeri, Courtney and I are all appraising our new situations. Kelly—who knows where she might have gone.

• Our last day with Parker, we go on the downtown tour, where we see the statue of Gassy Jack in Gastown and pose for photos under the steam clock that doesn't work, but yet is a landmark for no apparent reason. Courtney and I decide to take old-time photos, so we duck into a photo shop. All decked out in our saloon girl hussy outfits, we see three people peeking in the windows—our chaperones. They clearly disapprove of our getups, judging from the pointed looks from the window. Oh, well, the photos have already been taken. I wish I could sponge some cash off Marie to pay for them, but she looks mad.

• The next morning we get ready for the festival, our purported reason for making the trip. In our red and black dresses, we complement the Mounties, who we coax into posing with us. Mounties, it turns out, are not as hot as firemen, and will not allow us to ride their horsies. No Fun Mounties!

• Courtney and I get invited onto a parade float that's passing in the street by two men dressed in sailor suits. "Come on up!" they yell from atop the float. We are like Rose Parade queens as we wave and cavort on the float. The sailors grab us and kiss us, right in front of Amanda and Marie, who are appalled. What a riot!! I love being in parades! Reluctantly we climb down, our fifteen minutes of Canadian fame over, when Amanda threatens us with never-ending detention.

• A post-festival celebratory dinner comes with the tour package, and we are toasted as second-place winners. Jonathan digs wax out of the candleholders with his spoon and insults the waiters. "I wish there was booze at this festival," he snarls. When Jonathan gets bored, he can get nasty. I dodge Adamth, and Jonathan pretends to be my boyfriend to scare him off. The Aberdeenies are useless to me now.

- At the airport the next morning, Jonathan asks if he can sit separately from the rest of our group, as Charlie starts a chorus of "Do You Hear the People Sing?" from *Les Misérables*. Courtney merrily reads a Cosmo and paints her toenails, which are not dry when we board, so she goes barefoot onto the flight. Courtney and I settle into our seats, and Jonathan looms up next to me. "If you stay out of the Les Mis medley, I'll sit here," he offers ungraciously, plunking himself down on the other side.

- Marie sits with Amanda behind us, blissfully unaware of our presence as she remarks, "I think if Melissa lost a little weight, Jonathan would definitely go out with her." I'm wondering where she thinks I can lose it from—there's nothing to drop except my boobs, and they aren't going anywhere.

- My mouth must be hanging open, because Jonathan leans over. "That's not why..." he begins, and then turns away. "Why not then?" I demand, my face burning. "Look at what's out there for me! What's wrong with me? Why don't you want me?" I can't believe I'm finally asking him. I should have just asked Magic 8 ball if I wanted bad news. He sighs. "I honestly can't tell you. I just don't feel that way about you...but I don't feel that way about anyone else either."

- Courtney writes me a note and slides it over on her tray table. "Get over him. He's useless. He only kissed me once while we went out in 8th grade. Remember, the sailors loved you!" Courtney is the best friend ever. She can drop her pragmatism and cheer me up like no one else can.

- The Scam-o-Rama ends where it began: with Jonathan, hoping his feelings will change...or I meet someone else who <u>doesn't</u> need to join a mime troupe.

The Hitcher

Las Vegas, NV
May 1990

We've all caved to peer pressure. It's a fact of being a teenager, and at 17, I'm very susceptible. But some people's friends don't pressure them to do things that will get them raped, killed, or sent to military school. Mine, however, will do anything it takes to stay entertained. This was one of the few times I truly knew this was a stupendously bad idea, but went along with it anyways. Thank God my parents never found out.

Suggested Soundtrack*: "The Gambler"-Kenny Rogers. Over and over and over.*

- For the first time in my life, my parents actually go away together for the weekend to Catalina Island. My friends and I wait approximately two hours to see if my parents will get in a fight, turn around, and come home like they did last time, ruining a perfectly good party.

- After deciding we're home free, we celebrate by allowing Chad to drive my parents' Winnebago through the McDonalds drive thru, which he negotiates with surprisingly little trouble. As we slurp away at our milkshakes and sundaes, Chad turns to me. "I should fulfill my lifelong dream of taking the motorhome to Vegas, Melissa! Now is the time!" he cries dramatically, slamming his cup down.

- I feel dread flowing through my veins, imagining the horrific amount of trouble I will get in if my parents somehow find out. Plus, the plan involves me leaving my 13-year-old sister Rachel and her boyfriend home alone. Courtney and I call these types of plans Bad Idea Jeans, after the hilarious Saturday Night Live commercial advertising them. Bad

Idea Jeans describes this plan to a T. The peer pressure overwhelms me, though, and I agree with a sickening feeling that I will be off to military school come Monday. I have no idea how Chad talks everyone into his wild schemes, but I just can't stand when he's disappointed in me. I cave every time, as does everyone else.

- "How do high school students get into bars and casinos?" Penelope asks practically. Chad, as usual, advises: "Wear the sluttiest clothes you have, and it'll be fine..."

- Jonathan and Courtney, the pragmatists, want to know where we're getting the money for this adventure. Chad's plan: "There are tons of abandoned class rings in the office at school in the Lost and Found. We'll just pilfer them, take them to a pawnshop, and get cash for the gold!" This idea seems brilliant (although by the sick feeling in my stomach I recognize Bad Idea Jeans again) and Chad makes us agree to lift some of our parents' jewelry that they won't miss.

- "This pawnshop is the sleaziest place I've ever been, even counting the butcher shop where we got the check-cashing IDs," I remark disgustedly to Chad. It neighbors an adult bookstore, and we stare blatantly at the sheepish men coming out of it midday. The Bad Idea Jeans II plan nets us a couple hundred dollars and we are off to Vegas!

- Everyone has a different lie about where they are spending the weekend: at Chad's, at Jonathan's, camping with Charlie, etc. We leave a handwritten matrix of lies with Rachel to respond to any parents in case they call. She waves goodbye enthusiastically as we clamber into the motorhome (after packing an assortment of tiny halter tops and spandex skirts) and hit the 15 freeway.

- Jonathan seems edgy. "If we get caught, I'll be jailed for transporting minors over state lines. I'm eighteen now, don't forget." His goals in life right now are: not being jailed, having fun at prom, and graduating,

- Grouchy Jason, Chad's friend, immediately sinks into a surly mood and snaps at me, Penelope, Courtney, Jonathan and Chad. Courtney doesn't mind as much; she and Jason have hooked up before, so who knows...

- Jason could be surly because when he went to the bathroom, Chad made a quick lane change and the door un-Velcroed itself and came hurtling open, exposing Jason at his least attractive. Jason misses the seat all weekend, rendering the bathroom useless to everyone else. Penelope and I pretend to be reporters, speaking into the video camera Jonathan has commandeered. Jason has other ideas for the video camera, but that's not happening, you dirty boy!

- Chad commandeers the tape player and plays "The Gambler" over and over the entire way to Vegas, a song that will become deeply ingrained in our psyches. He begins yelling, "Second verse, same as the first" every time the song ends—and rewinding the tape, in a perverse exercise in control.

- Suddenly, through the pitch-black night, we see a man standing by the road. Jonathan, Penelope, Courtney, Jason and I all see The Hitcher. Chad sees a sad, lonely man and *stops to pick him up*. In my parents' motorhome.

- Jonathan predicts, "He's going to hold us at knifepoint and sell us to donkey bars in Tijuana!" Never the most charitable person, Jonathan sees no reason to start now when our lives could be at stake. Penelope tries to use her charisma against Chad's, pointing out, "This could be really dangerous, Chad," but to no avail. She caves to him, like the rest of us. Chad yells back, "Jonathan has no heart!" but in this situation, none of us do. Chad strides back to unlock the back door as we all cower on the sofa, except Jason, who just narrows his eyes and mumbles, "Snapperheads..."

- As soon as The Hitcher gets in the motorhome, Courtney, Penelope and I begin screaming bloody murder, not caring that we're being <u>so</u> rude by screaming right to his face. The guy doesn't seem fazed, alarming me even more. All too soon, our new friend settles himself in the motorhome and we roll down the dusty road, probably as accomplices to a prison break. Jonathan groans.

• The Hitcher introduces himself as Kurt Raper. Courtney says faintly, "Raper? Not like rapist, right?" Kurt grins. His teeth are brown from chewing tobacco and he's missing two prominent ones. He has scraggly long blond hair and a beard.

• Courtney sidles into the tiny bathroom in the back so she can flag down any passing motorists in case there's a bloodbath. I whisper to her, "No one will be able to see you; there's a wavy window so that no one driving behind you can see if you're going to the bathroom." She whispers back that she's really going to hide and survive the possible carnage and there's no room for anyone else. This reminds me of how she wouldn't share her water with Keiko in Death Valley—she'll let the rest of us die and then be on the news alone!

• In the meantime, Kurt has whipped his arrest warrants out of his boot like a deck of cards. He asks, "Wanna see something?...." We all shake our heads no, but he needs no encouragement and pulls a knife from his <u>other</u> boot, handing it around with pride. Jonathan shoots Chad an "I told you so!" look. "Can you believe I'm in all this trouble already? I'm only 18!" Kurt tells us. Penelope leans over and begins trying to counsel Kurt to change his ways and make something of his life. Especially starting right now!

• I wish I were wearing more than a halter top as Kurt's oily gaze slithers over my cleavage. Thanks, Chad. Luckily, Kurt loves Kenny Rogers and goes to sit up front with Chad and sing along with *The Gambler* 187 more times.

- Eventually, we get to Vegas and park the motorhome in the Mirage parking lot. Kurt lingers around the locked vehicle long after we have said farewell to him. "Chad, he's still hanging around," I mutter, looking back and offering a little prayer the motorhome will be there when we get back. I am an outstanding liar, but even *I* can't think of a plausible story to tell my parents about why their motorhome was stolen by a vagrant hitchhiker in the Mirage parking lot.

- Jason and Chad head off to lose their money big time, making Jason even surlier than ever. The astonishing amount of liquor he drinks doesn't help his mood, either. Jonathan and Penelope, who look 11, are targeted immediately by Security. We gamble at the $2 tables and drink all night at O'Shea's, after being asked to leave all the other casinos. Courtney and I didn't figure on the bouncers seeing exposed breasts pretty much every night of their lives, so our halter top defense crumbles. Penelope tried for a sophisticated older look with glasses and a librarian bun, but she just looks like a little kid dressed up as Betsy Ross. We hear Jason yelling, "Now, you listen to me, snapperhead!" at someone. Hopefully not a Security officer; they don't seem too laid back.

- How can they give away all these free drinks? I love free drinks!

- Courtney needs to get a jacket from the Winnebago, so we go back and discover we are all locked out of the RV. In fact, the keys are dangling from the ignition, where Chad must have left them in his haste to flee Kurt Raper. We search the parking lot for coat hangers, not knowing what to do with them if we find some. Luckily, Security comes by and we plead, "We're locked out of our camper!" Without questioning why teens dressed as hookers are trying to break into a locked vehicle, they simply jimmy open the door with a Slim Jim. "Maybe they're more laid back than I thought!" I marvel as we rejoin the group.

- We all decide to head off to Caesar's Palace, where the festive music they play on the moving walkways entices us inside. Chad and Jason sprint off to lose more money, although Jason actually lumbers along like a sloth since he's pretty drunk.

- Jonathan, Penelope and Courtney want to visit Caesar's Mall, but I want to stay by the entrance, where Max the Gladiator has started chatting with me. Penelope lifts her eyebrows. "Amen, sister," she comments respectfully, and drags Jonathan off, despite his insistence on "rescuing Melissa from that man-whore." My halter top finally proves its value! And maybe Jonathan will get jealous...

- I imagine that Max the Gladiator has some sort of suite here, with lots of drapery hangings and bowls of grapes. Reality rudely intrudes, as Max yaps on about being a business student at UNLV who only works here to put himself through school. He gestures wildly with his sword when talking about economics, and I am hurtling off the Cliffs of Boredom. I'm saved when his toga-clad supervisor wanders over, telling him he needs to greet all the guests, not just me. I bid farewell to his giant pecs and abs of steel, heading toward the mall. At Caesar's Mall, Jonathan buys silk boxers with $100 bills printed on them. If only they were real hundys, as we have no money but quarters for gas for that behemoth motorhome. Penelope, who borrowed $20 from my Bad Idea Jeans pawn fund, wins $50 in nickels! She carefully stashes it for gas money.

- Courtney announces, "I'm hungry. Chad and Jason better have won some food money." Chad and Jason meet us with this plan for getting food: "Show the Del Taco guy your breasts and get us free tacos!" There are not enough free drinks in the world for **that** plan to happen. Instead, we go to a keno parlor for $1.99 steak and egg breakfast. On all the keno monitors, the words "Magic. Music. Dancing. Abracadabra." keep flashing. Courtney decides, "It will be our mantra," and we keep chanting it over and over. Penelope begins using a weird accent to make it more dramatic. "Myoooo-zik. Maaaa-jik. Dahncing. Abra-ca-dabraaaah."

- Amazingly, thank God, the motorhome is still there, bathed in the flashing glow of the neon on the Strip. Courtney asks, "How are you going to explain away the 600 extra miles on the odometer to your dad?" This whole scenario reminds me of the end of *Ferris Bueller's Day Off*, and I can't even think about it, as driving the motorhome off a cliff just won't work. Jonathan and I sing "Amazing Grace" into the video camera as a plea for mercy if we get caught stealing a vehicle. Especially if Jonathan gets carted off to jail for driving us.

- Jason snarls, "Shut the hell up, snapperheads!" Chad finally loses it on Jason: "All you do with your life is drink, bitch and call people snapperhead!" This makes Jason laugh, perversely. Chad's too tired and depressed from losing all his money to drive home, so Jonathan takes the wheel. "Why are all these cars making obscene hand gestures at me? It's so rude!" Penelope, the eternal optimist, waves back at them.

- We call Rachel from the road, and she admits she made up some lie **not** on the matrix and my parents seemed suspicious when they called in. I start crying hysterically, lamenting how we're going to get caught. I cry for twenty miles. On videotape. Jonathan took Eduardo's video camera without asking so he's worried about that, but on the grand scale, it's nothing compared to taking a <u>motorhome</u> without asking.

- When we stop for gas for the 80th time, Jason notices that one of the hubcaps has come loose, and swings wildly back and forth. It hangs by a small wire, but everyone else on the road probably thinks our wheel is about to come off. Jason viciously kicks the hubcap back into place, and Courtney attaches some gum to the loose edge for good measure. "No wonder everyone was gesturing!" Penelope tells Jonathan happily. "It must have been the hubcap, not your driving!"

- On our 89th stop for gas, Chad announces, "We have 79 cents left for gas, and that won't get us home." I suggest scooping up change from the fountain at the outlet mall. I am innovative and figure we need the money more than the fountain. "The water is so cold!" Courtney chatters, shaking the water off the coins.

- Everyone waves at us on the highway. We wave back. Hi everyone! Oh, they are pointing out that the back door of the camper never locked, is <u>wide open</u> and swinging and slamming around precariously. As a result, all of Courtney's clothes have blown out and are scattered across the highway. Courtney leans back on the sofa bed, presumably in despair, until we hear her jingling. Jason and Chad force her out of the corner, and find Penelope's bucket of nickels hidden behind her! She hoarded nickels this whole time, but claims she hid them to keep them safe from Kurt Raper. Jonathan points out that Kurt was long gone *before* we started gambling. Her strong survival skills really just mask a greedy soul. But we blame her mother for raising her that way. Penelope generously shares the nickels. "It was just so exciting to win them!" she exclaims.

- We get home before my parents and clean everything up, using rolls of Scotch tape to mask all the damage, as the motorhome has self-destructed in two days.

- A week later, my dad comes in the house, brandishing a Kenny Rogers tape. "Who was listening to Kenny Rogers in the Winnebago? I want to know what's going on! Why would anyone sit in the driveway to listen to Kenny Rogers?" Mom completely diverts the conversation because she has been looking for the Kenny Rogers tape all week, and accuses <u>my dad</u> of taking it and then denying he took it!

It is a miracle! He is in trouble, not me! As he questions her logic, disbelievingly asking, "Why would I take it in the first place? Why would I want to listen to Kenny Rogers, ever?" I slip out of the room, unnoticed.

- Thanks a lot, Kenny!

3 States in 3 Days

Palm Springs, CA, Lake Havasu, AZ, and Laughlin, NV
April 1991

Jacob and I briefly got back together last summer after graduation, before he left for school in Colorado. We had the best, most romantic summer, followed by letters and packages all through the fall. When he came home for winter break, we finally slept together. Then, in February, right after I turned 18, I discovered via his ESL roommate (who didn't speak English well enough to be discreet or a good liar) that Jacob had another girlfriend at school. Heart. Broken.

Yet again, bad choices follow angst, and I rebound to Chad's friend Keith, who may as well be Darren's clone (as far as money and highlights go). Immediately realizing this is a huge mistake, I palm him off on Courtney (hey, she owes me for kissing Jonathan in 8th grade), who promptly palms him off on Glynis. I'm at loose ends, so when Spring Break rolls around, a spur of the moment road trip seems like just what the doctor ordered! It's not. It's the trip from hell.

__Suggested Soundtrack__: "I'm the One Who Wants to Be With You"-Mr. Big. Over and over and over. Can you tell Chad's in charge of the music again?

- Jonathan calls us from Spring Break in Palm Springs. "Will you and Courtney come get me and take me to Havasu? Keith supposedly has a boat. Or his friend JD does. Or something." Chad, Courtney and I leave for Palm Springs in Courtney's car. I'm dubious about revisiting Palm Springs in case I accidentally sleep with a stranger, but then remember that with Jonathan along, there's no chance of that happening.

- Courtney's car, a 1981 Toyota Tercel 4-speed hatchback, can only make it to 70 before it shimmies alarmingly. It has no air conditioning, and woolly seat covers. Chad begins planning to kill himself immediately if she doesn't drive any faster. I can feel Chad mentally calculating the extra time it will take us to get anywhere at a lower, legal speed. He silently wills her to speed up, but I can tell him from experience—it doesn't work.

- Courtney gets signed statements from us that if she gets a ticket, we'll split it with her. With Monopoly money, since that's all I have. I'm po folks (poor) as usual, despite my full-time job. $5.75 an hour doesn't go far.

- Chad restlessly begins pulling tufts from the woolly seat covers, and thrashing around, complaining about being sweaty already. I forget why he didn't drive us himself— perhaps a DUI or something? Eventually, he bursts out: "Courtney, seriously, did you go to driving school with the nuns? I think even nuns drive faster than you! I can't stand it one more second!" She retorts that if he wanted to drive, he should have offered, and he can shut it if he doesn't like it. Chad subsides, thinking obscenities to himself.

- We spot Jonathan at the Holiday Inn in Palm Springs, drinking beers by the pool when we arrive. I flee the hostile tension in the car immediately. We all join in, briefly forgetting we have to leave that night and shouldn't be drinking beers. Chad decides it's time to go when Jonathan almost burns a hole in his new shirt with a lit cigarette through sheer carelessness. He's acquired an "If You're Not Wasted, the Day Is" t-shirt, which he wears in the car, along with silk boxer shorts with playing cards printed on them.

- On the main strip of Palm Springs, a passenger in a Suzuki Samurai, dressed as the Easter Bunny, gets hauled out of the car and handcuffed by police. Courtney says breathlessly, "They're arresting the Easter Bunny?" like she just found out there was no Santa Claus. I snap a photo for posterity.

I'm always the photographer for anything we do—trips, birthdays, anything. I love having pictures of all our fun times together. Chad calls them "evidence."

- As we drive off, I ask, "Has anyone actually spoken to Keith? Do we know he's there for sure?" Keith's unreliability annoys me to no end. Chad waves airily. "He'll be there. He's obsessed with JD's girlfriend Natalie, and she'll be hanging out on JD's boat." This train of logic seems sound, so off we go!

- Jonathan begins flailing around in the backseat, eyeing the speedometer as we putter away. "Are hamsters running the engine or what?" he whispers. Courtney, who does not care for driving without directions or a map, asks Chad if he knows the route we're taking. Chad claims, "I know exactly where we are...Take that deserted, unmarked road over there." Courtney prays it leads to Arizona. We're in the middle of nowhere; there are no lights, and no call boxes on the roadside of the freaking desert. It seems perfect for an alien abduction.

- To entertain himself, Chad begins calling Jonathan "Gilbert Gottfried" and cawing, "Aawk! Jonathan is the parrot from *Aladdin*! Aawk!" I move to the back, putting Chad up front, to separate the children after Jonathan starts punching Chad in the arm and howling, "Stop calling me that! Stop it!"

- Unfortunately, this gives Chad access to the tape player, which he slots with Mr. Big's "I'm the One Who Wants to Be With You." He plays this one single over and over until we get to Havasu. "Second verse, same as the first." Jonathan and I wish Chad was still obsessed with one of the other songs he's been brainwashing us with this year. His most memorable song choices include: "Joy and Pain", "Life is a Highway", "Wishing Well", "Don't Worry, Be Happy", and "I Want to be Rich"—and he'd always yell, "Bitch!" at the end of the sentence.

- Before we get to the hotel, we crawl down a main road in town at "7 miles per hour," according to Chad, and notice a house on fire. Jonathan and Chad perversely want to drive up so we can "see it burn." Courtney pulls into the neighborhood to be looky-loos, and we feel guilty and bad when we see the sad family, watching their house burn down in their pajamas. Courtney peels out to flee the horrid scene, and Chad smirks, "Oh, now your car goes fast, doesn't it, Courtney?" Courtney gives him a filthy look.

- Finally, we get to the hotel in Havasu where Keith has a room. We all sprint out of the car, realizing the trip had better be really fun to endure the car ride with each other. Are we just tired of each other right now? Penelope and Glynis are tired of us right now. Glynis has a new boyfriend and Penelope has a new friend she wants to be her boyfriend, so that's all very time consuming. It will all work out for them, because they don't have my horrors life.

- Chad carries an economy-size bottle of Jack Daniels, probably stolen from his mom's liquor cabinet, and swigs from it in the hallway, singing, "I'm the One Who Wants to Be With You." Jonathan asks nervously, "Do you think you should be drinking out here?" Chad retorts, "Shut it, Gilbert," and takes another gulp. He begins to pound on Keith's door, yelling obscenities for no reason.

- Keith flings opens the door wearing *lime green Speedo underwear*. They are very shiny, and extremely tight on him, making his paunch look even more pronounced. "Oh my God," Courtney blurts out, and I cover my eyes and begin shaking with laughter. If Jeri were a man, she'd be wearing them.

- The whole scene totally reminds of this horrid experience I had right after I found out Jacob cheated on me. I bet Penelope that I could get my new personal trainer to ask me out, a bet I won. Over dinner, I found out he had spent the holidays in jail for cocaine possession, and was trying to turn his life around (by working in a gym at age 32). After dinner, we met up with some of my friends to go night swimming. My trainer shows up in a blue Speedo swimsuit, which, granted, he had the body for, but I was mortified, especially when he kissed me, and murmured, "You're making my Speedo grow," the worst use of rhyme ever. I fled and made Courtney tell him my parents had found out about his criminal past and forbade me to see him anymore. And I had to switch gyms, the worst part.

- Courtney stares at Keith in shock. "Where did you get that repulsive pair of underwear?" she asks, pointing at his crotch. "My mom got them for me," he snarls defensively, his excitement at seeing us literally deflating by the moment. Chad waits a moment, then mutters, "So THAT'S how it is in their family."

- I am <u>never</u> sleeping with Keith again, and in the bathroom Courtney says she's not hooking up with him ever again either. I can't believe someone would wear those underpants in private, let alone open the door in them. Neither of us can figure out why we hooked up with him in the first place, since he has Yeti Booty, the hairiest butt either of us has ever seen. I'll have to tell Glynis about this immediately when I get home. Between teaching dance and her new boyfriend, we don't see that much of each other, but she'll definitely want to hear this!

- Jonathan refuses to share the bed he's claimed, climbing in, spreading out, and putting on his sunglasses for no apparent reason. That's too bad, because there are only two beds, so Courtney crawls in between Jonathan and Chad, while I have to sleep with Keith and Natalie. Natalie sniffles, and sobs out that she and JD got in a huge fight, so she's staying with Keith now. Keith's generosity doesn't always have ulterior motives, but in this case, it does.

- I can hear Chad quietly slurping from his economy bottle in the other bed and wish I had some Jack Daniels, too.

He's clearly not tired yet, and keeps humming Mr. Big until Jonathan punches him again. Keith tries to cuddle up to me since Natalie's crying herself to sleep, but I'm irritated with the whole scenario. I snap his Speedo mercilessly, causing him to roly-poly up in pain.

- The next morning, Jonathan crawls into bed with me, pulling me on top of him and like Charlie Brown trying to kick the football, I somehow think there's a chance we'll finally get together. Not that I'm actively interested. I'm <u>retroactively</u> interested, from years of ingrained habit. No, nothing new—he only moved because Chad spilled whiskey in their bed and Jonathan doesn't want to sleep in the wet spot. I'm just in his way to dry land.

- I wonder if my parents will let me move to another state? Maybe there's a state that has better boys in it?

- We find out conclusively that Keith does **not** have a boat here, as he'd claimed, and that he wouldn't be invited on JD's boat since he tried to hook up with Natalie. We decide to flee Keith, and try to salvage the trip by going to Laughlin. The plan gets foiled when Keith urgently tells us we have to get him out of here, as JD and Natalie made up, and JD is now "looking for him."

- Chad stole a towel from the hotel, which he now uses to make various disguises to keep himself busy for the long, slow car ride to pretend Vegas. Courtney and Chad put a moratorium on show tunes as soon as we get in the car, leaving Jonathan and I with nothing to do for the rest of our lives. Luckily the Mr. Big tape has jammed and won't play anymore.

- Chad becomes Sahib the Oil Sheik, with his towel draped over his head and a scarf out of my bag tied around it.

- Jonathan complains, "I'm going to die of dehydration," as the combination of fuzzy sheepskin seat covers and no air conditioning raises the temperature to bikram yoga class levels of heat. Chad narrows his eyes and bursts out, "Oh, stop complaining, Gilbert Gottfried! We're all hot too, you know!" and then begins the Gilbert Gottfried taunting again for fifteen miles. Also, driving conditions are suitably worsened by the fact that Chad, Keith and Jonathan are all crammed into the tiny backseat together. I'm always smart enough to call shotgun so they are "touching each other" due to lack of space.

- On the way to Laughlin, Courtney's much-maligned cautious driving saves everyone's life as we drive up a steep, curvy grade. A giant big rig comes swinging around the corner, out of control, down the middle of the two-lane road. Courtney veers off the cliff (which is luckily a shallow embankment) and comes to a stop. "Is everyone all right?" she asks calmly. I turn around to see Jonathan, Chad and Keith clutching each other, eyes bugged out, and Keith screeches, "I can't believe we're not dead! If Chad had been driving, we'd have died for sure!" Chad agrees, and gets the Jack Daniels out for distribution among the backseat.

- All too soon Chad's bored again, makes a turban out of his towel, and will only speak in the voice of Apu from *The Simpsons*.

- We bicker about where to eat. Chad and Keith are in favor of McDonalds, Courtney and I want Carl's, and Jonathan wants Del Taco or Taco Bell. Courtney vetoes any Mexican food on grounds it will give everyone gas and stink up the car. Jonathan retorts, "What does it matter? Both windows have to be down the whole time *in the desert* because we don't have air conditioning! In the desert!" The drive clearly makes him flash back to riding around in Eduardo's various heaps, and he trembles with rage.

- Chad already wandered off to McDonalds so we just go with it and eat there. He wonders aloud if we think someone will really come kick him out of the Playland if he tries to play in it. Jonathan gets nervous, as he usually does when Chad potentially causes a scene that will likely get us thrown out of somewhere. Pushing the envelope is one of Chad's favorite things to do, so Jonathan stays perpetually agitated around him. I dissuade Chad by using the persuasive argument that small children probably pee in there like mad. He looks at the Playland with disgust. "That's sick! This place is SICK!" he shouts, frightening several children. Jonathan pushes us out and back toward the car.

- Jonathan and I quietly begin singing the score of *Les Miserables* in the backseat, feeling it appropriate for the occasion. Keith has fallen asleep, so no one will notice our flagrant disobedience of the car rule against singing.

- We arrive in Laughlin and are horrified to find there are only four hotels and none of them look nice. "This is not even *pretend* Vegas," I complain, looking at the horrid orange stucco buildings. As we get out, Courtney flips it on me, hollering that I will have to pick up every last one of the sunflower seed shells I dropped onto the seat. "They stick in the seat covers," she warns, stalking away.

- Jonathan sniffs, "This place is so trashy," as we walk into the Edgewater. Jonathan and Chad have very specific ideas about what's trashy and what isn't. The Waterfront Hilton in Huntington Beach= not trashy. The Edgewater doesn't stand a chance. Keith just seems grateful to be safe from JD.

- Courtney and I are only wearing bikini tops and shorts, so we fit right in, although we don't have the leathery orange hides most of the other women have. Jonathan, Courtney, Keith and I drink and play slots while Chad pretends he doesn't know us and plays blackjack. However, our fun gets cut off mercilessly by Security, who notices that we aren't over 70 years old like everyone else here, and asks us for ID. The check-cashing cards fail yet again. Chad doesn't get carded, mainly because he already has wrinkles at 19 from years of hard living.

- The four of us continue drinking out by the pool until the intense combination of sun and liquor drive us inside to pass out on a hallway bench, since Security will recognize us if we try to sneak back into the casino. Check in time isn't until 3 p.m. Sigh. Studiously, I avoid eye contact with any hotel employees, who might ask us if we're actually guests there. Finally Chad loses all his money, and joins us for an all-you-can-eat-buffet. It's so sad eating there, like being at Hometown Buffet during the early bird special. Almost all the food is pureed and mushy, definitely not worth the $4.99 each. Keith checks us into the room, since he pays for everything. We spend the night at the Edgewater holed up in the hotel room drinking Chad's whiskey and watching TV. We leave very early the next morning for home.

- By the time we get home, I never want to go anywhere with anyone again. Next year, I vow, we're going the have the funnest Spring Break ever! Without Jonathan! Without Chad! And definitely without Keith!

- Courtney and I make our pact over the last drops of the economy size bottle of Jack Daniels whiskey, and slug it down.

Uncle Upchuck

Sun City, CA
May 1991

After we all graduated from high school in 1990, some of us continued to do what we did normally, except we were doing it at community college in 13th grade. Mostly, this consisted of illegally drinking at a local Chinese restaurant, Peking Palace, where carding consisted of Bunny, the owner, asking, "You all 21, right?" and then waving us in. Some of us, restrained no longer by the social pressure of high school, were pursuing different interests and older men beyond the Orange County line. It was quite a shock to our little clique to get a wedding invitation from our friend Andrea from high school. I'm 18 years old! How can someone I know be getting married??

Suggested Soundtrack: *"I Got Friends in Low Places"-Garth Brooks, "Boot-Scoot Boogie"-Brooks and Dunn, Theme to Beverly Hills 90210*

- Jonathan, Chad, Glynis, Kelly, Courtney, Keith and I arrive in Sun City for Andrea's wedding. Glynis and Kelly pointedly ignore each other, animosity about Chad always bubbling just beneath the surface. In fact, I think Glynis does a push-turn when she sees Kelly and sashays off in the other direction towards me. "I haven't seen you in ages! I've been looking for you at school," she remarks, hugging me. She's highlighted her light brown hair, and wears it shoulder length, with bangs. So cute! Always tall, thin and graceful, Glynis has a commanding physical presence. No wonder Kelly hates her.

- I tell her I started out at the community college she's going to, but after a parking mishap, I couldn't go back.

  - My first car, a Chevy Citation that Keith had dubbed "The Ticket," had been in three accidents since I inherited it from my grandmother. All of them my fault. I had also pulled the fabric covering the ceiling off after Keith and I had left footprints in the ceiling while in the backseat. Only the dome light held the fabric up, creating an Arabian tent look, which went well with the bashed-in hood and dents on both sides.

• The power belts on the windows were broken, so to use a drive through or swipe my parking pass at school, I had to park, set the emergency brake, open the door, punch the parking card in and then I could drive away. Well, one day, I neither parked nor set the emergency brake when I got out of the car. It promptly turned into Christine, Stephen King's homicidal car, and drove itself away, smashing through the parking gate and through some landscaping, ending on the baseball field.

• I ran after it, dressed only in the sports bra and bike shorts I had worn to my aerobics class, and after bouncing all through the lot after my runaway car, with hundreds of people pointing and laughing, I did the only thing I could: I drove away and never came back to that school.

• Glynis, clearly over being tired of us, has recently broken up with her boyfriend, so she's eager to catch up on all the gossip. She laughs till she cries when she hears about Keith's Speedo panties. We determine we have no idea who Andrea's marrying, other than Chad heard that he's a truck driver and country music fan. His name is John Something.

• Apparently, they met at a country bar in the Sun Valley area, which is the Crapeteria of California. Keith can't believe that anyone we know goes country line dancing. "Haven't we all learned from *The Accused* that you'll definitely be gang raped in a country bar?"

- Our group elects to sit near the back of the recreation room at the apartment complex where they're holding the wedding. "Do Andrea and John even live here?" Chad whispers. We all dream of having our weddings at the Waterfront Hilton, and the rec room of an apartment building seems a long way away from that. Jonathan wrings his hands. "This will never last. She's way too young to be getting married! And she's not even pregnant—what's the rush?"

- Jonathan, to fit in with Marie and his sisters, spends most of his time with them going to church, shopping, cooking and watching TV shows such as Jeopardy. Chad theorizes that Jonathan has never had a real girlfriend because of Marie. Jonathan can't relate to his dad, Eduardo, at all. Eduardo spends most of his time camping in his van at the beach...alone. Or tinkering with his pedal scooter, which he actually drives around town, wearing a helmet that has stickers all over it. Jonathan lives in fear that his friends will see Eduardo on his pedal scooter with his sticker-helmet, and recognize him as Jonathan's dad.

- One side of the room is made up of a glass wall separating us from the pool area, currently packed with small children and tubby fathers. "Let's sit here, by the windows," Chad suggests, assuming immediately he'll be bored with the wedding. The music begins with a country-themed wedding march, and John and his groomsmen amble out from the sidelines. John's wedding ensemble: a black suit with fringe across the shoulders and down the pant legs, a white shirt with a giant bolo tie, and matching silver belt buckle. He has also sports a large black cowboy hat, which he wears throughout the ceremony, shading his thick mustache.

- Deanne comes in as the maid of honor, in a rodeo clown dress. I wonder if Deanne has considered the fabulous Halloween potential of her bridesmaid dress. She's Laura Ingalls without the bonnet! Her long, curly hair is the color that happens when Asian and black women try to dye their hair blonde. She apparently didn't have enough dye left to do her eyebrows; they're still dark brown. She could be bald for all anyone cares, though, since her giant fake breasts take all the attention away from her head. Laura Ingalls as a porn star—that's what Deanne looks like. Glynis looks over and widens her eyes, mentally saying, "Can you believe this?" Kelly and Courtney, who have the luxury of being natural blondes, are shaking their heads in unison. Keith stares at the boob job in fascination. We are already trying not to look at each other to avoid cracking up. Jonathan fails miserably, and Glynis elbows him, being much more discreet at laughing hysterically *on the inside*.

• Andrea begins her descent down the stairs, holding her long skirt up, displaying a pristine pair of white cowboy boots. Her rodeo gown matches Deanne's, except in white, and she has the matching cowboy hat to John's, except in white. Chad buries his head in Keith's shoulder and moans, "Oh, nooo," and I look up to see why: You can see clear up Andrea's skirt, all the way to her white lace panties. No one should flash at her own wedding, but it's a lost cause. The panties are there for all to see. And they are skimpy. Blissfully unaware, Andrea smiles and waves to beat the band, apparently not at all uncomfortable in what has to be itchy lace and only tiny ribbons on either side holding them up.

• She makes it down the aisle and takes John's hand. They look happy, but since he has a mustache and thus reminds me of my father, I feel like I'm watching an after-school special on incest.

• In high school, Jeri got this book from somewhere called *Kiss Daddy Goodnight*. It was a graphic account of this girl who had been molested by her father for years, and how she had supposedly grown to like it. I think it ended with them going to live in some other European country where they're more relaxed about incest or something. John looks just like the dad on the cover of that book.

- Meanwhile, in the back Kelly and I speculate about the rest of the guests, as we know very few of the people attending. Glynis provides lots of fun facts about the guests, as she's our historian. She can remember the most arcane facts about almost everyone we went to high school with, down to what she was wearing when she and Chad broke up years ago.

- At this moment, one of the tubby dads lumbers along by the window wall, dripping from the pool. Spectacularly fat, he resembles one of Chad's neighbors, Mr. Fat Man, who always calls the police when we have parties. He retrieves a large killer whale float and trots back by, only this time, all we can see is the giant whale float bobbing along the window, and cannot contain ourselves. It's like Shamu escaped from Sea World and is flopping his way to freedom, supported by a pair of hairy white legs. All of us are shaking with the effort of not laughing out loud, which is almost more obnoxious than just laughing. People begin shooting us dirty looks, but none of us can help it.

- Finally, John slips a ring on Andrea's finger and they kiss amorously, buried under his mustache. *Kiss Daddy Goodnight*, indeed.

- They hold the reception out by the pool area, so we celebrate along with the other random families who are using the pool that day. Deanne hikes her dress up and takes off her cowboy boots so she can soak her feet in the Jacuzzi. Keith hopes, "Maybe she'll flash her panties as well!" but she stops just short.

- A little boy stage-whispers, "Dad, are those bandits?" He obviously thinks the wedding is just a Western come to life, and who can blame him? John's groomsmen look like the sort who would shoot off guns just for fun. In fact, in Sun City that type of behavior might be perfectly acceptable.

We're sheltered, spoiled teens from Orange County, a snobby place to grow up.

- All the pool chairs have been pushed to the sides for dancing. All of us have to learn the Electric Slide, since there are no other normal musical options. Deanne, being a regular at country bars, already knows it, but the rest of us stumble around trying to follow along. Glynis' years of teaching dance come in handy: she holds an impromptu line dancing class so we can participate. Most of us would rather drink, but there are parents here who frown when we get near the coolers. "And one, two, three, four, five, six, seven, turn—no, Keith, what are you doing? There's no turn there!" Jonathan kicks Chad on the hopping part. Chad complains, "You broke my ankle!"

- John, Andrea and her dad wave goodbye, pile into a car the size of a Yugo and head off to their honeymoon in Vegas. We discuss the likelihood of her father actually accompanying them on the honeymoon, but someone tells us they're dropping him off on the way.

- After the wedding, we go back to the one seedy motel room we're all sharing and argue about who's going to get dinner and beer. Keith volunteers to get beer and Kelly and I offer to go to the liquor store with him. Jonathan and Courtney take Taco Bell orders from everyone and head off together. Kelly suddenly realizes that leaves Glynis and Chad alone together. She sees by the smirk on Glynis' face that she realizes it, too.

- At the store, only Keith can do the math involved to calculate seven people drinking (on average) seven beers each. He gets five cases just to be safe. Keith works for his dad's company in accounting, so I guess he has to be good at math. He makes bank and pays for everything. In a moment of candor, Courtney, Glynis and I realized that we probably all felt obligated to hook up with him at some time or another since he paid for everything we did. "We're prostitutes!" Glynis wailed, her eyes welling up with tears for our lost innocence. Courtney just rolled her eyes. She works as a waitress at the Newport Harbor Yacht Club, and after months of seeing 80-year-old tycoons come in with 19-year-old bimbos, she's jaded. I work for a physical therapy office, so all I see are the same 80-year-olds after they break a hip and the 19-year-old leaves them.

- Keith pays for all the beer, plus all the assorted snacks we dump on the counter. We load everything in his BMW (license plate: HPPYGUY) and take off for the motel. Some of John's groomsmen are also staying at the motel and ask if we want to smoke out with them. Those of us who don't smoke pot (me, Jonathan, Keith, and Courtney) head inside. Those of us who do (Chad and Glynis) stay outside, gladly accepting free pot. Torn, Kelly vacillates: She desperately wants to be with Chad and look cool and glamorous, but she hasn't smoked pot and doesn't really want to. Reluctantly she mopes inside, leaving Chad outside with Glynis, who handles her victory modestly again.

- "Now we have beer, so we can get in the hot tub," Keith proclaims. Glynis looks mortified. "Keith, this is the grossest motel ever—who knows what's in the hot tub?" Keith claims we can jump the fence to a nearby apartment complex he saw, and skinny dip like we do at home. "The police here might not be as nice as in Huntington Beach," Courtney reminds him. The police in Huntington are really nice, considering we're technically guilty of: trespassing, indecent exposure, underage drinking, and littering, leaving our bottles and cans at the pools we skinny dip in. This may also explain why we all hook up like rabbits.

- After the pot is gone, the groomsmen all drive off to a bar and the rest of us venture outside again to drink more beer. Chad gets bored of drinking with us, and befriends a transient named Chuck, who he christens Uncle Buck. Uncle Buck has been idly hanging around the parking lot, checking out all the pockets of his coat. Chad passes Uncle

Buck a beer, and says, "Uncle Buck, what's your story?" Chad loves this activity: approaching the oddest people he can find, becoming involved with them, then getting bored and palming them off on someone else. Uncle Buck begins drinking our beer and telling us the sad story of his life, which involves mostly drinking and doing drugs.

- Meanwhile, Jonathan pulls Chad aside and whispers he better not be sticking us with another Kurt Raper. Chad airily waves him off, insisting nothing bad happened with Kurt, and Jonathan needs to be more charitable to the less fortunate. Jonathan points out, "Uncle Buck isn't really less fortunate. He just does drugs and could stop."

- Keith tries to determine if anyone here will hook up with him, but the three of us pinky-swore we would not succumb again just to get free stuff. We'll let him pay for us without putting out anymore and see how it goes.

- The room is a complete dump, but Kelly and Courtney still think it's best to have their dinner on one of the beds. I prefer not to think what fluids might have seeped into the repulsive blanket. Kelly turns the TV on to *Beverly Hills, 90210* — the show of our generation. Jonathan and Glynis are sprawled on the other bed, avoiding Uncle Buck outside, and Keith tries his luck with Kelly, which will **never** happen. Especially not in front of Chad.

- Kelly's been obsessed with Chad for years, after they dated briefly. She has never found anyone else who measures up to him, but it's crystal clear to everyone else that nothing will come of this. As Jonathan always predicts, "it will all end in tears." Glynis' presence just adds salt to the wounds of love.

- Uncle Buck comes into the room and sits on the bed with Jonathan while Chad goes to the bathroom. Uncle Buck starts looking around and eyeing our stuff. Jonathan flips out and demands he go outside. We're all pretty shocked, since Jonathan hates conflict and rarely rocks the boat. Chad yells from the bathroom, "Uncle Buck is my friend, and if Uncle Buck goes, I go!" Keith, whose credit card is actually paying for the room, says Uncle Buck needs to go NOW. A generous person, Keith also likes that paying gives him some control, which he exercises right now. Chad pouts and goes back outside with Uncle Buck, who has left a stink cloud inside the room for all of us to enjoy.

- It's 3 a.m. and other rooms are beginning to complain about us, primarily because Uncle Buck and Chad are drunk and screaming obscenities about Jonathan and Keith. Kelly tries to wrest Chad away from the evil influence of Uncle Buck and Jonathan's shouting, "I hate Uncle Upchuck! Get him out of here!" Kelly narrows her green eyes at Uncle Buck. "You're pretty," he tells her, leering at her in her pajamas. She laughs snidely.

- Jonathan stretches out to sleep on his bed, and Glynis and I push in, despite his protests. There are leftover snack crumbs and salsa spills all over the bed. Kelly and Keith get in with Courtney, equally ruining her plans for solitude. Maybe she and Jonathan make a better couple than I think?

- Chad, inevitably, gets bored of Uncle Buck and comes in, but sleeps on the floor in a pile of towels. Kelly occasionally mumbles, "Stop it, Keith...", and he whines, "Wha-aat?" Jonathan flips out on Glynis. "If you're going to sleep here, you can't sleep in pirouette position! There's no room! Straighten your legs out!" Kelly finally slaps Keith's hand away. "Stop it!"

- On the drive home the next day, Courtney, Kelly and I speculate about getting married at 19. Courtney and Kelly are against it, but at the rate I'm going, I'll be dead before I have a good boyfriend, so I might cave and take the first proposal I get. Unless he's named Chuck or Buck— then I'll pass.

Vegas Goes Awry

Las Vegas, NV
December 1991

I moved out of my parents' house over the summer and into "The Grotto", as it was called, with several guys from my gym as roommates. I lived in their laundry room for $150 a month, and didn't mind that the dryer vent left a gaping hole in one of my walls. Courtney dated one of my roommates for a while. Penelope, Glynis and Kelly loved coming over to beefcake central, especially when we had parties that got broken up by police helicopters. The Grotto was a good place to make bad choices. Living with the inmates of The Grotto brought home how naïve I really was. I thought I was all grown up at 18. Boy, was I stupid.

Suggested Soundtrack: "High Enough"-Damn Yankees, "Winds of Change"-Scorpions, "Show Me the Way"-Styx, other metal/hair band music you're forced to listen to

- My roommate Kaiser asks me if I want to go to Vegas with his friend, Tony, because Tony asked him to ask me to go. Yes! YES! Tony, Kaiser's hottest friend ever, should be in one of those construction worker calendars, at least until we get married and he gets a white-collar job.

- I'm packed and ready to go when the van pulls up to our house at 10 p.m. on a Friday night. I get in and hear the slam of the door behind me. The van peels out before I notice I don't know a single person in the vehicle. I try not to panic, and tell myself we must be going to pick up Tony at his house. You'd think he'd already be here...

- I keep quiet until we're an hour or so out. "Wow, I had no idea Tony lived so far away." A creepy Menendez brother look-alike, wearing a black **mesh** shirt, chuckles, and says,

"Tony's right here, baby." He stretches his meaty arm across the back of my seat as if he owns me.

- I'm going to throw up in the van.

- Mesh Tony doesn't seem to sense my distress, despite the fact that my eyes dart nervously to every locked door in the van. How can my mother always be right! I can hear her: "If you do stupid things, like go somewhere in a van, bad things will happen to you." Eternally suspicious of vans, she'd have a coronary if she knew I was in one right now.

- I'm nervous about making a total scene—perhaps because I could be date raped repeatedly and left for dead in the desert, since Mesh Tony clearly does not have the chivalry of Hot Tony, who was <u>supposed</u> to be here.

- It turns out Mesh Tony bartends at the Play Pen, a nudie bar frequented by my roommates Kaiser, Memphis, Jay and Calvino, and everyone else they know. Mesh Tony has "wanted to meet me for a long time" based on glimpses of me he gets delivering illegal Mexican steroids to my roommates. More realistically, being a total cretin, he probably sits in the parking lot across the street from our house watching me, like in a Lifetime kidnap movie.

- Sadly for Mesh Tony, he had no idea I expected a totally different Tony, Hot Tony who I love, not yucky Mesh Tony. When I try to explain and ask to be let out, he acts puzzled by my reticence to randomly go away with him for the weekend. I stare at him in disbelief. "You thought I would just agree to go to Vegas with some nudie bartender I've never even met before? Are you insane?" He chuckles again and chides me, "Relax, you'll have a good time."

- This has chilling overtones of the last time I heard someone say this:

- Flashback to the time Courtney and I were offered a ride by this bunch of guys in a limo in Newport Beach, and since we had never ridden in a limo, even for prom, it seemed the opportunity of a lifetime. Our Bad Idea Jeans radar never went off.

- The guys told us they were in a band called The Subjugators. Look it up if you don't know what that word means, but it's not good. After driving around Newport Beach and drinking in the limo, they invited us back to a house party that we foolishly went to without retrieving Courtney's car first.

- The house was super cool, with slot machines, video games, a full bar, and I was having fun until I realized one of the guys had disappeared with Courtney into the basement and *locked them in*. I started screaming, "Let me in! You locked my friend in a torture chamber in the basement! Let me in there!" and pounding on the door.

- One of the other guys laughed and said, *"Relax, you'll have a good time,"* and handed me the most discolored drink I have ever seen. I poured it out into a plant and I'm pretty sure the plant passed out immediately.

- Finally, I noticed that you can see into the basement through an outside window and ascertain they are just making out.

- Courtney had no idea until they were leaving the basement that the door was even bolted and flips out that she was locked in. We have to threaten to call the police and tell them we are minors to get anyone to take us back to our car. Two other new guys on motorcycles offer to take us back, and we are finally free of The Subjugators.

- Once we arrive in downtown Vegas (ew), Tony gives me money to gamble with. He has no idea I hate gambling and pocket all the money, possibly for a cab or new hotel room, electing to just nurse my free drink and make the best of it. He keeps trying to talk to me about boring things, like sports, cars and guns. Once he mentions the guns, I'm terrified. "Is that why we rode here in a rapist van? So you wouldn't have to check firearms on the plane?" He chuckles again.

• Finally the whole group (Tony plus three male friends plus a couple) goes up to the suite to go to bed. I wake up about an hour later. Everyone has left, Tony looms over me and has removed the mesh shirt, which initially seems good, but it's actually not, because he has also removed his pants and underwear. What has awakened me was him fumbling with the button on **my** pants. While I'm asleep. A sleep-date-rapist.

• I finally snap and flip out on him, yelling about:

  • How he's a would-be date rapist

  • How raping a sleeping person basically makes him a necrophiliac (he scratches his head like an ape and looks puzzled again)

  • How I'd never have shown up if I had known he was the wrong Tony

  • How he's a total loser, and even worse, he works at the Play Pen

  • How I would never in the world go out with someone who would wear mesh clothing

  • How he looks like either of the murdering Menendez brothers

  • How he is dumb as a box of rocks and I can't hold an intelligent conversation with him

- Forgetting about his gun penchant, I push and shove him all the way back to the door, and then shove him into the hallway, naked. I consider re-opening the door to throw his hideous mesh shirt out after him but don't want to ever see him again.

- Bolting the door, I consider my options, the best of which I spot lying on the dresser. Tony has left his wallet behind (being thrown out unexpectedly) and he owes me big time. Still on the adrenaline rush of almost being date raped (as predicted), I call the credit card company to see how much available credit Tony has: $4000! I book a first class ticket on the next flight out of Vegas, lowering my voice dramatically on the phone to the ticket agent while impersonating Mesh Tony.

- Wishing I had more time so I could book a limo on each end, I empty the wallet of its remaining $120 in cash and call Security to escort me down to the entrance. By the time Tim, the security guy, arrives, Tony has disappeared like gorillas in the mist. I finally burst into tears, my bravado melted into a puddle of horror. Tim sympathetically tells me I did the right thing, and too bad I can't cash advance all the money off the credit card. He puts me in a cab with Arun, who I allow to run free with his horrible driving (which cannot possibly be worse than riding with my dad, especially in his motorhome).

- Where did I go wrong here? Ah, trusting Kaiser. There was my mistake. Kaiser, my most piggish roommate, has three girlfriends right now, and has unprotected sex with all of them. To get rid of the 6 o'clock girlfriend, Tammi, he tells her his mom came to town and he's meeting her for dinner. Then the 8 o'clock girlfriend, Ellen, comes over, not smelling the miasma of Tammi sex on him. He gets rid of her at 9 with, "My sister's flying into town, and I have to pick her up at the airport." Then Mimi comes over and spends the night. I just can't tell if he did this on purpose or really thought I'd like Mesh Tony.

- I call Courtney from the Vegas airport. "Pick me up at Long Beach Airport ASAP." She's at the gate with hot chocolate to go when I arrive. We drive around and talk about it and put things into perspective.

- When I get home, Kaiser looks apprehensive about what I'm doing back already. Perhaps Mesh Tony called collect (as he also left his room key behind). I have already armed myself with Jay's hockey stick from the closet, which I begin brandishing at him as I scream that his disgusting "friend" almost raped me! I see his arms come out as though to hold me off and the thought, "Let me explain" form in his brain. Jay wheels on Kaiser. "You let her go anywhere with Tony the bartender? With that pig?" Jay restrains me and pushes Kaiser into the living room, where I hear shouting and thumping. Apparently, even among the low moral standards of this pit, Kaiser crossed a line. Jay is the best roommate ever, despite his steroid use and using clippers to shave his back in the shower.

- Later, Kaiser limps in to apologize to me. Jay refuses to let Mesh Tony in the house and gets him fired from the Play Pen. In the meantime, I have called everyone Kaiser has slept with lately and told them how he has been cheating on all of them. And has VD. Which he actually does, as I saw the antibiotic pills in his filthy bathroom.

- The next week Hot Tony comes by a party at our house. Hot Tony, not too bright either, seems sweet as he kisses me in the backyard. Until the next day, when he comes over with his *fiancé*. And introduces her to me. I am pretty sure living here is warping my perspective on men; otherwise, they really are **all** asses.

- That night, as I'm shoving a chair against my door to block it (Kaiser found out about the VD calls) I realize I'm too young to be this bitter and jaded. I'm too smart to settle for a crap boyfriend (especially ones who cheat). My best solution seems to be going home and listening to my mother!

- So I do. I pack up, move out, and go home. It's so nice being somewhere people love you, no matter what. As my mom says, "These stupid morons will come and go, but we're your family forever." The other good part of moving home: getting to see Jonathan, Chad and Keith again. They all boycotted the "Den of Sin," as Jonathan (and his friends from church) called the place.

- I know "what happens in Vegas stays in Vegas," but this time it doesn't. It stays with me and makes me suspicious and fearful for a long time.

Pigs in the Trailer Park

Rosarito Beach, Mexico
Spring Break 1992

After nearly being date raped in Vegas and fleeing back home, I regard every boy I met with a high level of suspicion. Jonathan, Courtney and Kelly bolster that position until it becomes a given that no guy could be interested in me for anything but sex. Despite my resolve to stay home and get good grades and things, at 19 I'm easily distracted. So when Spring Break rolls around, the siren song of sun, beach, and boys overpowers me.

***Suggested Party Game for Reader**: Kelly was obsessed with the movie The Grifters at this time, and every time she would finagle someone, she'd call it a grift. Take a shot for every grift in the chapter, preferably of Jack Daniels if you have some on hand.*

***Suggested Soundtrack**: "Paradise City"-Guns 'n' Roses, "You Shook Me (All Night Long)"-AC/DC, "Brown-Eyed Girl"-Van Morrison, "Let's Go Crazy"-Prince, "Little Red Corvette"-Prince, "Vacation"-The Go-Gos and "Boys Don't Cry"-The Cure*

- Kelly, Courtney and I decide on the spur of the moment to go to Rosarito Beach for Spring Break this year instead of Have-a-Brew, Have-a-Screw, Havasu. Two hours later we're on the road, promised by Kelly's friend Craig Ensler that we could stay at his parents' beach house. He would meet us there at the Rosarito Beach Hotel tonight. Even though we're pretty sure Craig thinks one of us will hook up with him for the use of his beach house, that's definitely not going to happen.

- Our adventure begins with a pre-emptive bit of bad luck: a speeding ticket twenty minutes from home. Ironic, since Courtney drives so cautiously. People were passing

Courtney left and right, but it was easier for the police to catch us in her slow car. We have no money to help her with, so hopefully her dad will just suck it up and pay the ticket.

• Unfortunately, we can smell Tijuana well before we get to the border. The freeway jams with cars on their way to Mexico. We crawl to the Mexican border, assuming there will be signs directing us to Rosarito, and we are not disappointed. Viva la Mexico! The main street in Rosarito oozes bares tanned flesh! People are already hanging off their hotel balconies, riding on the roofs of cars, and drinking <u>while</u> driving. Courtney gets nervous and snappy. Kelly and I yell, "We want road sodas too!" but are banned by Courtney even from drinking while **she's** driving, which seems harsh. Road sodas are alcoholic beverages, cleverly disguised as Cokes, usually drunk out of Big Gulp cups. Highly illegal but very efficient.

• We get a room at the Rosarito Beach Hotel (at $70 a night, we can only afford to stay there one night) and go change clothes. Our room has a window that faces a brick wall. Why even bother having a window? We have seen neither hide nor hair of Craig Ensler, but immediately run into a girl from high school, Vera, who has a room. Grift #1: We file her room number away in case we need to crash there tomorrow.

• Start heading towards the beach until Kelly notices horseback riding lessons going on. "Being trampled by horses does not sound like fun," she points out. Neither does laying out in horse poo; diabolical brown pits litter the sand.

• Head back to the murky green pool at the hotel. Courtney fears that her hair will turn green from whatever gunk colors the pool. Kelly's hair has turned brown, so she's over hair maintenance. I have no worries, and dive right in. Some guy charges drinks to his buddy's room, so we put in our orders as well. Grift #2: Jack and Cokes for everyone! I love Spring

Break in Mexico! Everyone's fun and friendly! There are so many cute boys! The drinks (so far) are free!

- Mid-afternoon, we put on shorts and head to Rock and Roll Taco for lunch. Rock and Roll Taco, a fun bar, has a wooden cow with its legs crossed sitting outside the door. We insist on posing for pictures with the cow, who I name Bessie. I like this Bessie better than the Brig Pilgrim Bessies. We get tacos and head out to the bar's pool. It's the second murky green pool of the day (what is with the water here?) and sports a volleyball net. The losing team in the pool volleyball game has to buy a round of drinks for everyone! Grift #3: We put our orders in yet again.

- Grift #4: Kelly gets invited to a rooftop bar serving cheap lobster by a Nevada soccer team. She finagles them into paying for our lobster with promises of how we'll party with them tonight. She can make all the promises she wants, but I wonder what will turn out to be wrong with them. Will they lisp? Expect sex in exchange for lobster? She claims I'm too suspicious and we can always escape if needed.

- Easy for her to say—**she** wasn't living in The Grotto with one good roommate out of four (Jay). **She** wasn't the one pushing furniture in front of her door every night to block out the Mesh Tonys of this cruel world.

- "Let's go back to the hotel to nap and then shower before going out tonight," Courtney yawns. The shower may be unusable, it's *so* gross. You'd think for $70 the hotel would give you those pedicure flip-flops at least. But since I probably caught athlete's foot from the murky green pool, who really cares now?

- After much discussion of outfits and hair, we are off to the legendary Papas and Beer. I hope to frequent this bar in Heaven: low cover charge, $2 beers and fabulous dance music. I could live here from now on. And I may have to, if my mother ever finds out I'm here. I'm pretty sure I'm supposed to be at Courtney's writing a paper right now.

- A guy who looks like he might be a science or engineering major asks me to dance, so I shuffle off, casting looks back at the bar. Courtney raises her beer to me. Thanks a lot, Courtney. She mouths, "Survival of the fittest!" and turns to a muscular blonde guy who sits down beside her.

- What are the social rules when someone you aren't interested in asks you to dance and you do it because you're a nice person, and then the song finishes and they stare at you like a moose? I resort to chugging my full beer, pointing at the empty bottle, and weaving off through the crowd. Kelly resignedly dances with someone's chubby friend. She only talks to non-threatening boys so Chad won't think she's interested in anyone else. I'm pretty sure he barely notices but she refuses to move on. Or stop hating Glynis.

- I meet Courtney at the bar. She's keeping the soccer guys at bay, lamenting how she learned German in high school and now she can't even order any beer. I order cervezas for both of us. Grift #5: Some older divorced man, a Dad on the Scam, pays for the beers. Go Dads on the Scam! If only we could see his credit card number for future use....

- Dad on the Scam invites us to his hotel, but we'd rather sleep in the car if necessary. However, if Kelly gets drunk enough, we can pretend she might hook up with him if she were sober (quasi-Grift #6). Later, we can spring on him that she's only 16 and stay in his probably posh hotel room while he trembles in fear of Mexican jail!

- On our way up to the upper bar, this guy Brendan introduces himself. I can't tell if he said Brendan or Brandon, and after the embarrassment last month, I am determined to get it right.

- Last month, I met this hot guy at a Mormon skating party. But I didn't know it was a Mormon skating party, because they never tell you, so beware of being invited to any skating or beach events if a Mormon person, like a co-worker in my case, invites you. Anyways, he was the only other non-Mormon who was there, and he asked me for my number. He calls two weeks later on Valentines Day, a little presumptuous, but whatever, he's British, so maybe they don't have Valentines Day in Britain. I invite him to this party I'm going to that night, and introduce him to all my friends as Germaine. Only a couple weeks later, when I'm in his dorm room, I see an award that has his name on it. His name is <u>Tremaine</u>. Not Germaine at all, although it sounded right because of his fabulous accent. When I asked him why he didn't say something, he said he didn't want to be rude and correct me. So I basically couldn't go out with him anymore because I would have had to tell everyone I didn't even know the guy's real name.

- Establish it's Brendan, not Brandon, and he goes to SDSU. This means I'll never see him again, since nobody wants to drive two hours to hang out. But he really is cute.....Courtney sees my indecision and pragmatically takes charge, hustling Brendan's chubby friend off to the dance floor. Why can't hot guys always have a hot friend for your hot friend?

- We go up to the pool table area where we can talk. As soon as I sit down, I realize I'm teetering on the line between pleasantly tipsy and wasted. I crash right over onto the wasted side of the line with: "Look, if you're looking for some skank to have a one night stand with, keep looking!" Oh, here's my New Pact for dealing with guys: I will **NOT** sleep with them right away <u>anymore</u>, because they never call you again. If I can string it out longer, the relationship has a better chance of lasting. Or so my theory goes.

- He's either the nicest person in the world or studies psych, because he stays and talks to me instead of going to the bathroom and never coming back. Speaking of which, I am going to wet my pants right in front of him. He will take the opportunity to flee while I go to the bathroom for sure.

- The women's bathroom has a line all the way to back to America. I pee in a dark area into a planter instead. I love how bodysuits are so much more discreet for those times where you just have to urinate in public. And I love Mexico, where you probably wouldn't get busted for doing so, unlike America. Particularly if the Harbor Patrol catches you.

- He's still here? Doesn't he know he's cute enough to find someone who would sleep with him immediately? Who doesn't have a brand-new pact? In any case, he is funny, hot and smart and that's all that matters at the moment. There's no need to start worrying about later (not that there will be a later, but still...)

- He asks me to dance and fortunately proves to be a good dancer, not an embarrassment like that Marty Moose guy earlier. I think there must be a Spring Break soundtrack they give to DJs in every fun Spring Break city. Standards like "You Shook Me (All Night Long)", "Brown Eyed Girl", and almost the whole Purple Rain soundtrack seem to get played everywhere I go. Somehow, after dancing for a while, Brendan and I end up making out on the pool table. It's as though anything in between got fast forwarded, and suddenly we're in a movie scene of making out on a pool table while the crowd of hot extras drink and dance around us. While kissing me, Brendan notices a couple having sex in the bushes behind us—probably right where I just peed. I accidentally mention this. He starts laughing. "I thought you got back really fast!"

- Courtney and Kelly come to ruin my life and take me back to the crappy but expensive hotel. Why don't I have irresponsible friends who would just abandon me to a stranger and let me find my own way back? Brendan says he'll meet me in my hotel lobby at noon the next day. As soon as we're out of earshot, Kelly says, "You know he won't show, right?" Yes, Kelly, I know that.

- We all wake up in the morning in total hangover mode. Of course, Courtney and I have scored the bed. Kelly sleeps on the cold, tile floor, with nary a blanket, next to the door which has a one-inch gap under it. Dirt blows in on her. I shout, "What time is it? Where are my contacts? What's going on?" Courtney narrows her eyes against the light, and yells back, "Just pick up the phone and ask 'Que hora es?'" Courtney knows no Spanish at all, but has somehow channeled it through her hangover.

- We get up to eat, with no word from Craig Ensler. He better show up. Courtney and I go off to search for him, leaving Kelly as collateral on the floor. We literally start walking the streets, asking locals, "Donde esta la casa de Craig Ensler?" No one knows, not that we could understand the answer anyway.

- "What do you want for lunch? I'm hungry," I announce. We eat street tacos, despite hearing Jonathan's voice in our heads that we'd get horribly sick, perhaps even die. Jonathan's voice and my mother's occasionally mingle together in my head with dire prophecies about all the bad things that could happen.

- As we wander about, we pass by the Hotel California, the funnest hotel ever! A camper parks in the middle of the courtyard, and people just walk from room to room with beers. I imagine real college is like this, when you live in a dorm and know everyone. Unfortunately, we all go to community college except Kelly, who's still in high school. Speaking of college, Courtney and I **barely** go to school— we usually ditch class and watch *Little House on the Prairie* reruns and then get blue Icees and drive to Newport Beach. We are doomed when it comes time to transfer.

- There are no vacancies at Hotel California, which is also très cheap. We MUST find a way! I follow Courtney outside, feeling despondent, and overhear two guys talking about how they are dead broke. We perk up immediately.

- It turns out Jim and Ron, our new roomies, got pulled over by the cops on their way here. They had to use almost all their money to bribe the Federales, and now can barely pay for the room for the week they have it reserved. Grift #7: We offer to pay 1/2 of the room and we'll all four share the one bed. Courtney bets they are too nice to allow this and will take the floor, and as usual she is right. She also bets we can boot Kelly to the floor as well, as she is not part of the deal. In fact, we have not even disclosed her existence yet.

- Maybe I should just move to Mexico because the guys here are so much nicer than in Orange County? I'm fine sharing the orgy bed because neither Jim nor Ron are cute, and will not tempt me to break my new pact.

- We go back to our hotel to check out and move our stuff to Hotel California, my new favorite song. From the hotel, Kelly calls home collect to determine the whereabouts of Craig Ensler. We hear her yelling at the operator, "I just want to call America! Comprende, dammit!" She somehow gets in touch with Surly Jason, who tells her smugly, "Craig went to Havasu and I heard he's in jail with a bunch of other people for drunk driving. You're screwed, snapperheads!" he gloats as he hangs up on us.

- On the minus side, we have no more free places to stay, barely any money, and Kelly, being 16, could be deported at any time. On the plus side—I have actually met a fabulous guy who may not <u>only</u> be interested in sex. He may redeem all mankind if he actually shows up today! We head for the beach and lay out in a poo-free zone. I pretend not to notice the time about five times before Courtney grunts in annoyance at me.

- At noon, I walk back to the Rosarito Beach Hotel, hoping for the best but assuming the worst. I may put that on my tombstone—that's catchy. Kelly and Courtney had done their sighing, eye rolling thing when I got up, but I will always wonder if I don't go, even if I have to slink back alone. Brendan arrives right on time, in what has to be a documented miracle, like stigmata. When we arrive back on the beach, holding hands, Courtney and Kelly look suspicious, as though I may have cloned him in the night and then *planted* him in the lobby on time.

- He takes me to lunch at the lobster roof bar I went to the day before. I pray the soccer goons do not frequent this place. Also, this doesn't count as a grift, as I am in earnest. Brendan, a business major studying Chinese, wants to do business internationally. No problem, I'd be happy to jet set around the world and I love Chinese food! He also has three older brothers, who I'm hoping could appease Courtney and Kelly and put me back in their good graces. He seems appalled that I work full time and put myself through school which, I claim, builds character (but I think I have enough character at this point).

- Jim and Ron are very nice when Brendan and I return to the hotel, and we hang out in the room drinking beer and laughing. It's too bad they aren't cute, because now I want Kelly and Courtney to at least hook up a little with someone so I don't have to feel guilty for meeting the nicest guy in the country.

- Brendan goes back to the condo at Los Gaviotas that he and his friends had the foresight to rent, and we eat dinner with Jim and Ron and then go to Rock and Roll Taco. Courtney meets some mysterious biker guy who invites her into the rafters to share his bottle of Jack Daniels (Grift #8). I keep thinking, "Kurt Raper! Kurt Raper!" as he reminds me strongly of The Hitcher.

- Grift #9, 10, 11, 12, and 13: Kelly and I dance and do a lot of shots, gratis. The Liquor Gods are smiling upon me and I'm not the one barfing when we get home.

- Brendan invites us to dinner at their condo the next night, which turns out to be nicer than any of our houses back home. We drag Vera along in case we need her room later and figure we'll get points. She sequesters herself with Brendan's chubby roommate, Mario. Kelly flirts with his entertaining African American friend. I know his name isn't Lenny, but he looks just like Germaine/Tremaine's roommate Lenny. I <u>cannot</u> call him Lenny; that could be awkward for all concerned. Courtney will be hooking up with Chris, this guy who apparently believes he's the lost member of Guns'n'Roses, wearing a scraggly head rag "just like Axl's." I know this through some sort of telepathy with her. I don't like Chris, and Brendan says he doesn't like Chris either. But she likes him, so whatever. Kelly and I speculate that Chris hides a weird bumpy scalp, head lice, or a really tragic haircut under his head rag. Brendan tells us later, "He's prematurely bald." Yuck.

- Brendan barbecues vodka shrimp for us—so good! The shrimp was heavily doused in vodka, and that would explain hooking up with him a little more than planned that evening...Must keep the pact...must keep...the pact. It's working so far!

- All of us head out to soak in the Jacuzzi in the complex, totally buzzed from the vodka, but it still seems a good idea to drink more beers. All of a sudden, the water over where Vera sits on Mario's lap starts sloshing around suspiciously. Later, Vera confesses that they had sex, sans condom, in the Jacuzzi, and *Mario pulled out and came in the Jacuzzi*. With all of us in it. I desperately need a shower. With a wire brush to scrub myself all over with. I could say, "Eww!" forever and it wouldn't come close.

- Brendan calls the next morning to invite me to dinner. I tell him about the whole Mario-in-the-Jacuzzi incident so he can throw up along with me, which he does. I'm curious to see when this thing with Brendan will all end in tears. As it must, because this is <u>my</u> life we're talking about. "Don't hang out with that skank Vera anymore," he warns.

- Kelly and I go souvenir shopping the next day and find an excellent pair of bullhorns for Chad. We buy blankets, piñatas, and silver jewelry. I get two rings and a toe ring. Kelly haggles mercilessly for a heavy silver necklace (Grift #14).

- Roomies have spent all their money on silver jewelry. They think if they drink enough beer, they'll have enough in bottle return cash to stay an extra day or two. "That's a lot of beer," Kelly volunteers. "We could help..."(Grift #15, 16, 17)

- I go out for tacos with Brendan and his friends (I don't want to milk the lobster train again) and they pressure him into buying me roses from a street vendor. I am not sure what to do with my ill-gotten roses. Lenny has no advice on this. He just hangs his legs out the back of the truck and howls what sounds like, possibly, a Bob Marley song. We pass the restaurant where Courtney and Kelly are having dinner with Jim and Ron using Jim's emergency credit card. Hi, guys!

- Tragedy strikes on Saturday, the last day of Spring Break! Jim and Ron only made their reservation through Friday night because they have to leave to drive back to their school—and we realize we don't even know where they're from. I confirm Vera checked out of the Rosarito Beach Hotel, which means the last night of Spring Break has crumbled into a shambles. On the street, heading to pick up our stuff from Hotel California, I run into these kids Leslie and Phillip from my sociology class! They only came down for one day, and here they are!

- Courtney sidles up to Phillip. "We'll have to go home if we don't find somewhere to stay very soon...." Grift #18: He immediately offers for us to stay with them, and even to carry Courtney's bag for her. Leslie glowers at him but it's too late. We get our bags from the Hotel California, and deposit them in a small trailer in Chewy's Trailer Park. That's right, a trailer park. Oh, how the mighty have fallen.

- Courtney refuses to take responsibility for this rancid turn of events. She can't imagine how anyone who lives in Orange County could possibly stay in a trailer park in Mexico, with pigs running around free and squealing. "Did that guy think I would hook up with him after he brought my stuff to a *trailer park*??" she fumes. Chewy's advertising strategy fascinates Kelly. How could anyone from America have seen the ad?

- They both want me to finagle Brendan into inviting us to stay at the condo, and then we'll just pick up our stuff here tomorrow. I feel uncomfortable asking him, as I already seem like a shellfish gold-digger, having eaten a lot of seafood on his tab so far. Kelly and Courtney threaten me. "Grift #19 MUST take place!"

- Courtney and I meet Brendan and his friends at Papas and Beer later that night. Kelly wanted to stay in the trailer and eat Spaghettios she got from a store earlier. She cooked them *in the can* in the trailer. "You are bordering white trash, Kelly," I warn her. I went with her to the Spaghettio's store to buy razors so I could shave my legs, and every time I asked for razors the storekeepers handed me condoms. Do I have that "I need condoms and plenty of 'em!" look about me? I'm not having sex! I don't need condoms! Condoms will just tempt me to give in and have sex with Brendan!

- When I mention the word "trailer," Brendan goes white under his tan.
    - "What trailer?"

- "Oh, the one we're staying at. Everywhere else was booked up, so we met some people in one of my classes who are staying there."
- "In a trailer park? In Mexico??"
- "It's not so bad, aside from the pigs running and squealing."

- He takes charge immediately. "Absolutely not. You guys are coming to stay at our place. You can't stay in a trailer park. Especially with livestock." Behind his back, Courtney raises her fists in a victorious gesture, as this also assures her hooking up with Chris the Headrag Guy on our last night. She locates Chris and they slip out of the club and onto the beach, where, as Kelly predicted, they are almost trampled by a horse. Brendan and I spend our night drinking and dancing and keeping an eye out for Kelly. The place is big, but eventually you see everyone cycle through, like the original Dad on the Scam, and one of the soccer goons. Brendan and I hide behind a palm tree to avoid Vera skanking along.

- Kelly never shows up. I begin to worry.
  - "The trailer smelled like a gas leak. Maybe she's been asphyxiated."
  - "I'm sure she's fine."
  - "What if she got food poisoning from those sick Spaghettios?"
  - "I'm sure she'd rather throw up in the trailer than here."

- Finally we go back to the trailer park to get our stuff and collect Kelly's body. She isn't there. Brendan shudders as a herd of pigs runs in front of his truck. Courtney seems more philosophical. "She'll turn up tomorrow, or she'll have to get another ride back to America. I have a paper to write tomorrow." We collect our luggage and leave without Kelly. We are *horrible* friends.

- At the condo, Courtney and Chris unfold the sofa bed for themselves. A large black spider, freed from its prison, scampers over the pillow. Courtney screams and refuses to sleep there. They leave, arguing about where to sleep. Brendan and I check the rest of the bed for spiders and then settle in. We speculate about whether Courtney has actually seen Chris' bare head or not.

- He asks if I think she'll go out with him when we get back home. I scoff. "Please, it's not like anyone ever sees each other again after Spring Break hookups." I know this from experience, as Arizona Rob never came looking for me again. He's quiet for a moment and then says, "Well, I want to see you again after this one. Can I call you this week?" I shrug. "You can have my number. If you call me, fine. If not, fine."

- I am the Mowgli of dating.

- In the morning, even if that's it, it has been a pretty awesome week. I can't believe I made it the whole week with him without having sex! That's got to be a record of some sort. Courtney can't believe it either. She's more conservative than I am, so she doesn't have to make Pacts with herself.

- Kelly waits outside Chewy's Trailer Park with her bag in her hand as we drive by. I have never in my life seen her so flat-out pissed off. Not that I blame her in the least. We basically left her in a pig farm so we could have beds and clean air and hot Spring Break memories. The entire trip home cycles through dialogue of "I was there, so how could you **not** have found me at the club?" to "We never ever saw you and neither did anyone else!"

- Upon heading for the border, we repeatedly have to shout, "No, no, leave us alone!" to people trying to sell us things, children juggling oranges on the highway and people trying to wash our windows for money. As we get close, I discover

I lost both my real *and* fake IDs, and as I look ethnic (ranging from Mexican to Greek to Turkish, depending on the country I'm in) I have no idea how I'll get across the border with no official ID. I panic.

- The border guards ask us where we are from:
  - Us: "Uh, Huntington Beach!"
  - Guard: "Uh huh. Did you walk on any beaches barefoot?"
  - Us: (Yes.) "No."
  - Guard: "And the purpose of your trip?"
  - Us: "Spring Break!"
  - Guard: "And what did you purchase here?"
  - Us: "We got these great bullhorns and a piñata....oh, and toe rings!"

- They wave us through without checking our ID, but I still block my face with a donkey piñata I bought.

- Our original argument stops only when we arrive home to find out our friends who went to Havasu had five people end up in jail for drunk driving. Two of them were charged with public intoxication, which basically means you vomited directly onto a police officer. None of us plan on talking to Craig Ensler ever again.

- Brendan **does** call me, sharing his horrible border crossing story:

  - During the hour-long border crossing, Brendan sees a friend from SDSU walking towards the border. Lenny invites the guy to ride back with them since he has a bag of pot. By the time they get to the actual border crossing, everyone is severely stoned. When asked the purpose of their visit to Mexico, Lenny responds soberly, "We were looking for the elusive spotted iguana!" Border patrol calls, "Secondary inspection," which everyone except Brendan assumes means you're free to drive away now.

- After Brendan yells that the officer clearly meant, "Pull over at secondary inspection so we can search your car, you stupid stoned idiots," Lenny pulls off the freeway and into a Carl's Jr. parking lot so he can flip out on Brendan. Just then, five Border Patrol cars scream down the freeway in hot pursuit of them. Everyone declares Brendan the smartest one in the car and they hide at Carl's Jr. until things cool down.

- After the trip Brendan and I talk a couple times a week, and go out a few times. As soon as I sleep with him at the end of the second month, he <u>never calls me again.</u> I absolutely can't believe this! What the hell? Was he just playing me the whole time? You'd think he just wouldn't have called in the first place when we got back, instead of getting my hopes up that he was different.

- My office organizes a pool to guess why, and when I call and harass Brendan into telling me that he met someone else at school and didn't know how to tell me, Marilyn wins $38. Sue, my manager, knows how hurt I am. "Mel, someday the right one will come along." I shrug. "I didn't think he was The One, but I thought he liked me for <u>me</u>, not just to hook up with."

- By the time the right one comes, I'll be so hostile and bitter I'll probably be heartlessly grifting seafood wherever I can get it. The Pact was a complete waste of my time. In fact, if I had just given in sooner, I probably would never have gotten so emotionally involved.

- My friend Eric at work tries to cheer me up by taking me out to lunch. Eric clearly likes me and he's not that cute. He would probably be so happy to go out with me that he'd never pull a stunt like that.

- The New Improved Pact: Only go out with boys who will count themselves lucky to get you.

Road Sodas

Mammoth, CA
November 1992
Sue decides that our work holiday party should be a ski trip in Mammoth! At 19, I've never been skiing before because my mom thinks "it's very dangerous." She also thinks anything she doesn't know how to do, such as bike riding, or roller skating, "is very dangerous." It's time to start doing new things and having new experiences. Jonathan, an expert skier, offers to teach me to ski. The goal for the trip: Not to break my leg or asphyxiate Eric with a pillow in his sleep. What an ass he turned out to be...

Suggested Soundtrack: *"Mysterious Ways"-U2, "Friday I'm in Love"-The Cure, "All I Want"-Toad the Wet Sprocket, and other random radio hits you listen to on an eight- hour car ride*

• I invite Jonathan as my rent-a-date to my company ski trip. "I will die of embarrassment if I have to go alone," I plead. Jonathan snorts. "Under the circumstances, I would too. Does Eric's girlfriend know about you yet?" I can feel the bile churning in my stomach. "No, and hopefully she won't at the end of the eight-hour car ride either. We're driving up to Mammoth with them, so zip it," I warn.

• After Brendan slept with me and never called me again, Eric and I started seeing each other. Three months later when Sue found out, she pulled me into her office. "Eric has a girlfriend back home. Her name's Jill. Did he tell you he broke up with her?" I stared at Sue. "No, he never told me about her in the first place," I replied evenly, although I'm sure my flaring nostrils belied my calm voice. I pretended I was fine. She knew better, but he was dumb enough to believe me when I said I wasn't mad. Jill, unaware of this drama, **also** wants to be my friend now that she's moved all the way down here to live with Eric. She's one of those nice, boring girls that always have a boyfriend who cheats on them. "Eric's told me sooo much about you!" she squealed the first time she came to meet him at work. "Really?" I drawled, looking sidelong at Eric and making him as uncomfortable as possible. "You'll have to tell me *everything*." He wandered off, probably to throw up.

- On the drive up to Mammoth, Jonathan and I drink road sodas made of Diet Coke and Bacardi 151, a potent combination. Jonathan, thrilled to be on a free ski trip, happily sips his drink and sings along with the radio. "She mooo-ooves in mysterious ways, uh huh," he yowls along with Bono. We encourage Jill to drink road sodas with us, knowing Eric will flip it if I start turning Jill to the dark side. "Here you go, Jill!" I smile at her as I pass her a cup, my eyes watering from all the 151 I poured in there. She looks hesitant. "Jill, you want to be *fun*, don't you?" Jonathan coaxes her. I love him. She takes it.

- I also voted Eric as the driver, to punish him for being a lying ass and a cheater. He knows I'm punishing him, but can't say a word with Jill right there. "Can't you go any faster, Eric? You drive like my grandma," I complain, while Jill and Jonathan giggle. He shoots me a look in the rearview mirror, narrowing his blue eyes at me. I raise my eyebrows innocently and kick the back of his seat. The 151 starts to kick in, hard, so I kick his seat a few more times.

- At the gas station Jill buys us all a lot of candy, which also helps the time pass, because getting drunk and eating candy for eight hours is a pretty good way to spend a long drive. "Here, put this CD in," Jonathan requests, passing her the disc. She starts giggling at pretty much anything at this point, and begins singing along with the show tunes she knows. Eric sighs heavily whenever there's a break in the music. "The phaaaaaan-tom of the opera is there," she trills.

- We arrive at the cabin in Mammoth, and before I have a chance to introduce Jonathan to anyone, he falls down the stairs into the living room and lies there drunkenly, rolling on the ground, shaking with laughter. "This is my friend, Jonathan," I stammer, vaguely gesturing at him. Most everyone already knows him, luckily. Jill giggles at this too, and Eric elbows her. I hope *Sue* thinks it's funny that we've all shown up wasted, except Eric, our grouchy chauffeur. She just shakes her head.

- It turns out Jonathan and I have to share a room with Eric and Jill. Why am I being punished? For getting drunk in the car? Bad Idea Jeans abounds.

- Jonathan acts thrilled we have bunk beds so he "doesn't have to share a bed with Melissa," which also makes everyone look suspiciously at him. Especially when he leaves while I change into my bikini. I head out to the hot tub, grabbing a beer on the way, to drink more and sweat and forget my troubles, followed closely by Sue and Marilyn.

- Marilyn leans in. "You guys hooked up, right? You and Eric? Does Jill know? I knew it! I can't believe you didn't tell me! Who else knows?" Marilyn is like the Delphi Oracle. That's how she won the pot on Brendan last time. "Let's be clear that I never slept with Eric," I begin, moving over to make room. "The thing I'm most mad about is that I only went out with him because I thought he was too <u>pathetic</u> to do something like this!" I'm flailing my hands at this point, spilling beer in the Jacuzzi. It's the sort of mood I make my worst decisions in. Marilyn considers. "I don't know; he's kind of cute," she shrugs. Sue, the best manager ever, looks sympathetically at me, but she's busy being in charge of everything. Her two sons, Matt and Caleb, have come up with her and she's trying to keep an eye on them.

- Sue asks, "How did you all end up driving together? It seems..." she fishes for the right word. "Maybe not such a good idea?" she finishes. I explain Eric convinced me to come skiing, never dreaming Jill planned to surprise him by moving here. "She knew we were driving up together, so when she showed up, she figured we'd all go together. At that point, it seemed the best way to begin my plan of making Eric's life a living hell on Earth." I finish my beer, and Caleb offers to get me another one from the cooler. "Me, too," Marilyn calls after him.

•   My troubles come home to roost the next morning as I try to learn to ski with a wicked hangover and cramped legs from sleeping in a toddler's bunk bed. Jill also staggers out of bed, almost as ungracefully as I do.

•   Jonathan claimed he would help me, but he gives no instructions whatsoever as we get on the lift and it just jerks me up from behind. "Now, Melissa, I know you're totally uncoordinated, but literally all you have to do is stand up. OK? And turn when the mountain turns or you'll flip off the side of the mountain." How hard can it be to just slide down the hills? On skis? Plus, I'm wearing a totally cute jacket, which has to improve my chance of success!

•   On the lift, I find myself seated next to Peter Ono, our crew master from the Brig Pilgrim! He's there to snowboard and it's great to catch up with him. But I still don't have any interest in him, even though he's still the nicest guy ever. So typic.

•   Once I get off the lift, I just begin sliding down the mountain, as Jonathan's lack of instruction really kicks in and I don't know how to stop! I'm accelerating rapidly toward a large group of children! "Get out of the way! Move it!" I bellow, frightening a line of small children along a tow rope. Jonathan screams, "Snowplow, Melissa, snowplow!" I look around frantically as I hurtle down the mountain, yelling, "Where's the snowplow? Is it going to run me over??" I fall spectacularly, cartwheeling down and losing both skis and both poles to the four winds. I lay there on my back, waiting for the St. Bernard with the booze to show up. Dee-saster!

- Jonathan skis up in disgust, says, "There's no teaching you," and skis away. Jill skis up. "Come on, I'll help you out! It'll be fun!" Now I feel even worse about hooking up with her boyfriend, albeit unwittingly. Jonathan, Sue and I agree she could do a lot better, as frankly, Eric's a 6 at best. Jonathan swooshes around us and keeps yelling pointers that don't make any sense. "I have no control whatsoever over my knees or ankles! They feel like they shattered into a million pieces when I fell down, so yell something that doesn't involve my knees or ankles!" I snarl. He shrugs and bails again. Thanks a lot, Jonathan!

- Skiing along with me, Jill yammers, "Eric are I soul mates! It's just so great to have found him so early in life! I mean, I'm only 20 and I already know my husband!" This couldn't be any sadder, unless she asks me to be in the wedding. "I'm sure you will, Jill. I'm sure he really loves you and would never do anything to hurt you," I assure her. Except date me. The next step in the making-Eric's-life-a-living-hell will be hooking up with his hot roommate.

- Marilyn and her husband Bruce are also professional skiers, like everyone else at my company but me, swishing by in a cloud of powder. Sue tries to restrain herself and go slowly along with Jill and me, but eventually she can't stand it, and speeds off with Matt. Her sons are also good skiers, but Caleb, who's 13, slows down to ski with Jill and me. He's very sweet, but it's embarrassing that a 13-year-old feels sorry for me.

- Fortuitously, everyone knows I hurt my knee playing softball this summer, so when I head off back to the cabin, I can claim injury. Jonathan lectures me, "You see, I told you, you just don't have the coordination required for sports. You should just spend the rest of the trip at the bar before you hurt yourself." After skiing that day, we all sit in the hot tub and drink eleventy million beers. Eric blatantly ogles me in my bikini. Jonathan does not, Marilyn notes quietly. Jill looks jealous and hurt. Honey, it's not my fault he's averting his eyes from your Speedo tank suit and knit hat ensemble.

• Marilyn whispers: "Let's get a pool going on this one. I bet Jonathan comes out someday. Come on, I won $38 last time! How can he **not** be looking at your boobs? He's gotta be gay!" If only! That would explain why he never wanted me. But doesn't explain why even boring Jill has a boyfriend and I don't. I notice Sue looking at Caleb, who's looking at me. Oh, great. I'm probably going to get fired for contributing to the delinquency of a minor. Until I realize suddenly that Caleb embodies everything I'm looking for in a boyfriend. Why is my life like this?? I hear Courtney's voice: "Probably he's still nice *because* he's 13. He'll be a jerk by the time he's 20." I don't know though...maybe I could wait...

• Another co-worker, Jen, has shown up. She opts for the floor after discovering the only available bed was the baby crib. Jonathan vetoes my suggestion of offering her my bunk. "That would mean I'd have to sleep next to you." I idly wonder if he'll ever learn to share space with anyone. At this rate, he'll be living alone with cats by the time we're 30, yelling at kids to "Get off my lawn!"

• My legs truly feel like amputation would feel less painful than keeping them the next day, so I head off to read my book in the lodge bar. Are all ski resort bartenders hot as hell? This one floors me, he's so hot! He introduces himself as James, and gives me free drinks all afternoon. I love free drinks! James, my new best friend, also has a hot British accent. Not as thick as Germaine/Tremaine's, so I am positive I have his name right. After several free cocktails, I'm in love with James. I could live in this winter wonderland with him and become a professional skier. If I can ever learn to ski.

- Sadly, I'll never get to make out with James. I'd love to irritate Eric and Jonathan by bringing James back to the cabin with me, but we couldn't hook up in the toddler bunk bed, or the available baby crib. James would probably be fired if we hooked up in the refrigerator of the bar where he works, ending the free drink train right quick. The Ghost of Hook Ups that Might Have Been hovers near.

- That night at dinner, Jonathan mysteriously tells Jill, "I think you could do better than Eric, especially if you stop wearing hats with your tank bathing suits..." I smirk. I look *adorable* in hats (not paired with my bikini, obviously), and I have a gorgeous ski outfit. Of course, it masks a clumsy hippo skier, but who cares? The pictures will look great!

- Sue and I head out to the hot tub again. I can't get over how cool lying in the snow and then slipping into the hot water is. Also, the 151 tastes better in here. Caleb comes out to keep me company. Why God why can he not be a good six years older?? Caleb offers to get us snacks, and while he runs inside, Sue leans over. "I think he's fallen for you. He's got quite a crush going on." She smiles at me, so at least I'm not getting fired. I sigh. "Well, I'll probably still be single when I'm 24 and he's finally 18, so I'll call you."

- Jen comes out and since we're alone, I can tell her the whole story. She shakes her head disbelievingly. "What an idiot! I can't believe Eric didn't think you'd find out about Jill! You should totally blackmail him and threaten to tell on him." She glowers at the window where Eric passes by. "I hope he gets hit by a train"—she pauses for dramatic effect—"*and lives.*" Yeah, me too. In fact, there are several other people I'd like to get hit by a train and live, like Brendan, Jacob, and Mesh Tony, so I tell Jen and Sue all about them, too. Eventually, I must go in before I get so drunk I throw up in the hot tub. That would almost be grosser than that gross guy Mario who came in the hot tub—but not quite. Caleb sits quietly, eating snacks and commenting, "What a jerk!" at appropriate intervals. I hope we aren't setting bad examples for him. Maybe he'll turn out super nice due to all this instruction in what jerks men are. Except James.

- Jonathan hogs the bottom bunk, and I'm afraid to sleep in the top bunk in case I fall out. Also, I can barely move my legs to climb the little wooden ladder. But I'm still better off than Jen, who sleeps curled up in the fetal position in the crib due to the fetid carpet.

- Jonathan and I replenish our Big Gulps with 151 and pineapple juice and climb in the backseat. Eric self-righteously refuses to drink in the car even though Jill's driving. "You'll want to kill yourself pretty soon; Melissa and I are much too obnoxious to handle sober for eight hours," Jonathan warns. "C'mon, you always drink in the car if you're not driving," I remind him. Jill snaps her head around to look at him, while he turns red. I press on. "Remember when we all went out for pizza and you asked for a to-go cup for your beer?" Jill's face says she doesn't even know him anymore.

- Jill drives even slower than Eric. I'm going to throw myself out of the moving vehicle if I think about how long it will take to get home at this rate. It's like being in a *Flintstones* car, or Courtney's car. Eric keeps telling her she needs to speed up and be more "daring". I could hit him with Jay's hockey stick! Has he ever met her? I've met her once and I can tell you she'll never do anything daring in her life! You **had** adventurous, you stupid moron!

- Road sodas are sometimes the only things that help you keep it together. I swig my drink, hoping to pass out soon. Jonathan rolls his eyes and mouths, "Typical." I whisper my plan for hooking up with Eric's roommate, Jonathan cheerses me, and we start the chorus of, "Maybe this time... I'll be lucky..." as Eric groans softly to himself.

The Poseidon Adventure

Newport Beach, CA
June 1993

Some events you just know are going to be a train wreck. A full-on, complete train wreck and a damn funny one at that. The kind you'll all be talking about for years. So you wangle an invitation, show up and wait for the inevitable fireworks. Nina, a high school friend of Jonathan and Keith's, will definitely have an entertaining wedding. At 20, I'm over Jonathan. I'm back in school, working full time, and living back at home. Things are pretty even keel, so a drama-queen wedding is just the ticket to liven things up!

Suggested Soundtrack: "Whoomp! There It Is"-Tag Team, "I Would Do Anything for Love (But I Won't Do That)"-Meat Loaf, "What is Love?"-Haddaway, and other crap wedding music played by an unimaginative boat DJ

- Jonathan, Keith and Chad get invited to Nina's fiasco wedding. Kelly and I, sensing potential hilarity, insist on being rent-a-dates. I reconsider after finding out she's holding the wedding on a boat in Newport Harbor; we'll be effectively trapped at the wedding no matter what. After my unfortunate experience on the Brig Pilgrim, I'm leery of committing to boat events. Courtney refuses to come. "Even the promise of free drinks cannot lure me on the Love Boat of Doom," she tells me ominously. "It's taken Nina almost the whole eight months of her pregnancy to convince her Marine boyfriend to marry her. I guess now that she's finally triumphed, she wants a wedding he can't escape from," I tell her. Also, as Keith points out, they couldn't afford to get married at the Waterfront Hilton. He's totally right. I went to eat there on a debacle date once, and almost fell out of the booth when I looked at the menu prices.

- On the boat (which I secretly name *Titanic*), Nina's mother, who's evidently competing in a Liza Minnelli look-alike contest after the wedding, complete with long, sequined black gown and tarantula eyelashes, greets us. She grabs Keith and Jonathan and gives them major cleavage hugs. Jonathan resignedly hugs her, but Keith snuggles right into her rack. Captain Morgan, El Capitan, also greets us unsteadily. Kelly, looking blonde, tan and gorgeous, whispers, "I suspect he's had several of his namesake cocktails already." He stumbles prior to bringing in the gangplank, and winks at Kelly. She smiles halfheartedly, humoring him.

- Chairs are set up on the main deck for the ceremony and Chad offers me his arm, as I am his rent-a-date. Captain Morgan adds a priest's collar to his jaunty captain's outfit, and voila! He turns into a wedding officiant! Chad decides he might be seasick at this point, and leans over Kelly's shoulder with his mouth hanging open just in case. Kelly is willing to get thrown up on to have Chad nearby. She tucks her long blonde hair out of his way. Jonathan rolls his eyes.

- Nina, stuffed into her wedding gown like a sausage, weaves erratically down the aisle. We don't know if **she's** been drinking as well, or if her belly is leading her astray. Jonathan whispers, "Ick, her belly button sticks out like a light switch. They better take all the pictures from the waist up." Her mother cries hysterically, her thick mascara running down her cheeks in rivulets of gooey black. So much for the Liza contest. Unless she's entering as Boozy Liza.

- The Cap'n **definitely** has been drinking and giggles occasionally during the ceremony at funny things only he hears. Chad and I laugh along with him—he's so wasted! I love this wedding! The ceremony, mercifully brief, lacks emotion. Nina avoids vomiting by the skin of her teeth, and gallops back up the aisle, leaving Joe in her wake.

- After the ceremony, we crowd around the bar, where Cap'n Morgan has exchanged his captain coat for a tuxedo jacket and morphed into a bartender. If he's tending bar, who's driving the boat? Does he just jam the wheel with a broom handle and let us go in circles or what? We throw back all the cocktails we can fortify ourselves with. Surly Jason finally hacked into the DMV computers in Connecticut and made us all good fake ID cards. Cap'n Morgan doesn't question why quite a few of us are from Connecticut and all live at 123 Main Street. He may be too wasted to even see at this point. "Cap'n Morgan probably would have taken the check-cashing IDs," Chad remarks bitterly, sipping his drink. "It needs more Jack, Cap'n!" He hands it back, and the Cap'n just hands Chad the bottle. That's more like it! "I'll charge it to the wedding!" cackles the Cap'n.

- Boozy Liza comes swooping in like a crow, having cleaned up a bit, and announces, "Dinner will be served." Keith chooses a table for us. "Look! The little boxes on the tables might have chocolate in them!" We all fall into seats around him and tear into the favors. Except Chad, who still might throw up. I'm literally speechless when we open our boxes to discover *naked plastic babies*. Jonathan shoves one in his mouth in case they're made of sugar, but spits it back out immediately. What are we supposed to **do** with these? Kelly hisses, "Did the words 'good taste' never enter the conversation that made this wedding decision?" Jonathan reminds her, "We're at the wedding of a 19-year-old pregnant girl, her G.I. Joe husband, and her Liza-look-alike mom. What do you expect, a string quartet?" Chad flings his baby overboard in disgust.

- The rest of us leave ours in their boxes on the table to show group disappointment in the lack of chocolate, and Keith and I go scout the buffet. "So, what are you doing after we get back?" Keith leers at me. "I'm reporting my credit card stolen later—we could go out somewhere first..." I just smile and report back to the table, "Lasagna is served!" Chad leaps up—he loves lasagna! The wedding seems to be catered by Costco, and Chad can eat without fear of hidden veggies.

- Kelly turns to me. "Can we swim to shore?" I peer at the horizon. "It's too far. And remember how I got busted by Harbor Patrol after hopping over the side of Keith's boat to pee in the water? I think we'd get in trouble."

- After dinner, the DJ begins the first dance, but Joe can barely get his arms around Nina's girth, and Keith cannot control his mirth any longer. The DJ, sensing possible drama, rushes them into the bouquet toss, which some Amazon redheaded girl catches, and the garter toss, which Keith catches. He gamely dances with her, as expected. He immediately mouths, "She is so drunk!" over Big Red's shoulder, and squeezes her butt.

- Big Red falls down almost immediately, and lands with her skirt at her waist. Her privates are exposed through a thin screen of her $1.99 pantyhose, as she's going commando. Jonathan screams, "Oh my God! You can see her cooter!" and points until Kelly slaps his hand down. Chad smirks, "Well, we all know she's a **real** redhead now, don't we?" After her first flash, Big Red decides to basically turn the dance floor into a peep show, spinning about and letting her skirt twirl up so everyone can see her "cooter" whenever they want. Eventually she goes below decks with one of Joe's friends.

- Dancing and additional cocktails improve the event dramatically until someone screams, "Oh, no! Not Aunt Lucy!" A very, very old woman sprawls on the floor groaning, and suddenly we're in *The Poseidon Adventure*. Cap'n Morgan staggers off to call the Coast Guard or Harbor Patrol or someone; hopefully the same officers who caught me peeing won't respond. They might remember me shouting, "It's a free country! They let you pee anywhere you want in Mexico!"

- Harbor Patrol instructs the Cap'n to dock the boat at the Newport wharf. As we begin to dock, the drunken captain slams the docking side of the boat into the pilings, shattering all the windows in the dining room, and scaring Big Red and her half-naked Marine fling. Aunt Lucy screams in fear. Chad assures her, "Captain Morgan got wasted, and that's why he crashed the boat," which probably gives her a second heart attack.

- Nina's husband, Joe, exclaims, "Look! We're at Hooters! I love Hooters!" Nina bursts into tears and pushes past the Harbor Patrol and off the gangplank. Not that she had a dream wedding in the first place, but having your wedding end at Hooters really blows. The Harbor Patrol officers carry Aunt Lucy off, and she's successfully transported to a medical center.

- We elect to get off here in Newport and call Surly Jason to come take us back to our cars at the other end of the harbor, which he does with his usual bad grace. Over schooners at Mutt Lynch's, thanks to our new fake IDs, Kelly and I speculate on how Nina ended up in this mess. I mean, I've already been on the Pill for years. It's just not that hard to avoid getting knocked up, marrying some random guy and having your wedding end in tears at Hooters. Chad proclaims, "It's karma for giving us plastic babies as favors."

- As we drive home down Pacific Coast Highway, Kelly starts laughing hysterically and points to a car driving along ahead of us. "Look at that car! There's an inflatable shark hanging in the back window! Pull up, Chad, I want to see it!" Chad changes lanes and pulls up next to the car. It's a white station wagon with do-it-yourself window tint bubbling over the back windows, where the inflatable shark indeed dangles from the ceiling. On the side passenger door, someone has stenciled "Official Beach Wagon" in red paint. The piece de resistance: the driver has sawed the head off a child's rocking horse, mounted it to the hood like an ornament, and painted the head white, with blue eyes and red lips. Sparkly streamers attached to the handles on either side of the horse's head flutter, and an American flag has been stuck into a hole drilled in the top of the horse's head.

- Suddenly, we notice the driver waving at us. Eduardo, Jonathan's dad, smiles and waves to beat the band. He calls, "Hello, Yon-a-than! Hello!" Jonathan just slumps down in his seat, looking mortified as the rest of us wave back at Eduardo. Chad yells, "Cool car, Eduardo," and bursts out laughing. Kelly and I lay on the floor so Eduardo won't see us howling with laughter. Yeah, my life rocks compared to Nina's, and it's fantastic compared to Jonathan's...

- ...Until later that night, when Courtney and I end up going to Bobby McGee's with Keith and his friend Daniel. Daniel drives a red Porsche and seems to think he can get by in life with only his car to recommend him. He's been stalking me forever. Sadly, he looks like Mesh Tony after a wardrobe upgrade. I would *never* go out with him. Courtney sensibly murmurs, "If Keith plans on reporting his credit card stolen anyways, he's not *really* paying for us. Per se. So we can drink all we like without feeling like we owe him anything." Good logic!

- Daniel plies me with expensive Midori drinks. I love Midori, and drink about eleventy million Midori sours. I consider wetting my pants, since the bathroom seems light-years away, but finally decide to get up and go. I get the attention of all the bouncers when I fall backwards off my barstool. Daniel and Keith wave them off, saying they're taking care of me. As soon as the bouncers leave, Keith instructs Courtney, "Take her to the bathroom. We'll get kicked out if she pees her pants." Courtney drags me off, cursing a blue streak. She reports later that I peed and threw up simultaneously, but with spectacularly good aim, right between my own legs. Midori gives me the agility of an Olympic gymnast in the Throw-Up Olympics!

- She declines to wipe the leftover throw-up off my legs, reasoning that I'm wearing black pants that will absorb it.

I feel much better and climb back on the stool. "I think I'll just stick with light beer from now on. And maybe get some nachos. That will settle my stomach for sure," I slur to Daniel.

• An hour later, I fall off the stool again, hitting my head hard on the dance floor. "I think I have a concussion," I moan, lying on the dance floor amid people who can still walk. Daniel offers to take me outside to "get some air." He gets me right outside the front doors, where I fall over onto the lawn in front of the giant windows. To the chagrin of the family seated in the window, I begin noisily vomiting right in front of the windows. The parents are appalled at paying for an expensive dinner interrupted by a vomiting patron. The kids are dying laughing. "I think she ate the nachos, Dad," one of the kids yells excitedly.

• Daniel hustles me off to the parking lot. He obviously thinks better of letting me anywhere near his Porsche. We sit in my car, The Ticket. I'm starting to think more kindly of Daniel. He must *really* want to hook up with me if he's willing to put up with this crap. Then I pass out. When I wake up alone at three in the morning, still in my car and my hair wet with drool, Daniel has fled like gorillas in the mist. He's left a note: "Call me! I want to go out with you," and left his number. Yeah, I sure will, if I don't get killed driving home, still three quarters drunk and with a concussion. I would call Jonathan to get me, but I don't have any money. Thank God I didn't hook up with Daniel. Or did I? No, he wouldn't have bothered with the note if I had given in. How could he just leave me here like this? He could have hidden his face if he didn't want to be seen driving my beater car. The Ali Baba tent fabric roof hides everything anyway.

• I call Courtney the next day. She hooked up with Keith after all. She's leaving for school in Boston, and figured one last fling might be worthwhile. "It wasn't." Thinking about Courtney leaving the state makes me feel like throwing up again. I don't know what I'm going to do without her. "Well, don't get desperate and hook up with Keith," she reminds me, "and make sure to come visit me!"

• I will, but it won't be the same. In fact, things will never be the same. Does growing up have to be this hard?

Trapped on the Freedom Trail

Boston, MA
October 1996

Well, a lot has happened over the past three years. I finally transferred to Chapman University and finished college last spring. Who knew what a nightmare getting a job and having to pay for everything myself would be? But getting a second job as a cocktail waitress paid off, I have a boyfriend I met at school named Julian, and he's getting ready to move in with me. Julian likes being my boyfriend. He wants to spend time with me all the time—how refreshing. At 23, I finally have a real relationship!

Courtney moved to Boston for college in 1993 and I can't tell you how much I miss her. I can't believe I don't get to see her every day, know everything that's going on in her life, and I haven't even met her boyfriend. I always imagined us living close by and hanging out all the time. Somehow, Jonathan and I get it together to go visit her in Boston. I'm so excited to see her until Julian flips out that I'm going with Jonathan and he's not invited. Does he honestly think after 100 years of solitude, Jonathan magically wants me? But if he did, what would I do?

Suggested Soundtrack: *"Ironic"-Alanis Morrisette, "It's All Coming Back to Me Now"-Celine Dion, "Breakfast at Tiffany's"-Deep Blue Something, "Closer to Free"-Bodeans, "Just a Girl"-No Doubt, "As I Lay Me Down"-Sophie B. Hawkins. What a great mix tape that was!*

- Jonathan and I arrive in Boston, and immediately after we touch down Jonathan assures me he'll **never** sit next to me on a plane again. He got so irritated with me eating sunflower seeds, depositing the shells in the barf bag, and asking for more sodas, he attempted to change seats mid-flight. We did get to chat about him moving in with Kelly.

"She's a good roommate, but she doesn't want any cats. I'm getting some anyway after we get home." I wonder if they are just roommates, but Kelly scoffed when I asked her so I assume so. For now.

• Courtney meets us at the airport with Damon, her boyfriend, who has a car. Cars are commodities in Boston, but there's nowhere to park them and having to dig them out of the snow makes most students decide against owning one. Damon introduces the car, a purple Honda, as Barney. "I hope to get a new car soon," he tells us, pulling into traffic. "The purple wasn't as appealing as I thought."

• "Damon" happens to be one of my least-favorite names, but he seems to be really in love with Courtney, so I will overlook it.

    • I hate the name Damon because it reminds me of my loser ex-boyfriend Damon, who I dated my junior year of college. He was incredibly cheap, never wanted to have sex with me (which gave me a complex), and drove a lowered emerald-green truck. Penelope and I both hated it. Penelope hated Damon from the start and claimed his fingers weren't properly separated, resulting in webbed hands. I met him through a friend of his, Mike, who I met at a party. Mike claimed to be a construction worker, but was actually a porn actor. For gay porn. He claimed he was straight but I was just ill. So, comparatively Damon seemed better. Because that is what's out there. The last straw came when Damon took me to Claim Jumper, where Mike and Daisy, his girlfriend, were meeting us. It turned out Daisy worked as a <u>call girl</u>, and arrived at Claim Jumper in a peach bikini top and a belt, I mean skirt. Damon saw nothing wrong with this, so I left him at the restaurant. Both literally and figuratively.

• I plan to overlook my bad associations and like Courtney's Damon, until I get in the car with him. He drives like an

Egyptian cabbie. I see Jonathan has wisely closed his eyes and white-knuckles the door handle. The Big Dig diverts us through Chinatown, where we add Chinese cabbies into the mix of terror. At a stoplight, a homeless man with a flask walks up to the car, begging for change and cigarettes, and sticks his hand in through the open window. Jonathan pounds the lock down on the door and cowers. The light turns green, and Courtney says, "Sorry!" and rolls up the window. She turns to the back seat: "I don't think that's ever happened to me before!" Mr. Toad's Wild Ride finally arrives at Courtney's apartment, and we are truly thankful to be alive, as Damon ran two red lights and squeezed over the T tracks, narrowly missing the oncoming train.

- She lives in an old historic building, where Jonathan and I circle the radiator like chimps, scratching our heads and looking puzzled. It hisses at us and we retreat warily. Courtney goes into the tiny galley kitchen to make coffee and we hear Damon remark, "Your friends aren't too smaaht, eh? They don't even know what a radiatuh is!" She explains to us, "The radiator provides heat in old buildings; it's too expensive to put in heaters."

- We go to dinner at a fun restaurant near Fenway Park, where the back of the scoreboard butts up against the neighborhood. "How they can have a baseball stadium in the middle of a residential neighborhood?" I ask Damon. "Where do the fans park?" (Nowheah, Damon tells us, they take the T, Boston's amazing public transport system). "What if a ball goes out of the park?" (It breaks someone's window or flies into their living room if the window is open). "Why do they have uncomfortable wooden benches instead of cushy seats like at The Pond in Anaheim?" ("It's history!" Damon yells, pounding the table for emphasis). Still dubious, I order a peanut butter, banana and bacon sandwich from the menu, aptly called The Elvis. Jonathan, grossed out from my order, orders a drink to calm him down from the car ride.

- Drinks for everyone at an Irish bar next door! We find out that Damon hails from Woostuh, actually spelled Worcester, and I wonder why we don't all have Woostuh sauce. It's almost the same.

- Back at the apartment, Jonathan and I are given the living room futon to sleep on. Jonathan looks around wildly for any other available surface besides the hard wooden floor. He hates sleeping with me even more than flying with me. He still has never had a girlfriend. Every time the train rumbles by, I wake up and whisper, "What was that??" Jonathan threatens to throw me onto the T track if I don't shut it. He falls asleep. Involuntarily, I cuddle up to him in my sleep, only to have him elbow me in the ribs, and mutter, "Get off me!" I can barely breathe in this humidity. Throwing the window open makes the humidity worse. My hair immediately springs into Shirley Temple ringlets. Well, I definitely can't move here or I would look hideous all the time.

- In the morning, Courtney discovers that we drank half the new carton of orange juice, and being that she only makes about $50 a week, is bitter at the financial impact of juice replacement. Before leaving for work, Courtney gives Jonathan a T-map and explains how the T works and when you have to pay and when you don't, which somehow involves if you are going into town, or out of town. And, if you're above ground or below ground, that affects the price. I begin to panic. "How should I know which way the driver is going, and if he'll suddenly turn into Charon the boatman and take us underground on a ride to the River Styx?" Jonathan looks at me like I'm crazy. "I would never let you direct us. You have nothing to worry about as long as you don't get separated from me." I consider making a rope leash to avoid getting separated.

- We head off to Faneuil Hall for lunch and sightseeing. Faneuil Hall rocks! There are cobblestone streets, brick buildings, stores that aren't franchises, and in the Hall, food stalls like an old-time market. It's like Main Street in Disneyland! We order lobster bisque in a bread bowl, and go sit outside in the sun by the Sam Adams statue. Jonathan goes on about the history of the Hall and the surrounding area when all of a sudden...

- ...Ben Franklin pops out of a candy shop, followed by a horde of schoolchildren, telling them about how he flew his kite in a lightning storm. Some mothers look worried that their children will attempt a foolish stunt like this without the excuse of being a scientist or a Founding Father. I can tell Jonathan wants to be photographed with Ben Franklin, but he refuses to say so. I snap a photo with Ben in the background anyway.

- Jonathan asks, "What do you want to go see first?" "The Cheers bar!" I shout, full of lobster bisque and ready for "beeahs," as Damon would say. The Cheers bar, actually called the Bull and Finch Pub, is ok but there are no sassy barmaids or funny drunks, much to our dismay. I have nothing else I am dying to see, and whine about going anywhere. I'm so bored with the idea of seeing historical sights and getting lectured by Jonathan all day long. Jonathan fumes, "You are acting like a petulant child! Unless you know your way back home on the T, you are trapped on the Freedom Trail with me!"

- We start off down the Freedom Trail, a red line you can follow around the city and see important sights, for those interested in our nation's history. First, we hit the Boston Common, where important speeches were made and the Boston Massacre took place. I am completely shocked to discover only six people were killed in the Boston Massacre! I turn to Jonathan. "What kind of a *massacre* only has six people killed? Do these idiots even know what a massacre is???" He shrugs it all off as propaganda, continuing to read the little sign. Now we know where the concept of media spin comes from: Mr. Ben Franklin and Mr. Sam Adams!

- The trail leads into the Public Garden, which has adorable swan boats gliding across it. Jonathan bets the swan boat fare costs too much, and nixes a trip across the lake. I almost trip over one of the ducklings from the Make Way for Ducklings statues on the way out.

- Paul Revere lived in a tiny cold little hovel and we both feel sad for him. "What a dump," Jonathan remarks, looking around at the bare floors, little wooden stools and the wooden pegs to hang the clothes on. "My Gap sweaters would all be stretched out if I had to hang them on wooden pegs." As if Marie would ever live in a little dump like this. She has much better taste, and with three children, needs tons of storage space for all their junk. Who knew Paul Revere was a metal smith and cast bells? I thought all he did his whole life was yell, "The British are coming!" Fortuitously, he had other fallback talents. "I think the chamber pots could come in handy myself, when I am so lazy in the middle of the night and cannot imagine getting up to go pee," I ponder, wondering if they sell any in the gift shop.

- Jonathan drags me all over town. I swear we've staggered about fifty miles before we approach a giant bridge. "You cannot possibly expect me to walk all the way across this bridge! There cannot be anything to see that's so important it would require walking across this bridge!" I revert to full petulant child mode, and stop in my tracks. Jonathan claims the USS Constitution or some ironclad ship oozes history over there, but I flat refuse to go there. "There has to be some freedom on the Freedom Trail, Jonathan!" I cry, shaking my fist like a (fake) revolutionary.

- I offer to buy him a drink at the Green Dragon Tavern, where revolutionaries probably met, to appease him. With what money, I don't know, since I am, as usual, po folks. (Very, very poor). But I will have to somehow replace all the expensive orange juice I drank. Being poor reminds me of something. "How's Keith doing? Have you talked to him lately?" I only saw Keith a few times after Nina's wedding. He started dating someone and drifted off. Jonathan leans back in his chair and raises his eyebrows, so I know it's going to be good:

- Keith, apparently unsatisfied with his giant salary, had been embezzling money from his father's company for years. His father finally discovered it, called Keith in Paris while he was on vacation, and fired him. And kicked him out of the house. Keith then got a job at a car dealership, and moved in with Chad and Charlie in Los Angeles. Things evidently did not go well at the car dealership, and Keith ended up stealing Chad's credit card and a car from the dealership. He got arrested three days later, ironically by Lance Linder, who came a long way from his wall-punching days in Palm Springs and became a sheriff. Currently, he's in jail. We drink a solemn toast to Keith, hoping he will get it together.

- That night we go to dinner in North End, the Italian section of Boston, "the land of my heritage!" Damon informs us. The restaurant has a lottery where if you pick the "Free Meal!" ball out of the basket, they comp your meal! No "Free Meal!" ball, so we console ourselves with extra wine and desserts.

- Courtney, appalled I missed the rest of the Freedom Trail due to extreme laziness, remarks, "You'd think you'd want to know more about the history of our country, Mel." I swig more wine. "Why bother? It's all lies, like the supposed 'massacre'," I answer, making air quotes. Plus, I didn't really *miss* going, although I feel bad Jonathan feels cheated.

- After dinner, we go to a billiard hall in Harvard Square to shoot pool and drink. Seth, Damon's very entertaining friend, meets us. Seth confides his innovative strategy for picking up women: he pretends to be her gay best friend, and then eventually claims he has fallen for her, and she has "turned" him straight. This is a brilliant strategy, although deceptive, and Seth claims it "works like a chahm." Damon shakes his head, realizing he's the only one who has any clue about shooting pool, as the rest of us all got C's or below in geometry. As Courtney and I drink more, our lucky shots increase in frequency and we sort of hold our own in the game. Courtney confides she's hopeful Damon is The One and will propose at some point. I am hopeful for her, although this means she will never move back to California.

- Damon also knows lots of cute friends, but unfortunately we won't be staying long. Seth has already spread his deceptive cards on the table. Also, Jonathan's mere presence prohibits my quest to meet cute boys. Yet he still doesn't want me for himself, obviously. As I drink more, this begins to piss me off and I begin sniping at him about it. On the way home, once we hop off the T and begin walking back, the tension blossoms into a drunken fight on the sidewalk, which finishes with me screaming: "At least I'm not frigid!" and Jonathan shouting: "At least I didn't sleep with the whole world!" Damon and Courtney, shocked and dismayed, will remember this until their dying day. They start trailing farther behind us, trying to pretend we're not with them.

- We call a truce when we realize we have to sleep on the futon together again. Jonathan stalks off to the kitchen, and I smell juice and cookies on his breath when he comes back. He'll probably blame me for drinking the last of the very expensive orange juice. I make Jonathan sleep by the open window, hoping he will block me from the T sounds and the humidity. He turns to Courtney. "I hope you realize I fear for my life every night! I'll probably be catching malaria tonight, thanks to you—and her," he snaps, jerking his thumb at me.

- "Oh, don't even go there! You take up the whole world on this futon!" I shout, tossing my purse on the floor. "And you never turn off the lights! You just lie there and pretend you don't feel me kicking you to turn them off! And I smell juice on your breath, so you better not blame me when Courtney throws a tantrum tomorrow." He stares at me, shocked that I tattled on him. "Well, you ate a cookie, too. You have crumbs all over your boobs," he accuses me. Damn! Damon offers: "I ate five cookies before we left for dinner," in an effort to make peace. Jonathan and I cringe, knowing Courtney will flip. She does: "FIVE cookies? You ate FIVE cookies? Do you think I'm made of money over here? I can't afford for any of you to eat <u>anything</u>! Mel, you are on mango probation. Do not even *think* of eating my mangos. No more cookies for anyone!" I can't believe we're all eating the cookies and hiding it from each other! We all storm off to bed, but Jonathan and I start giggling when we remember Damon's startled look when Courtney forbade anyone from eating anything.

• In the middle of the night, I wake up very cold and notice it's pouring outside. Then I notice the rain has blown in from the window on Jonathan. He feels soggy as a bowl of leftover cornflakes. Do I wake him up and tell him? Or let him sleep and hope he dries in the night and doesn't catch whooping cough? I nicely decide to wake him up and he flips out on me, accusing me of *deliberately* placing him by the window, and preemptively blames me for future ailments he might contract. Somehow, Jonathan wakes up at the crack of dawn, and inconsiderately turns on the TV, blaring "The Facts of Life" and singing along, "You take the good, you take the bad," until Damon flings open the bedroom door. "Do you want to get us all killed? Turn that off before"—he glances nervously at the bed—"*she* comes out." Jonathan complies, and we both feel good that if Damon turns out to be The One, he knows exactly what he's getting himself into.

• In the morning, Damon goes to get us doughnuts and springs for half price leftover wings. Jonathan wonders, "Do you think they have salmonella from being left out all night?" I point out the spicy wing sauce has probably killed any salmonella. We all scrounge money to give Courtney for groceries so we can eat. In the spirit of generosity, she promises to make us homemade fudge, which will be excellent. Courtney and Jonathan are both great cooks. Damon gets stuck taking the trash out after Jonathan claims, "I don't know what to do with trash. I'm not a trash-handling type of person." I guess he makes Kelly take it out at home.

- Courtney, after vetoing Damon's suggestion of going to the dog track as a possible activity for the day, accompanies us to the Sam Adams brewery in Jamaica Plains, on the dreaded orange T line. Jonathan coughs occasionally on the T and throws me dirty looks. He fishes gum out of his pocket and I brace myself. "How is there only one piece of gum left? This is MY gum! Did you eat all my gum?" I nod apprehensively. "You eat it like candy! You can't have any more! That's it for you." I share my new diet plan: "They say gum doesn't digest for seven years, right? So if I eat tons of gum, it will eventually fill up my stomach, preventing me from gaining any weight, ever." Jonathan closes his eyes. "It's obvious why you were kicked out of Honors Science in high school."

- Jamaica Plains is sleazy, and Jonathan declares ominously we will be mugged. However, he does have a Chad moment, spotting an ancient black woman sitting on a stoop. "I want to meet her and sit on her stoop. She'll be funny." I disagree and drag him along. We take refuge and sanctuary at the Sam Adams Brewery, probably where he plotted his nefarious media schemes to incite people against the British. Not that the British were such gems either...

- Throughout the tour, we get to taste, touch and smell the various grains and things they put in the beer. When we arrive at the vats where they cook the beer, we get to meet Dirk the Beer Brewer, a total hotty in a Boston College sweatshirt. I am moving here immediately to live happily ever after with Dirk! I love beer! Damn this tour! Why are we moving out of the vat room! How will I ever find Dirk again!

- This happened to me once before, at Disneyland on New Year's Eve, where I fell in love with a gorgeous Pirate of the Caribbean. He put us in our boat line and smiled <u>significantly</u> at me. He must have switched with someone, because he also unloaded our boat. We flirted for like five minutes, and then arranged to meet at the fritter stand at 11:30, but the horrific crowds conspired to keep us apart. I never got there at all (also because Courtney refused to come with me, despite my siren song promises of other Pirates) and I never knew if he was The One. Alas, me hearties, yo ho.

- "Where was Dirk on the touching and tasting part of the tour anyway?" I'm reluctantly dragged off, and can only hope he will pop up again somewhere. Courtney thinks Dirk is hot too, I can tell, but keeps her thoughts on Damon.

- In the tasting room, we are served pitchers of taster beer. Free pitchers! After six or seven taste pitchers, we are "wicked buzzed," as Damon taught us. Dirk does show up, but turns out to be a complete troll, personality-wise. He's not The One, so I wander off to buy two glasses and a t-shirt for posterity.

- Since we are on the orange line anyway, we go to the Boston Museum of Science. The museum has tons of experiments, like stuffed taxidermy exhibits of New England animals, including a box you can stick your nose into and smell "deer musk," which Jonathan announces loudly smells like dog poo. After being forced out of AP Science our freshman year (for leaving the gas on *after* removing the Bunsen burner from the gas tap), even though no one was harmed, Courtney and I still don't really understand science. She struggled to get B's and I gave up the struggle. We opt for the IMAX movie rather than more science. "I still don't get it," I sigh as we leave the museum. "You're just smart in other ways," Jonathan kindly responds, his buzz making him friendly again.

- Back at the apartment that night, Damon fixes two broken shelves in the bathroom. How Tool-Time handyman of him! Jonathan wanders in to see, and asks, "Who keeps closing the curtain over the window in here? It's so dark." Courtney smacks her forehead with her palm. "We shut the curtain so the people directly across from us in the next building don't think we're exhibitionists! Have you been flashing my neighbors in here this whole time?"

- Courtney makes fudge while we pick up pizza for dinner and hang out and watch TV. Damon comments, "You know, it's totally unrealistic in these shows how people sleep so far apart. They might as well be sleeping in separate beds." I tell him, "The man probably has sweaty legs, like Jonathan does, and the woman doesn't want to get all clammy with leg sweat." Damon laughs. "So, where are you two going on your next trip together?" We simultaneously respond, "Never again." I look at Jonathan. "Jinx, buy me a Coke."

- I pilfer a shirt of Jonathan's and a belt of Courtney's I like. Holding them up, I announce: "I'm taking these home," and stuff them in my bag. "Fine, klepto," Courtney yells back from the kitchen. I know she's mentally deducting the belt from her inventory, like her mom used to do. I love having things that belong to my friends. It makes me feel close to them when I wear them, like love armor.

- Courtney doles out small pieces of fudge to each of us. Jonathan keeps trying to take more until Courtney literally smacks his hand. Damon whines, "But I want more too!" They are both denied large pieces, and lose out big time. I notice Jonathan getting up repeatedly in the night. In the morning, when Courtney discovers half the pan of fudge missing, he blithely admits to eating fudge while everyone else sleeps. She caves in completely and we have a Healthy Start breakfast of cheese, butter, fudge and cookies. Over breakfast, Courtney asks, "So, are you looking forward to getting home to Julian?" I'm startled, mainly because I had completely forgotten about him. Is that a bad sign?

- After making Courtney a record hour late to work, Damon takes us back to the airport. Jonathan and I debate whether to purchase a live lobster from Legal Seafood and take it on the plane, just because you **can.**

- We decide no because:

  - Neither of us knows how to cook lobster.

  - When the lobster guy explains we throw it in the pot alive, we're disgusted, hate all lobster eaters, and feel bad for eating the bisque.

  - We can't imagine how they sedate the lobster for plane travel.

  - We're afraid the lobster will come back to life on the plane, escape, and terrorize us with its large claws.

- Jonathan sits across the aisle from me on the plane and pretends he doesn't know me, discouraging my attempts at conversation by pointedly raising his book. On the plane ride home, I reflect on my long friendship with Courtney and Jonathan. I'm so happy to see her content, in love, and in a place she belongs. It's still bittersweet to be far away, but I think it's time I let go a little—of both of them.

- After we return home, Jonathan calls me. "Those stupid tourists who took our picture at Cheers? The camera wasn't even loaded! There are no pictures!" I just laugh and promise to send him copies of the ones I took. I realize if Julian had forgotten to load the camera for a trip, I'd flip it on him. I also realize that Jonathan and Courtney are a billion times more important to me than Julian; he'll never understand that he'll never be enough for me. I'm going to have to kick him out before he even moves in.

- Well, what's the rush? It can't hurt to keep going out with him—even if I know it's not going to work out. Can it?

A Moose Intervenes

New York, NY
December 1997

It turns out I'm horrible at just dating someone and then ending it. I tried to break up with Julian about ten times, but he just blew it off each time and pretended I wasn't breaking up with him. When he asked me to marry him last winter, I'd have said no if: a) it hadn't been in front of his whole family and b) on Christmas morning. Once the ring went on my finger, I just let it get out of control. Breaking my engagement was one of the most difficult decisions I've ever made. While I clearly couldn't marry Julian, I felt scared no one else would propose. I had one good cry and then determined not to settle. I'm 24 and I'm optimistic The One for me is still out there.

Suggested Soundtrack: *"Heaven Knows"-When in Rome, "Don't Go Away Mad (Just Go Away)"-Motley Crue, "I Never Loved You Anyway"-The Corrs, "It Must Have Been Love"-Roxette*

- How bad could it be to go to New York with your bitter ex-fiancé, who you've just broken up with six weeks ago, but you already had the plane tickets? As it turns out, *really bad.* This whole trip definitely falls into Bad Idea Jeans territory. Luckily, Julian sits quietly on the plane, so I can pretend I don't know him and just read my book, Stephen King's *It.* This book haunts me for life—I'm already terrified of clowns. In fact, one of the reasons I broke up with Julian was due to his announcing he wanted to become a party clown for his job. How could I live with someone who went around scaring people?

- When we arrive, I discover that Julian's brother, Sean, will *not* be meeting us at the airport after all. Instead, we'll be taking a bus to a terminal near Sean's apartment. Crippled by my giant suitcase, I hoist myself onto the bus, leaving

Julian to struggle with his own bag. On the bus, which smells like pee, I ask, "Did you call Sean to meet us, like I asked you to?" I can see the lie forming in his mind, so I just tell him to forget it. As Jonathan has pointed out many many times, "Julian lies about things that there's not even a good reason to lie about."

• Sean meets us in front of his building, which also houses a diner, decorated within an inch of its life for the holidays. Oh good, the diner has a bar! Julian keeps trying to hold my hand and act like we're still together. "Get off," I hiss as I extract my hand. Sean looks over and seems puzzled by my hostility. Why, I don't know. You'd think breaking up would be a clear sign of hostility.

• Our bags, stored directly next to the radiator, are sure to catch on fire. In addition, the living room is about the square footage of my closet at home. Sean goes to change out of his tour guide uniform. "We're going to dinner at a nice restaurant where I get discounts," he calls to us. We pick up his girlfriend Mandy, an investment banker, on the way. As soon as we're seated, Mandy bounces around in her chair. "I'm so excited to come to California in March! I just can't wait to get out of this cold!" I innocently ask, "Why are you still coming out in March? Did you already have plane tickets or something?" Like I did for this trip? Mandy and Sean exchange confused glances, while Julian looks at the floor, hoping to be swallowed up like Jonah. Charlie should be singing *In the Belly of the Whale* as background music. Mandy says, "We have plane tickets for your wedding. So we can come to your wedding." She looks concerned,

• I jump to my feet, knocking my chair over, and bellow at Julian: "Are you kidding me?? You didn't tell them we **aren't** getting married? Are you still pretending that it's happening? Who else haven't you told? Oh, no, your mother?" I snatch up my water glass, preparatory to dashing it in Julian's face, or possibly throwing it at him. The entire restaurant has gone dead silent, the other diners not even pretending not to watch, whispering at the drama unfolding before them. Someone mutters, "Is this real or performance art?" Maybe I should throw my glass at that guy instead. Julian's straight blonde hair hides his stricken face.

- Sean demands an explanation but when Julian's not compulsively lying he's not overly articulate, so Sean and Mandy turn to me. I inform them loudly, along with the entire restaurant, that, "Julian is a compulsive liar. He cheated on me, and never wants to have sex with me. He has bad credit. He won't get a real job and now wants a career as a party clown. In fact, the only positive thing I can think of about Julian right now is that he has a convertible. That's the sum of his current appeal." I drain my water glass. A Chinese woman nearby comments, "What a los-uh. No won-duh she dump him." Thank you!

- Mandy, who has only been dating Sean nine months, looks shocked. "I can't believe he won't have sex with you," she replies empathetically, laying her hand over mine and stroking my fingers. I may be off here, but I'm pretty sure she's hitting on me. Sean wonders aloud, as if Julian wasn't there, "Does he get the compulsive lying from our mom?" Possibly, as their mother, a stockbroker who hates me, recently married husband #6, only **he** thinks he's #2. He also thinks all seven of her kids have the same father. Another lie. All different fathers.

- Julian protests, "I only cheated on you once...a long time ago." Mandy squeezes my hand, and I think she's rubbing my foot under the table. Sean excuses himself and Julian sprints after him, frightened at being left at the table with me. I'm a little frightened at being left with Mandy! "I guess I'm just so surprised because I find you really beautiful," she begins. I feel like I can process this new development since I'm not really still upset over the cheating or the engagement. "Mandy, are you bisexual?" I ask her directly. She looks down demurely. "I don't know," she confesses, and looks up at me. "Are you?" Oh, there are so many days

I wish I was, but other than for novelty, I just don't see this happening. "Mandy, I'm still really upset about the breakup, so this wouldn't be a good time for me to explore. But I'm really flattered. Does Sean know?" She tosses her head. "He's going to find out pretty soon when I leave him for a waitress at one of the restaurants we go to. The no-sex thing must run in their family."

• After dinner, we walk to Rockefeller Center to watch the ice skaters. Everyone looks so graceful and happy out there, whirling around the ice while the music plays and snow gently drifts down. Maybe if I was an ice skater and just skated around and stayed single, I would achieve inner Zen peace? I wish I were here alone. Thank God Courtney will be meeting me here tomorrow. She's taking the train from Boston and I can't wait to see her.

• The next day, I take a cab to Grand Central to meet Courtney's train. All the men exiting the train look hot and successful, probably like the investment bankers at Mandy's firm. I spot Courtney's blonde head peering around in the crowd. She looks great, very classic in her wool coat and jeans. We hug. "How's it going so far?" she asks, pulling gum out of her purse. If only she had a flask in there. I mime hanging myself, making my eyes bug out and letting my tongue dangle from the corner of my mouth. She cracks up and drags me about seventy blocks to have lunch at a restaurant she knows. "Julian never told anyone we broke up, and Mandy hit on me over dinner last night," I begin as we walk, unloading all the drama over blocks and blocks of walking. "Moving on," I change the subject, tired of thinking about it, "How are you and Damon? Do you think he's going to propose at Christmas?" Courtney groans. "A Christmas proposal wouldn't be ideal. I want to be proposed to in a garden and it's barren everywhere in Boston right now." Plus, I ominously remind her, Christmas proposals are doomed: Julian proposed last Christmas, after being specifically told <u>not </u>to propose in general, let alone on a holiday in front of his whole family, let alone I'm Jewish. I relate the tale to her, a la *Scooby-Doo* flashback sequence:

- True to form, he gets his whole family involved with an elaborate surprise of wrapping a giant box, with tons of Styrofoam and bubble wrap in it, with a sign at the bottom. The sign, written by Sean, says, "Will you marry me, Mellisa?" The misspelling of my name adds a nice touch of comedy later when I open the box. Christmas morning, his whole giant family waits with bated breath for me to dig through the box and get to the misspelled sign. I tear off the wrapping paper, see that it's a pots and pans box, and snap, "You had <u>so</u> better not have gotten me pots and pans! I already told you, no appliances, no kitchen stuff, and no gift certificates!" Julian helps me start ripping the box open, and my patience wears thin with all the filler. I sift around, don't feel anything, and throw the box aside as some lame joke gift. He digs the sign out and holds it up for everyone to see and then says, "Well?"

- Oh, such a big decision: do I ruin Christmas for his entire family or not? I am tempted to yell, "No!" and run upstairs and pretend to cry, but cave to the pressure and nod, then bury my face in his shoulder and pretend-cry there instead. Clearly, the misspelled sign was a sign (literally) spelling doom for our relationship.

- I recklessly pay the bill, fantasizing about all the money I'll have when I dump Julian out of our bank account. We decide on The Slaughtered Lamb for drinks, daydreaming about really good proposals on our walk over. There are tons of people there drinking away their troubles, and we join them. We spend hours meandering around the Village, talking about her and Damon and how I'm never getting married, ever. Relationships are not worth the drama of having it all end in tears over and over. It's much easier just to hook up and not get involved. I learned that from

Arizona Rob. Courtney eyes me. "How often were you and Julian having sex anyway? I mean, not to be judgmental, but you've been kind of *wild* since you guys broke up."

• I put my hands on her shoulders. "Courtney, I've been engaged to a man who has not voluntary slept with me in a year and a half. Every three months or so, he gives in. Do you know what that's like?" She shakes her head no, eyes wide. "So cut me a little slack here. It's just nice being wanted again, ok?" Courtney confides that she never liked Julian anyway. I stare at her. "Maybe you could have said something while I was wasting two years of my life?" She reminds me, "That was the summer you had four boyfriends and you had just become friends with Brendan again. Who knew you would pick the only loser of the bunch? And then it was too late." She picks out a red scarf from a street vendor and ties it on, fluffing her hair. She's totally right; I have the worst instincts ever. The opposite of Basic Instinct. She turns back to me. "Can I also tell you candidly you picked the ugliest bridesmaid dresses in the world? Forest green lace? I'm 5'10"! I looked like the Jolly Green Giant in drag!"

• We meet up with Julian and Sean and a random bunch of people they've invited to dinner at Friday's. Courtney glares at Julian even though he acts friendly to her. Fridays' food tastes sick, but enough drinks make anything palatable. I call Jonathan from a pay phone at Friday's to report all the horrible news. I can mentally see him lying on his couch with a glass of wine nearby, scrunching into the cushions, anticipating the gossip.

• Jonathan *finally* came out this year. Yes, that's correct— after *eleven years* of wondering, I <u>finally</u> know why he never went out with me. Marilyn, yet again, was right when she bet he'd come out. I owe her another $38. He's roommates with Kelly now in Los Angeles, and is basically her gay husband. He has a boyfriend. He and Kelly have cats that Jonathan claims are their children. His life finally got good! He sighs when I tell him Julian didn't tell anyone we aren't getting married. "He's so in denial, Melissa—and I *know* about denial. Maybe you can chuck him off the Staten Island ferry or something. Tell him from me he needs a shrink." I close my eyes. "He already goes to one. All Psych majors go to shrinks." Jonathan makes kissing noises into the phone and hangs up. He must have had several glasses of wine then; he's usually not that demonstrative. Or he was making kissing noises at the evil cats.

- We go back to the apartment (except Courtney, who escapes home, feeling a lot better about her life) and I try to take up a tiny sliver of space on the futon in the living room, wanting to avoid making any contact with Julian. Last night, I had a very sexy dream about Jacob and my old boots and woke Julian up. I do want to hook up, but not with you, Julian. And not with any of the people I hooked up with since I threw you out:

  - A college friend I ran into at Chester Drawers, who came over after the bar closed. I got in the shower, drunk, but not too drunk to realize he would think prickly legs are gross. Shaving my legs badly and cutting them, I passed out in a pool of blood and vomit in the shower. He found me that way, dried me off and *hooked up with me anyway.*

  - Teeny Peeny, the hot guy I met getting my car fixed, who had only a tiny nubbin penis and yet lounged around nude all weekend, flaunting it. He also came in 2.5 seconds and generally was useless.

  - The Entrepreneur, who claimed to be "self employed" (he owned some vending machines). He turned off the fuse box in his apartment so I would think we were having a blackout, and after making out for like ten minutes, blurted out, "I want to have unprotected anal sex with you!" I asked for a drink of water first and fled while he was in the kitchen, fumbling around in the fake dark.

- Mr. Fixit, who I met dancing at a bar on Christmas Eve. The next morning, I found he had knife scars all over his back and chest "from knife fights." In contrast to Teeny Peeny, Mr. Fixit's was huge. But not worth knife fighting. I dropped him off and peeled out.

- Sunday I spend sightseeing with Julian as planned, which goes marginally better than getting anally propositioned by The Entrepreneur, but not much. We walk awkwardly around Central Park, Times Square, and go to the top of the Empire State Building. I need to be nice enough to him that he signs all the documents to close our joint bank account.

- Sean told us we had to have lunch at Jekyll and Hyde's, a fun bar in the Village, so we take the subway out there. I visualize Julian being mugged and getting amnesia. It's pointless to kill him off in my fantasies since I don't have any life insurance on him anyway. The paintings and other things hanging on the wall at Jekyll and Hyde's talk and move, like the rat head at Chuck E. Cheese. I worry that they will come to life and kill me, and then realize that may be a blessing. I am one phone call away from changing my flight home.

- Lunch takes a sad turn when I turn my attention back to Julian. He's sniffling, his black eyes all red and bloodshot. He's trying to convince me to give him another chance. Another chance at what? Lying? Cheating on me? Ruining my self-esteem by recoiling from having sex with me? I could give him eleventy million chances, but he would still be *who he is*. And that's the problem. He says, "I'll do whatever you want," and I lose it. "I'm not looking for a puppet!" The moose head on the wall behind me asks, "Who you calling puppet??" We turn around to look at it, and the moose says, "Look buddy, even **I** can tell you're done." Perhaps the talking moose head can convince him?

Obviously, an intelligent person lurks back there, making the moose talk and eavesdropping on our conversation.

- Bullwinkle agrees with me, shaking his antlers at Julian and telling him he needs more therapy, and maybe his moneybags mom will pay for it? This qualifies as the most surreal breakup ever: intervention by a talking moose head. Julian looks dazed as we pay the bill and stumble out into the sunlight.

- That night at dinner, Sean takes me aside and says, "Look, I just don't see why this can't be worked out. I mean, Julian says he's willing to do anything to get you back." I sigh. "Sean. Is he willing to get a lobotomy and a testosterone drip? That might help a little...but maybe still not enough." I explain to Sean I am so much happier living alone and being free of the tension and despair. He almost faints. "He's moved out? Where does he live? He said I could still call him at home. He lied to me!" Join the club.

- I nod. "Sean, he's a compulsive liar. I cannot imagine the horror of being married to him, or being related to your mother. That's it. It's done. I'm better than this." As I say it, I realize it's true. The One waits out there for me, and I'm going to find him! On the plane home, I begin making a list of the things I want in my new man, shielding my paper from Julian. "Wants to have sex minimally once a week, hot, has white collar job aspirations, does not have loony mother, hates sports, loves theatre, concerts and movies, hates stupid TV shows, dresses nicely, works out, smart, likes to travel somewhere besides Boise, Idaho to see his mom, gets me presents that I want..."

- I realize I have just asked God for a gay man. Or Mandy. I still don't know what to think of that. Maybe I could move in with Jonathan and share custody of his evil cats? Is it too late?

The Princess Bride

Kennesaw, GA
August 1998

Glynis' wedding, which I have been asked to be a part of, turns into Old Home Week. Me, Jonathan, Chad and Charlie have an awesome time hanging at the bar, drinking and laughing over old times. Jonathan in particular has become much less guarded now that everyone knows he's gay.

I also have a fabulous new boyfriend, Matthew, who I met online. Cross your fingers for me! At 25, I may have finally found The One! He's everything I wrote on my list on the plane, except miraculously he's not gay! It's amazing and probably too good to be true.

Glynis, with her usual flair for the dramatic, has chosen to have a theme wedding. Her theme: The Princess Bride, another of our favorite movies. I guess she thought a St. Elmo's Fire wedding would be too 80's. The clincher came when she insisted that everyone come to the wedding, in Georgia, in costume. It's a testimonial to her how everyone just put on their tights and serving wench gowns and shut it.

Suggested Soundtrack: *"Conviction of the Heart"-Kenny Loggins, "U Got the Look"-Prince, "Pride (In the Name of Love)"-U2, "Love Theme from St. Elmo's Fire"-David Foster, "Storybook Love"-The Princess Bride soundtrack*

- Jonathan and I arrive in Atlanta (after he ditches me on the flight, cautioning me not to annoy the other passengers) and we rent a car. Neither of us can possibly navigate the rural roads that just let you be lost for miles out in the Blair Witch forest. "Unless you want to hire a driver, one of us has to drive," I point out. Jonathan grumbles, but we Rock Scissors Paper and Jonathan gets stuck driving. "How can anyone tell where they are with all these trees?" he cries, wishing himself back in the concrete jungle of Los Angeles.

- Finally, I check us into the hotel Glynis recommended, conveniently located by a mall and a restaurant called Taco Mac. "Does this place have tacos *and* macaroni or what?" Jonathan looks skeptical. Taco Mac becomes our new favorite restaurant, being a) within walking distance, and b) has a bar. These are the only requirements we have. Chad and Charlie also check in to our hotel and then head over to Taco Mac, dragging along Wendy and Lee, other high school friends. Lots of excitement, since Wendy and Lee live in New York and no one ever sees them.

- "OK," Jonathan opens, "who exactly told Glynis we would all wear costumes? I even hate Halloween costumes! Who would have a costume wedding?" We all reply in unison, "Glynis!' and then crack up and cheers each other. Seriously, she is the only person who would think that a Princess Bride costume wedding is normal—and only she could get everyone to go along with it. "I like my outfit!" Charlie bounces around in his chair like Tigger on crack until Jonathan swats him, reminding Charlie, "That's because you didn't get an outfit that has tights with it, like Chad's." Chad narrows his eyes at Jonathan, swirling his Jack and Coke ominously. "Shut it, Gilbert Gottfried! At least I'm participating, unlike this lazy bastard." Lee just shrugs. He's unpressurable.

- Wendy and I, being The Princess Bridesmaids, have our final fittings for our bridesmaid dresses tonight. We all head off to Glynis and Trey's house in Kennesaw. On the drive over, I envision a beautiful gown with a square neck, and maybe a tall pointy hat with ribbons or veils or something coming off the top. Glynis effusively greets us at the door, hugging and tearing up when she sees everyone came to her wedding. Her organized side takes over quickly, and she hustles Wendy and I back to the bedroom to try on our "costumes." Wendy gets a dark green dress, reminiscent of serving wenches at the Renaissance Fair or Medieval Times. It looks great on her!

- I'm handed a maroon wall tapestry that appears to be hiding eleven months of pregnancy. With triplets. I look more pregnant than I ever will **actually** look when I'm pregnant. "Go try on your costume, Mel!" Glynis twirls around in excitement, swishing her gorgeous silky gown with corset lacing. Maybe I can request corset lacing so I have a waist? Nothing can be done about this tragedy/tapestry, so I shut it. Jonathan bursts out laughing when I return wearing the tapestry, which really says it all. "You look exactly like Grimace in the McDonald's commercials, if he was maroon brocade!" He falls over the couch arm, laughing helplessly. Charlie threatens him not to hurt Glynis' feelings. "What about my feelings, Charlie?" I ask evenly. "When it's your wedding, we'll care about your feelings, Mel," Charlie assures me.

- After the "fitting," we head off to Buckhead in Atlanta for Glynis' bachelorette party. She has made Charlie, Chad, Jonathan and Lee honorary bachelorette attendees. In the car, Jonathan and I speculate about how Trey, a traditional Southern male, feels about having two of Glynis' ex-boyfriends, Chad and Charlie, at the wedding. "I'm pretty sure Trey thinks Charlie likes guys," I offer. Jonathan rolls his eyes. Lee, also gay, rolls his eyes too, but Wendy looks amused. In the other car with Chad driving, Charlie hops around in the backseat and Glynis has her legs out the sunroof, stretching out preparatory to dancing all night. I can barely get mine to the dashboard.

- Most of the downtown bars seem to be shacks raised on stilts. We're nervous until we spot a Pottery Barn, knowing they would never open a Pottery Barn in a seedy neighborhood. Chad gets out of the car, revealing he has either brought plastic vampire teeth on the plane or acquired them somewhere. He wears them the whole night in all the photos. At Bar #1, Glynis climbs onto the bar and starts drinking out of a beer bong, starting the night off right! She gets up and starts dancing on the bar, after Lee shouts that in New York there's a bar called Hogs & Heifers where everyone dances on the bar! In fact, she has a choreographed routine she's performing on the bar top, to the whistles and applause of the other patrons.

- Tragedy at Bar #3: From her years of professional dancing, Glynis sustained a lot of injuries, and her left knee is the weakest link in the chain. Charlie loves dancing with Glynis, and finishes with a big dip onto her left knee, despite being specifically told NOT to do that. Her knee goes out, and she crumples into a dramatic heap. Jonathan and Charlie have to carry her off the dance floor. "My wedding," she whispers, "it's *ruined*." Chad grimaces with his vampire teeth in. "Don't worry, Glynis," Wendy reassures her, "Trey will still marry you in a leg brace." Lee and Jonathan both roll their eyes again.

- We get back to Glynis' house, Lee and Chad practically carrying her, while Wendy gets out the ice packs. Glynis sobbed in the car the whole way home, envisioning looking like a clumsy hippo on her wedding day. Welcome to my life, Glynis. She has perfected the art of letting her big brown eyes fill with unshed tears, making you want to do anything to keep her from crying. Even telling her the wall tapestry looks great, and of course no one minds having to wear a costume.

- After dropping Glynis off, the rest of us convene at the bar in Taco Mac to discuss the disturbing development. She'll absolutely kill Charlie if she can't make it down the aisle. And Trey might shoot him. Chad pipes up, "Charlie, you ruined Glynis' wedding. Now she'll have to gimp along down the aisle. Maybe in a *leg brace*!" Charlie feels horrible. Too guilty to hop around as usual, he quietly sips his beer, which Jonathan appreciates. Charlie's hopping always makes him nervous.

- Later that night, Trey arrives home from the local theater where they're holding the wedding. He takes one look at Glynis on the couch with ice on her knee, and says, "I don't even want to know." Glynis, fortified with several glasses of wine, smiles and calls "Don't worry! I should be able to walk by Saturday. I love you!" She's regained her optimistic equilibrium, thanks to Franzia.

- Back in our hotel room, Jonathan hogs up the phone yammering on to his boyfriend about all the dramatic wedding developments. I motion to him to snap it up, I want to call Matthew, but he just rolls over and ignores me. It's probably all for the best he's gay; he treats me like a slave. I call Matthew collect from a pay phone in the hall, and tell him all the news. He laughs hysterically, especially about my maternity tapestry. I miss him so much, but I am grateful he wanted me to just have fun with my friends and not worry about keeping him entertained. We make kissing noises at each other, and I go back to my room. Jonathan still yaps away, but I don't care anymore.

- The next morning, I get ready to go to the bridesmaid luncheon at the Kennesaw Country Club, located on a street actually named for Trey's family. Chad and Charlie plan on going to the mall to buy a wedding gift from all of us. "Chad, don't pick something tacky, ok? Just pick something nice from the registry and leave it at that," I warn him as I head to the lobby. "What are you saying?" he yells down the hall after me. "Just because I told your mom I liked her 'Dogs Playing Poker' blanket doesn't make me tacky!" Jonathan preemptively refuses to go to the mall, giving no explanation. He probably has to call his boyfriend again to yap on for hours. Now that I know he's gay, he's *so* gay.

- Maybe they were all gay? Everyone who never liked me from Scott Steinberg on…could all have been gay! Maybe that's why after I broke up with Julian and ran into Jacob at a bar, he didn't call me. Even though he said he would. I am so thankful to have Matthew. God, I will do anything You want if Matthew turns out to be The One. And not gay.

- At the luncheon, Trey's grandmother, Granny Fulton, announces she had *seventeen* marriage proposals before she agreed to marry Granddad. She sagely advises Wendy and I to "be picky and not settle." Wendy and I think it would be the equivalent of winning the lottery to be able to get one non-loser to propose. Granny Van Etton, Glynis' grandmother, tops her by announcing that she's killed three husbands "so far." The Black Widow Granny sips her drink and smiles deviously at us. She's more realistic; you may have to kill people, especially ones who don't call you back. After the luncheon, everyone meets back at Taco Mac. In the bar. After a few drinks, I want to drunk-dial, but everyone I usually call is here. Except Matthew, who hates being drunk-dialed and has firmly instructed me to "call someone else when you're drunk, like Chad."

- Chad and Charlie argue over whose rented costume is better. Chad rented essentially a jester outfit, while Charlie chose a red velvet Inquisitor robe. Jonathan, confident in his choice of a studded leather Bob Mackie vest worn by Cher, benevolently tells everyone else they look fine.

- The wedding rehearsal turns out to be a somber affair: Glynis limps badly due to her knee injury. I fear she might fall down the stairs while going down the aisle at the theatre. The fact that she's having the wedding in a theater adds to the surreal experience. Trey, too busy working on the lighting design for the wedding, can't help in the limping sympathy department. We haven't seen the final design or effects yet. I hope they don't have anything popping out at me, like clowns. Glynis' mom, Glenda, takes offense that Glynis runs the rehearsal like a drill sergeant. "You've obviously never taken a dance class with Glynis as the instructor, where she barks at everyone not keeping up," I murmur to Glenda. Chad invites Glenda to the Taco Mac bar with us to "take the edge off." Chris, Glynis' dad, holds up a bag with a pair of white tights for his costume and asks plaintively, "Can I come too?"

• Everything goes relatively well until the costume designers, Celeste and Susan, update Glynis on the status of costumes. Glynis panics. "You didn't say anything about the leggings for the guys." Celeste: "What leggings?" She and Susan look completely blank. Glynis retorts, "Well, they can't just go naked under their tunics! This isn't Scotland, you know!" The bad news about the leggings results in a midnight Wal-Mart run. Glynis, Wendy, Lee and I comb Wal-Mart. Hallelujah! We find two black and two brown stretch pants that will work. I cannot believe all the men in the wedding are, in essence, going to be wearing women's Wal-Mart spandex pants. Lee gets hauled out of the Men's section with a disgruntled look on his face. Who knew he wanted to have a midnight shopping spree at Wal-Mart?

• The day of the wedding starts off fine. I wake up on time and beat Jonathan to the shower. "Hurry up!" he pounds on the door. "Or I'm peeing in your luggage!" Glynis picks Wendy and I up at the hotel and off to the theatre we go! Glynis chose flower garlands for our headpieces, rather than the pointy hat fantasy that might have redeemed my dress. When we open the boxes containing our wreaths, Glynis' eyes almost pop out of her head. "They're huge!" she gasps, turning hers around in her hands. "They're the size of the Christmas wreath I hang on my door! I can't wear this on my head!" She sinks into a chair, her eyes welling up in her trademark style. Wendy roots her nail scissors out of her giant purse and comforts Glynis. "I'll just do a little pruning, I mean trimming here..." After a few snips, she has the wreath under control again and Glynis' neck can support her wreath.

• Glynis continues to sniffle at the near miss; also, her knee still hurts. Once we have her laced into her wedding gown, she forgets her troubles and sashays around backstage, twirling her skirts and giggling. She looks like the perfect medieval bride. I notice my shoes suddenly are too tight. When did that happen? I transform into Brocade Grimace, and squash the wreath down over my fluffy hair, which has freaked out in the humidity. Thank God Matthew didn't come! Meanwhile, back at the hotel, Chad struggles into his jester costume and bitches about wearing tights, Charlie tries to keep his robe hem clean, and Jonathan fusses with his ruffled shirt. Lee just laughs at them, as he's wearing a purple silk shirt and black slacks, choosing comfort over participation. Scott, Trey's brother, wins The Most Sullen Groomsman Ever award. He howls at Trey, "If I ever get married, you have to cut your hippie hair for **my** wedding, after making me wear tights and a dress to yours!!!" Trey storms around the corner. "How many times do I have to tell you, it's a tunic, NOT a dress!"

• Granny Fulton looks resplendent in a pink gown with the tall pointed princess hat *I* wanted to wear. She'll probably get proposed to again today. Granny Fulton proposals: 17. Me: 1 lame one. Mr. Fulton pulls nervously at his tights, and only seems reconciled to the event by getting to wear a giant medallion around his neck. He's a good sport but clearly worried all his business associates will see him in jumbo tights. Chris whispers, "I would do anything for my daughter, but I *never* thought I'd be giving her away wearing a pair of white tights." I don't try to sugar coat it to him, either. You raised a drama queen, you get a drama queen wedding, Chris. It's fun and everyone will be talking about it for years to come, so make the best of it. Glenda looks warily at Glynis; if she starts barking orders again, I think Glenda will smack her.

• Glynis hobbles down the aisle—the show must go on! Chris puts a big smile on his face and walks Glynis down the aisle, white tights and all. Once we're all placed onstage, I notice Trey has a giant saber attached to his belt. It sticks out behind him about three feet. I prophesy someone falling over it before the day is done, perhaps slicing themselves in half. Scott pouts, probably because he didn't get a saber, too. Just a little Friar Tuck rope belt.

- The ceremony starts well. Then, as the minister starts talking about the joining of "Lamar and Glynis," everyone realizes he's actually saying, "Lamar and Glenda." Glynis, named to combine her parents' names, Glenda and Chris, has always had trouble with people mispronouncing her name. But who could foresee the minister getting it completely wrong at her wedding! Glynis' mom, the actual Glenda, clutches Chris' arm in fear. The minister says Glenda's name twice before realizing his mistake. The whole wedding party leans towards him to *will* him to say the correct name. Trey appears to be considering shooting the minister. Is she really married if the minister calls her the wrong name? Trey's real name is *Lamar*?

- Scott has tied the little ring bag to his rope belt, and knotted the bag shut. He ostentatiously rips the bag free, and tears it open to get the ring out. Trey might shoot him as well if he doesn't stop pouting. Glynis and Lamar kiss and are married! (Side note: This will be the last time Glynis says the name Lamar, ever, in their lives). Charlie: "I can't believe that's his name. I feel like I don't even know him." Chad: "You don't."

- During their vows, a spotlight comes on, displaying a castle out of nowhere. Literally, a castle just appears onstage, although we know it's a backdrop and Trey set up a scrim. Wendy and I keep straight faces, but Jonathan curls up in his seat in the audience, shaking with laughter. None of us knew it was going to happen. It's very Disney, and I sort of expect a pumpkin coach to come rolling along as well, or jugglers.

- After the ceremony, Jonathan, Chad, Charlie and I get in the rental car and attempt to find the reception church. Glynis privately confided that the decision for the reception location revolves specifically around the "no hard alcohol" policy. We get completely lost, and Jonathan loses Rock Scissors Paper, so he goes into a gas station in his leather Cher vest to ask directions to the church. "If you see them gay-bashing me," he instructs, pointing at two men getting out of a pickup, "you need to come in and help me." The Jester, the Inquisitor, and Brocade Grimace all nod, still talking about the Magic Castle and the minister calling Glynis the wrong name.

- Charlie farts in the car, and Chad tells him he can't return the rental costume if it stinks. While Charlie worries that Chad may be right, Chad leans over into the front seat to scan radio stations, looking for "The Gambler," no doubt. "I wish we had a Newt Gingrich sticker on the car," Chad bitches, bored with the radio. "Everyone else has "Vote for Newt" stickers and we'll probably get beat up since we don't." Jonathan, having returned with directions involving, "Turn right at Old Oak Corner," challenges him. "Do you even know who Newt Gingrich is, Chad?" He starts the car and backs up, waiting for an answer. "Shut it, Gilbert," Chad answers sullenly. He only recovers his good mood when I miss telling Jonathan to turn at Pooh Corner or whatever. "I can't help you because there's no sign! There's only a giant tree on the corner!" Jonathan rolls his eyes. "It's an oak tree, Melissa, as in Old Oak Corner." I complain how they're too cheap to put up a sign and Chad starts laughing, forgetting all about Newt.

- We finally find the church and meet the MC, who's obsessed with the Renaissance Fair and feels the need to put on an accent. "Me lords and ladies," she trills, "give a waaaahm medi-eeeevil welcome toooooo.... Lady Wendy and Sir Scott!" I notice several bees have followed me into the church and are crazed with lust for my giant wreath, which I can't possibly take off now because my hair is destroyed from it. I swat bees away as Glynis and Trey move to the dance floor for their first dance, which is supposed to be "Theme from The Princess Bride." Instead, the instrumental piece from the swordfight between Inigo

Montoya and the Dread Pirate Roberts comes blaring out and I have to go over and change the track myself.

- During dinner, everyone who comes to the head table to talk to Trey and Glynis trips over Trey's saber, but he stubbornly refuses to take it off. "No!" he whispers to Glynis. "If I take it off, Scott will take it." She just shakes her head and says she hopes no one sues. We have authentic giant turkey legs and mugs of ale for the meal.

- Scott has clearly hit the spirits double-time and somehow manages to get through the toast. The toast, painful to watch, seems heartfelt. Glynis fumes, "Where did he get hard alcohol from? It's not allowed here!" We notice a steady trickle of men heading outside and opening their trunks, where they hide their liquor. Glynis' church ploy didn't work out as planned. Chad spots Scott on the dance floor with the hood from his costume <u>on</u> his head instead of gracefully settled on his shoulders, swinging his little Friar Tuck belt around. Rock on! Granny Fulton cuts in to dance with him, leading some senior gentlemen on a merry chase.

- After the wedding, Chad makes me drive. "You're the only one who didn't spend the whole reception drinking Coors." Jonathan sits up front and sings songs from *Les Misérables* with me on the way back to our hotel. Once we hit the Alabama state line, Jonathan sits up and starts yelling, "Where are we? Are we in *Deliverance?*" Chad yells, "Melissa, the hotel was literally fifteen minutes away! How are we in Alabama?" "I don't know," I cry, throwing my hands in the air. "There are so many trees. Everything looks the same!" Charlie moans, "Now we'll never get back to Taco Mac!"

- Jonathan and I are unceremoniously dumped into the back seat. We are all tired of each other by the time we get back to the hotel and pass out. No Taco Mac for us tonight. "Where did you all come from, a costume party?" the desk clerk jeers at us. "Shut it, Gilbert," Chad retorts as the elevator doors shut.

- The next day, on the plane, Jonathan sits in a different row. On the flight, I suddenly remember they never told me what they got Glynis for her wedding gift. It turns out to be a giant silver candelabrum. Chad actually says the word "giant" and Charlie spreads his hands out really far to show me the size. I look blankly at them. "Was that on the registry?" Chad flips his hand dismissively. "Please, I'm not getting her a stupid pizza cutter or something. I wanted a gift that every time she looked at it, she would think of us. We're her lifelong friends — she should remember us all the time." Chad was right. Every time she looks at it, to this day, she thinks of us. Turns out it was one of her favorite gifts.

He Never Gave the Signal...

San Jose, CA
April 1999

This trip was my first with Matthew, who moved in with me six months ago. Well, after we solved some privacy issues. He thought I was snooping when I was just innocently going through the drawers of his desk, looking for a pen. Also, I had a real problem with him locking the bathroom door. As my mother used to warn my sister and me, "What if something happened to you in there? If you lock the door, no one can get in and save you if something bad happens." This created an unnatural fear of dying on the toilet for Rachel and I, so we never ever locked the door. Smooth sailing so far.

I looked forward to going away together for the first time, and with one of his friends getting married, perhaps Matthew will see our relationship in a more serious light. Or he'll flee far from commitment if his friends hate me. No pressure...

Suggested Soundtrack: *"I Think I'm Paranoid"-Garbage, "Only a Lad"-Oingo Boingo, "Ask"-The Smiths, "Enjoy the Silence"-Depeche Mode, "The Metro"-Berlin*

- Matthew and I are going away to our first wedding together! His high school friend, Colin, invited us to his wedding in San Jose. Matthew seems confused by the invitation. "Why would Colin get married? I don't understand," he remarks, looking over the invitation carefully. I look up from my book. "Well, they've been dating for a couple years, and if they're happy together, they should get married." He eyes me warily. "My point exactly. If they're happy, why ruin it all by getting married?" He edges away to the bathroom, and I hear the click of the lock as he pushes the lock button. As a child of divorced parents, Matthew seems more paranoid than the average bear about getting married himself. I think his exact words were, "Why would I do something stupid like that?"

• Several weeks later, we fly up to San Jose with a friendly seatmate who wants to know if he can store his burritos under my seat. They are *special* burritos from some obscure taco stand in Los Angeles, so I agree that for forty-five minutes I can sit atop a beanfest. Matthew picks up our rental car and drives to the hotel/wedding site with no mishaps. Where was he when I got lost and drove to Alabama? We drop our bags in our room after checking into the mansion hotel and locate Martin, Colin's former roommate and Matthew's high school buddy. He's in the bar, as expected. Martin appears completely shell-shocked that Colin essentially dumped him for a wife. He's already been competing with Liz for Colin's attention, and now this! "Judging from the swank hotel, Liz's a wife with a wealthy family," I observe, noting the expensive elegance of the hotel. It's pretty much right up there with the Waterfront Hilton for ritzy. I'll have to call Jonathan and report.

• The Western-themed bar beckons us, and before long Martin nicknames me "Pardner" as we drink our Jack and Cokes. Colin comes to meet us, with other high school friends, Jose and Geoff, in tow. He keeps looking over his shoulder, as though fearing to be caught in the bar with his friends, and I have to wonder why. Is he marrying someone who would veto hanging out and drinking? If so, from what I've heard about Colin, this won't work out at all. They all catch up and reminisce over many more drinks, and are surprised I can keep up with them. Matthew boasts, "Oh, yeah, she drank a six-pack on our first date! She can totally drink you guys— except Martin—under the table." I understand this group has different, lower standards of acceptance.

• Colin reminds us that they're having a dinner buffet in his parents' suite and scampers off before he gets caught. "Ok, guys, what's the deal?" Matthew demands, putting his arm in a puddle of drink sweat. Geoff leans forward. "She's making him get a **job**, a real **job**, and everything!" Martin chimes in, "Yeah, and he's not supposed to spend all his money drinking anymore. He might have *an allowance.*" Jose looks reproachfully at them. "I think Colin's doing better than ever! He has a good job, he's living in a clean house," (Martin rolls his eyes) "and he's happy and in love. What more could he want?" Matthew looks confused. "So wait. If everything's so great, what does he need to get married for? Can't he just live there and be happy without getting married?" No, no, Matthew, he can't. But I can't be the one to say it, or he'll scent danger.

- Geoff scoffs at him. "What are you, new? Yeah, they pretend you can just live there and hang out and have sex, but eventually you have to pony up the ring, or it all goes to hell, buddy." He looks smugly at Matthew, as he knows but Matthew doesn't, that this will also be Matthew's fate sooner or later. Martin punches me in the shoulder. "Nah, my pardner wouldn't do that to you, man. She's cool." Eventually, we realize we need to shower and change and not reek of Jack Daniels at the dinner buffet, so Martin goes over to close the tab. "Charge all of this to Colin Finnerty's Wedding." Matthew and I head back to our own room to change for the dinner, Matthew pondering proposals. "Isn't it expensive?" Not as expensive at not proposing would become, trust me.

- Dressed and ready to go, we head to the Finnerty suite. Colin's parents, Jon and Brenda, are hospitable and welcoming. Not as hospitable as Colin's aunt, Jeanie Pie, who practically makes out with Geoff and Jose. She leaves Matthew alone out of respect for my presence. Liz, Colin's fiancé, and her friends are in a corner, waves of nervousness emanating from her. Colin laments, "I wish I had some pot from Uncle Tim's pot farm for tonight. It would have been so much fun!" Jose, Matthew and I breathe a sigh of relief, as none of us wants to be peer-pressured into smoking pot to make Colin happy before his wedding. Liz has to get her beauty rest so she turns in, shyly thanking us for coming and hoping to get to know us better soon. What a sweet girl! Martin rolls his eyes and spills his drink a little. "He's so jealous of Liz! He's like a comic book villain plotting against her," I whisper to Matthew. He's too busy watching Geoff flee Aunt Jeanie Pie to respond.

- Martin, Geoff, Jose, Colin, Matthew and I head back to Jose and Geoff's room for more drinking and pre-wedding revelry. I offer to leave them alone and go back to my room, but Martin slings an arm around my shoulder. "No way, pardner, you're coming to the party." Matthew begins eying him suspiciously, trying to determine if he's drunk and friendly or hitting on me in earnest. In the room, Jose disappears into the bathroom, calling that he's "getting comfortable" and emerges wearing flannel pajamas with horses printed all over them. They maul him mercilessly, calling him everything from Black Beauty to the Red Pony, with Ponyboy (from *The Outsiders*) winning out as his new nickname. Colin occasionally whinnies in Jose's direction.

- Finally, around 3 a.m., Colin, a 4.0 on the Breathalyzer right now, sits bolt upright. "Oh my God! What am I doing? I'm getting married today! Oh my God!" I'm thinking he's realizing how Bad Idea Jeans this is, being up at 3 a.m. and drunk the night before his wedding, and how he'll look like hell in the photos, but he's truly panicking. Martin, Geoff and Matthew circle in like vultures, stoking his wave of panic. "You're right, Colin," Martin begins, circling for the kill. "What *are* you doing?" Ponyboy tries to intervene, reminding Colin that he's *happy*, and Liz has turned his life around, unlike these losers. Meanwhile, Matthew and Martin are working out a hand signal: if Colin wants to flee during the wedding, he will swing his arm around in the air three times and then pull down, like he's pulling the emergency cord on a bus. Jose refuses to be a party to this disaster, and heads for the door. Martin calls, "Stay gold, Ponyboy! Stay gold!" I wonder if Jose has a girlfriend? He seems stable and not commitment-phobic...

- Colin curls into a fetal position on the bed, realizing the horrible mistake he has just made in voicing any nervousness whatsoever. Suddenly, Martin exclaims, "Colin, we never even got you a stripper for your bachelor party! You should have had a stripper!" Geoff and Colin look completely confused, and Geoff reminds Martin they went camping for Colin's bachelor party, not to bars. Martin sidles up to me. "Maybe you could be our stripper tonight?" Matthew's first response: he bursts out laughing, as he knows that my stripping will be as graceful as the Pink Elephant scene out of *Dumbo*. Then, he's affronted. "My girlfriend is **not** stripping in front of you! In fact, we're going back to our room to have sex right now! Alone!" He grabs my hand and tows me out of the room, weaving unsteadily as we're seriously intoxicated. When we get back to our room, I glance at him. "We're not having sex, are we?" He shakes his head and sprints for the bathroom, spending the rest of the night throwing up on the floor of the shower.

- The wedding starts the next afternoon, everyone slinking in with varying stages of headaches. Matthew and I are seated in the middle of the crowd out on the lawn, waiting for the wedding to start. He seems to be intently focused on the tableau at the front. Colin looks completely at peace and thrilled when Liz emerges from a horse-drawn carriage, escorted by her beaming father. I'm impressed! This is a class-act wedding. Martin and Geoff keeping glancing at each other, and I hope they haven't done something stupid, like planted a stink bomb near the priest. Jose seems calm, so if they have anything planned, he doesn't know about it.

- Liz looks absolutely beautiful and self-possessed, much different than the nervous girl we met last night. Matthew looks impressed. "Wow, she looks great! Hey, you would look good in a tiara like that! You have great hair!" But he doesn't want to marry me, obviously. Probably he never will. Suddenly, being at this wedding, I realize Julian was my only chance to get married. I will have to become the crazy cat lady as gracefully as I can.

- The ceremony goes without a hitch, and as Colin and Liz kiss, I see the shock on Martin and Geoff's faces echoed on Matthew's. "What's wrong?" I murmur, looking closely at him. "He...never...gave...the...signal," he stammers out. "He got married, after all." I sigh. "Of course he did. He's not an idiot. He was drunk last night and had a moment of panic. Only you, Curly and Moe thought he would give the signal. Don't you see? He wants to be Liz's husband! Plus, this wedding cost thirty grand, easy." As we head into the reception, Matthew's curiosity overcomes him. "Thirty grand, huh? How much did it cost to get wine glasses with their names engraved on them for everyone? How much does the food cost?" Luckily, this distracts him from being distraught that Colin got married.

- During dinner, Martin gets up to give the best man's toast. The gist of his speech is, "You're married now, so when I invite you to do fun things, you'll have to say no because you have a wife who wants you home. Boy, is your life going to suck." If only Ponyboy had made the speech...

- Martin and Geoff promise to come to the Winchester Mystery House with us the next morning before we fly home. The next morning, however, we discover Martin lying in the hallway in front of his room, completely passed out and unable to articulate how much he hates the idea of stirring to go to the Winchester House. The Winchester House turns out to be on a main street in a parking lot next to Keno's Restaurant. Matthew absolutely loves tourist attractions where there are guided tours full of arcane trivia. He also loves to read every single little placard in the museum area. Stairs lead into walls or ceilings, there are rooms you can't even get to, and tons of workmen died horrible deaths. Matthew springs for a Winchester House cup at the gift shop to commemorate our visit.

- On the plane home, Matthew still seems quiet. It's almost like he's being forced to grow up before my very eyes. I touch his arm. "Hey. Why don't you wait and see how it goes? Maybe Colin getting married won't be as bad as you think." Matthew sighs. "Yeah, maybe. We'll see. Hey, how much do you think the horse and carriage cost?"

A Double Double and a Strawberry Shake

New Year's Eve, 1999
Big Bear, CA

We've packed the car. We've quit our jobs. Matthew and I leave tomorrow for Baltimore, where I'll start a new job at Towson University. For the first time, we'll be living away from friends and family in a new place. Exhilarated and terrified, we plan to spend New Years Eve in the mountains with my family, and New Years Day having brunch with Matthew's family. We'll say our goodbyes, they'll promise to visit, and off we'll go on the coolest road trip ever! It's time to say goodbye to our old lives and start a new one on our own.

Suggested Soundtrack: *Auld Lang Syne, "Tiny Bubbles"-Don Ho, "Unbelievable"-EMF, "Hey Jealousy"-Gin Blossoms, "Closing Time"-Ben Folds Five*

- Matthew gets in the car and turns to me. "Where are the directions to Big Bear?" he asks expectantly. "I don't know how to get there," I reply, getting out of the car to use the phone. We're supposed to be meeting my parents at Tía Lupe's cabin. "Hey, Tía Lupe? Give me the directions to your cabin. I didn't look them up." I hear the clunk of the phone being dropped on the counter, and Lupe yelling, "Hey, Ricardo? Do you know how to get to our cabin? Melissa wants to know." Eventually, they cobble directions together, involving vague turns "at that church. We don't know the name of it, but it has a steeple." Yeah, thanks.

- Matthew flips out. "How does she own a cabin she doesn't know how to get to!? Do they ever go there, or can't they find it!?" I soothe him with a Double Double and a strawberry shake from In 'n Out, his ultimate comfort food. Unfortunately, he realizes afresh *there are no In 'n Outs* where we're moving and flips out again. This time, he won't be consoled. "We won't know anyone! Everything will be different! Maybe they'll have accents! Oh, God, what if I get an accent?" I touch his shoulder. "As long as it's not a Jersey accent, you'll be fine." He pulls himself together and we continue our journey. I'm cutting Matthew a lot of slack, considering he agreed to move sight unseen. He has never been to the East Coast, and was brave enough to just pick up and go. I admire him; not many people move away from home at all. He starts a conversation to distract himself. "How does your family even know Tía Lupe anyway? I know she's your mom's best friend, but she seems so involved in your family." I sigh. "Tía Lupe met my mom when they went to cosmetology school in the olden days, and Lupe has been there since I was born. But, never having married herself, she's definitely entwined herself into the family more like a relative. You can't be as honest with her as you would a relative...but she's always there in the middle of everything. Mom feels bad that she doesn't have a husband or any kids."

• Matthew pulls over. "I need a restroom break. Do you want anything from inside?" I shake my head no, and watch him through the window. He waits for about fifteen minutes, and then one small boy exits the bathroom. I'm puzzled to see him turn on his heel and walk back. "What's wrong?" I ask as he gets in and starts the car. "I refuse to go in there. What could that boy have been doing in there for *fifteen minutes?*" He pulls out and finds a Carl's Jr. bathroom. We finally arrive in Lake Arrowhead at the cabin and settle into our room, which has two twin beds. Lupe and her boyfriend Ricardo are already in bed. "See you tomorrow," Lupe calls from upstairs, turning off the lights.

• I lie awake in my twin bed. The pine trees make shadows on the walls that remind me of my cabin at choir camp. I wonder what ever became of Jacob? I've only run into him once in a bar since we broke up. I don't know if he never called me because I looked engaged, or because he didn't want to start seeing me again, or because I had gained about twenty pounds stress-eating while trying to dump Julian. I roll over, falling asleep to the familiar smell of pine and dirt.

• We sleep in till 10 a.m. "I'm starving," I announce. Matthew shifts under his blanket. "Well, go eat then and I'll see you later." I think better of waking him for good, since it's sure to be a rough day. I forage, and find two doughnuts; Matthew eats nothing when he finally gets up at 11 a.m. "I don't want to overeat now if we're having a big dinner." Tía Lupe looks doubtful; someone refusing food bothers her deeply. Although she eats next to nothing, she dislikes other people who don't eat. "You can eat now, and eat again later," she begins to argue with Matthew. "I mean, people eat all day long." The food-pushing battle between Matthew and my family amuses me. He cannot be guilted into eating, and Mom and Tía Lupe are often beside themselves as to how to **make** him eat. Matthew seems impervious to their old ploys of "The cow will be soooo sad if you don't drink ALL your milk," and "The chicken will be soooo sad if you don't eat ALL your eggs," which left me sobbing and stuffing my face all through childhood. I suppose the Hostess people would have been soooo sad if I didn't eat all my Ding Dongs, too, Mom?

• Ricardo keeps trekking to the store, ostensibly for food, but really to avoid everyone. He's terribly antisocial, and Mom and Lupe try to get Ricardo to talk like they try to get Matthew to eat. People who don't talk enough annoy them, too. As he runs out to his car for the sixth time, Ricardo mumbles, "Miranda and Stan should be here soon." Matthew grimaces. "The Poodle's coming?" All too soon, Ricardo's daughter, Miranda, and her boyfriend, Stan, do arrive. "Where's the beer?" Miranda demands, dropping her bag on the living room floor. Stan at least has the wits to say hello before he starts drinking. Matthew sidles outside to wait for my parents

- Mom and Dad show up after checking into their hotel room. Matthew wonders aloud if we should get a room there too. "Oh, no," Mom shakes her head, "there are no vacancies anywhere. And you can't stay in our room; I don't need you bugging me about smoking." She goes out to the car and begins unloading what appears to be an entire set of dishes, including cookware. As she carries a giant pot inside, she starts on Lupe. "I can't understand how you live with no pots or pans or aluminum foil. *Everyone* has aluminum foil." The answer to this mystery? All Lupe eats are frozen fish fingers. Lupe lifts her eyebrow, giving Mom a narrow look. "Don't even start with me, Vic. You can't just pressure everyone into cooking and eating all the time, like you." Matthew closes his eyes briefly; although he knows Lupe well, he's always mystified by her total lack of self-awareness of the hypocrisy inherent in her conversations.

- Ricardo arrives with some gum, and asks Miranda, "Where's your sister? I thought they were following you?" Miranda shrieks, "They couldn't keep up! They were going about twenty miles an hour, and they wouldn't speed up because of the baby! It's not my fault!" She takes a swig from her beer, and goes out on the balcony to smoke. Stan follows her, scratching at his acne. Ricardo pages his daughter, Katrina. Katrina calls back to report that she, her boyfriend Harlow, and their baby, Daisy, are stuck at the base of the mountain because they don't know the way either. Ricardo leaves to pick them up, despite Lupe's protests to "just give them directions over the phone." Ricardo sees a golden opportunity to be gone for hours, and he won't be swayed. As soon as he leaves, Mom starts in again. "Seriously, how much TV can you watch with someone and call it a relationship?" Lupe gets exasperated. "Vicki, there aren't so many great guys out there, ok? You've been married forever! Not everyone has someone like Sam!" They both look reflexively at my dad, who somehow manages to nap through the argument. He's not exactly looking like the epitome of excitement right now either.

- Everyone who hoped for snow (not us) got their wish as several inches cover the ground, making the roads up the mountain impassable. Miranda, who has spent her time smoking and drinking on the deck, comes inside out of the snow.

- "Lupe, where are the towels? I'm going to shower now so I'll be done when everyone else wants to use it." I've looked vainly through the tiny doll cupboards in the hallway, but no towels to be found. Lupe rounds on me. "Ricardo will shower when he gets back, so **no one...**" she looks around at all of us dramatically, "can use the bathroom until then, for anything." She teeters away on her stilettos. At six feet, she towers over everyone, including Dad. Matthew whispers to me, "Ricardo won't **be** getting back. I heard on the radio they closed the road." Matthew turns out to be a Prophet of Doom. Ricardo calls to say they are all stuck at the bottom of the mountain due to the snowy roads. Lupe starts crying. "I'll have to spend New Year's alone!" Then she starts yelling at Miranda, "This is *your fault*! You were too selfish to just let your sister follow you here! You've ruined New Year's!" Miranda starts shouting back at Lupe, and Stan begins to intervene. Matthew and I flee to our twin bed room, and I hear the door shut as Mom and Dad slip out.

- Regardless of Lupe's situation, Mom still wants to go out, so we get ready. Mom wears a sparkly twin set she wore to lunch at Marie Callendars. "Isn't that a little casual for New Years? You could wear that anywhere," I point out, looking critically at her. "And I do," she replies, giving me a look that says, "Shut it." Dad didn't bother to try on his suit before leaving home. "It doesn't fit, Vicki! I don't know why." Mom comes over to look at his limited fashion choices. "Sam, you can't go like that. You don't even match, and you can't

button your shirt collar. I don't want to be seen with some
hobo." Dad wanders away, muttering, "This outfit was ok
for lunch at Marie Callendar's, but suddenly I'm a hobo."
Matthew didn't try on his tuxedo either and the tiny neck
cuts off his air supply, but looks great in the photos. Lupe
wears a long black gown, reminiscent of Boozy Liza, and
has teased her long, dyed red hair into a drag queen wig.

• Mom rifles through her food bag in the fridge, snacks on
ribs, and gets busted by Lupe for spoiling her appetite for
dinner. "But I'm hungry now!" Mom complains. "Who
made an eight o'clock reservation? We eat dinner at six, not
eight. Here, Matthew, have a rib. You must be hungry, too.
No, Sam, none for you. You won't fit in your pants if you eat
anything."

• Ricardo, having purchased chains and bribed a flagman,
finally returns with Katrina, Harlow, and Daisy, their violent
baby. Ricardo spends his time in the bathroom muttering
about how he had to buy chains and he knows he could
have made it without them. No one cares; we're all just glad
he's here so Lupe won't complain all night. Daisy shows us
her new doll and begins whacking Baby Alive against a door
and stepping on her head. We fear going to sleep, lest we be
mistaken for Baby Alive. Dad looks dubiously at Daisy, and
asks me, "Why do you think she's all violent like that?" I
stare at him in disbelief. "Dad, you've met her entire family.
They're lucky she hasn't killed them all in their sleep!
Especially Miranda."

• At the restaurant, Lupe begins to dispel her gloom with
shots of tequila. Mom orders a martini, although she dislikes
them, because she wants olives. Dad: "You could just order
a drink you like and ask for a dish of olives." Mom refutes,
"That's tacky, Sam. I'm not doing that." Dad retorts, "At five
dollars a pop for martinis, you'll do it if you want more than
one olive! I'm not paying hundreds of dollars for drinks you
don't even like when I could get you a jar of olives for $4."
And then bring them into the restaurant? And mix your

own drinks from a flask? I don't even know what to say. Matthew may be catatonic at this point.

- At midnight, Harlow and Stan both propose, which gets *très* maudlin. Miranda yells, "Daisy, your mommy and daddy are getting married!" making the whole group of us seem like white trash, instead of just them. Ricardo, dressed in a loud yellow suit and purple shirt, nearly has a heart attack at the thought of paying for two weddings. His face turns as purple as his shirt. He runs a bail bond business and seems to do well, although it's a shady business. Matthew and I try to dance but the band is playing a bad rendition of "Tiny Bubbles." We learn they are a Hawaiian band, and they play *everything* as though it's written for the ukulele, even Auld Lang Syne. It's all clear now. Mom, who has a two-step for every occasion, is the only one who can fake it and dances around happily.

- The manager summons Ricardo, who's paying for this debacle. His credit card has been declined. His eyes literally bulge from his head. He obviously did not have the early life experiences I did, where I drove around looking for ATMs that dispensed $5 bills because I didn't have $20 in my account, and every credit card transaction was blessed by crossing my fingers the card would go through. I want to reassure him it's no big deal, but he clearly can't deal with this. They swipe it again. Declined. The manager tells him if it gets declined again, they will have to call the cops. Ricardo looks suspiciously at Miranda, wondering if she somehow stole his card number, and then appraisingly at Lupe. Providentially, it authorizes on the third swipe and exonerates him. Matthew and I leave with Mom and Dad, fearing further tragedy. There have been enough fiascos today without pressing our luck.

- In the morning, we all go outside to discover Dad betting the neighbor $20 that he can't put chains on his car by just letting the car slide downhill onto the chains. The neighboring "mountain person" (as Lupe calls them) releases the emergency brake, putting the car into an uncontrolled downhill slide, then jams on the emergency brake when the car rolls over the chains. The men present wince, as the emergency brake can't take this abuse, but as Mom points out, "It worked didn't it, Sam? Just because it's not how *you* would do it..."

- After discovering our car has gotten snowed in and egged, we finally leave Big Bear. "Evil mountain people," Matthew mutters grimly, trying to wipe off the frozen egg. We meet my parents for breakfast at a restaurant down the hill. They plan on moving to Israel within the next year to join my sister, yet they seem very nervous about Matthew and I moving to the East Coast. My mom expresses her worry by foisting food on us and admonishing us, "Don't go out with wet hair, or you'll get sick." Dad wants to show me how to change my own oil, but acknowledges it's too cold. Matthew cannot convince Mom colds come from **germs**, and she later finds an article that says our immune systems are weakened by cold, so indeed going out with a wet head can make you sick, to some degree. We try to leave without a dramatic scene, but Mom and I both cry a little, and as soon as we're out of sight, I cry hysterically, all the way down the mountain. I've never been away from my parents before, and even though they're leaving too, I'm leaving first. Also, I still don't know how to cook anything.

- Bob and Cheryl, Matthew's dad and stepmom, host our New Year's lunch, moving stiffly as they're bruised from skiing. Kristen, Matthew's sister, and Noah, her 7-year-old son arrive soon after we do. Noah disappears into the bathroom for twenty minutes, prompting Matthew and I to speculate that maybe all small boys are obsessed with the bathroom. When questioned, Noah tells us, "Mom says to take my time, so I do."

- Exhausted from the ski trip, Bob and Cheryl order pizza for New Year's brunch, and we all generally avoid talking about how Matthew and I are moving across the country today. They all claim they will visit, but let's get real. Who knows when we'll be back? After a couple hours, Bob says quietly, "Now is a good time to just say goodbye and leave. Don't drag it out."

- We get up to go, and everyone comes outside. When they all line up on the lawn, in their Johnson family tradition, and begin waving like the dolls in *It's a Small World* at Disneyland, Matthew starts crying. Oh God, let's go, let's go! I can't stand it!

- A Double Double and a strawberry shake, anyone?

What the Hell is the Sugar Bowl?

Cross Country Road Trip
January 1, 2000

Matthew and I decided to go the adventurous route and drive cross-country to our new home in Baltimore. Once we stopped crying, got ourselves some Double Doubles and strawberry shakes, and hit the road, we started to enjoy the excitement and freedom of cutting the ties to home. We also found we really enjoyed traveling together, which can be tough, especially on long road trips. Other than Tim's wedding, we hadn't really taken trips together up until now.

This adventure could have all ended in tears as Jonathan predicted, and Matthew could have flown home to California on arrival, but I think this trip really showed us that all we need is each other, an icy Hurricane, and some change in the glove box for the last night's hotel room.

Suggested Soundtrack: "There She Goes"-The Boo Radleys, "Just Like Heaven"-The Cure, "Wild Boys"-Duran Duran, "The Promise"-When in Rome, "Spiderwebs"-No Doubt, "The Devil Went Down to Georgia"-Charlie Daniels Band

California
- Making good time, we pull into Blythe by 8:30 p.m. I assert my shoes are too heavy and that's why I'm going 90 miles an hour, but really it's to make up time for when Matthew drives like my grandmother, may she rest in peace. "I swear, I've never gotten a speeding ticket," I reassure Matthew, trying to hide the speedometer from his prying eyes. It's no use; he can feel his car shimmying, ready to fall apart around us. We're both still shell-shocked from spending New Years with our respective families, and reality slowly seeps in like

a shot of Jack Daniels into the bloodstream. Somehow, we both feel like we might get grounded at any moment.

• Matthew makes more futile attempts to scrub off the car after being egged in Big Bear, where the egg froze onto the car and will probably never come off, ever. "I can't believe the mountain people egged my car," he wails, scrubbing furiously at the first gas station. I spill gasoline on myself while trying to pump gas with shaking hands, and the tiny car fills with noxious fumes for hours. We speculate on who will actually come to visit us in Baltimore, and realize almost everyone we know is too lazy to come see us. "Jonathan will come for the historical aspects of Baltimore," I count him on one finger, "and the proximity of Washington DC will be a draw. Courtney? No. Chad? No. Penelope? No. Glynis? No. None of them spend money traveling unless they have to. Bob and Cheryl? No. Kristen? No....No, I think hardly anyone will really come to visit. We're pariahs!"

Arizona

• The sign at our first rest stop boasts poisonous insects and snakes. Unfortunately, we don't notice this sign until after we'd wandered around for some time, and, for miles and miles, have the unsettling feeling that we may have a poisonous snake in the car. Every time the empty In 'n' Out bag rustles, Matthew twitches. At midnight, Matthew pulls over. "Come on," he invites me, holding out his hand. Is he taking me into the desert to kill me? He lies down on the ground, and I tentatively lay next to him, waiting for the glint of the axe. "That is the most beautiful starry night sky there ever was. God did a great job on that one," he murmurs, shifting closer to me. We lay there in silence, feeling peaceful and contented. I see a shooting star and wish on it. "Please let him be The One!"

• Matthew nicknames Arizona the "Not for Children State", as adult-only communities pepper the whole state. Not that we can blame them, after spending two days with the volatile Daisy and Baby Alive, who was missing her head by the time we left. We'd love to live in a kid-free community. Regrettably, we'll be living with college students, who behave worse than spoiled toddlers.

- "Denny's!" I yell, spotting the distinctive sign at 2 a.m. Matthew whips into the parking lot, fantasizing about grilled cheese. I'm all about the pigs in blankets, with hash browns and coffee. When we enter the lobby, I almost make the mistake of telling them it's illegal to smoke inside. "Oh, no," I groan. "People can smoke wherever they want from here on out. Yuck." California does have the best smoking laws, if you're a non-smoker. "I feel out of place," Matthew confesses. We stand out in the crowd, as we lack the Stetson hats needed to fit in. Too bad Andrea's wedding party isn't here. When the bill arrives, I fish around in my purse. "Do you have the credit card?" I ask nervously, fishing deeper. Matthew's eyebrows lift to his hairline. "No, you paid for gas when we stopped at that Texaco...two hours ago," he trails off. I frantically pat myself down, finding the card in my coat pocket and we agree never to speak of this again.

New Mexico

- Numerous signs advise against picking up escaped prisoners. Been there already, although Kurt Raper wasn't technically incarcerated. Matthew teases, "Would prisoners want to escape so badly they'd put up with your driving?" I shoot him a filthy look. "How often do prisoners escape in New Mexico that they have to **advertise** against transporting them? Are the guards that incompetent?" I rail, inching the speedometer up to 85 without Matthew noticing.

- In Las Cruces, the gas clerk berates Matthew for not pumping the gas or washing the windows, and letting me do it instead. What the gas clerk does not know: we spend our entire lives Rock-Scissors-Papering to determine who does what chores, and on that draw, I was the loser. Later on, while I sleep in the tiny back compartment of the Honda Civic hatchback, Matthew notices all indicators of the road have disappeared. He slowly follows other cars to see if their taillights suddenly vanish, or plummet over a cliff. The road canaries lead us safely along an essentially straight road. He gently wakes me to see the sun rise. Our first sunrise together. I love him.

- Matthew wakes me up to drive. I pull out the map, and he sees he missed his chance to go to the Grand Canyon hours ago. "What do you mean, it was back there? Where back there?" He remains blissfully unaware that I *never* planned on driving eight hours out of our way to go there on this trip. "You mean you missed the sign?" I feign sadness. "Oh, well, maybe another time."

Texas
- Nothing to report yet. Texas vistas are big and pretty empty, so I'm not sure I foresee any exciting news, other than I'm falling asleep at the wheel. The plan to drive straight through Texas to New Orleans turns out to be ambitious, given the state's massive size. Littering signs use the *Don't Mess with Texas* motto with gusto, which I like. At the next gas station, Matthew spills gas and almost self-immolates. Sprinting to the restroom to wash his hands (steeling himself against being in a gas station restroom), the horror becomes complete: there's no soap. He becomes borderline autistic, his cleanliness fetish overtaking all rational thought. "You could use the water in the squeegee bucket," I offer. "No, thanks," he snaps. I suggest he get hook hands, because he'll have to cut off his own if we don't find soap. This actually cheers him up, as he imagines all the clever attachments he could use if he had hook hands. "I could have one with a corkscrew!" I remind him I don't want a hook-hand boyfriend, despite an erotic story we read about a man with hook hands (who also rode a motorcycle in the story). "You're not as open-minded as the girl in the story," he complains, pulling into traffic. I can't wait to get out of Texas.

- We stop at an Outback restaurant in San Antonio to eat dinner and call home. No one can believe we already got this far. They have no idea that we have limited credit and no cash. All our money went to cashier's checks that will be deposited the **second** we arrive in Baltimore. As Matthew sleeps in the pod compartment, I pop in my *Phantom of the Opera* CD and sing along at top volume. Matthew can sleep through anything; it's definitely a plus about him.

Louisiana

- "How can we not be to New Orleans yet?" Matthew mutters disgustedly, rustling the decrepit map. I reply, "Louisiana seems to be the 'Optical Illusion State'; everything looks much closer than it is." I'm too busy negotiating a terrifying unfinished bridge, and then threading my way through a maze of detours that has to be a hidden DUI trap to bother answering his additional complaints. At 3 a.m., we pull into New Orleans.

- A man driving a booger-green Chevy Nova limps by. One of the tires has gone missing, and the man drives it on the naked rim, sending a shower of sparks into the street. "That looks just like the car I went to Senior Prom in!" I exclaim, pointing out the window at the decrepit hulk. Matthew tries to hide his curiosity, but finally caves. "How could you of all people have gone to Prom in that car?"

  - During senior year, after Jeri told me Chip liked me, I decided to take Courtney's advice and date someone nice. We went out for a couple of months, and then Prom rolled around. Chip insisted we shouldn't go to Prom together because he "always breaks up after a formal." I asked him if he wanted me to take someone else to my Prom, like Jacob or Cade. Considering it, he finally rejected my offer and promised to get Cade to go with Courtney.

  - On Prom night, Chip and Cade arrive at my house in his car, which Courtney and I privately call The Boogermobile. "You were supposed to be borrowing a Mercedes!" I remind him. He shrugs. "Yeah, that didn't work out." Then Courtney notices they're wearing the exact same tuxes. Cade looks guilty. "Well, we already had them from choir," he hedges. I put on my corsage, which doesn't match my dress at all. Chip flippantly tells me, "That one was closest to the door." I don't ask if he stole it or was too lazy to go inside. Cade and Chip disappear during dinner, the same restaurant Jonathan and his date (not me, as usual) have dinner reservations, and Jonathan reports that they were fighting because neither of them brought enough money. The final straw was when Cade directed Chip back to his house and they both went inside for ages. "They better not be picking up condoms—that's never going to happen," Courtney grumbles. I snort. "Courtney, Chip and I would have to move past kissing to even think about condoms, so no worries. And since Chip confirmed I scarred Cade for life by sleeping with him and not remembering it, I'm not sure he's back in the game." Eventually, we shamble off to Prom in The Boogermobile, take pictures, dance once or twice, and leave. Courtney and I are dumped unceremoniously off at my house by midnight, eating Lucky Charms and bitching.

- "The only good thing about that night," I conclude to Matthew, "was that Jacob heard about the fiasco and called me, and we got back together." He can't believe it. "The life you led," he muses.

- We learn there are no hotel rooms in New Orleans due to the Shugabull, whatever the hell that is, being played here.
  - Me: "What's the Shugabull?"
  - Desk Clerk: "You know—the shugabull!"
  - Matthew: "Is that the name of a hurricane?"
  - Clerk: "No, it's football. You know—the shugabull."
  - Me: "We don't want to watch football, we just want to sleep. Why is this football game relevant to there being no rooms?"
  - Clerk: "Everyone's here to watch Florida play Virginia

Tech. You know," he gestures to the restaurant, pointing to the little sugar packet holder on a table, "the Sugar Bowl," exaggerating so we can finally understand him. Is some stupid football game going to ruin our dream of New Orleans?

- Matthew: "I don't get it. Neither team is actually from here, so why is the game here?"
- Me: "And why would football fans want to stay in the French Quarter? It's not like they're sightseeing, so why hog it up for everyone else?"

- The clerk cannot be bothered to discuss city revenues with us, so he waves us off to a Holiday Inn outside the city near the airport. As soon as we check in, we race for the shower. Matthew wants his shower documented, so I take a photo of him with the shower curtain modestly covering his private area, although I predict he'll look like a drowned otter in the photo.

- Strolling through the lobby, I stop. "What's the pool here in the middle of the lobby, under this dome? Pools belong outside!" The coffee shop hostess overhears me. "Honey, it gets too cold here to swim outside. Where ya'll from, anyhow?" I'm not convinced. How cold could it get? This whole episode probably stems from a childhood bias against indoor pools. My dad took Rachel and I swimming once when I was ten, and she was six. Against my advice, he let her eat about twelve cherry tomatoes immediately before she went swimming. We're swimming around in the pool, breathing the muggy, chlorinated air that comes with indoor pools, when she swallows water, burps, and throws up all her tomatoes into the pool. The whole pool must be evacuated, tomato vomit floats like an oil slick, and I could die of embarrassment (except embarrassment is not fatal). The air now reeks of muggy tomatoes. I hate indoor pools.

- After a late dinner in the coffee shop and immediately passing out in our room, we arrive in the French Quarter the next morning rejuvenated, and triumphantly slap down our credit card for a room at The Monteleone, unexpectedly vacant. The "European suite", their name to dress up a teeny-tiny regular room, costs $190. I can't believe any Europeans are fooled by the name, and neither am I, but I don't care to complain. I'm just grateful to have gotten a French Quarter room.

• We have to park our car in the hotel garage. Matthew tries to teach Mr. Miyagi, the parking guy, how to operate the car's anti-theft device, but Miyagi-san gets huffy and kicks us out of the car. This car security has plagued us for years, because a) no one would steal a car this tiny and b) every valet, parking lot attendant, or sober friend cannot seem to *simultaneously* touch the two metal screws necessary to start the car, and end up grinding the starter to dust.

• Matthew initially wants to eat lunch at Hooters, home to Nina's wedding reception, but peeks through the window first. "None of the waitresses even *have* any hooters," he grumbles, feeling cheated. "I can see better hooters at home." Thanks, hon. I decide we'll eat lunch at La Boucherie, where we order our first gumbos, jambalayas and Dixie beers. Matthew strikes up a conversation with Charlie the bartender, who gives us sightseeing tips and draws up a map on my napkin, detailing areas to stay the hell out of. "This paht uh town?" he points out, stabbing a little square on the map. "You'll git shot out theah. Doan' go there, no matter whut!"

• I mention hesitantly, "I saw a Confederate flag flying on someone's house. We presume that means they're in the Klan?" Charlie, our guru, assures us we're wrong. We've never heard of "heritage, not hate," being from California and only studying the Gold Rush and the mission movement in Social Studies. I suddenly remember, "The Dukes of Hazzard had a Confederate flag on their car....the General Lee! Oh my God, my parents were letting us watch Klan propaganda!" Charlie just shakes his head. "Heritage, not hate!" he reminds me. Matthew volunteers, "My family descends from Robert E. Lee." Charlie might reverently bow down to him. Ultimately, Charlie tells us there are different views of the Confederate flag issue and not to judge either way too hastily.

- The stupid Sugar Bowl fans, Hokies and Seminoles, are totally out of control. Some of their cars are so covered in paint they can't even see out the windshield. They hang their heads out the windows like golden retrievers to drive recklessly around the French Quarter. I announce, "I have to have a tiara and some party beads as soon as possible!" Matthew warns me, "As long as you don't take your top off, that's fine." New Orleans is my Mecca: Alcohol can be drunk anywhere, on the street (or, it seems, in your car), and well drinks are $3! I could possibly live here! Matthew reminds me, "The only jobs available would be stripping or bartending if you want to live in the French Quarter." Boo! No fun! I forget about all that $3 liquor being vomited up haphazardly on the streets, until it happens right in front of me.

- We opt out of the Garden District trolley tour. We see all the same houses on our own but taking a fraction of the time, as we would die being trapped on what my mother would call "the slow boat to China" trolley tour. Matthew and I share impatience for wasting our time and tend to rush through things. I spot the first of a string of badly dressed vampire wanna-bes in a coffee shop. His black nails and sharpened teeth give him away. "Oh, how lame," I moan, remembering suddenly Anne Rice lives around here and has obsessive fans.

- Matthew picks Margaritaville, Jimmy Buffet's very colorful restaurant, for dinner. Coco, our waiter, snarls, "Ah'm backed up! You gotta wayt!" In the meantime, I notice three Hokie fans staring openly at my breasts, so I begin to root for the Seminoles. A TV camera comes in and, all of a sudden, fans desperate for their fifteen minutes of fame claw at each other to get on camera. Matthew: "I feel sorry for them.

They all look like total drunken idiots." What the hell are Hokies anyway? Oh, some sort of turkey-type bird. What a great mascot, almost as good at the Santa Cruz Banana Slugs. Coco reverses his former position and becomes our new best friend, besides Charlie. He can recommend the best of the strip clubs on Bourbon Street because he "basically lives there." Instead of hitting strip joints, we go to Café du Monde for café au lait and beignets, which are similar to funnel cake. I love funnel cake *and* beignets.

• Matthew, who loves tours, decides we'll take the Vampire tour through the French Quarter with Don the game show host tour guide, Brett the Bouncer, and Vlad the tubby little authentic vampire. He also loves vampire lore. The tour stops at Charlie's bar, so we wave and cheers Charlie with our potent Hurricanes. Matthew questions Vlad's credentials as a vampire when we glimpse him drinking a Hurricane and spilling it on his vest. The tour covers tons of scary haunted houses and murder sites. Seriously, I don't know how anyone in this town sleeps at night. The place has got to be crawling with ghosts. We also learn that all houses in New Orleans, when they burn down as they have many times before, must be rebuilt and repainted the same color for continuity so generations of tourists get the same effect.

• The tour wends its way to a burial ground, full of Haunted Mansion crypts. Don tells us, in a hushed spooky voice, that "corpses are buried in crypts above ground here due to the high water table." Or the low water table. Something about water and dead bodies= not good. We can't shake the feeling that we're really in New Orleans Square at Disneyland, although the prices are **so** much better here. The tour ends at a bar on Bourbon Street. We're immediately accosted by a man bleeding from a head wound and on crutches a la Ted Bundy. He claims to have been injured by renegade Hokies but we can't be sure. The police come over and spirit him off. "We cannot stay on Bourbon Street," Matthew cries, due to the massive public vomiting being done by the football fans. "Well, I don't want to be Bundy's next victim," I agree, and we scamper back to the hotel.

- I lead Matthew into the famous Carousel Bar. As we drink more Hurricanes, the bar slowly revolves around the bartenders. It's kind of cool and relaxing, other than the horrid fan rivalry following us here. Matthew leans over. "I'm getting motion sick from the bar circling. Ugh! It's like being on the Teacups at Disneyland. I'm going up to the room." I sigh and follow him, stepping off the Carousel Bar, which maybe goes one mile per hour.

- I wake up hungry hungry hippos (starving) at 9:30 a.m. and drag Matthew out to forage for food. Possibly at Café du Monde, although I'm not sure if I'll fit in my clothes if I keep gobbling beignets. Matthew, trying to retrieve our car, feels outraged that we have to pay for parking. In Orange County there are huge free parking lots, not tiny underground lots that cost $25 a day. When I describe this to the parking attendant, he salutes the idea of free parking. The new attendant does not have the Zen parking skills of Miyagi-san, and consequently grinds the starter to dust. After breakfast, we leave New Orleans via a long, narrow bridge across a major body of water. I keep a sharp eye out for alligators sunning themselves on the bridge, as it's truly that low to the water. Signs point out that we're on the hurricane evacuation route. "Shouldn't we be heading west, not east, if we're fleeing a hurricane?" I wonder.

- Matthew yells "Waffle House!" every time he sees one. He desperately wants to go inside and eat, but I ate at a Waffle House once in Georgia and am not anxious to repeat the experience.

- I insist on a stop at Mardi Gras World, "Best Mardi Gras souvenirs, low low prices," and score on beads, tiaras and assorted tchochkes. Due to the low low prices, I procure both an everyday driving tiara *and* a special occasion tiara!

An old gentleman (who looks like the grouchy old sea captain from *Scooby Doo*) wants to know if I think a man could wear a purple sequined vest "or is it just for the ladies, ma'am?" Here, I think it's anything goes, Cap'n! I slide on my new driving tiara and off we go—right into another DUI maze.

Mississippi

*   I'm stuck driving on a floating highway, a narrow strip of a road surrounded by water lapping at our tires. What is with these low bridges? Doesn't driving so close to the water freak anyone else out? I anticipate drowning in the car because, as Matthew points out, "We give important jobs like bridge building or space contracts to the lowest bidder." I get stuck behind a State Trooper who has his cruise control set to the exact speed limit and I almost gouge my own eyes out in frustration.

*   On a desperate quest for sweet tea, we finally find some at a deli. Sweet tea has been touted as "the drink of the South", so I'm totally gratified to find some. Over lunch at the deli, Matthew keeps saying, "When we get to 'Bama", and practicing the new accent he hopes to develop. I hope he doesn't turn into a redneck. Or a Klan member. "Let's get more sweet tea to go," I beg. I live for sweet tea!

*   I remark to Matthew that I'm shocked that we haven't gotten in any fights so far. In my family, fights begin almost as soon as the driver starts the car, and range from criticizing the driver's abilities to changing destination midstream to digging up age-old conflicts and rehashing them while going 70 miles an hour. Matthew confesses, "My friends had a secret betting pool, much like a cockfight, to see when we would snap and attempt to smother one another in our sleep." I am perturbed that I had no chance to win any money for myself, but mostly I am just interested in who's winning so far. He thinks a moment. "Vinay should

be the big winner so far. Andy thought it would happen on the first day, so he's out."

'Bama

There were no highlights of the time we spent crossing a small section of Alabama, except Matthew's continued use of his new accent.

Georgia

- According to the signs, littering in Georgia costs $1000, definitely not worth it. As we drive into Atlanta, we note that the capital building is topped with gold plate at the taxpayers' expense. We drive around their complex freeway system through the worst traffic in America (after Los Angeles) to find Kennesaw, where Glynis and Trey live. Glynis and Trey live in the Blair Witch Project forest, which makes me nervous about staying with them. I miss Glynis though, so I'll suffer in silence. (We later learn almost the whole East Coast has Blair Witch forests.)

- We finally arrive at their house, which Glynis describes as a "toddler's deathtrap." The stairs have gaps, railings a child could slip through and a deck full of splinters. Luckily, they have no children and no plans to have any. Trey refuses to inflict "Lamar Fulton the Fourth" on any child, but would probably be disowned if he didn't. It's easier to just not have kids. Glynis goes back and forth on the issue, but for now, the pendulum has swung to the No Kids side. Trey, who I only briefly met at the wedding, turns out to be a rabid football fan and obsessed with the Sugar Bowl. We still don't even know who won. He can't believe we were just there and totally missed all the Sugar Bowl excitement.

- Matthew realizes his dream of eating at Waffle House again for breakfast. Normally, he's a very healthy eater, but Waffle House just has some unknown factor going for it. As we eat breakfast, Glynis and I regale Matthew with tales from the past. Matthew can't believe the minute details Glynis remembers from high school or the incestuous relationships we all had. As we leave Georgia, Matthew, who did not attend the Princess Bride wedding, says, "I had no idea Glynis was so <u>dramatic</u>. It doesn't come across on the phone." I tell this to Jonathan and Chad later on the phone, and they burst out laughing. Chad makes me put Matthew on the phone, telling him more <u>dramatic</u> stories. I hustle Matthew off the phone and out of Georgia. No more skeletons just yet.

South Carolina

- Matthew reads aloud, "Penalty for speeding in work zones is $200 and 30 days. I pray you avoid jail." Everyone slows down to a crawl for the work zones, which proves **conclusively** that stiff and enforced penalties do work to prevent crime. Billboards in South Carolina also have clever messages from God on them:
  - "Don't make me come down there"- God
  - "Keep using My Name in vain, and I'll make rush hour longer"- God

- I see a man in the next car wearing a hat with a Confederate flag on it. "Matthew," I ask skeptically, "Does he really think the South will rise again, or is he just making a fashion statement?" Matthew contemplates adding MasonDixon as a new AOL screen name, while I am fearful of the IM's that will attract.

- After bickering about that for a while, suddenly, Matthew finds out he gets carsick from reading maps while the car is in motion. This grinds us to a halt because I can't read a map at all, under the best of circumstances. "How can you not read a map?" Matthew rails, conveniently forgetting he offered to read the maps. "Everyone can read a map!"

- I pull up my sleeve and notice that I have either been fed on by vampires on the tour, or slept in a nest of spiders, judging from the tiny fang marks and a giant welt on my arm. "If I die," I pause dramatically, "know that I loved you." Matthew wants to treat the bite with an unidentified ointment out of a first aid kit he got from a Japanese friend. When I challenge him, he admits he can't read the Japanese characters on the label and doesn't know what any of the things inside it are for. He just wants to use the kit for something. "Are you trying to kill me?" I demand, throwing the kit on the floor. "Because you're not the beneficiary on my life insurance policy, so there's nothing in it for you!" Someone may be about to win that betting pool!

North Carolina

- It would appear that in spite of the huge fines they've paid, the cigarette companies are not that apologetic for their business, judging from the giant signs and billboards. Matthew points out that people have to take responsibility for their own choices. He argues, "Chad hasn't sued Jack Daniels for making him an alcoholic and killing his liver, so why get all wound up about cigarettes?" Jonathan and Chad both smoke also, but I don't bring that up.

Virginia

- In Richmond, the party's over—we try to check into a Red Roof Inn and our credit card gets declined. It's hit the limit. Denied. To the chagrin of the front desk clerk, I bemoan buying all those purple and green Mardi Gras souvenirs and using up $40 of available credit.

- We literally make up the cash with change collected from the glove box and under the seats, leaving us with $4 for dinner. Hello, Golden Arches! The McDonald's cashier wears an enormous diamond ring. If I had the money for that ring, I sure as hell wouldn't be working at McDonalds, or anywhere else. We hole up in the room for the night, as we are terrified of spending any money. Plus, the area of Richmond we're in looks sketchy. "I feel bad for Robert E. Lee that his capital turned into such a pit," I remark. We go to sleep early. Tomorrow we'll arrive in Baltimore, our new home.

Maryland

- Matthew drives us into Baltimore, where we get lost immediately, thanks to the Beltway. What kind of freeway goes in a circle? "This doesn't bode well," Matthew remarks grimly. "I hate this freeway already." But he loves the beautiful green hills, the lush Blair Witch forests, and the rivers and streams.

- "There's Towson University! We're home!" I shout, ready to get out of the car once and for all. We check in, and everyone seems very friendly and welcoming. The Facilities Director offers to take us over to the apartment, and help us get our boxes moved over. The apartment, which I saw during my interview processes, is huge, and Matthew walks around like a kid in a candy shop, running his hands over the brand-new furniture and inhaling the smells of new carpet and paint. When we're alone, he puts his arms around me. "This place looks great. I love the apartment. I'm really excited to be here with you."

- Lila, my new boss, takes us to lunch at Panera Bread, a fabulous sandwich shop. It will take years for Panera to come to the West Coast anywhere by us. She tells us the local stories of the "Baltimore Hon", Café Hon, and local idioms like "dicey" and "kitsch." I plan to integrate "dicey" into my conversation right away—as in, "Our financial situation is very dicey. We need to find a bank immediately." Lila directs us to the bank near campus to open an account and address our dicey financial situation. The situation feels worse when we learn that all our checks, even though they are cashiers checks, will be placed on non-local holds for five days. Horrors! Philosophically, we head for Target to get all the new house stuff we need, writing a check. "Please, God, don't let this check clear for five days," I chant at the checkout. We return to our new apartment laden with Target bags, Matthew fumbling for his keys, and griping, "I still think we should have waited till the checks cleared to go to Target." In the meantime, Facilities has dropped off our boxes. Uh-oh. Five boxes of my clothes are missing and I have no shoes other than driving flip-flops. Matthew, who has gobs of shoes, sympathetically asks if I want to write more bad checks for new shoes.

- Lila and some of her friends invite us to dinner at Café Zen. I confide, "I *knowingly* wrote a bad check to Target today, since our credit card is maxed out from the trip, and all our checks we deposited are on non-local holds." Matthew points out later that the way to make a good impression on a new boss usually doesn't involve telling her you are a criminal. We all decide to go for dessert at Vaccarro's, the dessert shop of choice. Matthew and I have never had cannoli. Our first cannoli ever is orgasmically good! It's even better when we find out Lila plans on paying! I guarantee I'll return for the all you can eat dessert buffet offered on Monday nights- $10 all you can eat! I'm there! And down the street, there's a bar with $2 "Natty Bos" (National Bohemia beers)!

- Matthew unpacks till 2 a.m. I pretend I'll stay up and help but fall asleep immediately, surrounded by a houseful of brand new Ikea furniture (the nice stuff, not the pressboard crap you put together yourself). Hope rises as three more boxes arrive the next day, some of them containing my missing shoes! With my special occasion tiara and a decent pair of shoes, I'll be a Baltimore Hon yet! Cheers me with a Natty Bo!

The Boston Massacre Wedding

Boston, MA
April 2000

I can't believe Courtney's getting married. I'm so happy for her, but at the same time...we'll never go on another Spring Break trip together. We'll never go out to bars and pick up guys again. We'll never drive around in her Tercel from Hell and drink McDonald's shakes or Big Gulps and listen to the radio and gossip. Not that we would have done that even if she weren't married, but she's moving into a whole new phase of life that I'm not in yet. We've been best friends for 20 years. Now that I'm 27, I feel like she's leaving me behind again.

Suggested Soundtrack: "Shake Your Booty"-KC and the Sunshine Band, "Brick House"-The Commodores, "Play that Funky Music"-Wild Cherry, "Old Time Rock and Roll"-Bob Seger and the Silver Bullet Band— typical wedding music

- Matthew and I arrive in Boston for Courtney's wedding, and my old co-worker, Jen, meets us at the airport. We're staying with her for a couple of days before Courtney's wedding. Jen drops us off after directing us to the Freedom Trail, which has everything Matthew likes: a map with historical information, those metal signs along the way that tell you about the place you're looking at, and hours to kill.

- Matthew and I walk the Freedom Trail, where he discovers that most of our history was a ploy engineered by Sam Adams, the beer guy, to create a reason to revolt. "I've been duped all these years!" he announces, turning to me after reading one of the ancient metal signs. "I thought tons of people were ruthlessly murdered in the Boston Massacre."

I nod. "I know. And it wasn't even deliberate. Someone's gun just went off." He looks shaken, but presses on. I'm sympathetic, remembering my own dismay during my trip here with Jonathan. I walk the **entire** Freedom Trail, even though I fear my legs might fall off, to impress Matthew with my historical fortitude. We even see that boring old ship, which turns out to be as boring as I suspected.

- That night, Jen proposes going to Beerworks with her reluctant fiancé, Mark, for blueberry beer. Mark proposed to Jen with an engagement ring made up of three small diamonds in the shape of a Mickey Mouse head, because Mark loves Disney. Only a woman over thirty, with no other prospects, could pretend to like this hideous ring. This lesson makes an impression on Matthew, who whispers reassuringly, "I would **never** give you a Mickey Mouse head ring." Hurray! One less thing to dread! Wait—does that mean, "I will be proposing with a beautiful ring that does not resemble a Disney character," or "I will never, ever, be proposing, not *even* with a Mickey Mouse head ring?"

- I gallivant off to Courtney's bachelorette party, recklessly promising Matthew, "I'll be home around midnight." At the party I'm the only un-engaged woman there, a veritable leper in the nuptial world. Coincidentally, I'm also the only fun girl in the group. Dinner at the party: M &Ms and watermelon balls. I guess these engaged girls plan on giving their husbands takeout all the time?

- We all get cabs to Dick's Last Resort, a popular bar, and I buy t-shirts for Courtney and myself that say, "Contrary to popular belief, real women prefer Dick's!" This attracts substantial attention in the bar. We pose for photos with the restaurant staff. "Cheese!" Courtney yells, flinging a busboy's hand off her butt. I rack up a huge bar tab, as I find out the next morning when I find my credit card receipt in my bra. The huge bar tab proves necessary though, because I had to get the party started, and nothing says bachelorette party like a couple rounds of blowjob shots. "Go! Go!

Go!" I chant, forcing Keiko's head toward her shot glass. Courtney's friend Aimee catches the party spirit, but her future sister-in-law, Rochelle, seems skittish. More rounds of shots follow.

- The staff presents Courtney with a giant paper penis hat which she gamely dons, then slumps on the table, as if the hat weighs too much. Or possibly the weight of impending marriage? Is the hat a metaphor or am I just drunk? We hit the dance floor, and, as we have eaten no food except candy and watermelon to absorb the alcohol, everything strikes us as hilarious and we are the hottest women there! Some guy named Eric randomly writes his phone number on my new shirt, possibly after I danced on my chair and blew kisses to everyone in the bar, yelling, "Kisses for everyone!" After I fall off the chair and hurt myself, Keiko pulls it together and gets us a cab home. The cab ride blurs, as I have no recollection of it and believe I have discovered teleportation the next morning.

- Courtney tells me later she got dropped off a block from her apartment and had to drag herself home. She slept on the bathmat naked all night, because she couldn't find her way out of the bathroom, because she couldn't find the light switch. "The bathmat was so very soft and cozy...."

- I told Matthew I would be home at midnight. He flings the door open at 2 a.m. when I come in, and totally reminds me of my mom during my teenage years. He almost vomits at the stench of alcohol and cigarette smoke clinging to me. "You know," he begins, "some people would have had the decency to call if they were going to be late..." After I almost poke my eye out with my toothbrush, he stops lecturing me and competently puts me to bed after a quick hose-off. I am miraculously not hung over the next day, because the liquor gods love me.

- Matthew gets up the next morning and begins packing so we can check into the Parker House hotel. He stops when he picks up my Dick's shirt, holding it at arm's length and obviously considering burning it. "Who's Eric?" he demands. "What are you talking about?" I yawn, hoping Matthew will bring me some coffee. "If you don't know who he is, why did you let him write his number on your shirt...and when did you buy this dirty shirt?? You're **never** going back to that Dick's place, that's it!" Was Eric hot? I hope so! I'll have to stealthily ask Courtney later.

- Chad and Jonathan arrive and meet Matthew and I at the Parker House. Jonathan strides into the lobby, shouting, "I had to sit next to a man on the plane who ate jellybeans nonstop from California! He was just sucking them down, and when he dropped one, he would just fish it out of his crotch and eat it anyway!" I wonder how many drinks he might have ordered on the plane, since he always screams at the top of his lungs when he's drunk. The entire front desk staff becomes engrossed in this story because he truly talks so loudly. Chad looks weary. "I had to sit next to an Eskimo woman who immediately fell asleep on my shoulder. Then she started drooling. I could feel it through my shirt. It was sick." He motions to the front desk. "Where's the bathroom? I've been holding it since Denver! The airplane bathroom was sick." They silently point to the other end of the lobby. Matthew asks, "Why didn't you just sit next to each other?" They simultaneously say, "Don't ask." Chad sprints to the bathroom, and returns looking relieved. Jonathan ogles the lobby. "This is a nice hotel. I'm so glad the reception will be here and we can just pass out afterward."

- Matthew and I take our bags to our really nice room, which we booked online. Jonathan bursts into our room. "How did you get this room? We got a tiny Muppet room! It's literally designed for people who are less than four feet tall. Chad doesn't even fit in his bed." It's probably a "European suite."

- Matthew, Jonathan, Chad and I hit the bar before I have to go to the wedding rehearsal. Stretching out in the booth, Matthew remarks, "Melissa and I walked the whole Freedom Trail yesterday..." Jonathan interrupts, shrieking, "Oh, you walked the whole Trail with *Matthew*, but you just complained the whole time with me!" Yes, because he could be the father of my children, Jonathan, while you are my gay best friend. Not that I knew that at the time...

- I leave the three of them in the bar, and walk across the street to King's Chapel for the rehearsal. I feel very nervous, leaving Matthew with Jonathan and Chad, as they can be persuasive and may talk him into doing things that are very bad. They can also tell him lots of dirty stories about me that I would prefer not to dredge up. Seth, Damon's pretend-gay best friend, has just returned from a rafting trip around Cape Horn, and shows up at the rehearsal smelling of salt water. Better than smelling of Jack and Coke; I can tell I reek of it by the filthy look Courtney shoots me when she hugs me. I think my alcoholic perfume attracts Seth to come over and talk to me. As soon as Damon asked Seth to be in the wedding, Seth agreed. Two days later, he announced he was leaving on a rafting trip around Africa, and would try to be back for the wedding. Damon found this perfectly acceptable. Courtney did not. Especially as part of the trip involved swimming with sharks, so Courtney basically wrote him off since she was positive he would never survive.

- After the rehearsal, which I remember nothing about, except that Courtney's brother-in-law Jody and his wife Rochelle are both hippies, I collect Matthew, Jonathan, and Chad from the bar and we go to an Italian restaurant for the rehearsal dinner.

  - Just in time, as I overhear Jonathan recounting the time when we were fourteen and lying on his bed, reading magazines. Eduardo happened to walk by the window at this point, looked in at us and then knocked on the window. When we looked up, he shook his finger at us. "No hanky-panky, you two," he intoned in his accented English. Jonathan buried his head in a pillow, but I assured Eduardo he had nothing to worry about. Understatement of the century.

- "Was that the same day you guys found Eduardo eating a can of pumpkin out of the can because Marie wasn't home to make him a sandwich?" Chad asks, snorting with laughter.

- The morning of the wedding, Courtney discovers Damon hasn't checked the tuxedos, all of which came with cummerbunds instead of vests. She hollers, "No cummerbunds! This isn't 8th grade graduation!" and sends Damon out on a recon mission. He returns with a black vest and tie for her dad, which doesn't match anyone else's. Courtney flips out and screams, "I don't want my father looking like Johnny Cash at my wedding!" and runs out of the room. I encourage Damon to go exchange the vest, but Pete says he's fine wearing a black vest. I say a quick prayer Courtney doesn't notice and start flipping out during the ceremony. She's very detail oriented and obviously emotional—a bad combination at a wedding.

- We all slip into our yellow bridesmaid dresses. I look like I have jaundice. Rochelle, the hippie girl, also looks jaundiced. Keiko, who Courtney left to die in Death Valley, looks great in her dress, as does Aimee, a redhead. My dress barely fits across the boobs, due to poor measurements relayed to Courtney, and I look like I might be the quarterback for the Hokies or the Seminoles.

- In Courtney's suite, her mom, Carol, tries to help her into a boned strapless bra and a giant crinoline—and gets little cooperation. "Stop poking at me," Courtney crossly tells her mom. Carol just rolls her eyes and keeps poking. Damon's mom, Kay, runs in with fruit plates, resplendent in a hot pink tracksuit. I wonder if she plans on wearing the tracksuit to the wedding, as her sense of style runs to the Bedazzle side. Courtney finally struggles into her gown and veil and looks beautiful. I tear up, but don't want to ruin my perfect makeup. "You look so beautiful and happy," I cry, throwing my arms around her. She leans out far to hug me back, not wanting to wrinkle her gown. "Ok, time for photos," Courtney announces, and leads us all to the lobby. "Are you still taking mostly black and white?" I ask, thinking that would hide the yellow tinge on my skin.

• Suddenly, my gown bursts open from hip to armpit *in the lobby* with a horrid ripping noise. I have to be sewn back into it by the wedding coordinator. Courtney glowers at me as though I deliberately gained weight to ruin her wedding. I'm freezing and half-naked in the lobby, getting yelled at by Courtney, but Rochelle, Aimee and Keiko think I'm tacky already (after the Dick's excursion) and don't really seem shocked. The lobby staff whispers, "Yeah, she's with that jellybean-crotch guy...well, they're from California, what do you expect?"

• In the distance, we suddenly hear marching bands thumping along with their tubas, making me want to start singing, "76 trombones led the big parade..." from *The Music Man.* Courtney goes white. "What is that sound?" she hisses. One of the front desk clerks tells her, "The Greek parade starts in twenty minutes and they block off all the streets on the parade route." Courtney might faint. "No one can get to the wedding. No one at all. Is that what you're saying?" The clerk nods dumbly. Courtney starts screaming, "Those f-ing Greeks are ruining my wedding! Damn them all to hell!" Damon has a vein throbbing in his forehead but it could be from so many things....

• Eventually, Damon determines the wedding must start forty-five minutes late to accommodate the Greek parade, and Courtney slumps into a chair in the lobby. "No one will be able to hear my carefully selected organ music over their plate smashing..." she whispers to no one. Damon opens his mouth, probably to say something like, "No one cares about the organ music," but I shake my head threateningly at him. Courtney, the most organized person in the universe, has attended to every detail...except the Greeks and their damn parade. She determines that their overpaid wedding coordinator, the church wedding coordinator, and the hotel wedding coordinator were all totally ignorant of the Greek parade as well, even though that's their job. Courtney instructs Damon to have all three of them trampled by Greeks as punishment. "Of course, right after the wedding," he nods, "I'll have them all put to death." She smiles at him. I'm not sure she's kidding.

• Matthew, Jonathan and Chad, not being in the wedding party, walked across the street to the church on time and got locked in. The minister lectures them about the history of the church and religious oppression in New England for the whole forty-five minutes. Jonathan listens raptly, but Chad hunts for a sharp object to hurt himself with. They can see the bar just across the street, so close, yet so far away. Finally, the wedding starts, despite *Louie Louie* being played outside on the tuba throughout the ceremony. Courtney makes a beautiful bride and Pete almost bursts with pride in his Johnny Cash vest.

• At the reception, Matthew and I are, ironically, seated at the Boston Massacre table. Jonathan and Chad are at the Boston Tea Party table. They have a man from Kentucky at their table who has a fake English accent. Chad dubs him Talented Mr. Ripley. As Chad chats up Mr. Ripley, Jonathan tries to carry as many drinks as possible to take full advantage of the time-limited open bar. Seth joins us at the bar and starts talking about the tribal issues in Africa.

• At our table: Courtney's hot friend Nathan from college. I have never met him, but I **wished** I had gotten to hook up with him before I met Matthew. Now it's too late. Matthew whispers, "I can tell by your laugh that you're flirting with him. Stop it! It's rude!" I apologize to Matthew, but I can't seem to help myself. Despite the fact that I look like a linebacker suffering from jaundice, Nathan flirts with me too. The

open bar has just closed, which is a real shame, as Matthew's
hostility towards Nathan increases by the minute.

- Damon's best man makes a toast where he basically says
  that at each wedding he's been getting closer and closer to
  being the groom, like being in line to walk the plank and
  realizing you're next. His girlfriend of five years scowls
  at him. Courtney scowls at **her**, since she's sitting at the
  head table in black pants with fuzz pills on them. Ugly
  ones. Damon makes a fabulous toast, where he says that in
  his eyes, Courtney is always the most beautiful girl in the
  room. I tear up again at this point, because I'm so happy
  she's with someone wonderful.

- Jonathan and Chad scamper over to report on the doings
  of Mr. Ripley. Everyone at their table has just graduated
  college, and discusses politics, literature and art. Chad,
  bored to tears, grinds the conversation to a halt. When
  someone asks his opinion of a new novel, he hangs his head.
  "I never graduated high school, so I don't really follow what
  you're talking about." They freeze, as though a GED may
  be catching. Matthew asks, "Why would you lie about not
  graduating?" "Because it's funny," Chad replies, sipping out
  of my drink and exchanging smiles with Nathan. Courtney
  and Damon's DJ provides us with sparkly maracas, which
  Chad and I use as props in our dramatic choreographed
  dance routines that Glynis taught us in 11th grade.

- We all decide to go out to this gay bar Seth and Chad have
  picked after the wedding. All of us except Matthew, who
  doesn't *feel* like going out. Especially with Nathan. I feel
  bad, but I'm not staying behind and flagellating myself all
  night for flirting. Matthew can stay home and sulk if he
  wants to. The doorman, an otherworldly-hot blonde, wears
  silver lamé shorts and nothing else. Inside, Chad disappears
  immediately, which seems odd. Why did he want to come to
  a gay bar in the first place? Jonathan, of course, disappears
  right away, too. The stage has a barn set and the exotic
  dancers are dressed as cows and pigs. Next week's theme:

Egypt and the Pharaohs, but we'll be gone by then. I find myself in a maelstrom of beefcake who wants nothing to do with me. Except Nathan-hmmm.

- I find Jonathan talking to a cute boy in glasses at the bar. "Jonathan, what are we doing here? Why would Chad want to come here? Can we go somewhere else?" Jonathan slams his drink on the bar. Drunk and sweaty, he shouts, "Wake up, Melissa! Chad is gay! That's why we're here, because Chad is gay gay gay!" He claps his hands over his mouth, realizing he's just outed Chad. "Do NOT tell him I just told you that!" I won't, but how can I keep from telling Glynis? She will go berserk. Thank God I was never obsessed with Chad! One love-of-my-life turning out gay is enough for any girl to take. Poor Glynis and Kelly.

- "I'm so ready to go," I announce to Nathan. "Well, I'll go with you. Let's share a cab," he invites me, slinging his jacket over his arm. I say goodbye to Jonathan, who merrily lifts his drink glass to me in a mock toast. Realizing I'm leaving with Nathan, his face changes. "Don't do anything stupid," he advises, nodding wisely. "You have a good thing with Matthew, even though he's no-fun boy for not coming with us." Yeah, cheers. Nathan tries to kiss me in the cab, but really, what's the point? I just want to go home to Matthew, who might not give me another chance if I kiss Nathan tonight. Matthew looks skeptical when I tell him, "Nothing happened with Nathan. I missed you." I kick my shoes off. "Guess who else turned out gay besides Jonathan?" He ponders for a moment. "Seth? Seth seems the likeliest one." Flopping on the bed, I shake my head. "We went to a gay bar, and Chad is gay. Jonathan blew it and told me." Matthew can't believe it. "You can't tell anyone else though," he cautions me. "I'm not, I'm just telling Glynis and Kelly." Glynis isn't home, so she's saved from the news. Kelly yells, "The gays are ruining my life!" She's already Jonathan's pretend-wife, and now she knows for certain Chad will never get back with her.

- Two years later, *Nathan* comes out. Matthew skips around the apartment while I disbelievingly read him the email from Courtney. Chad and Jonathan are in tears over their lost opportunity. "I can't believe I didn't see it," laments Chad. "He's perfect for me." The gays may be ruining Kelly's life, but luckily not mine. I have Matthew, and that's all that matters to me. And if Matthew ever proposes, I will make *damn* sure the Greeks don't ruin my wedding.

Don't Bother Me, I'm Crabby

Baltimore, MD & Washington, DC
May 2000

My parents are our first visitors in Baltimore, and I'm excited to see them and I can't wait to hear about my sister's wedding. Rachel is four years younger than I am, but she's been living in Israel on her own and has gotten married in a whirlwind courtship. I will probably have to pay Matthew to propose to me, and we're still living in an on-campus apartment. At 27, as my mother says, "You're not getting any younger. The clock is ticking, you know." Yeah, cheers.

Suggested Soundtrack: Anything by Barry Manilow, Julio Iglesias, Neal Diamond, Perry Como or Tom Jones, since those were the tapes my mom brought along for the car rides

- My parents decide to swing through Baltimore on their way back from attending my sister's wedding in Israel. I couldn't go, because Rachel met Avi in March, and I have no vacation time accrued. Mom and Dad plan to visit for a week. It's so unfortunate that it usually takes less than two hours for us all to get on each other's last nerve, so a week will probably end in the silent treatment.

- Their flight arrives on a Sunday night, but they don't call to tell me they've arrived or when they plan to come over to our house. Instead, some stranger from the airline leaves a message saying, "Your parents will call you later," but the person barely spoke English, so I don't know if they were kidnapped by terrorists and held for ransom, or if they just didn't bother to call themselves. I pity the terrorist that kidnaps my mom; he would probably turn the gun on himself after she offers him food for hours. "You like meatloaf? No? Well, you could probably get pancakes. You know what pancakes are? How about pizza? I could warm up some pizza. Maybe they have some of those Hostess fruit pies here. Those are pretty good."

- Dad finally calls at 10 p.m. from their hotel, saying, "We're too tired to come over. We'll call in the morning." But not so tired that they don't call at 7 a.m. and wake us up. I invited them to stay with us, but they both nixed that plan so they could smoke freely, without me quoting cancer statistics at them. As my dad puts it, "We don't need your hocking all day and all night. We're getting our own room."

- Matthew and I meet them for lunch in Towson at a deli. Fun, other than my mom trying to wrap her sandwich in a napkin "for later" and carry it out in her purse. We peruse my sister's wedding photos as a distraction. Rachel looks beautiful and happy. Her husband, Avi, looks intense but happy too. My sister has become very religiously observant since she's moved to Israel, and our family is still getting used to it. I guess most parents want their kids to stick with their religion, but not become more religious than the parents are. My mom points out a hundred times, "I didn't really want to wear a scarf over my hair, but I had to. That's the law, you know? Women cover their hair. But it doesn't look so cute on me." Dad: "You looked great!" Mom: "Sam, just stop it, ok? There's no need to lie!" Dad (to Matthew): "I can't catch a break, no matter what I say. It's always the wrong thing." Matthew, whose family tends to silently simmer with tension when they have problems, squirms when directly confronted, especially in public when my mom starts shouting.

- They regale us with tales of how all the guests crowded around Rachel with candles. Mom feared Rachel would catch on fire, since she couldn't see at all and had to be led around by Mom and Avi's mom, Etti. My mom tells us the whole ceremony was in Hebrew ("You know, like nobody speaks English! We might have wanted to understand it!"), and she had to "sit on the women's side since there was separate seating and I couldn't even sit with Dad," also the law. My dad looks wistful, as though he would welcome separate seating in more places. And possibly people speaking a different language so he doesn't even have to pretend to listen to anyone.

- I take them to Reisterstown to shop and hang out. My mom won't let my dad have any money "because he just spends it on stupid stuff." I choose not to remind her of a straw donkey she once bought in Mexico that had a wine bottle carrier on either side. Like you would put a straw donkey on your dining room table and serve guests wine out of it. I took it to a white elephant party as a joke gift—it was the hit of the party! Three years later, Mom still blames Dad for the loss. "I know you did something with it, Sam, just like my Kenny Rogers tape. You won't admit it, but I know it was you..."

- She admires the sweater I have on and, when I tell her Matthew got it for me, she sighs and pointedly comments, "Well, that's nice that you have someone who buys you nice gifts, not just what they have leftover at the store at 7 o'clock on Valentines Day." My dad spends all his time pretending he can't hear. I can't believe he hasn't bought a fake hearing aid to make the illusion complete.

- Matthew gets off work, and we take them to Little Italy for dinner. Little Italy may be the cutest neighborhood in all downtown where they have tons of Italian restaurants, row houses with stoops, a bocci court, and Italian flags all over. My blood freezes when my mom remarks, "What a cute neighborhood. I could live here." Apparently she plans to live alone, because my dad has no interest in living in any more ethnic neighborhoods after his youth in New York. At Vaccarro's, during the Monday night $10 all you can eat dessert buffet, Mom comments, "If I lived here, I would get so fat! How much can you come here and not gain weight?

Is that what happened to you, sweetie?" I close my eyes and take deep breaths. It's only the first day.

- We spend about 80% of our time during their visit getting lost; no one but Matthew can read a map, and he's at work. I took a couple days vacation, but the rest of the week I check email and voicemail. Mom: "What is the point of your job if no one even knows if you're there or not? You couldn't have much to do. Why do you always say you're busy when I call?" I speed the car up. "Can we just find the exit before you criticize me? You'll have plenty of time to nag me when we get there, ok?" I assure her. This time, we're circling endlessly on the Beltway again, having missed our exit yet again. My mom loves that you can just circle around and in about forty-five minutes you can try your exit again. My dad grumbles, "How can you not know how to get **anywhere** besides the mall? You live here, you know." Ah, but I don't have a car. I don't drive well on deserted Blair Witch Project roads. I don't drive well on ice or snow. As we circle around again, my dad wonders, "Why in the hell would you make a freeway go in a circle? How are you going to get **anywhere** going in circles?"

- They have no curiosity as to why the dome light in the rental car never turns off. I point out that it will eventually kill the battery. Mom retorts, "Then they'll have to bring us a new car if they gave us a defective one. Sam, why did you let them give us this car? It doesn't work properly!" When he wearily points out he had never seen the car before either, she presses on. "You could have asked them. It wouldn't have killed you to ask, 'Does everything work or are you giving us a junky jalopy?'"

- In the morning, I go with them to Fells Point. My mom wants to get a nightshirt with a grouchy crab pictured on the front that reads, "Don't Bother Me, I'm Crabby." My dad bursts out laughing, and encourages her to get several "so you can wear it all the time. Then everyone will know what to expect." I groan inwardly. He always goes just that one step over the edge into annoying her. To spite him, she buys the nightshirt, plus several other lovely knickknacks that "will look great by the fireplace, above the straw donkey. Whenever I find it...Sam, you must have taken that donkey somewhere. You had better bring it back!" The knickknacks include: a crab made entirely of seashells, a blown glass seahorse, and a set of large, wooden, gaudily painted clownfish. They are all so hideous, and I ache to go home and start throwing things away. Mom's acquisitive nature has turned me against owning any possessions. I constantly, to Matthew's chagrin, throw away items we don't use, fearing my house will turn into the pack rat nest from hell I grew up in.

• I take them to lunch at The Cheesecake Factory, where my parents lecture me for eating shrimp and bacon in my pasta. Great, now that they've seen my sister, I'm The Black Sheep Jew. They're here, aren't they? It's not like they're Mr. & Mrs. Kosher. "But we're eating beef," Mom points out righteously. "Beef is kosher." Dad clears his throat. "Well, technically, Vicki, it's only kosher if you buy it from a kosher butcher, which I doubt The Cheesecake Factory does. So you're almost as bad as her," he points at my last shrimp, which I shovel defiantly into my mouth. We go back to the apartment. My parents both think it's very nice, "although a little bare," Mom mentions disapprovingly. "If you want, you can have my wooden fish to liven it up, and I'll get something else." Why can't my simple candle arrangement and carefully chosen photos be enough for her?

• The next day, we take a bus tour of Washington DC. The tour guide has a fairly limited vocabulary, so the tour isn't very interesting. Mom: "I can't believe we're touring the capital of America, and we have a guide that doesn't even speak English!" She harasses my dad into photographing any body of water, including a large mud puddle, which she initially mistook for a pond. She becomes agitated that we can't "get off the tour and walk around," so at the end, we get off and walk around. The walk lasts for about five minutes, at which point she slows her pace to a crawl, complains her feet hurt, and accuses me of taking her on a forced march. It must be nice to make up your own reality like that, and not have logic or reason ever factor in. Wait, I don't want to be judgmental—obviously, she suffers from a short-term memory problem where she immediately forgets what she *just said* one second ago, and behaves as though she didn't demand to be let out to walk around.

- She claims she could also live in Washington, and my dad tells her, "If you don't start walking faster, you *will* be living here, because I'll leave without you." This obviously leads to drama and recriminations, which I see coming miles away. My dad either doesn't think these things through, or deliberately toys with her. It may vary depending on his mood. We hit several Smithsonian museums, until Mom discovers the gift shops carry what are essentially copies of the museum pieces. Within five seconds of being in the gift shop, she can tell whether she wants to bother walking through the museum itself, saving her tons of time. "Is this the Hope Diamond? Well, forget it then. It's tiny compared to what I thought. I thought it would be as big as my head. Not that I would know what a diamond looks like, Sam. Sam?" Dad sidles out the door, gesturing with his cigarette and using his smoking as escapism.

- We barely get home in time for Passover Seder. Being Jewish seems to be an occasional habit for my parents, such as when they want to lecture me at The Cheesecake Factory. Matthew, wearing oven mitts, flips out. "Dinner's burned, thanks to nobody calling to tell me when you were coming back. You'd think no one cared about Passover!" He doesn't want to hear anyone's explanations, because he knows we're late due to one particular member of our party dawdling around, airily assuming there would be no traffic. Matthew gets really buzzed on the four cups of wine during the Seder. I actually can't believe he didn't drink *more* during this week! My dad also looks pretty buzzed, but I think he may have drunk more than his allotted four cups. After dinner, as we wash the dishes, Matthew bursts out, "It drives me nuts that you revert back to being either a compliant child, or a sullen teenager when your parents are around." I hang my head. I don't know why I do it, either. "Why can't you just deal with them reasonably? Just be rational, and don't get caught up in all the emotional drama?" he berates me.

- My parents leave the next morning for their road trip back to California. My mom has won this battle, winning my father over with the argument that they can't smoke on the plane, so it's better to drive cross-country and "see a little of the sights." I wish I could leave a tape recorder undetected in the car, in case I have to go back to counseling. I need evidence! Mom tries to convince Dad that Charleston, West Virginia, "is a quaint Southern city." She actually means Charleston, South Carolina, but my dad announces he has no plans of going to either place, as he hates the South. Too bad he has about eight states' worth of it to drive through. Short visits are the key.

- I call Jonathan to tell him about my parents' visit, but he has no sympathy for me. "Tell me, Melissa, are they driving cross-country in a car with a horse head glued to the hood? Because until you have driven in Eduardo's horse-head car, you have nothing to tell your therapist! Nothing!" I realize Chad will have no sympathy either, having had to drive around with his mom, Honey, in her convertible with the "XR Honey" (that would be X-rated Honey) license plate. Or Courtney, whose mom plotted to cut off Courtney's hair while she slept to put in an art piece and argued, "You're *my* kid, so it's really *my* hair!" Or Kelly, whose mom got liposuction and offered to give all her "fat clothes" to Kelly. Or Glynis, who still bears a grudge about all the Spring Break trips she wasn't allowed to go on. Or Charlie, whose parents have become swingers.

- We all just deal with our parents the best we can, I guess. I relax, opening the extra bottle of Passover wine, until I realize Matthew and I go home to California in a month— and we'll do this all over again.

You Can't Go Home Again

Orange County, CA
June 2000

We decided to make our first trip home to California so Matthew could go to his graduation at Cal State Fullerton. We assumed friends and family would be flocking to see us, lining up outside like a candlelight vigil. But we learned that for everyone else, life goes on. Everyone just seems to have their own things going on, and trying to make plans with people makes us feel bad. No one really seems willing to drop everything to hang out, and considering we're not exactly in the neighborhood anymore, it seems like we're not a priority. I guess we're lucky to have each other, huh?

Suggested Soundtrack: "Old Apartment"-Barenaked Ladies, "Chains of Love"-Erasure, "Tragic Kingdom"-No Doubt

- As soon as we arrive in Orange County from Baltimore, Matthew narrowly dodges an airport bus. He has forgotten that you can't just dart into traffic here and expect people to stop for you. There are no pedestrians in So Cal.

- Prophet Bob, Matthew's dad, prophesies during the car ride home that we will buy a house and have kids one day. We scoff that we'll prove him wrong and live like nomads forever, but he has a history of turning out to be right about everything. Our families are excited to see us on our first visit home, except Noah, our 7-year-old nephew. We invite him to a movie and he blows us off, commenting, "I'd rather ride bikes with my friends." This becomes a theme for the trip. In retaliation, Matthew decides to become Crazy Uncle Matt, who sends Noah weird gifts from Spencer's and embarrasses him in front of his friends.

- My mom doesn't tell my dad we're coming over for dinner the first night. She shrugs. "He never listens to a word I say anyway." Dad shows up late and becomes irritated that we're all having dinner without him. Tía Lupe can't make it down because "it's too far. I'm not driving that far." Relatively speaking, a two-hour drive is a lot closer than a four-day drive, which is how far you'd have to drive to see us if you miss this visit, but whatever.

- Everyone in both of our families (including me) weasels out of going to the early morning all-school graduation at Cal State Fullerton, so Matthew has to get up at 5:30am and go alone. He brings two books just in case the ceremony is boring. I tell him it's a sure thing the ceremony will be boring, but he feels compelled to go anyway. He discovers I am right, as usual, but productively reads a significant amount of *The Three Musketeers* so it's not a total wash.

- In retrospect, I don't regret going to my own graduations, boring though the ceremonies were. For undergrad, my college boyfriend and I each drank a bottle of wine, and then sat with the baseball guys, who were passing flasks of whiskey back and forth down the row. Through a miracle, Jonathan, who had gotten bored and gone to a bar, returned just as I was lining up to go onstage, and took photos, in which I mercifully didn't fall down. For graduate school, I had spent all my time writing my thesis and studying for comps, and had not taken care of the vitally important factor of buying a dress I could wear under the gown. Frustrated with my faulty wardrobe, and running very late, I threw my graduation gown over a black lace bra and panty set, put on some boots, and marched off to graduate. Matthew was horrified and titillated to discover that I graduated basically naked later that day.

- My parents meet Matthew's parents for the first time. Shocking revelations ensue, as all the lies Matthew has told since meeting me to cover up that he was living in sin with me unravel at once. Everyone is stunned but polite. My parents give me their worst look, as they discover Matthew used to be a smoker (I hate smoking). "He quit because he loves me!" I accuse them.

- We all caravan to graduation, held in what seems to be the middle of the Sahara, and swelter for hours, craning our necks to catch a glimpse of Matthew, as they announce graduates...in no particular order. Prophet Bob has to be an aggressive paparazzo to get photos of Matthew. He takes a couple photos of Matthew on the giant Panavision screen of graduates as well for good measure. Post-ceremony, I tell Matthew, "The jig is up! Our parents know everything." He plans to order cocktails at lunch, despite my pleas that my parents will think he's a drunk on meds on top of everything else—like being an ex-smoker and a liar.

- Prophet Bob takes tons of photos in front of the restaurant at lunch. Matthew will later refer to these photos as his "Jabba phase." He gets angry no one told him he's fat, NOT buff, as he previously thought. The photos will spur Matthew to diet like mad, even though I try to convince him everyone's face looks like a beach ball when wearing that stupid pointy hat. Once inside the restaurant, Matthew takes off his graduation hat and we all burst out laughing. His forehead sunburned in the shape of a point, so he looks like Satan.

- After lunch, we need a nap bad. Our bed at Bob and Cheryl's still has Noah's old bedwetting sheets on it, making squeaking noises whenever either of us moves. Each time it squeaks, Matthew freezes, terrified his parents will think we're "doing something in here." Alas, we are not, and will not for the rest of the trip, either. Matthew has serious issues with having sex when people might hear us. I could care less, but I can't force him.

- Matthew and I spend the next day driving around Huntington Beach and Placentia, discovering that everything has changed since we left. New stores have gone up, new housing tracts have been built, and a rival high school turned into a Home Depot. We're even too old for Java Jungle, the coffee shop we both hung out at during high school. Everyone wears shorts and holey t-shirts, and we look like parents picking up our kids.

- Later that night, we drive up to Los Angeles to have dinner with Jonathan, Kelly and Chad. Chad bemoans his fate of having roommates who do nothing but smoke pot, listen to Blues Traveler, and eat Hot Pockets. One of them has acquired a wolf dog, which growls at Chad and scares him. He refuses to move because there's a bar in his room, and where would he ever find that again? Better to live in fear of being eaten by the wolf dog.

- Kelly still can't meet any good men because she hangs out with only gay men. "The gays are ruining my life!" is still her mantra. Jonathan tells Kelly that their cats are her children, which makes her feel even worse, especially because one of the evil cats, Tasha, hisses and spits at Kelly.

- The restaurant lacks lighting, and Chad complains he's going blind trying to read the menu. Kelly tells him to get glasses, and he bursts out laughing. Jonathan tells him just to order a hamburger with ketchup, as usual. He has little patience for Chad's food issues.

- The next night, Matt's friend Vinay takes us out to the Ritz in Newport for coffee and dessert. He's the classiest person we know, although surely the scariest driver. Vinay gloats over having won the betting pool on our road trip to Baltimore. I have never been to the Ritz and, frankly, it's well worth the money for their heavenly tiramisu and great service. Vinay looks appalled Matthew has never taken me to the Ritz. Matthew insists he would if he made Vinay's salary. We'll see.

- Ultimately only four of our friends, plus our parents, miss us enough to make time to see us. We pack for our flight home the next day and board our plane home at 3 p.m. California time. I'm seated next to a small boy named Jordan. Jordan is five years old. Jordan is going to visit his mom. Jordan has a Pokemon watch. It will be a long flight.

• Matthew puts in earplugs and abandons me to my fate with Jordan, possibly in repayment for ditching his first graduation ceremony. He still looks like Satan with his pointy sunburn. Jordan wants me to take him to the potty, but I'm terrified of being implicated in some sort of pedophile lawsuit later, so I ring for the stewardess to take him. The stewardess crabbily tells us if we're going to sit next to him, then we are responsible for his potty trips. I try to tell her I didn't invite him to sit next to me but I don't want to hurt Jordan's feelings.

• Matthew has no such qualms, and promptly tells the stewardess she needs to move him. We aren't willing to be responsible for a child we don't know, and why would the airline or his parents let him fly alone? I love Matthew so much for being able to speak up. I knuckle to guilt in these scenarios too often. She seats Jordan next to a kindly old lady, who will presumably take him potty and listen to his boring stories about Pokemon. I feel horrible that Jordan might think he's a bad boy and am wracked with guilt all the way to Phoenix. Arrive in Phoenix and glower at Jordan's bad mother.

• Leave Phoenix and, en route back home to Baltimore, smell something burning. Other passengers belatedly notice the smoke smell, and a wave of panic sweeps the plane. The flight attendants begin running around and ignoring our questions, a sure sign something went wrong. An 8-year-old girl (traveling alone due to the irresponsible parenting running rampant in this country) starts crying for her mommy. Sadly, little girl, your mommy and daddy didn't bother to accompany you on this flight. The captain's comforting announcement: "We will be making an emergency landing just as soon as possible due to an unidentified fire on the plane."

In the crapshoot of passengers, we avoided the crying baby on this flight, but got stuck next to the woman who starts shouting, "Hallelujah! Jesus, take me home!" over and over, like she's *glad* the plane might be going down.

• I start saying my own prayer, namely that a falling bag will knock her unconscious, but she continues to appeal to her Lord until we emergency-land in Indianapolis. Matthew assures me, "If I have to get killed, I'm glad it's with you. I would be bored and lonely without you. I hope all the people who didn't visit us will feel very, very bad."

• We begin strategizing our escape route, plotting who can be shoved aside and run over if necessary. Matthew realizes all that time in college was a complete waste if he's going to be killed less than a week after graduation, and fumes about that. He could have just traveled the world or become a regular at a bar or something. The stewardesses demonstrate the kiss-your-ass-goodbye emergency landing procedure. We land amid police cars and fire trucks. We both grab our carry-on bags, despite orders *not* to do so. Are they kidding? I'm going to leave my purse to be stolen in the melee? That will be the first question my mom asks, if I ever tell her about this.

• In the terminal, we begin classifying the other passengers:

  • **Thurston and Lovey Howell**, both wearing knee socks and Bermuda shorts, looking for cocktails in Indianapolis at 11 p.m.

  • **Sherlock Holmes**, who uses his deductive reasoning powers to determine the cause of the fire and wants to share his logic with the rest of us.

  • **The Paparazzo**, who videotapes the whole thing and hopes to sell it to the media. We hate him and hope he gets detained by security.

- **Cruella de Ville**, who smuggled a Chihuahua on board under her jacket. It yips around the terminal and looks for somewhere to pee.

- **The Japanese Card Sharks**, who have removed their shoes, as though they are moving into the terminal, and are playing a complex card game to keep occupied. They display no curiosity as to what may have happened.

- **Burn Victim**, a horribly sunburned girl carrying no aloe or Noxzema. Matthew uses first-aid skills learned in the Navy to help her.

- **Little Orphan Annie**, the 8-year-old traveling alone. The staff tries to reach her parents to tell them their worst fears have come true: their daughter was alone in a scary situation crying for them. She will be spending the night with strangers in a strange city. Luckily Jordan got dropped off already.

- **Colonel Mustard**, who keeps demanding to know what happened, and why, and when it's going to be fixed, and when he's going to get home, and so on.

- Matthew decides immediately we are not getting back on that cursed plane and we settle into the local Ramada Inn courtesy of America West. An hour later, all the other passengers straggle into the hotel, after trying to force the flight crew to let them back on the plane for their abandoned carry-on bags. Matthew and I raise our glasses to toast them from the bar, pleased that we defied the rules and have our carry-on bags already and didn't waste an hour listening to Colonel Mustard bitch. I call the airline and find out that if we want to take America West to Baltimore, we have to fly all the way back to Phoenix, do not pass Go, do not collect $200. This cannot be happening, America Worst!

- Back at the airport the next morning, we get on a TWA flight to St. Louis, and then Washington, DC. Then we can take a forty-five minute cab ride home from DC. "Do no airlines fly to Baltimore? Is BWI the Bermuda Triangle of air travel?" I angrily ask the desk agent. He shrugs. Flying to St. Louis goes without incident, but the autopilot on the plane to DC is broken, par for the course. I want to know why the pilots can't just **fly** the plane the whole way as that's, presumably, their job. Why is autopilot a must? Isn't that why we have <u>two</u> pilots? Matthew just shrugs as I ask pointless questions, and I stop right before I turn into my mother, asking unnecessary and unanswerable questions. They supposedly fix the autopilot in about three minutes, which seems totally suspect. We board the plane very dubiously.

- Arriving in DC, we get a crazy Russian cabbie we'll call Dimitri, who speaks about two words of English. He pantomimes that he can't take us home; he'll only take us to BWI airport because our taxi voucher only pays that much. We agree, because we are not paying one dime extra on this trauma. He screams into his CB radio in Russian the whole trip, yelling, "Nyet! Nyet!" and slamming the receiver into the dashboard occasionally. At BWI, we receive a new cheapo voucher. This cabbie, Mohammed, speaks only Farsi, but takes direction through pointing and grunting when we want him to turn. He freaks out when he discovers Willie, the taxi dispatcher, has pocketed our taxi voucher and he may not get paid. He curses Willie (the thief) in Farsi. Mohammed makes us write a statement, on the back of a pizza coupon, affirming we **did** have a voucher and gave it to Willie the thief. He lets us go after scanning the coupon.

- My mother, upon hearing this story, admonishes us for not taking her advice to rent a motorhome to drive back and "see a little of the country", completely oblivious to the concept of PTO and how you can't just gallivant off for weeks. When I try to explain this to her, she says, smugly, "Well, then this is what happens to you." Like it's our fault this happened.

- You really can't go home again, and it's best not to even try.

Too Po to Travel? Use Your Credit Card!

East Coast Adventures
2000-2001

Since the point of moving cross-country was to broaden our horizons, Matthew and I travel up and down the East Coast during our sojourn in Baltimore. We discover there are some parts of America that are as diverse as being in a foreign country, and other places where the people still live with relics of two hundred years ago.

Living in Baltimore itself, or "Balmer," as natives call it, has its own language. "Downy ocean" translates "Would you like to go down to the ocean this weekend?" (The answer: No, because Ocean City is totally crap, with only miniature golf courses, Subways, and a gross seafood place called Jonah and the Whale.) The beer of choice: "Natty Bo," or National Bohemian. We might not live and die here, but we're learning a lot!

Suggested Soundtrack: *"I Would Do Anything for Love (But I Won't Do That)"-Meatloaf, "Pour Some Sugar On Me"-Def Leppard, "December '63 (Oh What a Night)"- The Four Seasons, "The Thong Song"-Sisqo*

New York City- March 2000

- My first and only time on e-Bay, I win the auction for a treadmill. "Yess!!!" I shout, jumping up out of my chair. "I beat your ass, MissMickey!!!" Then I realize how terrifying and addictive e-Bay can be and swear never to visit there again. "Matthew!" I shout from the other room, while he's in the shower. As usual, he doesn't answer. He claims he can't hear me in there. I stride into the bathroom. "Matthew! We're going to New Jersey on Sunday! I won a treadmill!" He pulls the blue and green striped shower curtain back.

"Really? We're getting a free treadmill?" I back out of the steam. "No, no. We're paying $1000.00 for it, but I won the auction. You see?" He yanks the curtain back across the rod. "I can't hear you. I definitely didn't hear you say you bought something that costs $1000.00."

- On the way to New Jersey on Sunday, I scream, "Watch out!" My eyes bug out. I sounded exactly like my mother. Matthew lets it pass. "That's odd," I remark calmly a few minutes later. "Why would cops just run out on the freeway in front of cars like that?" Answer: because if they run out and wave at you on the freeway (risking life and limb), they expect you to pull over. However, they have no signs or anything to explain, so we have to wait until they speed after us in their car to pull us over to understand the whole thing. Matthew gets a whopping speeding ticket. "Next time an officer waves you over," the policeman grumbles, "you pull over." I can see Matthew forming a comment, probably about how they all looked like potential suicides, but thankfully, he refrains.

- He flings the citation into the pile of garbage in the back seat and speeds off. "You seem pretty relaxed for someone who just got a ticket," I observe, as he begins humming along with the radio again. "Oh, I don't plan to pay the ticket," he assures me, explaining that since he still has a California license, the Delaware DMV won't be able to find him. I'm skeptical, but it turns out he's right. He never pays, and it never shows up anywhere on his driving record.

- "How much was your last speeding ticket?" Matthew asks, checking over his shoulder to change lanes, and switching the radio station from "I Would Do Anything for Love" by Meatloaf to "The Thong Song" by Sisqo. They play the same five songs over and over again here. "I've never gotten a speeding ticket," I retort, popping a piece of gum in my mouth. Matthew stares at me so long I'm tempted to tell him to watch the road, but my mother must not surface again today or he'll never propose. He rails, "The worst speeder in America has never gotten a ticket, but I get one....There's justice for you."

- Eventually he trails off as we pull up in front of a scary graveyard. The treadmill lady lives <u>directly</u> across the street from a giant *graveyard*. "How does she sleep at night with all these dead people around?" I shudder. "In fact, how does she sleep at all? Doesn't she know anything could be waiting to kill her? I would spend all my time at the window, waiting to see The Haunted Mansion graveyard rising up one night and floating toward me." Matthew remarks dryly, "I think Disneyland has shaped way too many of your perceptions of the world." As we walk up to the front porch, Matthew reminds me, "Besides, we live not two blocks away from The Asylum."

- I shake my head rapidly in denial. "Why do you have to keep reminding me? I try to forget The Asylum." It's true. We do live right by a mental institution Matthew dubbed The Asylum. There's a little stone caretaker's cottage at the entrance to The Asylum, where we often see a single candle burning in a window, as though inside The Asylum, the year remains 1646 and electricity hasn't been discovered. In my mind, the caretaker looks exactly like Riffraff from *The Rocky Horror Picture Show*.

- The treadmill lady limps to the door and points us up the stairs to her bedroom. Somehow we fold up the treadmill and jam it, barely, into the car, where the handles jab me in the back through my seat, and flee the graveyard. "I know how to redeem this day!" I exclaim as we pass a road sign for New York. "Let's go to New York!" Matthew loves spontaneous and exciting plans, so without hesitation, changes lanes and heads for NYC. "When do you get paid?" I demand as we stretch our legs in the $20 parking garage. Matthew looks at me. "In a week. I'm po (poor) right now." I nod. I'm po too. "What are we too po to do here?"

- We're too po to go to the Empire State Building and pay the $32 to go to the top and look over.

- We're too po to see Bernadette Peters and Tom Wopat (formerly Luke Duke on *The Dukes of Hazzard*, who I loved as a kid, but now realize I may have been brainwashed with Klan propaganda) in *Annie Get Your Gun* on Broadway.

- We're too po to take a carriage ride in Central Park.

- "Look," Matthew jerks his chin toward a tour bus. "We can afford to do that bus tour leaving right now from Times Square." We sprint to the bus, and breathlessly climb aboard. Matthew takes tons of photos through New York, on Wall Street, the World Trade Center, the Empire State Building and Flatiron Building, Times Square, Broadway, the Village, Chinatown, and all the other reasons tourists flock to New York. "It's so much bigger and more spread out than I thought it would be," he confesses. "Wouldn't it be exciting to live here?" I nod, smiling. We're on the same page. "The Statue of Liberty looks like a paperweight out in the water," he complains, trying to get a good shot. He imagines as you get closer, it gets bigger, but he thought it loomed over the city, like in *Ghostbusters 2*.

- After the tour, we walk through Central Park for free. I'm in a dream of romance, walking and talking, holding hands in the park. It's what I always dreamed having a boyfriend would be. As we sit on a bench by the carousel, Matthew looks at me for a long time and kisses me. It's too bad he wasn't planning on proposing today; this would have been perfect.

- On our way to lunch, Matthew nearly chokes when he sees a sign to rent a one-bedroom apartment for $1800. In Baltimore, a one-bedroom in a brownstone rents for $400. "Are they kidding with that?" he asks hoarsely. "No, that's how much all the excitement of living here costs. Still think it's worth it?" I ask teasingly, leading him into a kitschy deli in Times Square. "I'd rather have fourteen hundred extra dollars a month. I can buy a lot of excitement with that much money," he answers seriously as he settles into a booth. "I wish Jonathan was here so we could sing, "New York, New York...it's a helluva town!" I tell Matthew wistfully, seeing the movie poster from *On the Town*. I always wish Jonathan were here when I'm having fun. Before leaving we call Roger, my friend from work, who can direct us home from any road in a tri-state area. "Do NOT attempt the George Washington Bridge! It's a traffic deathtrap!" Roger commands. He quickly gives us directions. I can hear *Survivor* coming on TV in the background, so we wrap it up quickly.

- On the way home, Matthew chuckles. "Do you realize I've traveled to more places since meeting you than I have in my whole life before you?" He squeezes my hand. That's what love should be—a door to a new life. One that involves tour buses and New York delis, but cheap rent.

Philadelphia- June 2000

- Our first stop in Philadelphia: the Liberty Bell (after driving past the library stairs Matthew points out were made famous in *Rocky*, which I could care less about). "Look!" I point at one of the signs around the bell. "Did you know Paul Revere made this bell?" Since moving to the East Coast, we've realized our historical education contains gaping holes, thanks to California schools only covering the stupid missions. And then we got to visit Mission San Juan Capistrano and get pooped on by swallows. Wahoo.

- Matthew reads the sign for himself. "I thought he just rode around yelling, 'The British are coming!' Oh, and he lived in that little house on the Freedom Trail with no closets," he shudders, sharing Jonathan's poor opinion of wooden pegs. Matthew also points out that "Cronyism clearly came into play here. Paul obviously got the commission from hanging around in pubs with Ben Franklin and Sam Adams."

- Our other visitors to the Liberty Bell include a Japanese tour group, and an elementary school. "Why would Japanese people care about our Liberty Bell? I don't know a single American who cares at all about how Japan became a nation," I ask Matthew quietly. He discusses the cultural isolation of island cultures, but bottom line, they are a more curious people than we are. Maybe we could all have a little more curiosity, like the Japanese? Matthew itches to pepper spray the elementary school, especially one boy that keeps nagging the Bell employee to "ring the bell! I want to know what it sounds like! Can I just tap it? Why did it get cracked? Are you going to fix it? I bet my dad could fix it…" He steers me away from the boy, whispering, "What happened to 'Children should be seen and not heard?'" I just shake my head, thankful neither of us actually wants to have children. Can you imagine answering annoying questions like that all the time?

- At the State House, we notice the chairs are tiny and uncomfortable looking. I tug Matthew's sleeve. "That's how they decided things so much quicker then, and if the chairs in Congress, Senate and courtrooms were rickety and uncomfortable, they might stop wasting our tax dollars on these lengthy trials and filibusters and so on." I feel so political here! Matthew sighs, and wonders if I can wait till I become *informed* on any current events before I start spouting off. That's doubtful. It drives my mom crazy that I refuse to watch the news or read newspapers, citing bias and sensationalism. Plus, they only show the horrible and depressing stuff. Why would I want to watch that? Everyone I know complains about how the media lies about everything, yet they keep watching anyway. Stupid waste of time.

- Near the State House, there's a gallery showing Norman Rockwell paintings and art. We don't know what to expect, but we absolutely love it! What a cool guy! Matthew takes about eighty fliers for other art shows and stuffs them into his jeans pocket. "I'm going to get more involved with art, I think," he comments, zipping up his jacket to leave. Great—that's all he needs, a couple more totally random hobbies. He's always interested in the most random things for weeks or months at a time. I suppose it could be worse— last time, he became obsessed with meditating and I had to keep tiptoeing around since I couldn't tell the difference between meditating and napping.

• Hit the Public Market for the famous hoagies. "These are overrated," I announce, brushing crumbs off my chest and checking my turtleneck sweater for stains. "A sandwich should have more filler than bread, that's what I think." I can only imagine my mom ranting in the Public Market: "You call this a sandwich? I mean, where is the meat? This is 90% air! And bread! Who wants all this bread??" Handmade fudge more than makes up for the hoagies.

• We walk hand in hand along South Street, admiring the architecture of the buildings and homes, and how cool the stoops are, and how pretty all the parks and trees are. I wonder aloud if we would have a more happening life if we lived here, and if we'd go to bars at night and see cool bands, instead of staying home to watch *Dawson's Creek*. Matthew guesses no—he thinks the lifestyle you lead is dictated by how motivated you are to find the unique things in your own city, and we're just lazy. We're both enamored with Philly as we have drinks in the South Street bars, but later realize their murder rate nearly exceeds Baltimore's. We need delis, cheap rent, and low probability of being killed. These are the new criteria.

Williamsburg, Virginia- November 2000

• Depressed at our first Thanksgiving away from home, we decide to make a weekend of it and reserve a room at the Williamsburg Inn. My parents have followed my sister and moved to Israel. Matthew's family just doesn't want to travel over the holidays and won't visit us. Neither of us can believe we both got ditched by our entire family.

- Matthew points out that Williamsburg's age and history make it a perfect place to spend Thanksgiving. "Are you going to go authentic and leave your hair gel at home?" I ask sweetly. He narrows his blue eyes at me. "Of course not! Have you gone mad?" He checks his hair in the mirror, as if I've offended it by asking this question. The lack of sun here has darkened his hair and he bemoans his fate of being a "dirty blonde."

- Arriving in Williamsburg, we notice everyone dresses like *Little House on the Prairie*, with bonnets and shoes that button. Do they dress like this all the time, or just for the tourists? And do they just have old-time underwear or do they order from Victoria's Secret on the side? Matthew exclaims, "Hey, they have Blackbeard's skull here! They made it into a mug and it's in one of the bars!" I veto going to bars where we might be drinking out of shrunken heads, so we find a regular cool pub. Over ales, Matthew begins peppering me with facts about the town he just happens to know (from doing copious research exactly for moments like these). I interrupt, "Are you aware how many of our conversations begin with you saying, "Well, I happened to be reading this book...'?" He sips his ale and smiles at me. "Why? Do you miss those illiterates you used to date?" No. I don't, so I shut it.

- We arrive that night for our tour of Williamsburg, in pitch darkness. The tour guide, Annie, apologizes, "We normally have lights, but we had a blackout." A woman blurts out, "Oh, I just thought you didn't use electricity here at all." Annie gives her a dirty look and hoists her candle a little higher. The tour takes us through some of the businesses of Williamsburg, such as a blacksmith shop, a tailor shop, and a dairy. Matthew walks into a hitching post in the dark. Luckily, it has a horse head for its top, not unlike the one on Eduardo's car, so the muzzle punches him in the stomach before he hurts any other areas. He coughs quietly in the dark, not wanting miss any of the tour guide's fun facts about horses.

• Thomas Jefferson lived in one of the houses we go through! When told that after dinner, the Jefferson family would tell stories, read aloud, or sing songs, a little girl asks, "Was their TV broken?" Her parents think that's funny and precocious; we think it's sad that their family obviously never talks to each other. Matthew mentions that he's relieved he didn't live then, as the tall boots and capes would make him look even shorter. I think they're sexy. Perhaps I can convince him to get some anyway?

• The next day, our hotel begins their giant Thanksgiving meal at noon. I consider making myself throw up my breakfast so I can stuff myself with pie, but decide the last thing I need is the slippery slope of an occasional eating disorder. Somehow, we manage to discipline ourselves from running around like it's a relay race in the dining room. "This food looks so spectacular!" I enthuse, making room for my third plate.

• As we sit down to eat, Matthew wants to know why our table at home isn't decorated with glass turkeys and votive candles and sprigs of greenery. "Considering that the only things we eat at home are peanut butter and jelly sandwiches and steak made on the George Foreman grill, I can't imagine how we'd really dress those up," I reply defensively around a mouthful of turkey. "We mostly eat in the dining hall on campus, so you can ask Miss Debbie there why there aren't any decorations." Matthew, I am learning as we live together, admires all of these little details, but when it comes time to fork over $49 for glass turkeys he decides it's not worth it, and the cycle begins again. "I'm not asking Miss Debbie!" he retorts, shoveling beans onto his fork. "Obviously the students would steal them from the dining hall."

- We have a fabulous Thanksgiving and a fabulous time toasting and eating pie. We waddle out of the dining room, and go back to our room to pass out. As we fall asleep, Matthew whispers, "We're each other's family now." It feels, for the first time, like we might be enough for each other.

Orlando, Florida- February 2001

- To celebrate our <u>engagement</u> (!!!!) and our three-year dating anniversary, we elect to fly to Orlando and visit Disney World. I am definitely the most excited fiancé in the world!

- Since we are very very po, just having come back from visiting my family in Israel and Matthew shacking out for an engagement ring, we stay at a small motel in Kissimmee. Roger, who goes to Disney World at any opportunity, warns us against staying "off-park" and that the only way we'll possibly have fun is if we stay in a themed Disney Hotel. "Sorry, Roger, but you know how much I make. No way can we shell out that kind of money for a place to sleep. Matthew would sleep on the beach for free if I let him," I confide over lunch at the dining hall. He laughs until he sees something questionable in his pudding.

- Upon check-in to our hot-pink motel, we are offered the opportunity to get "free" Disney World passes. Matthew whispers, "I will sell organs at this point to avoid paying the hundreds of dollars on entrance fees. We're doing whatever we need to do to get free passes, except stripping." Upon learning we only have to listen to an hour pitch for time-shares, he signs us up. I warn him, I do: "I am the worst person in America to do this with. I am easily persuaded, and will buy anything I am offered. Slap me if you must to break the time-share trance." He waves me off. "Of course we're not buying a time share. Don't even worry about it."

- Later that day we tour the time-share model, which has a Jacuzzi tub and fresh chocolate chip cookies. I could live here forever, on cookies and champagne, in my Jacuzzi tub! I love the time share! I must have it! Matthew takes me firmly by the hand, possibly to keep me from eating more cookies, and drags me outside. "Look!" I gasp, "It also has a deck! Look at the tray of margaritas and a chip and dip!" I can already envision myself out there, sipping margaritas in the sun and waving to my friendly neighbors. I fall into their trap, hook, line and sinker.

- We arrive back in the office, Matthew reminding me I don't even really like margaritas and looking worried. I whip out my own pen to sign the contracts. Matthew twists my wrist viciously to get me to drop the pen. "Stop it! You're acting crazy! We don't want a time share!" We are passed along the chain of salespeople, Matthew steadfastly telling them we just came for the free tickets, and we want them now, please. I am close to tears by the third guy. "I hate you! You're ruining my cookie/hot tub dream!" I hiss at Matthew.

- Finally, we arrive at the last salesperson. I break down. "I want this time share more than anything, but *he* won't let me have it. I mean, I don't know how we'd pay for it, since we're both quitting our jobs and moving to San Francisco in three months, so the Evil One there can go to grad school, but I'll do <u>anything</u> to have this time share!" The salesperson exhales. "So basically, you will have no income, or prospects of income?" I shake my head sadly. Matthew rolls his eyes. Immediately, we are shuttled out of there, Disney World tickets in hand.

- Matthew looks shell shocked on the shuttle to Disney World, like he might need a couple of drinks. Do they sell liquor in Disney World? I skip merrily towards the entrance of Disney World. "What do you want to do first? Ride rides? Get churros?? I love churros! Who needs cookies when you've got churros?" Ashen faced, Matthew turns to me. He can barely speak. "You just told me you hated me!

You called me The Evil One! You still want to go to Disney World with me?" As we board the boat to get to the park, I explain, "Now that we're not in the time share, the spell is broken! I am totally over the timeshare, and you were <u>brilliant</u> for not letting me buy it!" I kiss him soundly to emphasize this point.

- He sags against the boat seat, looking seasick. Or like he's plotting to throw me overboard without attracting notice of the boat captain. Once we're inside Disney World, saving hundreds on entrance fees as planned, he rallies admirably and decides to start with Alien Encounters, which we don't have in California. I point to the sign out front. "Look, it says it might be scary for some children. Are you sure *I* should be going on this?" He scoffs that it might be too scary for me, forgetting about the time I opened a can of Poppin' Fresh biscuits. The can made an explosive popping noise, and I burst into tears and dropped the can on the ground, terrified evil clowns were going to spring out of it. I have a wide variety of irrational fears, stemming mostly from seeing scary movies and reading Stephen King as a child.

- The Alien Encounter ride involves sitting in a chair which you're strapped into, and then a frightening alien thingy appears in a glass capsule in the middle of the round room. Then, the glass shatters and the room goes pitch dark, and you're trapped in the room with an angry, escaped alien—my worst fear coming true. Ever since (mistakenly) watching *Alien,* I fear aliens. I am also afraid of creepy people who might **be** aliens, and when Matthew sometimes gets a weird look on his face, I suspect even **he** may be an alien.

- My chair vibrates, presumably from the alien shaking it so he can carry me away to kill me in peace, and I feel a hot puff of air, his molten breath, on my neck. I have my eyes closed as tightly as possible, trying to convince myself, "It's just a ride. It's not real. Disney would not want the publicity of having a guest killed by aliens in their park." I won't wet my pants if I don't see it. Objectively, this is actually the closest I've been to peeing my pants as an adult, even counting the near miss I had in Mexico when I had to pee in a planter.

- Once we are released from the horror of Alien Encounter, I fling myself flat on the exit ramp and begin to cry. A little boy, skirting me, queries, "Mom, did that lady not like the ride? I want to ride it again!" Matthew somehow convinces me to go on living, probably by making my new diamond ring sparkle in the sunlight, and we head off to ride less traumatic rides. "Why don't they have Fast Pass in California? Fast Pass is genius!" I exclaim, happily collecting my Fast Pass ticket instructing me to return to the NASCAR track ride between 4 p.m. and 4:30 p.m. Then I can hop right to the head of the line, saving me hours of waiting with increasingly little patience. We ride the Winnie the Pooh ride in the meantime, and I sing along merrily to "Heffalumps and Woozles," planning to buy the soundtrack ASAP. The other small children on the ride follow my lead and sing as well, to their parents' chagrin. The fake NASCAR ride also gets two thumbs up!

- The next day we hit Epcot, and we may not even have to go to Europe! Epcot has staged tons of fake country villages, which are clean, have ample rest rooms, and are staffed by English speakers. "I love fake Europe! This place rocks!" Matthew yells, trotting off to fake France's crepe cart. Matthew wallows in temptation to buy a giant beer stein in fake Germany, until he gets near the register and sees the $149 price tag. "For a cup??" he shouts, eyes bulging. This falls under the Glass Turkey Principle as well: It's all fine and good until you actually have to pay for these items.

- We ride on some sort of Viking canoe ride in fake Norway, which appears to go over a waterfall and plays *Flight of the Valkyries* throughout the ride. Matthew gets misty over his presumed Scandinavian heritage. "Don't look!" Matthew shouts, shielding me from a parade of giant puppets that accost us as we browse in a teashop in fake England. I snap my head away. "You'd think they'd consider how many people are afraid of things like clowns and puppets, and staff accordingly," I mutter accusingly, fingering a sachet. "Fake England is my favorite so far, but I why do they have puppets? English people hate puppets! They should just have a fake Queen to pose with for photos."

• The Chinese acrobats perform an amazing show in fake China. There are other cool shows, some of which involve nutrition, genetics, international cooperation and so on, mostly staffed by cartoons or animatrons. Matthew loves it. "I'm learning so much!" he tells me happily, munching on a churro from fake Mexico. I can feel a "Did you know that..." conversation coming later, probably regarding dental hygiene or riboflavin that we learned about in our last show. After eating more churros and cotton candy preparatory to getting on the boat home, Matthew throws up immediately upon returning to our motel. Upon checkout, Florida's enormous tourist tax tacked onto the motel bill makes him almost throw up again. We fly home with him muttering about "hidden fees." Not even reminding him about our coup on the free passes helps; he just gives me a filthy look.

Washington, DC- March 2001

• "We must visit our nation's capital! We only live forty-five minutes away!" Matthew insists, cutting into my protests. I extract a promise that he will not require me to read every single little placard on every exhibit of all the Smithsonian museums. I also extract a promise that we can stay in a romantic bed and breakfast. Matthew finds a lovely one within walking distance of the museums. After unpacking and taking a longing look at the deep, claw-foot tub, I'm ushered off the to Natural History museum.

• The Natural History museum kicks off with an impressive mastodon, which strikingly resembles Mr. Snuffalupagus on *Sesame Street*. "OK," Matthew cautions, holding my arm, "if we get separated, we meet back here at Snuffy." The museums quickly become a blur as we see more and more extraordinary sights. I remind Matthew repeatedly that he doesn't have to take a photo of *every* single exhibit. He subscribes to the theory that it's better to take all the photos you might possibly want and then discard the ones that are useless later. I subscribe to the theory that we end up with tons of crap photos in our albums this way.

- Matthew feels compelled to photograph a blown glass replica of the White House, despite my warnings that it won't come out. As he takes multiple shots "in case the first one doesn't come out," we both agree living in the real White House would be horrid, with all those people peeking onto your lawn and lining up to tour it.

- I look wildly for a chair on which to park myself in front of the Crown Jewels on display. I lust after the giant necklaces and brooches from all over the world. I sparkle my engagement ring at them. Hello, little friend! "Oh!" I gasp, jumping up. "The Hope Diamond lives right over there!" I wait in a gigantic line, tantalized with promises of the biggest diamond ever, the Hope Diamond. When we get there, Matthew goggles at it. "That's it? That's the Hope Diamond? It looks like the necklace from *Titanic*! I thought it would be huge! It's a rinky-dink James Cameron prop!" I steel myself against looking for a replica to purchase in the gift shop. I don't care how tacky the Hope Diamond looks—if it sparkles, I want one! "You are not buying that tacky fake Hope Diamond pendant," Matthew grimaces, dragging me out of the shop to the next museum.

- One of the museums has crap modern art pieces. I think it's called the Museum of Modern Art. Our two least favorites are a white door with a red doorknob, leaning against a wall, and a giant stick of fake butter. Matthew decides, "I'm just going to leave trash in our yard, call it modern art, and charge admission! Are these guys just screwing with us? Are we on Candid Camera or do people actually think this is art? And are we paying for this crap with our tax dollars???"

- We love the National Gallery, with its audio tour about all the old masters paintings, although we hate the creepy icon paintings where the baby Jesus looks like he's forty years old and has a Donald Trump comb-over. We also love the National Archives, even though we are whisked through the Declaration of Independence room at light-speed to accommodate the throngs of bored schoolchildren. "Well, at least we got to see it," Matthew yawns on our way to the Mall.

- Matthew's Big Dream of climbing the Washington Monument gets thwarted, as it's under construction, but still pretty striking. I'm relieved. I mean, they have an elevator for a reason, you know. "There's no glory in going up the elevator," Matthew fumes, stomping away. I patiently follow him. "So you don't want to go inside at all?" I ask nicely. He gives me a filthy look, again.

- The Lincoln Memorial feels so gigantic! Matthew points out, "Lincoln looks like he's sitting in one of the uncomfortable chairs from the Philadelphia statehouse. But larger. Much larger." Here's my question: Why did all our good presidents come at the beginning? Why have we had so few inspiring presidents since Lincoln? Or did the people in Washington and Lincoln's day disparage them as much as we do our presidents now?

- The magic of the Metro—a few dollars and you can go anywhere you want all over this city! The Metro is phenomenal, and if they installed one everywhere, it would solve all our gas and pollution problems!

- Disappointed, we learn you had to book a tour of the US Mint months ago to go inside, although we fancy we can smell the money from outside. "How do you get a money-printing machine?" I wonder aloud. Though not in hearing of the security guard.

- Using the fantastic Metro again, we're able to hit Georgetown for dinner, walking, shopping and drinking. According to the plaques, the houses in Georgetown were taxed based on their *face* value, the amount *facing* the street, so they built them very narrow but deep to avoid taxes. Even then, Americans were bitching about taxes!

- Back at the bed and breakfast, we thoroughly enjoy our wonderful tub. "I love making memories with you," I murmur appreciatively as he scrubs my back. A rubber duck, courtesy of the hotel, floats by.

In June, we ship our stuff and move to San Francisco for Matthew's graduate school. Our first home: a sublet <u>way</u> out by Golden Gate Park. The sublet literally has clowns everywhere—clown masks, clowns hanging from the ceiling, clown sheets. "I am in hell," I whisper in terror, looking at all the creepy clowns. "You have to get rid of them. All of them," I lean very close to Matthew, so the clowns can't hear me and organize an ambush. He stuffs them into the closet and firmly closes the door. They lurk there and plot to kill me. Also Bad News Bears: the place has a rat nest somewhere, as I discover one night while innocently sleeping. I wake to find my arm dangling out of the bed, and a rat sniffing my hand with its long whiskers. I jerk, and the rat strikes, biting me hard.

Now, with no job, no insurance, and a possible case of rabies, I have to go to La Clinica, the sliding-scale clinic in the Mission District. I'm ready to leave San Francisco at this point, but we both get offered great jobs in August and find an apartment. The rental agent calls it a one-bedroom. I call it a studio with pocket doors, but we'd be on Nob Hill. Things may be looking up!

Everything Happens at Irish Bank

San Francisco, CA
2001-2002

Matthew and I live in San Francisco for a year and a half before I threaten to leave him and go live with Prophet Bob and Cheryl if he wants to keep living in this hellhole. Months of dealing with our rent-controlled, rotten-fish-eating Filipino neighbors, drunks on the bus every day, transvestite hookers propositioning Matthew every time he does laundry, and trying to ride the cable car with ten bags of groceries have taken their toll. I'm 28, and I deserve a little peace and quiet. Before we fled, we did have a couple of memorable visits from friends.

Suggested Soundtrack: *"Thank You"-Dido, "Lady Marmalade"-Lil Kim, Christina Aguilera, Mya, and Pink, "Superman"-Five for Fighting, "Breathless"-The Corrs*

2001- Jonathan and Chad

- Chad breezes into San Francisco to work on a mini-Cooper promotion. "I'm wining and dining with the Mini-bigwigs," he relays over the phone. "Is Matthew coming out with us tomorrow?" I shift the phone to my other ear, and comb out the other side of my wet hair. "No," I answer absently, deciding whether I should get it cut or not, "he's in graduate school. That means he can't go anywhere, apparently for the next several years."

- Chad calls the next day, and he and I head off on the cable car to the Coppola wine bar. It's a gorgeous day for a change, and we look glamorous hanging off the side of the cable car. We drink excellent wine served by a very attractive bartender. "Which one of us do you think he's flirting with?" I giggle to Chad. This is San Francisco, after all. Notice the Amish have <u>not</u> put their community here. "I hope it's me," he leers, casting an appraising eye over the bartender's firm rear end.

- Both of us get really buzzed on wine and decide to move on to the Tiki Lounge. The Tiki Lounge has thatched hut booths, a river flowing through it that promises some sort of water-theme show, and torches flicker on the walls. "In the Tiki-tiki-tiki-tiki-tiki room," I sing, in between sips of my fruity tropical drink. Chad and I end up drinking many, many drink specials out of giant Buddha-shaped glasses at the Tiki Lounge, resulting in me drunk-dialing Jonathan, demanding to know why he never slept with me. Chad encourages this, even though he knows the answer, because he thinks it'll be funny. "You deserve to know the truth!" he yells, gesturing with his drink umbrella.

- Now everyone else at the bar also wants to know why Jonathan never slept with me too, since I'm shouting into the phone, "What was soooo wrong with me? You had a million chances and you never slept with me, not even once! Even though you lied to everyone and told them we did, but we didn't!" Jonathan, baffled by how I could still be hanging on to this after fifteen years, reminds me, "I'm gay. I've always been gay. There's nothing wrong with you... although you did have horrible haircuts...and those granny glasses...anyways, I'll see you when I get there. Ok??" OK. Oh yeah. Jonathan's coming to town tomorrow.

- Chad deposits me back home with Matthew, and they stand chatting at the door until Matthew notices I'm throwing up into our magazine rack, all over his BusinessWeeks. "Well, see you guys tomorrow," Chad beats a hasty retreat at this point, leaving Matthew to steer me into the bathroom and place me gently on our freshly laundered bathroom rug.

- Jonathan arrives in San Francisco the next day. He and Chad check into the W Hotel, the sort of swank and trendy hotel I always feel I don't belong in. "You look great, honey," Matthew assures me as we arrive at the bar. Chad immediately launches into how this boy he's in love with can't commit, and he's *traumatized*. Jonathan dismisses Chad's trauma. "You're unrealistic, Chad, and you'll be fine if you stop dating toddlers." (People who are under thirty). Chad snaps, "What would you know? After you broke up with He-Who-Shall-Remain-Nameless, have you even been on a date since?" Jonathan makes a face, signaling the bartender.

- After closing the bar tab, we wander down the street to a weird BBQ restaurant. Chad rejects most of the restaurants we pass based on their names or the appearance of the food visible in the windows. "Is that guy eating vegetables? That's sick. We're definitely not going to eat there, if they serve vegetables." Jonathan and I look longingly at all the ethnic cuisine we're passing up, but Chad only eats easily identifiable food. Even so, he puts Heinz ketchup on everything he eats, including prime rib. "This place seems kind of quiet, like there was a food poisoning scare here a couple weeks ago," Matthew observes nervously. Predictably, Chad hates all the food and orders a hamburger, which meets his requirements of being 1) easily identifiable and 2) good with ketchup.

- After dinner, Matthew and I suggest we go to our favorite bar, The Irish Bank, for more drinks, presumably as a stop-off before Jonathan and Chad go to the gay bars in the Castro. Jonathan loves Irish pubs, and Irish bartenders with accents, so we know he'll like it. After a plethora of drinks and a few tasty tropical shots, Chad begins waxing poetic about the Ricky Schroeder look-alike I lost my virginity to in Palm Springs, and how he thought Ricky (Rob) was hot, even then.

- I can feel my mouth hanging open. I never knew he coveted <u>my</u> hot spring break fling. Now it all makes sense! Now I know why he wanted to hear all the details! Now I know why he climbed up on the sofa bed next to Rob! Chad sees my face, slams his drink on the table, and yells, "Oh, grow up, Melissa! Get it together! I've always been gay!" Where have I just heard that before?

- Matthew stands up. "I'm totally uninterested in hearing any more of this conversation," he announces, getting his jacket. His own features bear some resemblance to Ricky Schroeder, and now he suspects me of some type of subconscious obsession. Since we only live three blocks from the bar, Matthew feels comfortable walking home, leaving explicit instructions for Jonathan and Chad not to, under any circumstances, leave me alone at the bar. Once Matthew disappears from sight, Jonathan yells, "More shots for everyone!"

- Thirty minutes later Jonathan and Chad catch a cab to the Castro, leaving me drunk at the bar with no cash, a sizable bar tab, and a strong desire to take my top off. I'll surely wake up with a credit card receipt shoved in my bra, wondering, "How the hell did I spend $153? And where's my top?" Instead of stripping, I close my tab and stagger out of the bar into the sea of fog. I can't remember if cabs take credit cards here or not, and I have no coping skills for being yelled at in Russian or Farsi right now. I'll have to stagger the three blocks home.

- In the fog, I'm gripped with panic, due to the fact that we saw the movie *From Hell* the other day, and I'm positive I will become Jack the Ripper's next victim. I almost wet my pants when the scary lion statues at the gates of Chinatown loom suddenly out of the fog, and imagine I hear the Ripper's carriage wheels in the distance. Literally holding on to the buildings and sliding along the walls, I finally get home without falling down one of the many steep hills. I am way-hay-hay-sted. Crying hysterically, I pound on the door. When Matthew opens the door, he looks in the hallway for Jonathan and Chad, then pulls me inside.

- Our conversation:
  - Matthew: "Are you ok?"
  - Me: Sob, sob, "I don't know," drop my purse on the floor, spilling its contents all over, including the receipt for the $153 bar tab.
  - Matthew (annoyed): "Where are Jonathan and Chad?"
  - Me (sniffling): "They left me all alone (sob sob) with no money and no way to get home...and there's Jack the Ripper..."
  - Matthew: (worried): "Did something (swallows hard) *bad* happen to you at the bar? Did someone try to hurt you?"
  - Me: "I don't know!" (wailing, sinking to the floor, crawling to the bathroom).

- I begin throwing up noisily, which will continue for hours. Matthew tries to help, but eventually becomes infuriated with my total inability to communicate anything and tries to go back to bed. I panic: "No! I want you to lie here in the bathroom with me...it's so cool here...the rug smells so good..." I finally pass out. Matthew, free to return to bed, tosses and turns, too angry to sleep well.

- I wake up on the bathroom floor, miraculously hangover-free, at 8 a.m. After showering and brushing my teeth, I meticulously clean the bathroom of all traces of throw-up. As I tentatively crawl into bed, Matthew opens one eye warily:
  - "Let me smell your breath..." (minty fresh)
  - "Did you shower?" (I swing my wet hair around cheerfully)
  - "Is the bathroom clean?" (I nod affirmatively)
  - "Are you hung over?" (I shake my head no and smile beatifically)

- He sighs. "I hate you sometimes. You don't even have the good grace to have a wicked hangover after what you put me through."

- Jonathan calls later that day. "Did you get in trouble?" he whispers, although no one else can hear him. I whisper, "Yeah, and Matthew got really mad you guys left me at the bar." Jonathan dismisses this. "Please, you were fine. Matthew just hasn't seen you like this very often. He'll get used to it." He might, but I think I should probably take Chad's advice and get it together. I'm getting married in February (Thank you, God!) and I'd like to keep it that way.

2002-Rita and Sharon

- My college friend Rita calls me in alarm. "Mel! Me and my friend Sharon are driving up from Orange County to audition for *The Real World*! Can we crash with you?" Of course you can! In our pretend one-bedroom, where you and Sharon can share a futon in the living room. It'll be college all over again.

- As soon as they burst through the door, Rita groans, "Where's the bathroom? I have assthrax!" She sprints off to the tiny bathroom while Sharon, who we have never met before, explains they made an ill-fated stop at Taco Bell, wreaking havoc on Rita's digestion. Matthew, who loathes any reminder that everyone poops, closes his eyes at the unmistakable sounds of...assthrax emanating from the bathroom. Sharon adjusts her headband in her short brown hair, smiling apologetically. She's trendy, and a perfect fit for *The Real World*.

- After a lengthy stay in the bathroom, Rita emerges. "There's no fan in there, by the way," she informs us, rummaging through the fridge for Pepto-Bismol, which she swigs from the bottle, "so I left the window open. Are you guys ready to hit The Stinking Rose for dinner? I'm starving." She and

Sharon are thin, tall, and gorgeous. Normally, I might feel threatened, but I know Matthew still reels from the horror that permeates our bathroom. Any attraction he might have had has literally been suffocated.

• Since finding parking by our house would take a bona fide miracle, we elect to move Rita's car to the Whole Foods parking lot. She points nervously to one of many signs plainly stating that she will be towed if she's not a customer. "It makes my stomach ache to think about having my car towed from here," she admits, rubbing her flat, exposed midriff anxiously. Sharon waves her off. "That's not the parking, it's the Taco Bell." Matthew shakes his head back and forth wildly, chanting, "Etch a Sketch! Etch a Sketch!" and tries to erase any mental images of Rita using our restroom.

• We may have to move apartments now; he will never voluntarily enter our bathroom again. I want to get him that children's book, "Everyone Poops!" but what's the point? He prefers everyone pretend that we have no digestion and not talk about our bathroom issues. He refuses to pee in front of me, and requires that I close the bathroom door completely when I use it. He also runs the faucet whenever he goes in the bathroom, no matter what he's doing.

• The bus ride to The Stinking Rose turns into a fiasco, as a large Mexican man boards and presses up against me. He's wearing a belt buckle of a preserved cobra head, its mouth open and fangs waiting to strike. The buckle happens to be on eye level with me. What if the cobra comes back to life and kills me?

• Rita and Sharon sit across the aisle from an elderly Chinese man, vigorously picking his nose. He wipes his findings not *under* the seat, but *on* the seat next to him for some stranger to inadvertently sit in. They stare at him in fascination, watching his boogers pile up on the seat. "We could be sitting in boogers right now," Rita mouths to me. "Would you rather be sitting in boogers or maimed by a cobra belt buckle?" I ask her urgently, offering to switch seats.

• Matthew turns red from holding his breath. He sits behind a homeless man who has peed himself at some point that day, judging from the eye-watering smell of urine wafting through the bus. I hate living in San Francisco. Some of the people that live here are like that drink the bartender makes out of all the leftover drinks at the end of the night. "The second grossest bus ride," Matthew reminds me. The first grossest bus ride was our first night here, when someone on the bus threw up into his beanie and then held the dripping beanie aloft until his stop.

• The Stinking Rose smells yummy and garlicky. It's famous for its heavy garlic dishes, a la the name The Stinking Rose. "Garlic smells so good compared to that bus," Sharon observes. Matthew inhales deeply through his nose, trying to obliterate the pee smell. Over dinner, Sharon and Rita try to plan their *Real World* audition strategy. Matthew advises them, "Make out with each other in line! You're both hot and MTV viewers definitely want to see hot women make out." Even the assthrax wasn't enough to completely turn him off these two. I elbow him and jerk my head toward several angry butch lesbians at the next table, who give him filthy looks for being honest. He sighs and mutters, "You only have freedom of speech here in San Francisco if you say offensive things about straight, white people, preferably men."

• After dinner we eschew the bus and walk to The Irish Bank, the best bar ever, for drinks. Rita casually refers to our waiter as her future husband. As in, "Could my future husband be any hotter?" and "My future husband has the cutest accent ever!" I remind Matthew, "If you ever go bald, you'll have to develop an Irish or English accent, you know. Only bald men with accents are remotely appealing to me." He retorts, "You are as shallow as a mud puddle! Could you be any shallower? No!" But yet he'll marry me anyway. We have fun laughing and drinking at the bar. I miss Rita and all my friends. It's so hard to make new friends in a new city, and what's the point? We're moving from this hellhole as soon as possible.

- Back at the apartment, Rita and Sharon bed down on our futon in the "living room." We occasionally hear blankets flapping and cries of, "Pull the blanket back if you're going to fart, Share!" Matthew shudders and I know we're getting a new futon as well. This may be an untapped strategy for both getting new things I want, and also getting rid of things I hate. "Oh, your Hooters tank top? Well, I hate to be the one to tell you, Matthew, but...Rita farted on it. Yes, yes, get a stick and throw it out the window immediately. That's a great idea!"

- The next day, after finding the car still at Whole Foods they drive off to the auditions, which do not go as well as hoped. Matthew sighs, "If you had just made out like I told you..." That night, our drinking has a more somber quality to it.

- In the morning, we walk outside and Rita gasps in horror. The car, wedged in by two other cars, turns out to be parked on a steep hill. She gets in to try to inch it out. The battery has gone dead. How this happened overnight, none of us really understand. Rita gets nervous again, since she needs to be back at work tomorrow and Matthew gets nervous that she might have an assthrax recurrence.

- We flag down passing motorists who are brave enough to stop on a steep hill and jump her car without rolling away. No San Franciscans will stop, but finally a carload of Dutch tourists helps. Yay for helpful tourists! Yay for the Dutch!

- Rita can barely take her foot off the brake to try and inch out or she'll hit the car behind her. We debate if there's a law that says if someone parks too close to you, you aren't liable for hitting them on your way out. Matthew thinks you get busted, but I assert that if they're so stupid as to park that close, it's their own fault if they get hit. Rita sides with me, mainly because this will enable her to leave. Sharon shouts decisively, "There is no such law! I will **not** be a party to a hit and run!" The Dutch tourists explain that the car is so close that even if they do roll into it, there's no momentum to actually damage the car. Using this "no momentum" principle, Rita and Sharon are able to escape and leave the city.

• Soon! Soon, my friends, we will follow you back to southern California. But for now, we'll just go to the Irish Bank, have a couple of beers, and then go to the futon store...

They Can Eat at Fuddrucker's

Buena Park, CA
February 2002

Wedding bells are finally ringing! After three years of dating and a year-long engagement, we're really getting married! Matthew and I decide that it'll be easier for everyone concerned to hold the wedding in Orange County, so Prophet Bob and Cheryl find a hotel that looks nice within our budget: The Holiday Inn, Buena Park. Fuddrucker's, an excellent burger restaurant we suspect Chad might slip off to, sits right next door. My parents fly in from Israel and mistakenly elect to stay with Tía Lupe. Matthew and I fly down a week early to handle any potential fiascos and then sail off on a week-long honeymoon cruise to recover. Prophet Bob predicts, "You'll need a year to recover from this much drama."

***Suggested Soundtrack**: "Crazy for this Girl"-Evan and Jaron, "Come What May"-Nicole Kidman and Ewan MacGregor, "Recipe for Love"- Harry Connick Jr., "When I'm 64"-The Beatles, "The Prayer"- Andrea Bocelli and Celine Dion*

Suggested Drinking Game: Take a shot of anything handy whenever anyone gets into a fight. You'll be wasted by the end of the chapter.

- Matthew and I arrive at LAX from San Francisco, collect our bags, and bitterly board a shuttle. "I cannot believe no one would pick us up from the airport," Matthew marvels, buckling his seat belt. "I know," I mumble, letting my head thunk against the window. "It's too far from Lupe's house when she has to pick us up, but not too far when she's flying somewhere good." Mom, Dad and Tía Lupe act all excited to see us after we're dropped off on their doorstep with no inconvenience to anyone. Except us, which turns out to be a theme for our wedding.

- Matthew stares in horror around the living room, where the sofa and the loveseat have little sofa blankets thrown over them. "Is that where we're sleeping?" he asks incredulously. Mom begins to backpedal. "Well, Dad and I are in the guest room—it's so *cute* in there, with all the music boxes and collectibles I gave Lupe—and then Lupe and Ricardo are in their room, so...there's nowhere else for you two to sleep." I feel a pulsing headache beginning behind my eyes, joined by the surge of bile in my stomach that signals rage. "Why, then," I begin slowly, trying not to sound angry, "did everyone <u>insist</u> we stay here, where there's nowhere for us to sleep? We could have stayed at Bob and Cheryl's and had our own room and bathroom!" Mom looks at me like I'm an idiot. "Well, we wanted to see you," she assures me. Apparently her desire to see us immediately overrode any common sense that we would have nowhere to sleep.

- "I'll Rock Scissors Paper you for the couch," Matthew offers wearily. I shake my head. "They're my family. I'll sleep on the loveseat." Is God punishing us for getting the good room at Courtney's wedding? The loveseat looks about the size of the Muppet beds everyone else got. I curl into a fetal position to sleep on the leather loveseat, but it's too short, too sticky, and this house feels like an oven. It has to be 85 degrees in here! On the plus side, I may sweat out a few pounds, since I resolutely refused to ruin my engagement by dieting for my wedding. I keep peeling myself off the leather to toss and turn.

- Fight #1: Mom, Matthew and I demand the next morning that the heat be reduced to something below sauna level. Lupe, Dad and Ricardo insist the temperature feels "comfortable." Mom whispers conspiratorially, "I'm going to leave all the windows open to let the heat out." Dad winces, hating the idea of "wasting" the heat, and also probably calculating how much the wasted heat will cost, like he did when I lived with them.

- Fight # 2: Mom makes a whole turkey for lunch, and Dad and I, knowing the drill, sit down and eat turkey whether we want it or not. Lupe says she's not hungry.
  - Mom: "Well, what have you eaten today?"
  - Lupe: "Nothing. I never eat breakfast and I'm not hungry for lunch yet."
  - Mom: "But you like turkey!"
  - Lupe: "I know. I just don't feel hungry yet. I don't want any turkey."
  - Mom: (encouraging) "You should just try a little turkey. It's good for you. It came out so nice and tender!"
  - Lupe: (testily) "Vick, leave me alone! I don't want turkey, ok? You don't need to force feed everyone all the time! Just leave me alone!"
  - Mom: (Pause. Pause.) "Lupe, just have <u>one bite</u> of turkey." (Pandemonium ensues.)
  - Matthew: "I'm leaving." (Walks out the door, unnoticed by anyone but me, and I don't have the heart to drag him back into this mess.)

- Fight #3: Dad snaps at Mom that she should have stopped nagging Lupe four sentences ago, and "she's an adult and if she wants to starve, let her starve." Mom yells how he "never supports her" and he'll take "anyone's side besides hers." Lupe yells how she's not coming to the wedding anymore if Mom's going, and Mom tops her by yelling that she's not going if Lupe *or* Dad attends. Lupe rounds on Dad, even though he took her side (stupidly), and yells at him that she knew he never cared about her if he'll just let her starve.

- I dash upstairs, lock myself into the bathroom and start crying, since I can't believe they can't act nice for even one day. Predictably, no one even notices, and they all continue ranting and raving downstairs.

- Fight #4: Mom, realizing Matthew has escaped from the loony bin that houses our family, makes Dad go drive around in the car looking for him. Dad finally locates him, and admires how far Matthew walked to escape and find a bar. Matthew peers at Dad warningly: "I don't lose my temper very often, Sam, but I am losing it already. I am going to tell your wife and her friend exactly where they can take their yelling and their selfish attitudes." Dad cheers him on.

- Matthew stalks back into the house. I crack the bathroom door to watch. He walks right up to Mom and Lupe and tells them, very quietly and very coldly, that if they yell at **anyone** within our hearing one more time, neither of them are *invited* to the wedding at all anymore. "I will not have your petty problems upsetting Melissa before the wedding, and if you're both so selfish that you can't keep your mouths shut, don't come. Either of you." Dad grins in the background. He's probably been dying to say the same thing—and mean it—for twenty years.

- Lupe and Mom band together against Matthew and try to convince him he's wrong. "It's OK for us to yell at each other (or whoever else happens by)," Mom assures him, but he stands his ground and keeps threatening to bounce them both from the wedding. Dad silently roots him on. A tense silence follows for the rest of the evening. Matthew collects me from the bathroom and takes me out to dinner. "I've only been with them for one day, and I'm already beaten down," I sigh, swirling my pasta around the bowl, regaining any weight I sweated out last night. What the hell—I order dessert too, and another cocktail.

- The next day, after another sleepless night on the sticky leather loveseat, but sporting brand-new leg cramps from lying in a crouching position, we hold the family bridal shower. The shower, postponed till my mom arrived, occurs a week before the wedding. Not that anyone even wants to have the shower anymore, with Lupe carping about how it's Superbowl Sunday and how early can we get everyone to go home so she can watch the game? "Nice hostess," Dad grumbles, putting out bowls of M & Ms. My cousins and great aunts start to arrive, and we all pretend everything's fine. Cheryl arrives last, and she's the one I'm happiest to see today: someone who will finally be on our side!

- During the shower, Lupe repeatedly retreats to the family room to watch the Superbowl. We have lunch and open gifts with her popping back and forth in and out of her own party. "Should I cut the cake?" I ask Aunt Norma uncertainly. "Absolutely," she reassures me. "If someone can't be bothered to be at their own party, there's no need to wait for them." I call out to Lupe a couple times, letting her know I'm cutting the cake, then begin to cut and serve under Aunt Norma's expert direction. She's been cutting my birthday cakes since I was born, so she knows exactly how much everyone gets, and who wants a rose and so on.

- Fight #5: Lupe pops into the dining room. "You cut the cake without me? You should have waited till I got back to cut the cake!" she cries, nervously eyeing Matthew to determine if he'll consider this yelling. "Lupe," I point out, taking a deep breath to control the bile in my stomach, "everyone else shouldn't be kept waiting while you watch TV during a party **you** are hosting! You need to decide what's more important." Matthew gives me a thumbs-up for handling it well. Lupe grumbles about how she wanted to see the National Anthem, but finally shuts it, sensing no one agrees. Aunt Norma shakes her head in disgust.

- After the shower we drive down to Orange County, where we're staying the rest of the week. Mom and Dad mercifully don't fight or smoke in the car on the way down. We drop them at their hotel, and flee to Prophet Bob and Cheryl's house. Cheryl has tea waiting, and there are towels laid out on our cool guest bed. "Don't worry," she consoles me. "It's only a week, and the important thing is that at the end of it, you two will be married." This becomes her mantra of the week.

• We all make a trip the next day to the bridal shop to see the dress I'm renting, and for Dad's tuxedo fitting. Dad picks out a fedora with a long feather in it to wear with his tuxedo, and I see Mom gearing up for Fight #6, but he's only kidding. I try on my gown, and my parents exchange looks. Not like, "Oh, there's our baby," looks, but "Hmmmm..." looks. It's a lovely off the shoulder gown with beading, corset lacing up the back and a gigantic full skirt and long train. The ultimate princess gown. Plus, it comes with a matching tiara! So why the Hmmm look? Dad finally speaks. "I will not accompany you down the aisle unless you get some sort of bra that doesn't show any cleavage whatsoever! That dress looks obscene!" Mom amends, "Well, it's obscene where we live in Israel, honey." Fortunately, Matthew got detained at the tuxedo shop and misses this exchange. He loves the dress.

• Off we go to Fredericks to waste $70 on a corset that manages to strangle my breasts enough to be pronounced publicly acceptable. Off we go back to the rental shop to try on the gown with the horrible new torture corset. The corset digs into my sides painfully, but Dad seems happy and relieved, so that's all that matters. My personal comfort on my wedding day? Not important. Obviously. Matthew wanders back in, looks questioningly at me, mouths, "Where are your boobs?" and starts to say something. I give him a warning look and he shuts it.

• Mom randomly asks, "What will you do if people who haven't RSVP'd show up? Did you order extra food for them?" I panic for a moment, trying to decide if she's invited people we don't know, and just testing to make sure they'll be fed. Would she really do that? Of course she would. People she would claim I knew. "Remember so and so? Of course you know them. You met them when you were a baby." And haven't seen them since. Matthew declares, "If someone rudely shows up without RSVP'ing, I'll tell them, 'You can eat next door at Fuddrucker's.'" I start cracking up, probably because Fuddrucker's sounds funny, but maybe because I'm at the end of my rope. Mom looks askance. "Oh, you wouldn't really say that!" Then she looks at Matthew's grave expression and rethinks that comment. I judge she doesn't look nervous enough to have invited random people, so I breathe more easily, though still confined by the corset.

• Throughout the week, we do all the finishing up errands, go places with Mom and Dad they haven't been in ages, and actually have some time to relax and have fun. Until Thursday. Thursday night our wedding rehearsal begins, and people start to wander into the hotel bar a little early. It's so exciting to see all my old friends together again! Jonathan and Chad arrive in plenty of time to get cocktails. Courtney and Damon stroll in holding hands. Kelly and Jeanine slip in with matching blonde highlights. Penelope calls to say she'll come in tomorrow. Charlie's on tour with his band, but sent a funny card. Glynis strides in, ready to start directing the rehearsal. We're ready to start except for Colin, Matthew's last groomsman. "I was on time for his wedding," he complains as he makes the long trek back to our room, the Governor's Suite, to call Colin.

• Meanwhile, I drink my third Jack and Coke and try to collect myself. Mom keeps bugging me about what shoes she should wear, and Lupe keeps asking what she's supposed to do as the matron of honor. I snap, "Just stand there," but she clearly wants to feel important. I finally tell her to hold my ribbon bouquet from the shower and make sure my train falls straight. Glynis moves towards me. "She still doesn't know your mom made you ask her to be matron of honor?" she asks sympathetically, holding her drink with one hand and fluffing her bangs with the other. "No, I have to take that to the grave," I answer, closing my eyes briefly. Mom and I had this conversation during my engagement to Julian. "You have to ask Lupe. She's never been in a wedding before, and she loves you." I yelled over the phone, "I don't care! She just wants to be the center of attention, and I can't deal with it on my wedding day." Mom pulled her trump card. "If you don't ask her, I'm not coming to the wedding." This time, I just knuckled from the start, and now I have a loud-mouthed, redheaded, six-foot Mexican woman as my matron of honor. If the shower was any indication of her "helpfulness", I'm in trouble.

- Fight #6: Colin's flight got delayed and he won't be arriving for the rehearsal as far as we know. I flip it on Matthew, who apparently did not specify to Colin that he couldn't fly in after work on Thursday night and have any hope of getting here. Matthew defends himself: "How important can this rehearsal be? I mean, Colin knows how to walk into a room already." Jonathan slips me Jack and Coke #4 and tells me to calm down. He knows I'm inches away from completely unloading on everyone there. Chad comes up with a tablecloth and stuffs it down the back of my jeans for a pretend train. "Now you're a bride!" he cheerses me.

- The rehearsal swirls into chaos. No one listens to Glynis. Someone complains the song we chose for our aisle walk seems "too loud" and "not traditional enough." Fueled by four strong Jack and Cokes, with a tablecloth stuffed down my pants, I stamp my foot and scream, "Now all of you listen to **me** for a change! You are <u>all</u> going to listen to Glynis, and you're <u>all</u> going to do what she says or you're out of here! I don't want to hear anything from anyone about the music! Just wear the clothes we picked out for you, stand there and smile for the photos! Ok???" At this moment, Colin shows up in a Wedding Miracle.

- After the rehearsal, which suddenly goes rather smoothly, we all truck over to Prophet Bob and Cheryl's for the rehearsal dinner. Everyone finally mellows out over lasagna and wine, including me. Everyone loves the attendant gifts. Everyone loves us. No, I wasn't too harsh on everyone. Definitely not.

- The next morning, Tía Lupe calls me. "So, last night after the dinner, Ricardo was in the bar by himself and your friend

Glynis came in with someone. She sat there and talked smack about me! Right in front of Ricardo! Of course, she didn't know Ricardo's my boyfriend, and of course he told me everything she said! What are you going to do about it?"

• Fight #7: "Nothing. I am going to do absolutely nothing about it. You know why? Because it's a free country and she can think whatever she wants about you. You were a pain in the ass at the rehearsal! You were a pain in the ass at the shower with the Superbowl! And if Ricardo cares about you, why would he tell you things he knows would just upset you?" I sigh and switch the phone to my other ear. "Look, Lupe, I'm sorry your feelings got hurt, but my wedding is not about you. None of it. It's about Matthew and I and I'm not spending any more energy dealing with anyone else's crap this week."

• As soon as I get off the phone, I head straight for the bar, where all my friends are congregated, even though it's only 11 a.m. "Glynis," I bark, "if you are going to gossip and talk smack about anyone even *remotely* involved in the wedding, do it in your own room. Lupe's boyfriend Ricardo heard everything you said last night, repeated it to her, and now I'm getting phone calls demanding I deal with it. Do you think you can shut it about her? Because I'd really rather not be having these conversations." Glynis nods mutely.

• Jonathan tells me later she started to cry in their room right after and felt horrible about the whole thing. "Her big doe eyes just filled up with tears, Melissa. You know how that goes. Then she wanted me to hold her." I snort. "Did you hold her?" He nods. "I can't resist her big doe eyes. I just can't do it...hey, what's this?" He rifles through the stuff on my dresser, trying on my tiara and making my necklace sparkle. I can't believe I'm letting him wear my wedding tiara while he's drinking Jack Daniel's. If he spills on my veil...

- I calm myself by getting a manicure and pedicure with Courtney, enjoying just hanging around and chatting with her. Somehow, she manages to put it all in perspective. "At least the Greeks aren't parading through playing 'Louie, Louie' on the tuba, Mel," she reminds me, picking up a bottle of red nail polish. "Besides," she continues, "I'm policing for you. This morning, I was wandering around the hotel while Damon watched hour twelve of the Olympics, and I noticed the door to Jonathan and Glynis' room was open. They were swigging Jack Daniels right from the bottle and bitching about Tía Lupe and chain smoking. I barged in and demanded they stop chain-smoking right near your wedding gown because you'd flip it." I feel the stomach acid start to churn again. "I specifically asked Jonathan to have it steamed. It's just hanging up in their room?"

- Courtney, realizing she has entered the Danger Zone, and that perhaps sharing this information was Bad Idea Jeans, backpedals. "No, I think Jonathan was hanging it in the bathroom and letting the shower steam it. Anyways, they scattered and freaked and opened the window. I smelled it, and you can barely smell the smoke or whiskey." Courtney pays her bill and flees. I elect to stick around for a facial by myself. If I just stay here and let someone rub cream into my face, nothing bad will happen. At least that's my theory.

- That night, after a huge prime rib dinner at the hotel with the whole wedding party and all our friends, Mom beckons me over in the bar. "Matthew didn't say goodnight to us last night. He just yawned and went upstairs. That was rude. You tell him that was rude. I expect an apology."

- Fight #8: "Mom, Matthew has shown admirable restraint in not becoming physically violent with any of the wedding participants so far. He has been as pleasant as he can and he's exhausted. He obviously didn't mean to be rude."
  - Mom: "Well, he was, and so was Glynis."

- Me: "Mom, don't even go there. You know Lupe has been pushing my buttons this whole week, and Glynis was angry that Lupe has been causing problems for me."
- Mom: "Well, Matthew and Glynis are both rude. Lupe can't help how she is." (!!!!)
- Me: "But everyone else has to be the model of decorum? Lupe is as responsible for her behavior as anyone else! Don't start with me too, or I'm putting you on the next plane to Israel!"
- Mom: "What, you want the terrorists to get me??"
- Me (quietly): "Sometimes."

- Matthew agrees to be conciliatory, but claims, "We're moving to a deserted island as soon as the wedding is over." He's got his own drama dealing with his mom Linda, who's crying that her friend got demoted from her faux wedding coordinator position, crying that Cheryl's dress doesn't match hers, crying that Kristen won't wear heels, crying that she has to walk in with Prophet Bob and Cheryl, etc. "If I tell my mom you said Kris could wear Doc Martens under her bridesmaid dress, she'll need to go to a mental hospital," he warns me. If only she'd take my mom and Lupe with her, I'd do it just to be free of them all.

- The day of the wedding, Matthew escapes everything after breakfast and goes to the gym for about three hours. Lucky duck. I spend the day at the hair salon with my bridal party: Lupe, Courtney, Kristen, and Glynis. My hair comes out perfect, curling beautifully all around my tiara. No one else gets so lucky.

- Lupe, glowering at Glynis the whole time, gets a French twist. She looks like the Bride of Frankenstein, thanks to her startling black and red highlights. She also discovers her tan lines from Cabo San Lucas "haven't faded like I thought they would" and her strapless dress shows her tan lines in perfect relief. Perhaps I can make her a cape out of my train/tablecloth? Glynis bursts into tears, as her stylist performs some sort of intricate weaving or braiding at the back of Glynis' head. "Too tight," she squeaks out. Kristen's tears roll slowly down her face as well. She looks like Shirley Temple after electroshock therapy. Her straight brown hair has been tortured into gigantic sausage curls all over her head. "You have to start completely over because there's no way the pictures are coming out like that," I demand. Kristen nods vigorously. Poor Kristen. She's been the most cooperative person in the bridal party. Her only request: flat shoes. I told her to wear whatever she wanted under her dress. "It's floor length. You can wear bedroom slippers if you want!" Courtney looks on sympathetically, congratulating herself on styling her own hair. Survival of the fittest.

- Back at the hotel, Rita arrives, ready to shoot candid photos of me getting ready. She documents every step of strapping me into the Iron Maiden horror corset, Glynis and Courtney dressing me as I'm now immobilized, and my breakdown when I admit my silver shoes did not break in as I had hoped. I elect to wear black comfy shoes instead since I can't even pretend to hobble along in the beautiful silver shoes. Ugly shoes turn out to be another wedding theme.

- Meanwhile, Matthew and his groomsmen are headed downstairs to start the photo sessions when he spots Linda's mother, Grandma Ginny, in the lobby. Fight #9: Grandma Ginny tells him off, in front of everyone, about how mad she was that he didn't come to visit her last time he was in Chicago. Mortified, Matthew apologizes and flees. I come downstairs with my bridal party and we take all the photos. I hate having to wait around for bridal parties to take photos, so we elected to go the practical route. "Besides," Matthew pointed out pragmatically, "we don't want to miss any of the open bar!"

- The walk-down-the-aisle music starts playing, the doors open and...nothing. Matthew stands there like a deer in the headlights. Linda pokes him hard in the kidney and he starts forward with Linda on his arm, followed by Prophet Bob and Cheryl. The groomsmen enter, Colin having been expertly coached, and they spread out the chuppah across the stage area. The bridesmaids follow, holding candles. My mom on one side of me, my dad on the other, I enter the room. I am so glad Judaism has both the parents lead the bride and groom to the chuppah. Why should mothers get dumped off in the front row? Moms do at least as much, if not more, to prepare the kid for marriage, and then they get sidelined.

• The ceremony turns out to be a long one, and I see the groomsmen begin to droop. The chuppah starts to droop too! I wonder how much it weighs? In the middle of our ceremony, a quinceñera across the hall bursts into life, its mariachi band playing very loudly right outside the door. There's nothing to do but snicker. It's almost a Greek parade band playing "Louie Louie" but not quite. After the ceremony, Matthew and I leave the room. "I'm starving," I whisper. "I hope they serve dinner right away!"

Other impressions from the night include:
- Rita and Sharon, joined by other college friends, dancing on the speakers and grinding up against each other in a scandalous lesbian manner right in front of Grandma Ginny
- Being lifted in my chair and carried around turns out to be very scary
- Damon borrowing Jeanine's fur coat and looking like a pimp in it
- "Show the Del Taco guy your breasts for free tacos, Courtney," Chad screams somewhere, and I see Courtney pull down the top of her dress as someone snaps a photo
- Jonathan tying someone's tie around his head preparatory to dancing like a sweaty wild boar
- Chad and I doing our choreographed dance we do at every wedding

- Matthew being reluctantly persuaded to dance with me and his mom, and then retreating to reminisce with Colin and Martin the whole night
- A tray of glasses smashing somewhere, then Colin apologizing profusely
- Sue and Penelope comparing notes on all my previous bad boyfriends
- Matthew starving all night, while I wolf my food down immediately before plunging into the crowd again
- Not being able to find the alleged open bar and alleged punch bowl
- Never being able to find my parents for anything, like speeches or photos, because they're outside smoking cigarettes the whole time
- Kelly and Jeanine making their peace with Glynis over her stealing Charlie and Chad
- Courtney being thankful for having Damon after hearing Kelly's mantra of "the gays are ruining my life."
- Kelly and Jeanine speculating about Penelope's hot husband

- After the wedding ends, Chad, Jonathan, Kelly, my parents, Lupe, and a bunch of other people head off to The Flying Dutchman, a local skeezy bar. Chad spots a bicycle parked outside, and gets on it. Jonathan clenches up, hoping the bike's owner won't see this, but Chad completely disregards him and rides the bike inside the bar and then around the bar in a circle until he gets yelled at to take it back outside. The bartender, an obese woman wearing spandex shorts and a jog bra, lines up shots on the bar. An overly tanned Dad on the Scam sidles up to Courtney. As she reports later, "He chats me up for a few minutes, and then offers to buy me a drink. I let him, because why not? Then he gets all in my face, going 'Where have you been all my life?' So I start looking around for Damon to rescue me from this creep. He's totally engrossed in some Golden Tee golf video game and can't be distracted from it to save me. So I have to pretend to pee to shake him."

- They head back to the hotel, where Chad has stashed stolen bottles of wine in the lobby plants, and now makes them appear like a magician. Courtney, Damon, Chad, Jonathan and Kelly lay around on the lobby couches, swigging away at pilfered Chardonnay. (Matthew, later: "So that's why we had a $4000 bar bill?")

- Matthew and I make the long trek back to the Governer's Suite. "Do you feel like having sex?" he asks, yawning. "No, but we should, otherwise we'll always regret not having sex on our wedding night," I answer, yawning. "Why did we invite people to breakfast and to the gift opening tomorrow?" he moans. "We can't even sleep in—we have time to eat, open the gifts and then we have to leave for the cruise ship." He considers. "I wish we were eating breakfast at Fuddrucker's, just so we could say we ate there." I grimace, the idea of a hamburger making me feel like throwing up.

- We barely make it through having sex, then pass out immediately, with Cheryl's adage running through our heads, "At the end of the day, you're married, and that's what counts."

- Yeah, that, and a whole bunch of presents to open in the morning!

Honeymooning in Muumuus

Mexican Honeymoon Cruise
February 2002

After four years of dating Matthew, we're finally married! I am married before age 30! I can't believe it! We can't wait to escape the crush of family and flee off by ourselves for the first time in weeks.

Suggested Soundtrack: *"Hot Hot Hot"-Buster Poindexter, "Celebration"-Kool and the Gang, "Get Down Tonight"-KC and the Sunshine Band, "YMCA"-Men at Work, "Old Time Rock and Roll"-Bob Seger and the Silver Bullet Band, "Piano Man"-Billy Joel, "Margaritaville"-Jimmy Buffet*

- Vinay drops us at the cruise terminal, where we relinquish our bags to Boris Karloff, the porter. He wears a hairdressing smock, has missing teeth, and possibly cuts his hair with a Flowbee. Boris points to a long, depressing security line. "You wait there," he instructs through his gap teeth. We wend through the Security line behind a man in a "Right to Bear Arms" t-shirt. He skates right on through, but a senior citizen tour group gets pulled out of line and frisked. But we shouldn't profile or anything...

- We finally reach the head of the line. "We're the Johnsons," Matthew announces proudly, looking adoringly at me. "Yes," the clerk replies dryly, "I can see that by your Mr. and Mrs. Johnson t-shirts. We like all honeymooners to attend our free cocktail party." Wearily, she slides two tickets with champagne glasses printed on them to Matthew. "I knew these shirts would be worth their weight in gold!" I gloat, fingering the free tickets. "Now, keep shamelessly mentioning our honeymoon to anyone who will listen. Who knows what freebies we'll get?"

• My new husband (!!!) stifles the urge to kick the people dawdling around watching to see their luggage being unloaded into the harbor. "Will they just move it already? How slow can they go?" he whines. "Also," he continues conversationally, "when men get old, do they have to wear NASCAR jackets, Hawaiian shirts, and straw hats? All those guys are," he points broadly to a group of octogenarians. "They all look like the time Jonathan dressed up as Eduardo for Halloween one year," I observe. Matthew stops short. "Where did he get the clothes?" I pass him breezily. "I think from Eduardo's closet. Those were Eduardo's actual clothes." A pleasant Filipino cruise employee directs us to the "evilator", which will take us to our cabin. Or to hell, as "evilator" sounds rather sinister. If only our San Francisco neighbors had been as pleasant...

• "Wait, two of our bags are missing!" I fret as we approach our cabin. "Are they mine or yours?" Matthew worries. I narrow my eyes. "One is our shoe bag. We'll have to attend the formal dinner in these flip-flops." Why do I have missing shoes wherever I go? Shoes have become a bad trend for me. We open our curtains onto a blank wall, reminiscent of the view out the window of the Rosarito Beach Hotel. Matthew says optimistically, "I appreciate at least having a pretend window." He pivots quickly into the tiny bathroom. "I *knew* eating those jalapeno poppers from Jack in the Box was bad news, wasn't it?" I call through the door. No answer. "Do you have assthrax?" No answer and a scowl when he exits.

• I force Matthew to participate in the lifeboat drill. Supposedly, the life preservers also double as travel pillows. Matthew whispers, "I'll only use my lifejacket whistle in a **true** emergency." I look over—his whistle has deep chew marks in it. Possibly it doubles as a teething ring? For rabid vampire babies? Captain Gellati welcomes us to the ship via intercom during the drill! Then he dismisses us back to our cabins, claiming he'll see us at dinner.

- At dinner, all the waiters are completely unintelligible, like Martin Short in *Father of the Bride*. No matter what accent they have, we can't understand them "Let's try and figure out what country everyone's from!" Matthew proposes, until he realizes he's never heard of most of the countries. "Are they even real countries? Where is Latvia, anyway?" How can he be an international business major and not know where Latvia is?

- After dinner, we stroll by the New York, New York piano bar. Sitting alone in the deserted bar, Sandro, the pianist, complains about people who frequent piano bars and always request Piano Man. "How about some show tunes? I'll have show tunes," I venture hopefully. Sandro rolls his eyes, but begins to play. When we wander off to participate in other fun shipboard activities, we get stalked by paparazzi everywhere we go. Matthew complains, "These photographers pop out of the woodwork! Don't they know we'll only buy the photos where we look exceptional?" They photograph us in dirty sombreros they clap on our heads.

- We ditch Game Show night when we discover the prizes are just stupid pins. People who are evidently desperate to win tacky lapel pins flood past us. Back at Sandro's piano bar, Matthew learns that the words to "Bad Moon Rising" are "There's a bad moon on the rise," not "There's a bathroom on the right," as he has always thought. We liberally use our Sail'n'Sign cards to ply ourselves with drinks. "Am I drunk or is the ship rocking like mad?" Matthew asks tipsily.

- We're in *The Perfect Storm*, and Matthew takes Dramamine, hoping to stave off nausea the first night of our honeymoon. The violent rocking of the ship enhances my daiquiri buzz, but makes Matthew sicker and sicker. Plus, the jalapeno poppers probably don't help things. "Don't worry," I call through the bathroom door, "we can wait till the second night of our honeymoon to have sex. You can sleep by the pretend window!" He just groans.

- In the morning, I decide we'll skip the "How to Avoid Gaining Weight" seminar. "They'll just tell us to stop eating all the time. I already know that," I comment to Matthew. "Don't mention eating," he commands weakly from the bed. Maids start scampering around at 7 am, not that we can tell for sure since we have no clock and no window to see light by. The limp curtains don't help us. At the breakfast buffet, Matthew perks up and eats bowl of ice cream #1. "See? The weight gain seminar would have just told you not to eat that," I point out.

- We locate the only two deck chairs blocked from freezing gale-force winds and in a patch of sun, and hog them all afternoon. "This is the life!" I smile from under my sun hat. "Take a picture of me. This is the first time I've been relaxed in months!" Matthew refuses to take a picture of me in my bathing suit, nervously claiming, "The angle's bad." Translation: I could have a lucrative career as Free Willy's stunt double. After paying for the wedding, maybe I should make big bucks as a stunt double? I guess I should lose weight...after the honeymoon.

- Matthew satisfies his gambling urge by losing $100 in ten minutes. "I'm defeated and hungry. Let's go to Tiffany's Café." He gobbles down ice cream #2 at Tiffany's Café. After a nap spent sleeping off our ice cream buzz, we get ready for the Captain's Gala. Matthew can't believe we won't be sitting with Captain Gellati, but only seeing him from afar. *The Love Boat* has warped his perception of passenger relations.

- Getting ready for the Gala turns into dee-saster. Matthew panics. "My neck has grown! I can't button my shirt!" He tries to cover the naked neck patch with his tie knot, but to no avail. The tiny bathroom lacks an iron so he wears his wrinkled suit with dignity. Meanwhile, I'm like Cinderella's ugly stepsisters, trying to jam my feet into my ill-fitting silver wedding shoes. "I can't hide the black shoes in this dress, it's too short," I wail. After using sunscreen for the first time ever today, my chest broke out in red hives. "I hope those paparazzi aren't lurking around anywhere," Matthew growls, looking both ways down the hallway as we stagger to the evilator.

- Kim, our Korean waiter, and the epitome of why stereotypes exist, calls Matthew and me "honeymoona" the whole cruise long. He pressures Matthew into ordering champagne to go with the free cake he promises us. Kim then wonders aloud if we plan to "makee babee" while on board the ship. He tells us he's been married five times, and has twelve kids. "He probably works on the ship to avoid all of them," I murmur wonderingly. Kim serves us cherries jubilee (ice cream #3) with much fanfare. Then Matthew orders strawberry ice cream and orange sherbet (#4 and #5). Kim brings me chocolate cake out of pity.

- We return to the cabin to change and discover Rhoda, our "cabin steward," has fashioned a striking cobra, complete with eyes, from the towels in our bathroom. "Why does she hate us?" I'm puzzled. "It's not like we undertipped her. We aren't supposed to tip till the end of the week." At this rate, she'll be getting nothing from me. I can't believe she's turned our honeymoon cabin into literally a snake pit. In our snake pit, we both sleep till 10:30 a.m. and miss Matthew's chance at glory in the men's ping-pong tournament. I console him. "Yes, honey, I know, you would have been the ping-pong champion. Let's try to make it in time for lunch—you can have more ice cream!"

- At lunch, we have brief drama with Kim, who insists it's "cheapa" to order a bottle of wine instead of individual glasses. We explain repeatedly we don't drink the same kind of wine. Matthew: "You don't carry Franzia by the glass for my wife here, do you, Kim?" Kim stalks off to spit in our food. Later, Kim, who missed his calling selling used cars, returns to sell us cookbooks and drink guides with ship recipes. We fend him off, insisting we received multiple cookbooks from the wedding. Not that we'll use any of them. After lunch, we attend the "Shopping in Mexico" lecture. I mostly go because our cruise director has a British accent and I like to listen to him talk. Matthew realizes belatedly, "It's all a thinly veiled pitch for shops that provide kickbacks to Carnival! We're not shopping at any of those places!" On our way out, the paparazzi accost us, posing us with a scary Samoan pirate.

- "Let's nap in our cabin," Matthew suggests, yawning. We need to regain strength exerted in avoiding Kim, so we nap till dinnertime. Steeling ourselves for our next encounter with Kim, I accidentally eat three desserts and Matthew puts away ice creams #6 and #7. "I just can't take the pressure," Matthew shovels spoonfuls into his mouth around his words. We sprint out of dinner to view the photo gallery.

- "I want to buy the picture from Gala night! They airbrushed out my chest rash!" I call delightedly to Matthew. "I look shiny," he remarks critically, but resignedly pulls out his Sail'n'Sign card. All the other pictures of us are hideous, so we surreptitiously drop them in the waste bin.

- "These are the only seats available," I resignedly tell Matthew as we survey the theatre for the comedy show. Matthew slumps into his seat, located in front of a family with seven kids, who punch each other and "tell" the whole time. In the meantime, we watch fiddle great Billy Armstrong play "The Devil Went Down to Georgia." The comedy show isn't funny, so luckily Billy Armstrong was really good. "The punching and telling was kind of funny, mainly because they weren't our kids," Matthew, the eternal optimist, comments on our way out.

- I return to the cabin to get our camera, only to find a sea tortoise made of towels on our bed. Our dinner companions got an elephant and a swan. Maybe tomorrow we'll get a tarantula? "Rhoda definitely hates us," I announce upon my return. "What, did we get a towel clown or something?" Matthew grins. Why would he even say that out loud? I shudder. As penance, I make Matthew take me to the Mardi Gras party with DJ Chaser, who sings a bad version of ACDC's "You Shook Me." I have fun dancing and drinking Hurricanes, while Matthew just hopes I don't take my top off. After dancing with DJ Chaser, we return to the trashy crowd at the piano bar with bitter Sandro. Standouts: woman who keeps yelling "Whiskey!" during "Margaritaville", a teenage girl, Tammie Faye, who hits on Matthew, and her mother, Carol, dressed in three arguing leopard prints and laughing like the Wicked Witch of the West.

- We pretend we're leaving to have sex, but sneak off to the crepe buffet. "Did we wait too long to get married, and now we'd rather eat crepes than have sex?" I ask Matthew, butter running down my chin. He shakes his head. "No, I think four years was just the right amount of time to wait." I disagree, but with my mouth full of blueberry crepe, I can't say anything. Once we do have sex, we can barely move. "Don't joggle me, I'm full of crepes," I warn Matthew, who tries to finish quickly before I throw up crepe on him.

- We wake to the ship crashing into the dock in Puerto Vallarta. "Are we sinking or docking?" Matthew mutters sleepily, flinging back the curtains out of habit. The pretend window gives us no clues.

- On shore, Matthew notes that the closest he's been to a beggar is a decrepit donkey wandering the streets, unfettered. I spot a purse cart and run over. Matthew declares me "the worst haggler ever, paying $5 for a purse I wouldn't have paid a cent over $4 for." He takes charge of all shopping, wangling a lovely wool cape for $20. Tacky magnets of sombreros with beers in the brim are purchased as gifts for our parents and friends. I could never survive in Mexico. I'm nearly killed numerous times by falling down slippery stairs, almost being hit by a bus from Ixtapa, and crushed by peddlers. Matthew berates me for buying chicles to ward off a begging child and pop them all day like an addict. "Stop criticizing me," I command, throwing a fresh package of chicles in my mouth. "They're healthier than fifty bowls of ice cream! Now where do you want to eat lunch?"

• "I saw Hooters back there, and at least we know the food there is good," Matthew remarks, instantly changing course. I don't bother to argue that Hooters' food could only be called good in comparison to Fridays' food. Matthew chivalrously declines to takes photos with the waitresses, as "I'm on my honeymoon, after all." Yeah, with Free Willy's stunt double. He still refuses to photograph me at all. I can't believe I'm at Hooters on my honeymoon. I'm clearly being punished by God for making fun of Nina's Poseidon Adventure wedding, which also ended at Hooters. Jonathan will love hearing about this horror. Other morons at Hooters are hoisted up by their ankles, spun around and then given shots of tequila. They could not be any more stupid, even if they were dropped on their heads. Skanky blondes in cowboy hats cheer the morons on.

• "Let's go back to the ship and go to the Dr. Ruth Quiz show," I suggest, having done all the shopping I plan to do. During the show, a 6-year-old makes it to the finals with her mother's help on the hard sex questions. Why doesn't this seem fun anymore?

• For the first time, we have the dinner table to ourselves! "What a relief, not having to make conversation with people we don't know!" Matthew hates small talk, so getting seated with other passengers has been his worst nightmare. Kim blames us for the others not showing up. We are served only one dessert each (ice cream #8). After dinner, we head to 24-hour pizzeria, as we're not used to eating only one meal. Matthew ignores pizza in favor of ice cream #9. We run into Tammie Faye outside the restroom. She hits on Matthew while I wash the pizza grease from my hands. I hear someone yacking in another stall. It turns out to be the mother of seven from the comedy show. I'd vomit if I had seven kids, too.

• Back in our cabin that night after a fruitless evening with Sandro at the piano bar, we find Rhoda's latest creation: a towel pig on the bed, which she posed wearing my sunglasses. Am I in *Carrie* all of a sudden? Has Rhoda seen me in my bathing suit and making a statement about it? I throw my clothes on the floor and pass out, exhausted from the stress of the cruise staff.

• We wake up in Mazatlan, where we rapidly discover the taxi fare to the city costs $40 per person. "Is it worth it? We don't fish or snorkel. Parasailing just attracts sharks, so we're not doing that, either," Matthew muses. "Why don't we just relax at the pool? Everyone else will be on shore," I remind him. We high-five and go back to the cabin to change. I notice my new shorts do not fit as well as when purchased (meaning that they only barely zip now). How much weight have I gained so far? I comfort myself that Matthew has gained weight too, so he can't be too judgmental.

• We have the whole pool to ourselves while everyone else gets eaten by sharks in Mazatlan. We lie out and swim for hours. "Finally, the pool with no kids peeing in it!" I exult. Matthew notices a grille separating the two sides of the pool. "Look at that!" he points out. "Do you think maybe one side is a shark tank? Hey, why are you getting out so quickly?" I can never swim here again.

• We can't tell if the many seniors lying out in all their clothes are just napping or if they have died. They haven't moved for hours. We skitter past the possible corpses on our way to lunch. The main dish at lunch is jerked pork butt. We both opt for fish nuggets and baked beans instead. Matthew shares later, "Fish nuggets and beans don't sit well together, just like the jalapeno poppers." I read in the library while he goes back to the cabin.

• Our cruise dates include Valentine's Day and my birthday. In our cabin, we exchange gifts—Matthew gets a leather journal to record the genius of his early years. I get a large leather jewelry case to hold future loot! We're feeling lovey and romantic, so we go to a classical music concert and sip wine. A small boy clad only in a swimsuit scampers through the classical music concert we attend, shivering and trying to locate his parents and room key.

• The next morning, I get up at 6 a.m. so we can leave the ship at 7 a.m. I shake Matthew awake. We eventually go ashore to Cabo San Lucas in a rickety boat and discover no shops are open, only disreputable fishing tours. "They know it's our last stop," Matthew ventures when I worry that the vendors don't haggle much. "I just wish they'd stop calling me 'amigo,'" he laments. We flee back to the ship in a different but equally rickety boat. We bask in the sun on the deck like manatees until we're interrupted by a Navy serviceman, who wants to talk about being in the Navy with Matthew. We pretend we're leaving to have sex. The worst part: we aren't actually **having** any sex on these pretenses, just moving to another part of the ship. Our priorities are out of whack. Instead of having sex, we hit Sweet Treats at Tiffany's. Matthew eats two sundaes (#10, 11), and two pieces of cake, so I feel disciplined with my one sundae.

• The big show that evening, *Spin!*, appears to be a dance show based on the cities of America. Matthew, the international major, gets annoyed that they include Puerto Rico. "It's not really America there!" I shush him, looking around to see if anyone's offended. "I know, but they wanted to have a salsa number. Come on, we can make the midnight buffet!" I lead the way to the buffet, where Matthew photographs a model of the ship done in a variety of cheeses. "I have a stomachache," he groans as he eats two plates of food.

He then decides he must C-section his jeans to make more room. "At this point, I think we need maternity pants," I tell him honestly.

- Orca and Jabba the Hutt waddle back to our cabin. "I can't wear pajamas tonight," Matthew tells me as he fumbles for the room key. "Why? Because you want to <u>have</u> sex instead of just pretending to have it?" I joke, half-seriously. "No," he replies testily, "because I'm not sure I still fit in them." We plan a water and rice diet when we return home. After changing into drawstring pants, we venture out to attend the audience participation show. A couple married **59 years** confesses to having sex on the Lido deck the night before! We then learn the husband is a retired minister! I point out, "We've only been married a **week** and we aren't that adventurous. I'm concerned." Matthew sips a Diet Coke. "I'm too fat to have sex, even in a dark cabin with no window. I promise—we'll have sex when we get home." He orders another Diet Coke.

- We return to the cabin to pack. "Should I pack these?" I ask tentatively, holding up my silver shoes. "No!" Matthew answers. "We're not taking anything home that doesn't fit. Maybe Rhoda will make new animals out of them." We leave a new wardrobe for Rhoda in the closet, including Matthew's no-neck shirt. Matthew goes to pay off our Sail'n'Sign card with our wedding dance cash. He reports, "The mom with seven kids was having a heart attack. She gave cards to the kids, and I guess they ran up a $3000 bill ordering tons of Cokes. We're never having kids."

- In the morning, we get little colored tags to determine who gets to get off the ship first, and they call out color groups, like on Romper Room. We are the last luggage color to be called, and search desperately for our bags, which have been thrown carelessly onto the sidewalk. A very different experience than the excitement of boarding the ship, when they still treated us nicely. Except Rhoda.

- I can hear my parents arguing in the car the minute we get off the ship. "You can't park here, Sam! It's red for a reason!" Mom wails, blowing smoke out the window before we get in. Dad retorts, "I'm not parking! I'm just rolling by *very* slowly..." I turn to Matthew. "Remember your deserted island plan? Is it too late to make that work?" He laughs. "It would be the perfect diet!"

Jack Daniel's Distillery: A House of Worship

Nashville, TN
January 2003

Matthew and I plan a trip to visit Glynis and Trey in their new home in Nashville. She's my first friend to buy a grown-up house and settle down. They have a whole different life than ours in San Francisco. Their life involves drinking coffee on their back deck, making weekend plans to fish on the lake, and watching the dog run around the yard. We have a fire escape, our sole access to outdoors in our apartment. It's hard not to feel pressured to be on the same plan as anyone else. I'm about to turn 30, move (again) to San Diego, change jobs (again) and Matthew will be changing graduate schools. Will it ever be time for us to put down some roots?

Suggested Soundtrack: *"Rocky Top"-a cappella, any rockabilly music*

- After two flight delays courtesy of a "light that won't go off here in the cockpit, folks," Matthew and I finally arrive in Nashville, where Glynis and Trey pick us up at the airport. "Oh my God! It's so good to see you!" she calls, running up to hug me. "You look really good," she observes, leaving Matthew to walk behind us with our bags. "You lost a lot of weight since your wedding!" I've lost ten pounds on Weight Watchers so far since the ill-fated cruise honeymoon. It's nice to know it's so noticeable.

- First stop: liquor store! The store has a Live Bait vending machine, which actually sells packages of worms for about $2 — the early fisherman's friend. Matthew, fascinated, asks Trey, "People here like to fish enough that they'd buy worms out of a machine?" Trey chuckles, "Oh, yeah, fishing's big around here. We get out fishing on the lake sometimes, and if the bait shop isn't open yet, this machine comes in real handy." I am so grateful for Matthew's irrational hatred of fishing. Julian's family lived in the mountains, skiing, hiking and fishing all the time. Majoring in Psych was an odd choice for him, but considering his total lack of ambition, I guess it made sense. I hate fishing, too. Glynis, a transplant to Tennessee, has morphed amazingly well with Trey's hobbies. She's always had this chameleon ability to become engrossed in her boyfriends' interests. Thus, the dancer from California now watches NASCAR, goes fishing, knows all about lighting, and owns a truck.

- Upon arriving at Glynis and Trey's house, we find out that there are <u>three graves</u> on their front lawn, complete with headstones. Glynis explains, "The property was an old family piece of land when the developers bought it and there were people already buried there. They couldn't just dig them up, so they sold the houses with the graves intact." Glynis, who has a New Age side as well, assures us Dagney, their dog, "would have sensed ill-will from the dead." I hope Dagney knows what she's doing. "I bet that comes in handy at Halloween," Matthew points out optimistically, knowing Glynis and Trey go all out with their Halloween décor. She flashes him a grateful smile.

- It's so much fun to drink beers and reminisce with Glynis about old friends, old times, and old loves. Matthew and Trey mercilessly mock us, especially when we pull out the photo albums. "Shut it! A 15-year friendship is nothing to mock, boys!" I yell, lifting my beer high in a toast. However, her perpetual dance moves, my collection of odd vintage outfits, my horrible orange hair color and her 80's mullet are fair game. And how we were both obsessed with gay men for years. And our *St. Elmo's Fire* addiction.

- Saturday morning, we all visit the Jack Daniels Distillery and take the tour to learn how to distill whiskey. Trey and I are highly interested, as both of us have donated quite a bit of disposable income to the Jack Daniels Distillery over the years. Matthew insists on reading all the informational placards in the entryway to the Distillery. Placards include: history of Jack Daniels, who died from foot gangrene after, I kid you not, *kicking his safe* because it wouldn't open. Glynis and I burst out laughing, because we could both see our husbands dying the same way. Except now they can cure gangrene. Trey admonishes Glynis, "Lower your voice, honey! We're in a house of worship here." He almost genuflects in front of the life-size Jack Daniels statue.

• Our tour guide, Morgan, a colorful man who sounds just like Boomhauer on *King of the Hill,* may as well be speaking Latvian. We're only able to catch every third word, so we must piece the information together while walking from building to building to make a coherent tour. We're allowed to sniff the mash, watch the charcoal filtering, and visit the barrel storage area. We don't need to drink the whiskey; it penetrates via osmosis through every pore.

• Matthew flips out quietly in the labeling area, where we learn that they label each bottle by hand. "They aren't using automation to its fullest potential! Do they know how many more bottles they could label if they used machines?" Morgan looks puzzled. "But why would we want to work faster?" Matthew thinks everything should be done faster and more efficiently. His frustration with the slow-moving Southern ways will become a theme for the trip. Morgan tells us how the employees fish for catfish in the Distillery lake. "When you only catch crawdads, that's a bad day, because crawdad's what we use for bait." Bait also seems like a theme.

• We can't purchase nor taste any Jack Daniels on the premises of the distillery, because Lynchburg counts as a "dry" county. Matthew finds this "logic" mind boggling and flips out again. "Why build a whiskey distillery in a place that doesn't allow liquor consumption?" he fumes, clenching his fists. I turn to Trey. "I don't understand this dry county business either. Basically, they just make people go out of their way to buy liquor? Believe me—if someone wants a drink, they go get one." Trey says it has something to do with religion, but he's the one who called the Distillery a house of worship, so I'm even more confused. "That's just the way it is," he finally concludes, steering the subject deftly towards lunch.

• We decide to have lunch at BBQ Caboose instead of Sonny's BBQ, due to the life-size pig sign for Sonny's saying, "Go down the road a piece and meet my brother." Glynis and I feel like cannibals, and boycott Sonny's on principle. Matthew notes, "The main square of Lynchburg looks like the town in *Children of the Corn* before the travelers are all murdered." Glynis and I both give him nasty looks. We are both huge fans of Stephen King, but then get scared afterwards. BBQ Caboose has a small band playing, and they willingly swing into "Rocky Top" on request. Glynis occasionally bursts into singing it in the car as well. Matthew, used to my random Broadway serenades, goes with it. The restaurant also serves "Cabooze Cookies," which have gallons of whiskey in them. Being baked goods, they slide in under the dry county wire. Goo-Goos, heavenly chocolate and marshmallow pies, are also very popular.

• Everywhere we go, we're encouraged to "Come back and see us, y'hear!" Other funny Tennessee sayings: "We love the 90 degree heat and 90 degree humidity—it smokes out the Yankees." Also, "You're from California? (Deep sigh) Oh well, it could be worse—you could be a Yankee." At these funny stores, I also buy some Tipsy Cake, whiskey-soaked fruitcake, and other Jack Daniels memorabilia. I beg Matthew to let me buy multiple Tipsy Cakes, but he firmly rejects my plea. "We're supposed to be watching our weight," he reminds me. So were the Cabooze Cookies and Goo-Goos diet food too, then? But he's right. I definitely need the guilt and shame of Weight Watchers when we get home.

- Glynis made reservations at The Melting Pot, a fondue restaurant in downtown Nashville. It's a madhouse tonight due to the Titans game. Glynis warns us: "Do NOT make comments like, 'Football? What a stupid waste of time watching that sport is!' OK? Football is religion here!" So whiskey and football=religion. The food at The Melting Pot tastes phenomenal, but Matthew gets frustrated at the concept of cooking your food bite by bite. He wants to request "a whole bunch of skewers so we could put all the meat in at once," but I'm pretty sure they would kick us out and restrain him. His nightmare unfolds: a Greek chorus of people asking, "What's the rush? Just relax and take your time, y'all." He realizes all too soon that if he keeps trying to rush, he will burn himself quite badly on the boiling hot fondue pot, so he begins drinking to calm himself. "Just enjoy sitting and having dinner with us," Glynis suggests brightly. "We're not in a rush." Matthew grumbles, "It's not the time. It's just not *efficient* to eat this way."

- As we walk to the Wild Horse Saloon, a fireworks show to rival Disneyland's light up the sky. "Yeah! Titans won!" Trey yells, and Glynis hugs him. The Wild Horse Saloon seems like a really fun bar, jam-packed with revelers celebrating the Titan win. We get drinks and a table right off the dance floor. Suddenly, everyone in the bar spontaneously gets up and begins to do the same dance. "I feel like we're in a movie where no one gave us our lines," I laugh to Glynis. She assures us we can learn the dance quickly. "We're not professionals like you," I remind her. She knows firsthand it takes hours to teach me any dance steps, being the choreographer of several high school musicals I performed in. We drink and dance our way through the first couple of sets by the rockabilly band.

- Four college guys ask me to take their photo in front of the bar as we leave. One hands me their camera and they pose as though they are all humping the wooden horse in front of the bar. Matthew tells me, "The short one totally wants you." I'm so grateful to be married if there are only horsehumpers out there to date. At a nearby souvenir shop, I almost buy a hot pink cowboy hat and Bud Girl tank top, but am thwarted by low funds, as usual. "Not by good taste," Matthew and Trey point out. "Hey, I'm just getting into the spirit of Nashville!" I defend myself. Matthew yells to Trey, "Who would buy these hideous belt buckles?" as a cowboy troupe enters the store, and we leave. Quickly.

• On Sunday morning, Glynis, Matthew and I visit The Hermitage, the plantation of President Andrew Jackson who, it turns out, was a real ass. Trey stays home to watch the football game, unmoved by our promises of historical enlightenment. He still gets a laugh out of how we didn't know what the Sugar Bowl was. I get trapped in the museum part of The Hermitage, cornered by a docent who thinks, mistakenly, that I want to know **everything** about the Jacksons. "I'm just a tourist. I'm not doing a school report," I plead. Matthew and Glynis ditch me. Matthew buys an ill-fated biscuit mix at the gift store. I hope there are explicit instructions within that decorative bag. I kindly decide not to mention that biscuits, like Tipsy Cake, are not exactly health food, either. I predict, "We will never ever make those biscuits," and I am right. We never do.

• Glynis makes dinner at home that night, and we hang out and watch movies and heckle, just like we used to do. Only more mocking from Matthew and Trey keeps us from a Brat Pack block of *The Breakfast Club* and *St. Elmo's Fire*. She wants to hear all about Charlie, who's a musician now and living back in Orange County with his girlfriend. "Did you ever hook up with Charlie?" she asks, straining to remember. "Nope, especially not after you dated him," I remind her.

• Monday morning, we head to the Belle Meade Plantation. "The property stayed within the family for four generations, until the children had to sell the property to the state to pay their debts," the docent, dressed in colonial costume, lectures. On the grounds, they preserved the family mausoleum, which looks very much like The Haunted

Mansion at Disneyland. For some insane reason, we feel compelled to march right up to the gate at the door. Glynis screams, "Oh my God!" and I start running away, because clearly a zombie or something has popped out. It turns out to be a metal raven statue, right above the gate on the inside, just waiting to peck your eyes out. Matthew examines it fearlessly. "You guys should be embarrassed," he tells us upon returning to where we cower, twenty yards away.

- Glynis takes us to the Opryland Hotel for lunch. They have their own river and boat cruise. Very Vegas, with a fountain show. There are also some wooden horses, cousins to the ones at the Wild Horse Saloon, so Matthew and I take photos with them. We, unlike some people, do not pose in a bestiality showcase.

- We also get to visit the Sam Davis House, the home of a Confederate spy, who got caught and hanged when he was twenty years old. Matthew and I both wonder why he didn't just make up some name when they caught him. I mean, it's not like they had databases or fingerprinting. Glynis says softly, "He was too honorable to lie." It's all very *Gone with the Wind*. Also, the Sam Davis House has a display of medical instruments—and I use this term very liberally— that shows how revolting Civil War surgery was and why nearly everyone died of being "treated" with rusty scalpels and dirty needles.

- "I had a great time visiting with Trey and Glynis," Matthew announces on the plane home. "But it's also like being at the kids' table in life. They're where they want to be, and we're just meandering around with no clue of our next steps." I push the snack package away. "My next steps are back to Weight Watchers." I reflect on our latest taste of American culture. "Well, in the grand scheme of things, our lives could be worse." Matthew raises a questioning brow at me, and I laugh, "It could be worse—we could be Yankees."

Someone Else's Naked Husband

San Francisco, CA
July 2003

Matthew and I wanted to visit our friends in San Francisco and have a rockin' party weekend. Instead, we got drama, drama, and more drama. At what point in your marriage do you deal with being propositioned by other women, becoming friends with exes, and seeing someone else's naked husband?

Suggested Soundtrack: "Bring Me to Life"-Evanescence, "Rock Your Body"-Justin Timberlake, "Hey Ya"- Outkast, "Stacy's Mom"- Fountains of Wayne

- Matthew and I show up at Oakland Airport, and wait for Giorgio, my former co-worker. Eventually, he calls us. "I'm stuck in horrible traffic! It's horrible!" He finally arrives and we head into the city. Giorgio confesses over pizza, "I had to invite Jasmine to the party tomorrow night. She found out about it, and I don't want her to be mad at me." I throw my hands up. "Come on! You know I hate her! Can't you invite her to some other party after we leave town?" I'm tempted to threaten not to come to the party, but that flirts with Mom and Tía Lupe territory. Actually, I'd prefer to skip the party, considering:

  - Jasmine regularly flashes people all over the office, despite having droopy water balloon boobs. Several lectures from HR have made no impression.

  - She lies compulsively. She declined a wedding invitation, supposedly because her ex-boyfriend had *kidnapped her daughter and taken her to Syria*, where she could not get the child back without flying to Syria and making a daring rescue. The day of the wedding, Giorgio spotted her in a park with the child. Jasmine claimed her ex had brought the child back as a surprise, all the way from Syria! FYI, Jasmine, we have all seen *Not Without My Daughter*.

- While not a lesbian per se, she enjoys hooking up with various women at the office, and brought a call girl to our holiday party. She also hit on me several times, a detail I never mentioned to Matthew or Giorgio. This generally happened when she did drugs, while at work.

- After his wife goes to bed, Giorgio suggests, "Let's hang out in the Jacuzzi up on the roof. I'm ready for my nightly soak." I get up immediately. "That sounds great," I declare. "I'll just change into my bikini." Matthew yawns, "I'm pretty tired. I think I'll go to bed. See you guys in the morning," and traipses off, leaving Giorgio and I to soak in the Jacuzzi. If I change my mind now, it'll look like I don't trust Giorgio, so I get my suit on, bemoaning my inability to handle awkward situations. As I climb the steps into the water, I realize Giorgio has *skipped* the step of wearing a bathing suit. Matthew has left me alone with <u>someone else's naked husband.</u>

- If I make a scene, the whole weekend could get awkward. Oh God oh God, he's smiling at me and shifting around. Can I say I have to get out and pee, never to return? Plus, like many Italian men, Giorgio appears to have a Sasquatch-like pelt. He's probably shedding a furry miasma of hair, bubbling and swirling in the water all around me. After about twenty minutes of silence and nervously avoiding looking at Giorgio, I yawn and scamper off to the guest room, deliberately jostling Matthew. He sleeps blissfully on, which makes me even more irritated.

- In the morning, Giorgio drives us into the city and lets us off at The Crêpevine. Matthew and I piggle out on sugary whipped creamy crepes, especially the Curious George, which has bananas and chocolate all over it. Piggling, for those not familiar with this activity, means basically pulling your chair up to the trough and starting to oink. "By the way, if you ever leave me like that again, I'm going to kill you in your sleep," I announce, licking chocolate off my fork. Matthew peers curiously at me. "Why? What happened?" As I fill him on my Yeti horror, I can see he's kind of mad, but mostly trying not to laugh. "I promise, I'll stick close from now on," he assures me, kissing me on my chocolate-sticky lips.

- After breakfast, we take the bus to the Haight, planning to spend a good amount of time shopping at Amoeba Records and browsing at Buffalo Exchange. "Are you sure you want a bus? You hated buses," I remind Matthew. As soon as we get on the bus, he remembers. "Why didn't I get a cab? We fled the city to be away from these people." It's only about 11 a.m. and half the people on the bus are wasted already. Some are drinking and doing drugs <u>on the bus.</u> "Let's agree to spring for cabs the rest of the day to shield ourselves from the homeless, the drunk and the mad. Basically, everyone," Matthew remarks plaintively, casting a look of fear over his shoulder as we exit the bus.

- At Buffalo Exchange, I realize that while I want sparkly, furry, edgy clothes I really have nowhere to wear them. "I am Old No Fun Girl!" I wail to Matthew. He looks over. "Well, I can start taking you to either raves or junior high dances, if those are the clothes you're buying." I scowl and march for the door.

- At Amoeba Records, the heavens have opened and are pouring their glorious light on Matthew. "I need an extra piece of luggage! Do they sell luggage here?" he shouts, loading tons of CDs into a basket. He only regains control when he discovers they have a website. He dawdles around for an hour, lusting after gobs of CDs I hate. "OK, I have to go. Are you sure you don't want to come to lunch with us?" I ask, kissing Matthew goodbye. He grimaces. "No, you go and see if it's awful. If it's fun, I'll come next time." I'm running late and catch a cab to meet Brendan and his wife Leah for lunch. In case you're wondering, I refer to the same Brendan I met in Mexico on Spring Break eleventy million years ago. How, you may ask, did we get from hating him for sleeping with me and never calling me again to meeting him *and his wife* for lunch?

- Three years after Marilyn won the office pool, Sue, my old manager, calls me at school in my dorm room. "You will never in your life guess who just called here! Never!" She's right. I can't guess. "Brendan! From Mexico! He wanted your phone number, but I flatly refused! So I told him to leave his number and I'd give it to you, as if you'd ever want to talk to <u>him</u>." I break out in a cold sweat. "Oh my God, Sue, you know what this means, right? It means he gave me VD! He's calling to tell me he has AIDS! Maybe the doctors make you call now! My brain could be turning to mush from syphilis right now!"

- She reminds me that I'm the biggest hypochondriac ever. "You've been to the doctor at least eighty times in the last three years. You don't have undetected STDs, OK?" I calm down. "You're right. Well, maybe he joined AA! I **soooo** don't want to be step 3 or whatever. I hope he's in AA, not Narcotics Anonymous. I don't need to know he was slamming heroin and that's why he went out with me." Sue sighs. She doesn't want to hypothesize with me anymore. In the end, curiosity killed the cat. I called him after exhausting all possible speculation long distance with Courtney. ("What good could possibly come from this?" she cried, frustrated. After tucking her own past firmly away, she doesn't enjoy dredging up mine. I should have called Glynis.)

- Brendan apologized. "I called to apologize for not calling you back in the first place. I should have been honest with you, and I wish I had handled it better. I know it's been a long time, but it's always bothered me." I'm suspicious. I want to ask if he's dying or something, as I can't figure out why he would be doing this otherwise. Guilty conscience only stretches so far. Maybe he's making peace with death? Ah, he's doing this because the girl he dumped **me** for just dumped **him**. I have four other boyfriends right now, so I can afford to be charitable and listen to his sad story and be a good friend. I liked the guy a lot, and I'd like to be his friend anyway. Although not if he gets back with his ex, who sounds like a complete loony, the sort who might try to run me over with her car.

- We start hanging out here and there, but he's not attracted to me anymore; we're just friends. "I figured he'd at least be into a rebound hookup, but he's not interested," I shrug to Glynis over the phone. "That's really weird. I bet he's just not over the breakup. Not everyone gets over a breakup by hooking up with someone new," she muses. "Luckily I have a good lineup of other guys right now to entertain me," I point out optimistically. "Plus, he's going to China anyway, so no point in getting worked up over it." At least Brendan doesn't promise to call when he leaves for China on a UN scholarship.

- That's it until eight years later when Matthew and I move to San Diego. The only person I knew here was Brendan, and I look him up online. Even though he lives up north now, I email him, he calls me that night, and it's like not a day has passed. When I mention we're coming up to visit, he suggests all of us meeting for lunch. Curiosity kills the cat again, so I go.

- In the restaurant, I see a pretty, slim blonde I suspect may be Leah for some reason. I haven't seen a photo or anything.

Who knows if I'll recognize Brendan either? I mean, it's been eight years; he could be bald by now and have a gut the size of a basketball. Brendan comes up behind me and taps me on the shoulder. "You look exactly the same," I exclaim as he hugs me. "I can't believe you look the same!" I wonder if I look the same? Or am I just barely recognizable? He still has the perpetually tan skin, and friendly brown eyes, but his hair has gone all brown, instead of half blonde and half brown. He directs me to the blonde's table and introduces me. Leah strikes me as quiet, self-possessed and poised. She looks like Kelly, but without the frenetic pace Kelly keeps.

- They are vegetarians and order green beans and some other vegetables and some sort of healthy tea for lunch. I order chicken skewers and beers and wish Matthew had come so I wouldn't be the only carnivore at the table. Leah turns out to be a very good listener, so I ask questions to get her to talk. "So how did you guys meet?" I ask, sipping my beer. This results in relatively divergent points of view on their relationship, as they met while studying abroad in Australia and had been on/off due to location and distance. Leah's dating experience prior to meeting Brendan sounds like peaks and valleys. The deepest valley: dating an ex-con convicted of armed bank robbery. I mean, my dating life was Parade of Morons, but I don't think any of them were incarcerated for anything (except Mesh Tony, but I didn't date him). Oh, except for Keith. But I didn't really date him either.

- The nosy question I **want** to ask, but don't: How Brendan convinced her to come to lunch at all. Not many women would want eat lunch with their new husband's spring break hook-up friend.

- I mention that the last time I saw Brendan he planned to go to Asia. He rolls his eyes. Uh-oh, maybe not a good topic? "I did go to China to study Chinese, but when I got there, the Chinese officials confiscated our passports. They then told all of us who won scholarships the university we were supposed to be studying at hadn't been <u>built</u> yet. They just duped us there to teach English in rural schools in the Chinese countryside for six months. If we didn't stay, we'd have to pay thousands of dollars to get our passports back from the shady Chinese officials." He regales us with the whole drama of applying to the US Embassy for help, but they can't do anything or they'll go to a secret prison or something.

- "So you were a hostage?" I gasp. Leah nods emphatically, but Brendan, like Matthew, makes the best out of a bad situation. "I figured I could stay and learn and have a great trip or I could complain the whole time. I decided to make the best of it." I finish my beer. "Well, I'm glad you had a good experience being held hostage. I would have complained, and they would have shot me so they could sell my organs on the black market, saving a Chinese criminal from execution for one more day." Leah cracks up. Conversation flows freely and we have a great time. Brendan generously pays for lunch, and we promise to hang out again. I know Matthew will like them, so we'll see.

- I catch another cab to meet Matthew at Tad's Steakhouse on Powell. I wonder if Matthew will notice the similarities between Brendan and himself if we hang out again. He still doesn't like Ricky Schroeder since Chad spilled the beans. "Mmm," I pick up a fork and take bites of Matthew's steak, despite having just eaten, because Tad's, while a scary place where I've personally witnessed assaults, has the best steaks in town. He looks accusingly at me. "I didn't have dessert at lunch," I defend myself. I figure I am practically owed a piece of chocolate cake and go to the register to get one.

- Matthew spent his afternoon all around town, stopping in Irish Bank for beers with his friends, and taking the proverbial sentimental journey. "I'm not as sentimental as I thought about San Francisco," he informs me, finishing his steak. "There are some fun places, but I'm so glad we moved."

- We go back to Giorgio's apartment via the last cab and get ready for the party. When Jenn, my old boss arrives, I confide the naked hot tub incident of the night before. She agrees with me. "When other people might see you, that's a no-no. It's a communal hot tub on the roof—anyone could get in!"

- As darkness falls, Jasmine arrives like a vampire to suck the life from the party. She immediately latches onto Giorgio, flirting and putting her arm around him. Giorgio, for some insane reason, has an ongoing flirtation with Jasmine. But this really pushes the envelope, considering his wife, Annie, has a black belt in karate. Annie, who's Chinese and probably could get officials to sell Jasmine's organs on the black market, finally rounds on them and snaps, "Why don't you two just go get a room?" She smirks. "But I guarantee, Jasmine, you'll be back in five minutes or less." Giorgio grabs Jasmine's hand and shoots back, "Maybe she'll do something besides lay there!" Annie laughs dangerously. "Be my guest, it just takes the burden off me"—looks at his beer belly—"literally." It's a Mexican standoff for a tubby husband.

- Giorgio and Jasmine head down the hall to the bedroom. "Who does these things but disturbed people? Are they just sitting in there waiting for more than five minutes to elapse or are they really hooking up?" I whisper to Jenn. "I don't know, but I'm out. Annie seems nonchalant, but she has a bad, bad temper." She hugs me goodbye and slips out the back stairwell. Giorgio and Jasmine come back and we all pretend nothing bad happened. Jasmine and a couple of other women get in the hot tub and start flinging their clothes out. Is this why Giorgio doesn't see any problems with flaunting himself?

- Matthew and I announce we're going to bed (to flee the discomfort). Annie, narrowing her eyes at Giorgio, calls flirtatiously, "Don't lock your door, I might decide to join you two!" I snap, "Your husband may be *for share,* but mine

isn't!" In bed, Matthew claims I was rude to our hostess. "I think that unless our hostess runs a <u>brothel</u>, her comment was totally out of line first, and I'm not planning on being invited back, trust me!" I rail, changing into my pajamas.

• The next morning, Matthew and I hit the Jacuzzi by ourselves. Giorgio comes out and gets in, flagrantly removing his shorts and flinging them out. Matthew shoots me a "Can you believe this?" look. I shoot him an "I told you so!" look.

• We may have lost some old friends, but hopefully I've made us some new ones. "So lunch was fun," I begin on the plane home, "and I'd really like to hang out with Brendan and Leah again."

Canada with the Jordan Bear

Seattle, WA & Victoria, Canada
September 2003
Liz and Colin are the first of our friends to have a baby. Matthew and I bemoan their terrible fate; they'll never get to go out again, never have privacy again, and they'll have no money. But when we see them, we realize they couldn't be happier. Are we missing something here? I'm 30, and if we should be thinking about a baby, shouldn't we start thinking now?

Suggested Soundtrack: *"The Elephant Goes Stomp Stomp Stomp" and "Down in the Meadow"- Wiggles and Giggles*

- "Why did we choose such an early flight?" Matthew yawns and stretches. "I need coffee. You want some?" I shake my head, planning on falling asleep as soon as we get on the plane. He walks off, right into the metal bar between the two rows of seats, and lands flat on his face. His legs immediately swell up and turn purple, with deep indentations in his shins. "Owwww! That hurt so bad!! Owww!" he yells, laying on his back and displaying his mangled legs to me. I remind him, "If you're crippled, you can use the electric carts at the grocery store!" He cheers up and limps off to Starbucks.

- First leg of the flight: we sit next to very young baby, mercifully a happy and quiet one. Suddenly his mother, who looks like Jabba the Hutt in a wig, starts breastfeeding the baby right in her seat, no coverage. Matthew closes his eyes and whispers, "My eyes! I want to claw out my own eyes!" Second leg of the flight: Matthew sits next to an ancient Chinese woman with a fold-up cane. He wonders aloud, "Do you think she'll whip out the cane and stick-fight the other passengers?" She doesn't. She just falls asleep.

- Colin picks us up in Seattle and Matthew relates the story of the breastfeeding woman, winding up with, "If she were hot, it would have been a different story," and then apparently remembers I'm in the car. "Right, hon?" I shake my head no. "Naked boobs belong in a private area. At least use a blanket, honestly!"

- Colin turns onto his street and we both gasp in envy. They live in the cutest neighborhood <u>ever</u>! Sadly, even if we lived here, we'd still have our same crazy life, not the Finnertys' Perfect Life. After touring the house, Matthew rounds on me. "Why doesn't our house look as nice as everyone else's?" I remind him, "It's just like the glass Thanksgiving turkeys. You don't want to pay for all the things that make this house perfect" Liz shudders, holding their son, Jordan. He's adorable. The Finnertys' Perfect Baby.

- Liz and Colin can't agree the next morning on when we need to leave to catch the ferry to Victoria. "Colin," she begins patiently, "we don't want to rush on at the last minute. We need to leave early if we want to go out to breakfast." Colin assures us we have "plenty of time. And we can eat at a local restaurant." These will be famous last words. Colin misses the off ramp (also soon to become a theme) for the restaurant, but instead of getting off at the next one, he keeps going, saying hopefully, "We'll see a sign for *something*." Jordan kicks the back of his seat, as if to disagree.

- We do. It's Denny's. At Denny's, I pretend I've never heard of Weight Watchers. "I'd like chicken fried steak and biscuits, please," I order, handing the harassed waitress the menu. Matthew begins to give me the "Are you sure you want to do that?" look, but I give him the "Zip it!" look first.

- Jordan, who recently turned one, begins to fuss in the car. "Put in *Wiggles and Giggles*!" Colin begs Liz, flinging a CD holder in the shape of a dog at her. *Wiggles and Giggles* hits include "Down in the Meadow" and "The Elephant Goes Stomp Stomp Stomp." These lyrics will become burned in our brains, and despite our own lack of children, we find ourselves humming these catchy tunes at home, in the car, in meetings..."Jordan seems to **really** enjoy kicking me in the kneecap during The Elephant Goes Stomp Stomp Stomp," I inform his parents. He gives me a filthy look for telling on him.

- "The directions say to go here," Colin says defensively, looking at the end of the dead end residential street we're on. "The ferry's going to leave in twenty minutes!" Matthew panics, twirling in circles to look for any body of water. Liz and I ask various pedestrians if they know how to get there. We get careful directions and jump back in the car. I notice the ferry confirmation letter says to arrive an hour before departure and that it's the last ferry of the day, but I don't say anything. Matthew completely despairs that we might miss the ferry already. We race onto the ferry with minutes to spare and go straight up to the cafeteria for lunch.

- To pass the time, Liz asks, "Do you want to play Loaded Questions?" Colin, Matthew and I gather around her, while Jordan occupies himself by throwing playing cards on the floor. Here are some sample answers:

- "What is a great evil in the world?"
  - Liz: Child molesters
  - Melissa: Terrorists
  - Matthew: Carnies

- "If you had to have a Siamese twin, who would it be?"
  - Colin: My wife
  - Matthew: Stephen Hawking

- We mutually agree on mimes for the most disturbing street performers. And that Matthew's choices suck. They decide to nap while I watch Jordan, who wanders off to the cafeteria, where he points urgently at the cookies. "What?

You want a cookie? Ok, what kind? Jordan, if you just point maniacally at the whole rack, I don't know what kind you want. That one? That one?" I buy two giant cookies at random. He eats three bites of each one and gets bored, leaving me to finish them. I consider throwing them away since I shouldn't eat two giant cookies and expect a Weight Loss Miracle, but I can hear my mom calling me a "waster" if I throw food away. I eat them, giving in to the unhealthy subtext of my upbringing.

• We arrive in Victoria and speed off the ferry to the hotel. "What's the name of the hotel, Colin?" Liz asks, peering at the line of hotels around the harbor. Colin admits he has neither directions nor the name of the hotel, assuming "we'll see it when we get to the water. The website said it was right on the bay." We're all quiet and Matthew asks, "Colin, isn't this an island?" Colin begins calling the various hotels we spot. "Yes, do you have a reservation for Finnerty, by chance? No? Ok, thank you!" Eventually, something jogs Colin's memory and he suddenly knows the name of our hotel. "Ok, great, you have our reservation!" He flashes Liz a triumphant look. "Now, where exactly are you? Goose Racing Bay? Hmmm. How do we get there?" It begins to rain on the way to the hotel, which we find only by chance. Liz sighs repeatedly and asks questions like, "Did they say how far to go on this service road? Or why they are off a *service road?*"

• Colin keys into our bungalow. "Hey! A fireplace that lights up on a switch!" Liz sighs again. "The bedroom has stairs leading down to it. Jordan might fall." I doubt it, since Jordan seems fascinated with the fireplace that lights up on a switch, and could care less about the stairs. Matthew looks outside. "Hey, we have kayaks! Two Fisher Price 'My First Kayaks' are right on our porch." He glances at the drops of water on the window. "Not that we'll be using them if it keeps raining the whole time."

- "It's so cold in here," I complain. "Where's my jacket, Matthew?" It turns out no one but Jordan was smart enough to bring a jacket, so the hunt for commemorative souvenir sweatshirts begins. Matthew and Colin buy matching Canada sweatshirts, and then adopt fake Canadian accents, mostly consisting of saying "Eh?" after every sentence. I have to admit, they do sound exactly like Parker, our bus driver during my senior year choir trip. "Perhaps Jordan might like Poulet McCroquettes for dinner?" I ask Liz hopefully. She and Colin exchange a look. "We try not to feed him junk food," Colin answers finally.

- We go downtown for dinner at a place that our hotel recommended for people traveling with kids. Yes, I too would definitely recommend a ritzy steakhouse with lots of stairs and dim lighting, so if the baby wanders off you can't find him. Liz tells us urgently, "We have to pen him in so he doesn't wander off! He'll get bored and fall down the stairs!"

- Matthew and I observe Colin and Liz's precision racing team, deftly handing Jordan off to each other while eating the hot parts of their meal and keeping him from playing with the best toys on the table, the steak knives. I also can't reach my water anymore, as Liz corralled all the water glasses in the very center of the table. "Jordan can't knock them over if he can't reach them," she explains patiently. We are so ill-equipped to handle children. Or a child. Or a cat. Or a plant...

- After dinner, we stroll around downtown Victoria, adorable with its hanging flower baskets and gas lamp streetlights. It's very romantic, apart from Liz pointing out Colin changed Jordan's diaper incorrectly after we ate. Also, the strolling commences at a snail's pace since Jordan wants to look in every shop window and meanders about all over the sidewalk. "I love how he's so interested in everything!" Matthew envies Jordan his fascination with the world. "Yeah, it's great, especially when you're in a hurry," Liz jokes back.

- At breakfast the next morning, two piggly Danish children woof down all the sweet rolls. Their father yells at them in Danish (sounding a lot like the Swedish chef on *The Muppet Show*) and they waddle off outside to wait by the car in the rain. Matthew seems impressed with the training of the Danish children. "You know, I think Captain Von Trapp in *The Sound of Music* had the right idea. Maybe a whistle <u>would</u> come in handy if we ever have a baby."

- Jordan, Liz and Colin arrive. Jordan makes his dining preferences known by pointing and yelling, "Dat!" However, he picks based on color alone and shows his disgust with his choices by closing his mouth and trying to twirl his head as far around as it can go to avoid the offensive food Liz tries to feed him. She even tries to make it more appetizing by singing little songs about cereal, but he can't be fooled. "You have to eat something," she begs him desperately.

- We drive back into Victoria, planning to have high tea at the Empress Hotel, but at $50 a pop for tea and cakes, it's not worth it. "Are they charging $50 in yen or rubles or what?" Matthew bursts out in rage. "Well, let's head back to the ferry. We'll see *something* on the way," Colin says optimistically. I hope it's not Denny's again. "Look! A butterfly garden!" Liz calls, pointing, and Colin pulls off. "Is this ok? Jordan will love it!" Colin asks us. Jordan makes a beeline for a parrot that lives in the garden near a sign that says, "Don't feed me—I bite!" The butterflies are beautiful and the gardens themselves are very tranquil and peaceful.

- We make it back to the ferry on time. Colin hands the booth attendant his credit card. "Cash only, eh," the attendant grunts. We have to root around behind the seats for enough cash to pay the ferry fee. "You **might** want to have a sign and a drive-up ATM here if you only take cash," Liz suggests helpfully. The ticket guy has no interest in process improvement. This time we all sleep on the ferry, even Jordan, and get home in time to eat dinner. We liberally drink wine with dinner and go to bed early.

- On Monday, Liz drives us into Seattle to meet Colin for lunch in the Pike's Place Market area. Oddly, there aren't any good restaurants in the surrounding area of Pike Market: pastries at Piroshky Piroshky, crumpets at The Crumpet Shop, Mee Sum Dim Sum, a place where everything on the menu is in French, or bagels next to the Communist bookstore. We end up in the Bad Service Restaurant inside Pike Market. "I'll have a banana, peanut butter and chocolate spread sandwich, please," I request, putting down my menu. I'll go back to Weight Watchers next week.

- Liz and Jordan head home for naptime. Matt and I go to Pioneer Square and walk around with Colin. Matthew finally bursts out, "OK, so do you really like Jordan? Is being a dad fun <u>at all</u>? Why would people do this??" Colin promises us, "One day, you won't see parenting as indentured servitude." He claims we'll voluntarily give up all our freedoms for a small person who has no control over his bodily functions. Hmm. Prophet Bob said the same thing, but I'm not too sure.

- Colin drops us at the airport with promises of coming down to visit soon. He reminds us Jordan is "great on planes!" I wish we had Jordan on our flight when I see the rest of the passengers on our plane. As we sit down, arguing over who owes what money for the trip, Matthew laughs and remarks, "Colin's crazy. We're way too selfish to have kids. I can't imagine spending money on all the stupid toys kids want. I bet that elephant-stomp CD cost $18, same as a real CD!"

- Becoming selfless enough to be a parent seems an unattainable goal, especially since when we get on the plane Matthew ducks into the window seat, leaving me squashed in with a bag lady trying to stuff four illegal carry-on bags under the seats. "Real selfless, Matthew," I mutter, lifting the armrest and shoving over into half of his seat. "Real selfless."

A Wicked Good Time

Pennsylvania and Massachusetts
April 2004

When our friend Roger from Maryland calls to say he's getting married, Matthew and I agree it's the perfect time to plan an East Coast road trip. That's the one trip we skipped when we lived in Maryland (being short on money and eventually, credit). We've realized experiences stay with you long after the credit card bill gets paid off, so don't pass up opportunities! Besides, even though I'm 31, I still miss Courtney. Who's pregnant.

Suggested Soundtrack*: "Let's Get It Started"-Black Eyed Peas, "Breakaway"-Kelly Clarkson, "It's My Life"-No Doubt, "24"-Jem, "Dancing Queen"-ABBA, "Sweet Caroline"-Neil Diamond, "Thank You"-Dido*

Suggested Drinking Game*: Every time we head off down an unmarked service road, take a swig! That's what I felt like doing, but I'm too old for road sodas.*

- Preparatory to the wedding, Roger's fiancée, Karla, goes to get their marriage license. The county clerk asks her:

    - "Are you both over 14? You need a judge's consent if you're under 14."
    - "Does your fiancée speak English?"
    - "Are you related more closely than second cousins?" which should make people think twice about marrying in Pennsylvania.

- We wake up at 5 a.m. to go to the airport. I trip over our suitcase in the living room, and Matthew falls down getting off the shuttle bus when we arrive at the airport. "It's too early for motor skills," he yawns and crashes out on the plane to Baltimore.

- We still can't figure out the Beltway and end up on a weird service road, which will be the first of many unmarked roads on this trip. "Matthew, you have a magnetic force pulling you towards roads that lead absolutely nowhere!" I cry, hoping we'll stop in time to avoid hitting a fence at the end of this road. "Do you want to drive?" he snarls. Then his eyes widen. "This is how someone turns into your dad! Oh, honey, I'm sorry!"

- Once back on the main road, I spot a sign for Popeye's. "I don't know about that place..." Matthew hedges, looking for somewhere else. Despite his reservations, he loves Popeye's after one bite. "Maybe we should buy stock?" he marvels, biting into his fluffy biscuit. He bases this opinion solely on the potatoes and biscuits. We only eat vegetarian now when we eat out in an effort to keep (more) kosher. I lament that the beans, which smell amazing, have bacon in them. "That's what makes them smell amazing. How do people only eat vegetarian?" Matthew wonders wistfully. I'll have to ask Leah and Brendan.

- No one answers the door at the Summer Dew Inn, our bed and breakfast, (which Matthew has been calling The Tampon Inn for months) when we arrive in Langhorne three hours later. Peeking through the window and knocking, I freeze. *Hundreds* of the most creepy angel figurines are staring maniacally at the door, waiting to kill us. It is the scariest house in Pennsylvania, hands down. "I am not staying here," I whisper, backing away from the window slowly. "Those things are just waiting for nightfall when they'll come to life and kill us in our sleep." Matthew sighs, but he knows better than to argue.

- Matthew offers to sneak us into Sesame Place, the *Sesame Street* amusement park, for the night as "The Grover costume will probably be warm." I stare at him disbelievingly. "An amusement park full of <u>puppets</u> is NOT a viable option!

We just escaped the angel statues!" I keep looking over at him in the driver's seat. Does he even know me at all? Puppets — brrr.

- Matthew pulls into a Hampton Inn located in an abandoned business park. Dinner ends up being free cookies and milk they put out, plus Cokes and M & M's from the vending machine. "Look! M & M's are kosher! We're in luck!" I shout. Matthew almost cries in gratitude for a hot shower — and takes a lengthy one that fogs up the whole room. We watch *American Idol* in our hotel room, and I tell Matthew about how Roger says Karla loves to sing and thinks she should be on *American Idol*. Even though Roger keeps telling her she can't sing, she scoffs and tells him, "I sound just like Celine Dion, and you know it."

- Matthew follows directions the next morning to the church and gets diverted onto service road #2. As we pass a giant graveyard, I fervently hope the wedding is nowhere near this area. We find a little local pancake place and have breakfast there. As usual, I am enchanted with small towns, and imagine living here, eating pancakes, and greeting everyone by name. "You'd get bored only having like five shops in the whole town," Matthew predicts.

- Highlights of the wedding:

  - Reverend Theo wears a colorful stripy stole, which Matthew swears he bought from a kid at the Mexican border crossing. He flings the stole over Roger and Karla's shoulders, appearing as if he might strangle them as they kneel.

  - Reverend Theo tells us we should pray together as couples, then takes it that one step too far and accuses us all of having **sham** marriages if we *don't* pray together.

- Reverend Theo: "My gift to Roger and Karla is my ability to speak from the heart about the Lord." Roger: "Can I have the gift receipt for that?"

- During the 7th inning stretch, we are asked to meet other people and say "Peace be with you." Matthew stubbornly says, "Shalom!" when he meets a new person, reasoning it's essentially the same thing and will pre-empt anyone from expecting him to take communion. I notice the single people are seeking out other singles to wish peace on, so maybe they'll be hooking up at the reception!

- Our pew is the <u>only</u> pew where everyone does not get up to take communion. We have two couples who are pissed about being called a sham marriage, two Jews, and two lesbians. Matthew, after shushing *my* funny comments throughout the service, goes, "Mmmm," as people start taking communion.

- Karla and Roger look happy as they are pronounced man and wife. Matthew squeezes my hand to let me know he's happy to be married, too. He's turned out to be a far better husband than anyone predicted!

- The reception is beautiful, held at the Washington Crossing Inn. If only that Inn had hotel rooms, we would have been set last night. Matthew loves the gold chairs at the reception. "Why didn't we have gold chairs at our reception?" he wants to know. "We spent our gold chair money on our muumuu honeymoon," I remind him. He makes a face. "I wish we would have had the chairs instead," he mumbles. "I gained eleven pounds on our honeymoon!"

- I sample cannoli, chocolate cake and cookies at the various dessert stations of the buffet before Matthew catches me. "Sweetie, we ate cookies and M and M's for dinner last night. I think you should watch the desserts," he reminds me gently, leading me away. He's right. I can't expect Weight Loss Miracles when I keep eating dessert all the time.

- We hang out with Lila, having fun dancing and watching Karla try to lift her arms in her dress, an impossible feat. "Help!" she calls to Roger during YMCA. We're sad to leave the reception, but have to move on to Massachusetts.

- We leave Pennsylvania directly from the wedding, and head towards Massachusetts to visit Courtney and Damon. Our Mapquest directions are 90% good, so we have to ask around to get the other 10%. We stop at a gas station. Cuarlo, the attendant, has an accent we can't place. I assume it's fake.

  - Matthew: "Do you know how to get to Newton?"
  - Cuarlo: "Yes..." stands there like a moose staring at us.
  - Matthew: "Can you tell me how?" Aside—"Does he want a tip?"
  - Cuarlo: "You are customer?"
  - Matthew: "Oh, I can't get directions unless I buy something? Ok, I'd like some gas, please. And directions."
  - Cuarlo: "This is a gas station."
  - Matthew: "*I know*. That's why I'm here."

- The freeway on-ramp misleads us and we end up down service road #3 that actually says Do Not Enter halfway down. "Why would anyone build a road that no one should enter? And why don't they tell you till you're halfway down it?" I ask disgustedly. Matthew glances at me to see if I realize I am asking pointless questions with no answers... just like my mom. Why do we mostly turn into our parents in the car? See, another pointless question!

- Near Miss #1 occurs when a metal utility ladder flies out of the back of a truck, bouncing across all highway lanes. Horror movie of the day: *Final Destination*.

- Near Miss #2 occurs when a truck (a different truck), towing a car by a length of chain, realizes it's about to miss its exit and veers over three lanes, leaving the towed car to sweep along behind it like a drunken water-skier. There is no one in the towed car to steer it, and the rest of us swerve and screech around it.

- Matthew feels deceived when we arrive at Plymouth Rock, one of our historical stops on the road trip. "It's the size of an ottoman! How could the Pilgrims land on it?" he growls, squatting down and peering through the metal bars. Also, 1602 has been *etched* onto the rock, not chiseled with pocketknives or whatever they had then, so it clearly wasn't the Pilgrims who did it. "As usual, the history books are all lies," he mutters angrily. I try to appease him with salt-water taffy, but he can't get past the idea it will taste like seaweed, so we eat ice creams instead.

- We arrive at Courtney and Damon's in Newton, bitching about Plymouth Rock. I've been dying to see her since she called eight months ago to say she and Damon were expecting a baby! I can't believe she's about to have her first baby this summer! It's so exciting! I'm so glad she's doing it first to pave the way. We're hugging and sniffling while Matthew and Damon look on indulgently.

- I'm shocked to learn she got pregnant two weeks after tossing her Pill packet in the trash. "Oh, yeah," she remarks, seeing my look of horror. "I thought it took a month for the Pill to leave your system. But it doesn't. And you CAN get pregnant the first time you try!" Damon nods smugly. Matthew edges away from me on the sofa.

- "I'm craving Legal Seafood," Courtney announces around dinnertime, so we head off in our car so Damon can avoid backing their car up their steep driveway. "Never buy a house with a steep driveway," he advises us wearily. At the restaurant, Damon doesn't know our kosher restrictions, and consequently keeps offering us calamari, lobster, clam chowder, and shrimp. We tell him we're sticking to vegetarian when we're not at home. He looks horrified. "What's the point of even eating then?" he wants to know.

- Stories from dinner include:
  - Courtney, even blinder than I am without contacts, stooped down and petted Damon's black shoes in lieu of their cats. "But at least we're not still wearing hideous plastic glasses, like in fourth grade," she shrieks. Damon sniffs her drink surreptitiously to make sure no alcohol got in there by mistake. "Maybe see if you can get Lasik before the baby comes, so you can see it," Matthew advises her.

  - They have gotten no baby advice whatsoever from either of their parents. "They're boycotting us until we tell them what we're naming the baby. We're going to hold out! It's no one's business what the baby's name is yet!" Damon's competitive streak, mixed with his stubborn Italian heritage, means Courtney's pragmatic Dutch parents don't have a prayer of finding out anything.

  - This winter, Damon's mom Kay invited the whole family of eight to a resort, and then got only two rooms, so one couple had to sleep in the parents' room in the second bed. "Did you Rock Scissors Paper for it?" I laugh. "No, we got there first, so we took the second room with the hippies," Courtney replies, rolling her eyes in annoyance at Damon.

  - All of our retired parents feel a trip to the bank or the post office is a time-consuming activity that takes up the whole day. In answer to, "So what's going on?" they might answer, "I saw a squirrel today!" or "I made a sandwich." Then a long pause. "Don't they remember how they used to do maybe five or six errands a day?" I ask Courtney wonderingly. "How did this happen? Then they want me to have the life of a rock star so they can hear about it and live vicariously through me!"

• Damon tells us, "I'm so excited about the new baby! I'm going to be a total baby-hog, and never let Courtney even hold the baby!" Courtney looks suspicious, as we have all met Damon and know his intentions are good but...

• I tell her about how Chad's dating life turned into a shambles. "According to Jonathan, he basically won't go out with anyone over 22. And we all know 22 year-old boys are idiots, so he lives in constant tragedy and turmoil." She shakes her head sadly. "How's Jonathan doing?"

• Since Jonathan and his boss broke up years ago, he lives the life of a monk. Kelly moved out a while ago, so he bought a condo in Los Angeles and lives with his friend Angie. Angie has become his surrogate wife, replacing Kelly. But she did draw the line at the evil cats, so they were relocated to live with Marie and Eduardo now. "Good for Kelly!" Courtney nods sagely. "She was never going to meet anyone living with Jonathan. The gays *were* ruining her life."

• We're both a little envious of Kelly. She ended up getting a job coordinating shows and events all over the place, gets paid bank, and travels all over the world. "Of course, you can only do that if you're single," I point out. Courtney and I look fondly at our husbands, who pick that unfortunate moment to be ogling our waitress, a gorgeous blonde like Jeanine. "Oh, yeah, I think Jeanine got back together with Allen! Remember Allen from high school?" I consider ordering dessert as the Jeanine look-alike hovers near our table. She looks at Damon for his order, but this time he's looking at Courtney, smiling and holding her hand.

- Matthew, meanwhile, somehow turns into my mother while we're at the restaurant. He lets me drive home, but gasps and flings his arm out every time I brake. I turn into my father, who has just received his driver's license in Israel after three years of attempts, and demand, "Do you want to drive? Do you? Here, you drive, then." We're all horrified, but don't know how to escape this new development. Back at Courtney and Damon's house we ponder it. "Maybe one day we'll just go to the post office, and then come home and take a nap! Gah!" I feel suddenly anxious, so I go get cookies from the pantry. In the living room, Courtney practices, "I see a squirrel! Nope, I can't even imagine calling you or the baby when it's grown up and saying that." It's hard to leave not knowing when we'll see each other again, but Courtney promises to call as soon as the baby comes. I promise to visit as soon as I can after that.

- We check into the Lord Wakefield hotel, since we're too large to sleep in Courtney's baby's crib. The "hotel" has no elevator, and a series of dangling wires indicate where the smoke detectors have been removed but not replaced. In our room, the smoke detector lies in a puddle of wires on the dresser. "I hope none of the other guests are smoking in bed and passing out," I comment to Matthew after he turns out the lights. "Are you going to start talking right now, when I'm trying to fall asleep?" he demands, flipping over onto his stomach. I'm quiet for a moment, then venture, "Do you think our parents have this conversation too?"

- I wake to the sound of dentist drills in the hallway, but soon identify the noise as a wheezy vacuum that needs replacing. Lord Wakefield would be spinning in his grave! Mercilessly, I shake Matthew. "Come on, if we're going on a sightseeing tour we have to get up now." He buries his head in the pillow. I would set off the smoke detector, but it's still just laying there on the dresser.

- Matthew makes good time to Concord, home of Louisa May Alcott, Nathaniel Hawthorne, Ralph Waldo Emerson, and

Henry David Thoreau. "I am totally bitter that the people here got to live next to all these famous historical figures, while we live next to losers who have the police called on them for domestic violence," I announce in Louisa's study. A Japanese tourist takes a photo of me.

• At Walden Pond, Matthew flips out. "They charge for parking! That's ridiculous." He announces we'll park without paying and risk the $25 fine. "First off, that's unethical. It's stealing. Second, that's the pond across the street. See that scummy lake?" I snap, pointing. Matthew feels guilty. "Maybe the parking money goes to cleaning the pond? That looks like a kid's aquarium when they never clean it."

• Matthew, disgusted that Thoreau wrote about being out in nature, but in fact was within walking distance of all his friends and family, maintains, "I'll just tent out in our yard and maybe English teachers everywhere will make **my** book required reading, too." I remind him we don't have a yard, only a balcony, not to mention he doesn't have a book, either. I also point out, "We're almost out of gas, and while Thoreau could have walked home, I don't want to." Silent blame permeates the car for almost running out of gas. The last straw of this adventure comes when I turn the wrong way onto a one-way street into traffic and Matthew loses it and shouts, "PULL OVER NOW!" He takes over, gets gas, and we head off to Salem with gas and an agreement to never speak of this incident.

• Salem's Visitor Center refuses to recommend any attraction over another, so we opt for the tour of Salem. At the Salem Witch Museum, I flee the tour after hearing shrieks from the audience of the film presentation they show. I can't do the walking part either, due to the scary wax figures that might come to life and kill me, or really even hang out in the gift shop, just in case they have toy torture devices. I buy a t-shirt that reads, "Salem: A Wicked Good Time," with a picture of a witch on a broom on the front. We head off toward the airport. On our flight home, Matthew reflects, "I can't believe Roger just married. I can't believe Courtney's having a baby. And I can't believe that little punk Thoreau!"

"Yeah," I reply, reclining my seat back. "But we had a wicked good time!"

The Ruler

Israel
July 2004

Family visits should go like this: You live within an hour or two of your family. You stop by once a week, possibly for dinner. You stay an hour, maybe two. Then just when everyone starts to get on each other's nerves, time to go! You flee to the sanctuary of your own home and complain about how everyone annoyed you.

In my case, my sister moved to Israel after graduating high school and got married shortly thereafter. Considering their retirement, my parents decided the married sister with the already-in-production grandchild was a safer bet than the single girl with no prospects. "Besides, you can afford the tickets to come visit us, and your sister can't," Mom reasonably pointed out. Now Matthew and I visit every other year for an endurance test of nerves and flaming tempers. But seeing my little nephews makes it all worthwhile.

- Neither of us gets any sleep on the red-eye flight to JFK, so we arrive in New York looking like crack addicts, red-eyed and bleary. "JFK International Terminal may be the biggest dump we've ever landed in," Matthew marvels, struggling with our bags. "Is this the message we want to send to international travelers? 'You probably just came from a 3rd world country, so you'll feel like you're still at home in our airport'?"

- "Look," I nudge him. To save salary costs, the airport employs cardboard cutout people to direct us, all of which have been moved so they aren't pointing in the right direction. "Good luck finding your way out of this place — the exit dummy points you right into the wall." We board the air train, accompanied by an Indian guy talking on a cell phone. Two stops later, he finishes the call and begins *driving the train.* I whisper, "Who was driving before?" Matthew stares after him in disbelief.

- On the flight to Tel Aviv, I discover that Nyquil, while a handy sleep aid for flying, makes me feel like throwing up for some time after waking. Especially if omelets are for breakfast. "Ugh, get those eggs away from me," I whimper as Matthew happily forks eggs into his mouth. "But I'm eating them," he points out, offering me some juice instead.

- In-flight movie: *The Cat in the Hat.* I feel like throwing up more than ever.

- My parents meet us at the airport, and my mom begins pushing food on us immediately: "You want some pizza? Look, the menu says they have pizza. No? How about some ice cream? The menu says they have ice cream too." Any hopes Matthew has of losing weight on this trip are crushed instantly. "Of course," I tell her resignedly, "we'd love some pizza." Eventually we eat enough to please her and are allowed to leave the airport.

- My dad rented a car for our trip, but instructs us, "All the cars here look the same. Look for a car with 51 as part of the license plate." Mom rounds on him. "Sam! You don't remember where you parked the car?" Dad looks curiously at her. "You were in the car when I parked it. Do *you* remember where it is?" She waves him off airily, telling us, "When you're just riding in the car, you don't have to notice where you park. But the driver should remember…" Matthew spots a car that looks promising, and my dad confirms, "Yes! Now I remember! I parked right here!"

- Speeding along the Israeli highway, Dad overshoots our destination by 25 miles, prompting my mom to wonder aloud why he was ever given his license. Matthew concurs, whispering "Your father is the worst driver in either the US or Israel. Possibly the world." Dad doesn't hear him, but retorts to Mom, "You're damn lucky I got my license at all or all your gallivanting would be curtailed." She shakes her head.

• We spend our first night in Netanya. "Isn't this where that suicide bomber blew up that car on our last trip?" I ask. Dad chortles, "Yeah, and he was the only one killed. I love when that happens—that's karma for you!" He whips into a space, insisting, "Blue and white curbs are open parking." The sign on the curb, in Hebrew, that none of us can read, probably says whether that's true or not. Mom requests, "Maybe we should try to figure out what the sign says, Sam?" He just walks off, and we all trail after him. After four hours of sleep, we meet for a breakfast of fish, cheese, rolls, seven kinds of salads, olives, and shot glasses of juice. Matthew asks for a bigger glass for his juice, and the waiter laughs, "No wonder everyone gets fat in America." Bleary eyed from arriving at 3:45 a.m., Matthew just gets multiple shot glasses of juice and glowers at the waiter.

• I try to change money at the hotel, but the lady claims, "We're out of money. You must come back later." I report this back to my family. Mom: "How can that be? Are they sure? Did they even look? They *must* have money. I bet she didn't look very hard." I don't reveal that the lady didn't look at all, and I just assumed she knew whether they had money or not. Then we hear Dad yelling out in the street. He has, as predicted, received a parking ticket, which none of us can read. He huffs, "Did all the other people who parked there get tickets?" Matthew peers up and down the empty street. "Well, since they all left, Sam, I guess we'll never know." My mom triumphantly points out that *she said* we should try to find out what the sign said...

• My dad drives into farmland, wondering aloud, "I wonder if I'm on the right road?" Why does he say that in front of my mom? It just encourages her to "help" him drive. Finally, after major detours and three more arguments, we arrive in Tsefat. "You'll love our friend Shlomo's hotel," Mom promises us. We get room 13, which carries no superstition in Israel. Our room has a small iron bedstead, a wardrobe and a balcony with two chairs. "It's great!" Matthew announces, dropping the heavy bags he's had to carry up three flights of stairs.

- To shower, you have to turn on the boiler thirty minutes before you want actual hot water, and the shower, basically a nozzle sticking randomly out of the wall, has no curtain or enclosure, so the entire bathroom gets soaked. "You definitely want to take the toilet paper out of the bathroom before you shower," Dad reminds us. Matthew looks longingly at the shower, but we're going straight to my sister's house.

- As we climb the steps to Rachel's apartment, we can hear the kids already screaming, "Where's Uncle Matt? Where?" Shimon, my 3-year-old nephew, overcomes his shyness and starts shouting, "Aunt Mel! Uncle Matt!" over and over as he runs up to us. We give him big hugs. Natan, my 2-year-old nephew, runs over, hits Matthew in the legs, pokes me in the arm and then runs away. We last saw him as a baby, so he doesn't really remember us. "He likes you!" Rachel declares, hugging me.

- Both kids return to their pizza lunch and then run over to Matthew with sauce all over their little faces. Matthew flinches, even though I told him to bring clothes that wouldn't stain. "Should we get more pizza?" Mom asks happily, finally having everyone together again. "Of course, Mom, we'd love more pizza," I tell her, putting my arm around her. Gedalia, two months old, looks like he wishes everyone would just *calm down*. He is a tranquil baby in a turbulent environment. Or else he just wants some pizza also.

- The older boys race around the living room on their tricy-cles like it's a NASCAR track, dodging furniture, clipping the baby's swing and almost tipping it over. Rachel seems completely unperturbed by the noise level or Gedalia's narrow escape. **Gedalia** looks a little unnerved, though. A kid from across the hall, Levi Yitzchak, drives into the living room through the open front door on his scooter, like a special guest star in a sitcom. The noise level jumps another notch, but my sister continues blithely talking to us as though we can hear her. "What are you saying?" I mime. "Can't hear you with all the yelling!" She just laughs. "Oh, you'll get used to it in a day or two," she tells us wisely. My mom looks like she might comment on that but doesn't. All the riding and crashing clearly alarms Matthew, who mentally adds, "Build fenced-in yard" to the List of Things to Do Before We Have Kids.

- I wake up early Tuesday morning with a rash of horrific mosquito bites. "Look! Look at this!" I yell, making Matthew sit straight up in bed. "I look like I have chicken pox." He examines me. "You're right! You do look gross!" he confirms sleepily.

- My dad picks us up at the hotel and drops us off at Rachel's. He then promptly vanishes; apparently my parents were fighting earlier and they're a little grouchy. However, Shimon and Natan are grouchier than my parents. Their issues are:

    - They aren't allowed to hit each other with sticks they've found. They are also not allowed to poke or hit the baby, who looks relaxed for a change.

    - They have a thousand toys, but only want to play with the **exact** toy the other one has, and they will fight to the death for it.

    - When my sister threatens to give the tricycle away if they don't stop fighting over it, Shimon tells her, "Give it away, Mom, so Natan can *never* have it!"

- One grabs a toy from his brother and starts walking away as if there will be no repercussions. The other smacks the thief in the back of the head. The thief turns around and pushes his brother to the ground. The one who falls down starts to cry and says, "I had it first!" in Hebrew. Rachel takes all toys away until they apologize, and then ten minutes later (which is two hours in kid time) allows them to pick one toy. Begin again.

- Matthew adds, "Buy all toys in exact duplicate if we have more than one child close in age" to his list.

- Rachel asks Shimon, "Get Natan a bottle of juice, would you?" He graciously offers Natan the mostly empty one he drank, keeping the new full one for himself. My sister doesn't notice, but Natan does, and starts wailing. Shimon hastily swaps the bottles before anyone else sees besides Gedalia and I. While holding the baby on my knee, I feel him vibrate. "Why does he vibrate?" I ask hesitantly. Rachel asks, "Does he smell like waffles?" I sniff around the baby, thinking maybe she uses waffle baby shampoo or something. "Kind of...." I reply suspiciously. "Oh, he went to the bathroom, give him to me," she laughs, taking the baby to diaper him.

- Shimon enjoys flying (while Matthew holds him up in the air) so much he drools all over Matthew, who almost drops him in a reflex action. Natan looks interested in joining, but Matthew knows to be wary of Natan's proclivity for violence. "Oh, just lift him. His feelings will be hurt," I implore Matthew. He gives in and starts to lift Natan. Rachel comes in from diapering Gedalia and exclaims, "No, don't do that, he'll kick you in the face!" just as Natan kicks Matthew in the face. Matthew becomes rumpled and dirty after the boys dog pile on him and throw toys all over him, using him as their track to run their little cars on. He's such a good sport! After a while, he suggests, "Maybe we can go to the park and...I don't know, let them run around or something?" We take the boys to the park. I ask Shimon <u>five</u> times before we leave home if he has to pee. No. As soon as we arrive, he announces he has to pee. We have to quickly carry them home uphill, and Matthew observes, "These kids aren't light, you know," as if I loaded them with ballast.

- In the meantime, Mom has made pizza, grilled cheese sandwiches and egg salad. She guilts Matthew into eating a sandwich he doesn't want: "You don't want to waste it, do you, Matthew? It'll be such a waste. Here, it's just a little sandwich." I have noticed that both kids point their index fingers and shake them at people, and now I see where they get it—my mother, who is currently shaking her finger at me. "You have to eat! You'll waste away to nothing!" I look disbelievingly at her. "Look at me! Do I look like I am in imminent danger of wasting away? I could actually stand to lose a few pounds." She looks me over. "Well, maybe you wouldn't waste away right away," she concedes, "but eventually, if you keep starving yourself..."

- Natan randomly leaps off a chair toward Matthew, his little face shining with the clear expectation of being caught. Matthew drops his sandwich on the floor to catch Natan, causing my mom to point out, "You didn't finish your sandwich, Matthew." After observing what the kids have dropped on the floor all day, Matthew declines to invoke the five-second rule and eat the sandwich. My mother gives him a sad look. "What a waste." Besides leaping on people unexpectedly, Natan's other hobbies include throwing things (like his shoes) out the window, and watching them land several stories below. Then he announces, "Mom, I can't find my shoes." I look at him, shocked, but he's already moved on to trying to climb on top of the dresser to retrieve some toys that were put in time-out.

- At 7 p.m., Shimon announces he was promised a trip to the zoo, and he wants to go <u>now</u>, not tomorrow. The fact that the zoo closed an hour ago makes no impression on him.

"Later" means nothing to a child. Gedalia starts crowing, the first sounds he has made in days. Possibly he also wants to go to the zoo now.

- We return to the hotel to have tea with my parents, and Matthew sprints upstairs to turn on the boiler. "Thirty minutes from now, I'm having my first hot shower in what feels like days," he gloats. We get clean with a race-against-time shower, worrying the whole time the water will run out. "Showering this fast stresses me out," I fret, shaving rapidly and cutting my ankle. "Don't bleed on me!" Matthew orders, pushing my bleeding ankle closer to the drain. "Here, let me get you some toilet paper...oh, no, we left the toilet paper in here! It's all soaked!"

- Due to the mosquitoes (and screens being an unheard-of commodity), we spray ourselves with Deep Woods Off before bed and go to sleep smelling like 8th grade camp. "Why are some places so resistant to screens?" I ask drowsily. "San Francisco didn't have them either." Matthew sighs, and I hastily roll over. "I'm going to sleep! NO more talking, I promise!"

- The next day, Dad calls and commands us to go buy diapers for the baby. "What a fiasco! I can't convert kilograms to pounds—do I need to multiply or what? I'm buying based on the photo of the baby on the package." I resolutely take my diapers up to the counter and give the lady all the shekels I have in my possession, letting her decide what change to give me back. When my dad picks us up, he gets irritated. "These are the wrong diapers! These are for much larger babies! You'll have to exchange them." I throw the car door open. "It's not my fault the baby on the package is anorexic! I can't do math, ok?"

- We finally leave with the correct diapers and go pick up the boys for the trip to the zoo. They built a pen with the dining room chairs and are currently pretending to be lambs. Rachel is the Ruler of the Lambs, but they don't listen to the Ruler and just keep doing whatever they want. Natan retrieved his shoes after learning he couldn't go to the zoo without them, and they put on their shoes obediently. Rachel snorts. "They listen to the Ruler when she's telling them they're going somewhere fun," she remarks dryly. We're delayed in getting to the zoo because the kids refuse to wear seat belts. Shimon stops crying when he learns Natan has to wear one too. My dad tells them, "Neither of you goes anywhere without a seat belt, so you can either go home or put them on." He's lost all patience and the kids hear the annoyed tone in his voice. They buckle up right away.

- "Whatever birds they have in this zoo sound like the poison-spitting dinosaurs in Jurassic Park," Matthew murmurs, looking around nervously. Shimon and Natan sprint off immediately, probably to go look for the dangerous birds. Gedalia smiles and chatters, obviously thrilled to be in a peaceful place where his brothers are otherwise occupied. So is Rachel. We lounge around in a grassy area and put Gedalia on a blanket, where he rolls back and forth happily. Eventually, the boys return and we head for the zoo playground. I sit down on a swing Natan vacated, and he wheels around instantly. He screams, "Nooooooo! Nataaaaaaan's!" I get up, but not quickly enough to avoid a finger shaking, a smack on the leg, and having a shovel full of rocks dumped on the swing to discourage other interlopers. "He gets a little possessive of things he likes," my sister tells me unnecessarily. She tries to explain the concept of sharing to Natan, but he's heard it before and still doesn't care for it.

- Back at home, my mom feeds the boys rice soup. She's told me, "They eat so nice for me, no fuss at all. They *always* fuss for Rachel." Now I see why: Mom lets them bring little cars to the table and run them around their bowls, while Rachel does not permit this behavior. "You realize you just make it more difficult for her when you let the boys do these things, right?" I ask my mom, raising an eyebrow. She shrugs. "So?

She makes things more difficult for me too sometimes. She'll live with it."

- My dad goes to get a haircut and returns as a shorn sheep because he hasn't learned the Hebrew for "Not that short." Mom's eyes bug out. "Sam! That haircut looks terrible! I can't go out with you looking like that...unless maybe you wear a big hat." I start laughing, as my dad wearing a giant floppy hat to mask a bad haircut would make things go from bad to worse. He gives me his worst look.

- Rachel and I go to run errands and get dumped out of the car, with no cell phone and no meeting time or place as my dad zooms off. This will prove ugly later. We go to my sister's optometrist, where we're greeted with a giant Out of Business sign. "When did he go out of business, do you think?" she asks distractedly. I shrug. Rachel, who has been wearing only one contact lens for weeks, takes her remaining lens out to reposition it and a gust of wind blows it away. We both just stare down the street after it. "Well, come on. I guess we'll just walk around town looking for another optometrist," she says philosophically, taking my arm to lead her. I am now Guide Dog for the Blind.

- We locate another doctor on the street who agrees to do an exam on the spot. Can we get an Amen! He gives her contacts right away and orders glasses to be ready. She can see again for the first time in ages! "You see how it all worked out?" she asks me, happily swinging her new bag of contacts. I don't point out how we could have wandered around aimlessly all day, because what's the point? Rachel uses the doctor's phone to call my dad. I can hear him yelling, "I've been circling the town looking for you! You never met me! You never called!" My sister looks puzzled. "But we're calling now, from the optometrist...and we didn't have a meeting time or place because you threw us out of the car before...no, we're ready now. Thanks." Matthew, due to additional miscommunication, has been waiting for twenty minutes outside the diaper fiasco shop. "I'm mad too," he announces when we pick him up.

- At home, we find Gedalia hungry and crying, Natan trailing his diaper behind him, and Shimon happily pedaling the tricycle around the living room. My mother has almost cracked under the strain. "How could you leave me alone with them for this long? You know I can't take this," she begins wearily. Rachel expertly changes Natan, feeds Gedalia, and restores order. She's the Ruler!

- Shimon starts crying when he sees we are going in the "auto auto" without him, and I'm tempted to bring a 3-year-old to a Chinese restaurant at 9 p.m. "I'm sure he'll be very good and quiet," I plead. Dad's eyes narrow so much I'm not sure he can see. No one else is tempted. My parents stuff me into the car and leave to eat our first Chinese food in about a year. Mmmm.

- Dad and I take the kids to the park the next day, where Natan kicks me in the rear to get me out of the way on the slide, Shimon rides a chicken he named Auto, and the seat belt debate rages on. "No! Nonononon!" yells Shimon. Dad warns, "You have one more chance to get in the car and put on your seatbelt." No movement. Dad starts the car and begins driving away. Natan nearly passes out; he cannot believe Baba would leave Shimon. "Baba! You forgot Shimon!" he shrieks. Meanwhile, Shimon has begun to sprint after the car, wailing. Dad slows down. "You'll listen to me now?" Shimon, white with fear, nods. Dad allows a small smile to creep over his face. "Still works," he reminds me. As a veteran of being threatened with being left behind, I know for a fact it works. When we arrive home, Rachel asks, "Where are Natan's sandals?" Somehow neither of us noticed he's barefoot. Dad and I head back to the car.

- We get Natan new sandals with dolphins on them. Shimon tries to throw *his* shoes out the window so he can have dolphin sandals as well. Fortunately, he forgets about the sandals with the appearance of a second tricycle. "Now maybe they won't fight!" Mom declares shortsightedly as we have dinner that night.

- On Friday, on our way back to the park, I eat a toffee and Shimon bursts into tears that Aunt Mel took **his** toffee, as though the whole bag was intended for him. I believe he's yelling, "Mine!" but I don't understand him. What does he want me to do, spit it out? Matthew confides, "I'm so happy to go to Dr. Levi the chiropractor, instead of the park in the blazing sun. It was almost worth throwing my back out!" In the blazing sun, the park feels like an oven; I have no idea how the kids play there. But they play on and on, Natan stubbornly refusing to switch his black boots for the new dolphin sandals. "He hates change," Dad mentions philosophically, smoking in the wretched baking heat. The boys are also not interested in drinking bottles of water, only cola. My dad will not give them cola in this heat. "Only water or we go home!"

- Eventually, we pick up Matthew from Dr. Levi's. He enthuses, "I've learned homeopathic remedies for all our ailments. The first one includes sleeping without a pillow. Apparently, pillows are terrible for your neck and back." I tell him, "We can start curing our ailments on Monday. Until then, I want a comfy pillow." I put on a red velvety dress for dinner, dirtied soon after when Gedalia's waffle-diaper overflows on me. Matthew sprints out of the room when he sees what happened. I may have to burn this dress; he definitely won't allow it in the suitcase with his clothes. "You know, Matthew, when you have your own kids, you're going to get pooped on!" Mom calls jovially to him from the living room. Since I'm sure he's got his ears plugged, I just go about getting cleaned up.

- Saturday morning, I make the mistake of arriving without Matthew (he sleeps in and shows up at noon). The kids wander around going, "Where is Uncle Matt?" every five minutes. "They sure love Uncle Matt," Rachel observes, feeding them breakfast as they zoom around the table on their tricycles. "Pit stop!" she yells suddenly, spooning cereal into their mouths like little tricycle-riding baby birds. Matthew arrives in time for lunch and immediately gets a plateful of lamb from Mom. "Just try it," she coaxes. "Everyone likes lamb!"

- I take all three children to the park by myself. Rachel claims, "I'll be right behind you," but shows up twenty minutes later after chatting with the neighbors. In the meantime, I'm left alone with a crying baby, no stroller to put him in, and two toddlers throwing dirt clods at each other. Rachel handles this calmly. "Don't throw dirt in each others' faces. Everywhere else is OK to throw dirt, but not faces," she cautions them. Now that they are *allowed* to throw dirt, they lose interest completely. Rachel smiles triumphantly. Matthew rescues us at the park, as neither child wants to lug his own tricycles home. "Thank you!" I offer tiredly. All my bones hurt from all the playing. He smiles, liking being appreciated.

- We return to the Chinese place for dinner. My mother's moment of glory has come: at some point, she returned to the restaurant and had someone *handwrite a copy of the whole menu into English*. I cannot imagine a waitress back home taking the time to translate a whole menu. Mom begins to **read aloud** the entire menu to our table. I beg her to skip the noodle section since no one wants noodles, but this is her moment to shine and she takes it. We order Cokes. The waitress says, "You will drink Pepsi," and we can't tell if it's a statement or question so we just nod. The translated menu helps immensely and we're all very happy with our dishes. "I'm full of lemon chicken and love," Matthew whispers to me in the car.

- Dad drops us off at our new hotel, the Hotel Adar. We have four steep flights of stairs to climb, so we elect to only take a small plastic bag full of clean clothes, rather than schlepping our giant suitcases up the stairs. Hot water comes on immediately, for which we are so grateful. It's nice to be grateful for things we normally take for granted. We go to sleep peaceful and happy.

- "Let's stop at the bakery for breakfast," I suggest in the morning, sniffing the wonderful baking smells. We go inside and Matthew considers. "I'll have a chocolate milkshake," he tells the waiter. "That does sound good," someone behind us remarks. Suddenly everyone in the place wants one. I buy a box of muffins and take it back to Rachel's for the family to share.

- We hang out until lunch, and I offer to help my sister prepare. She asks me to cut almonds in half for a salad, and I almost cut my hand off trying to slice them lengthways. She gives me a look. "Like this," she demonstrates, placing it flat on the table and cutting it in half to demonstrate. Matthew pipes up, "I've never seen her chop vegetables. Maybe she doesn't know how?" She dismisses me in favor of Matthew, so I go to watch the kids. I do a terrible job: before I can stop him, Shimon goes over to Natan and bites him in the back hard enough to break the skin. I have no idea how my sister restrains herself from smacking him, because I am itching to! Instead, she gives the old "Animals bite, boys don't bite" lecture. Shimon apparently tries to explain the injustice of whatever Natan did to cause this reaction, but Rachel doesn't buy it and puts him in time-out. We all have to kiss Natan's boo-boo. Matthew puts "Muzzles?" on his preparing-for-kids list.

- Matthew holds Gedalia, while I cut the ends off beans. Gedalia makes waffles loudly, and Matthew struggles with his instinct to drop him. "I feel like I should offer to change him, but I just can't. I just have this poo block." Rachel takes the baby away to diaper him, and Matthew shrugs apologetically.

- Shimon asks for pictures of all of us together. I promise to send them to him, and he smacks my leg and says, "No

Shimon! Shimon, Natan and Gedalia package." I don't explain all their names will never fit on an envelope. I'll promise anything, as long as no one cries when we leave for the airport. They don't. Everyone tries to be stoic, but it's so hard when we don't know when we'll see each other next. We're going on a cruise with Mom and Dad tomorrow and then go straight to the airport when we get back. "Say shalom to Aunt Mel and Uncle Matt," Rachel instructs. Then she smiles. "Maybe next visit I'll be Aunt Rachel?" I hug her hard. "I sure hope so," I reply. "I can't wait to be the Ruler!"

Wild Boars

Turkey, Greece and Cyprus
July 2004

My mother, the ultimate adventuress, ironically married a man who hates to leave home. In her wily way, she uses visits from Matthew and I to pry my dad out of his house and onto the high seas (cruises being her best travel option so she can smoke). We decide on a four-day cruise to Turkey, Greece and Cyprus, leaving from Israel, and pack our bags! Little did Matthew and I realize that international cruises aren't as accommodating as our "honeymoona" cruise.

- "I think we bought too much stuff," Matthew remarks nervously, eyeing all the unpacked items. "There's no way we can fit everything into our bags." I decide, "I can fly home in my bathing suit and leave all my other clothes behind to make room for our souvenirs." Matthew rubs his eyes. "I doubt they'll let you on the plane in a bikini," he remarks dryly. Our second unpleasant discovery: we don't have enough clean underwear for the cruise. Our laundry plans were thwarted when the boys poured a bottle of garlic powder into Rachel and Avi's drawers, so all their clothes got pushed to the head of the line. Mom: "You see? I give her things, like garlic powder, and she just wastes them."

- We leave for the port in Haifa with Avi, my brother-in-law, at the wheel. It turns out he doesn't know the way. He's just following signs in general to Haifa, and then asks random other drivers where *they* think the port is, leading to twenty-minute conversations amid blocked traffic and honking horns. At the parking checkpoint, the soldier says: "Did you bring any weapons?" Avi shakes his head. "No," we reply honestly. "Ok, then." And lets us go as though we couldn't possibly be lying. Mom shouts indignantly, "That wasn't a very good check! We could be lying!" but Avi sped away so quickly the guard didn't hear, thank God.

- This turns out to be the last security break we catch. After they scan our bags, Matthew and I are escorted into an interrogation room with a soldier. I can hear my mom going, "What's happening? What's happening?" outside the room and peeking in the little square window. The soldier frowns menacingly at her and continues to interrogate us.

- At Passport Control, they ask for these slips of paper we were given on the plane ride to Israel (although not told what to do with them). If we don't have them, we can't go on the cruise. I frantically rifle through my purse, but Matthew doesn't even bother to ask why no one mentioned this when we **booked** the cruise. By a lucky chance, they happen to be in a side pocket and we can go on. Dad steams, "What kind of place doesn't tell you if you need papers before you arrive?" but Mom doesn't answer. She's too busy going wild in the duty-free cigarette shop. I just cross my fingers she won't ask strangers to use their cigarette allotment for her and somehow get in trouble with security.

- A crush of people congests the little turnstile gate to get on board, frenzying like wild boars at feeding time. The cruise workers optimistically refer to this mad crowd as "the line." One person saunters in to check four hundred people onto the cruise. Dad begins cursing under his breath. We are told three times, "Come back in twenty minutes." It's like being at a nail shop where they claim they'll take you in "Five minutes, five minutes" when ten women are ahead of you. We finally, wearily, board the ship. Mom: "Isn't this exciting??" I'm too busy looking for a bar to answer her.

- Miraculously, our bags rest outside our cabin and we can shower as long as we want. "Did your father book us two twin beds on purpose?" Matthew demands accusingly. "I don't think so. I mean, we're married," I answer, dropping my purse on one of the beds. "I think we just make the best of it."

• The ship, called The Magic 2, sets sail. We assume the Magic 1 sank because of people disregarding the <u>Captain Only</u> sign and pushing buttons at random on the bridge. Just like they are doing here on the Magic 2. There are No Smoking signs *everywhere,* with people smoking directly beneath the sign. A theme for the trip: everyone will flout the rules except us. Upon boarding, we're issued our cruise charge cards, and are told "everything will be explained." They do explain everything, in Hebrew, which we don't understand. My mom reassures Dad and Matthew, "Melissa and I already know what charge cards look like and how to use them, so it's fine." Sadly, they both already know and fear this fact.

• Our cabin apparently doubles as a meat locker for the kitchens. "I think the numbers are in Celsius, so I can't figure out which way to turn the knob!" I wail, twirling the dials fruitlessly. Mom triumphantly crows, "I told you to bring a sweater in case you were cold! I told you!" I don't point out that everywhere else has been 95 degrees or hotter, and the AC knob clearly broke off at its lowest possible setting. Because what's the point, she's *always* right.

• At dinnertime, we're waved into the dining room by the head waiter/bouncer. "Sit where you like," he invites us graciously. We start walking toward a table when another family literally sprints in and starts grabbing chairs. Getting seating at dinner turns into musical chairs; those who don't run in fast enough have to wait for the other diners to leisurely finish their coffee and chatting. "Don't they know other cruise lines do seating at specific tables at specific times to avoid this?" Matthew asks Dad incredulously. "They don't know anything here," he snaps, shoving a portly man out of the way and snatching a chair, "and they don't try to figure it out, either." Our waiter introduces himself as Mykos, from Bulgaria. Matthew, despite getting his degree in international business, did not know Bulgaria existed. "I thought they just made it up in Chitty Chitty Bang Bang." Mykos worked for Carnival Cruises and looks shocked and horrified by both the buffet dining system and the wild boars galloping through the dining room.

- Every time he comes to the table, he says, "A thousand pardons for interrupting…" Matthew wants to know why I don't say that every time I interrupt him. "Because I didn't grow up in a Bulgarian gulag," I reply sardonically, pouring myself some coffee. "Oh, sorry, I mean Chitty Chitty Bang Bang Land." He gives me a grim look. We all like the healthy food, and there are no sundae bars or 24-hour pizza shops, so we may avoid gaining back the ten pounds we gained on our last cruise.

- After dinner, all of us separate to get massages. When we booked them, I yelled, "That's it? Only $40 for an hour? That's so cheap! We'll take two hours!" like the requisite ugly American. Matthew whispered, "You are staying in the cabin from now on if you keep doing that."

Alanya, Turkey

- I get shoved into a wall by the people running into the dining hall at breakfast. I gingerly rejoin "the line" for the buffet. There are two plates left, and a morbidly obese lady wearing a T-shirt reading "Don't You Think I'm Sexy?" in rhinestones reaches in and snatches them <u>both</u> away from me. My dad motions at me to snatch them back, but I prefer not to sink into that sort of behavior. Matthew ventures, "I don't think she can read English or she <u>never</u> would have bought that T-shirt." Mom turns to read it, and then whirls on Dad. "So you don't think I'm sexy?" she demands out of the blue. When we all stare at her, befuddled, she explains, "If you did, you should have bought me that T-shirt, Sam." Dad wrests four plates from the fresh pile. "I would never buy something so tacky, and I would never allow you to wear something so tacky," he announces loudly, earning a dirty look from the Rhinestone Cowgirl herself.

- Our surly waitress only gives us coffee in intervals, like she's doling out medication. We want Mykos! Undeterred, Mom gets up and gets the whole pot herself and brings it back to our table. I'm a little nervous she's fitting in so well with this aggressive crowd, but I do want more coffee...

- After breakfast, we go out to the pool (the size of a large hot tub) to check out the aerobics class going on at rock concert decibel levels. Matthew covers his eyes to avoid seeing the hairy Yeti-men doing aerobics in Speedos. Even the little boys have Speedos, but aren't quite so hairy. Yet. "Giorgio would fit in perfectly here," I whisper to Matthew. He answers from behind his hands, "Yeah, he'd love it."

- Dad lies and says, "I'm running down to the cabin to change. I'll meet you soon." Instead, he goes to the duty-free store to buy a DVD player without asking Mom, and to the casino without telling anyone. Mom grumbles for hours until he returns and cavalierly admits where he went. Matthew and I immerse ourselves in our books as they fight. "You pilfer away all our money on crap..." "I'm not the one who bought the straw wine donkey..." "That donkey was cute! I still want to know what you did with it!"

- We begin docking in Alanya, Turkey, and a crowd of people disregard the CREW ONLY signs and open the doors to the crew area so they can see better. We go downstairs, so if the ship starts listing because of all the people hanging over the bow, we'll be nearest the exits.

- Upon boarding our tour bus, the tour guide begins shouting at us. "You should have been here at 1:30! Where were you?" Dad snaps back, "The schedule says 2 p.m., not 1:30." The guide continues to mutter and hate us. He speaks Hebrew for five minutes straight, and then in English says, "There are olive trees here." We suspect we are getting screwed on the English tour, as our tour brochure claims we're on the ancient Silk Road to Asia, and passing a Seljuk fortress, the Red Fort. The guide: "There were Christians here, then Arabs came in and everyone became Muslim," as though voluntarily. He should write fairy tales.

- Mom begs to be let off on a deserted mountain road when she spots a stall selling scarves. She fervently assures us she'll catch up later. The guide pretends he doesn't speak English, even though we've seen him do it. Mom presses her nose to the window, sadly watching the scarves retreat into the distance.

- After driving through winding mountain roads at top speed, the bus screeches to a halt at a piknik restaurant. Throughout Turkey, these restaurants, called pikniks, seat you in the middle of a river or stream. The tables and chairs are in the water, so you can wade out to your table and sit with your legs in the water. Then the waiters wade out to serve you. This one also has a swimming hole with a rope swing a little further downstream. "I've never seen anything like this," I marvel to Matthew and he hugs me. These kinds of places are why we love traveling.

- They also have little floating barges with canopies, and you sit on cushions on the floor of the barge. I'd love to get one of those, but Mom claims she'll never be able to get out of one so we choose a regular table. As he sips a Turkish beer, Matthew becomes depressed. "We could make millions opening a place like this in California, but some idiot would slip into the water and drown and his survivors would sue." I look around and scope out the hole-in-the-ground toilets, which I can't negotiate due to poor balance. "If we do open one, our customers would have a moral dilemma: pee in the river around everyone's feet or hope not to slip into the hole-in-the-ground toilet and fall in?" I head for the toilet, white-knuckling the little handrails as I crouch clumsily. If only there were doors...or a handy planter.

- We return to the port area on Mr. Toad's Wild Bus Ride on mountain roads with 100-foot drops and no guardrails. Thank God I used the hole-in-the-ground or I would probably wet my pants. I spot a shop with things that sparkle and run off, eager to begin my shopping spree! I grab a pair of curly-toed slippers, but I see 40 written on the bottom. I ask the salesman, "Does that mean they're $40?" He laughs heartily. "No, they're size 40 and they cost $4." Matthew only allows me to buy one pair even though "they're so cheap." I compensate by buying a lot of other things. The owner of the shop invites us to tea. My dad asserts, "He probably invites everyone so he can sell tea sets." Matthew says it's a hospitality thing and please don't embarrass him. Too late, because Mom tells Palet, the owner, she doesn't like tea and could he make her some coffee instead since she couldn't get any at breakfast, because we had a rude waitress...

- We end up buying two tea sets. My dad shoots Matthew a smug look. As soon as we board the boat, Matthew laments not buying an authentic Turkish rug. Someone overhears him and assures us, "Oh, they make the Turkish rugs in Greece, so you can get one tomorrow." Matthew orders another Turkish beer. "At least I want something authentic from Turkey," he says defiantly.

- The only announcement in English on the ship so far: "All passengers need to return to the ship. We will be sailing in five minutes." How could you hear this announcement unless you were, in fact, already on the ship? And why in *English*, since the four English speakers are **not** the ones with the punctuality problems?

- We beat the wild boars to dinner, feeling like Olympic champions. On the way out, we see them clamoring and pounding at the door like they have Golden Tickets to the Wonka Factory. The bouncer shouts angrily at them and flails his arms. Fleeing to the Captain's Club lounge, Matthew tries cognac and becomes depressed that neither of us likes classy liquors, like brandy or cognac. The Lionel Richie music supports his depressed mood. Then we go back to our twin bed cabin, which depresses him further. "I hate having sex in a twin. I feel like I'm in high school," Matthew complains afterward. I'm too sleepy to answer.

Rhodes, Greece

• I drag Matthew out of bed at 7 a.m. to beat the crowd to breakfast. We get Mykos to wait on us again and get coffee refills to our hearts' content. Matthew heads out to the pool for his morning swim, avoiding the Yeti Aerobics class by coming early. We arranged to meet my folks at 9:15. They have apparently adopted Middle Eastern punctuality, as I call at 9:15 and Mom is just getting out of the shower. "This does not bode well for you," I warn Dad. He just hangs up on me.

• We're among the first on our tour bus today, a complete waste of our time, because we find out eventually that the bus can't leave without forty-six people. Forty-six people have not yet *purchased* the tour package, so we all have to wait for people to arbitrarily buy tickets at the last minute. Finally, the people who bought tickets ahead of time flip out on the bus driver and he leaves, reiterating the idea that if you throw a loud enough tantrum, you'll get what you want. We can't get out of the dock gate because of Olympic security. Matthew: "Aren't the Olympics on a completely different island?" Finally, a guy whose job involves riding around on his motorcycle and smoking, unlocks the padlock and chain on the gate. Then it's a free-for-all, par for the course here.

• On the tour, we learn the Colossus of Rhodes, one of the ancient wonders of the world, was destroyed by Arab invaders and sold for bronze. Maybe they "became Muslim" here too. Later on, Matthew feels a little disappointed in the ruins of Athena's temple (literally two pillars in a field). He thought there would be more complete structures, but plainly that's why they are called *ruins*. Our first stop: a ceramic factory, where we watch them make vases and plates by hand. Matthew whispers, "This would go so much quicker if they had machines. They're just like the Jack Daniels bottle people." He buys two vases and a plate, and I buy Jonathan and Courtney vases too. As we re-board the bus, we determine one person is missing. The bus driver leaves anyway, shrugging and remarking, "Cab fare back to the port costs a lot." I'm shocked at his callousness, but then remember Greeks left sick babies on a hillside to die. We can't expect too much sympathy.

• Our bus driver, blasting the *Evanescence* CD, drops us off at Lindos, the home of the Acropolis. My family bails on the Acropolis after learning it will take the whole hour we're allotted in Lindos to get up there on a donkey. "We've seen what the bus driver does if people are late," Dad tells us ominously, looking especially hard at Mom. She ignores him. "Who wants to ride a donkey anyways? I bet they don't let them in the shops." Once in the city, we almost get stampeded by a herd of escaped, angry donkeys. A chubby little man runs after them, but he doesn't have a prayer of catching them.

• I dodge into a shop, where I break a perfume tester. "I'm so sorry!" I cry, embarrassed. "Your whole shop smells like Happy now. I'll pay for the perfume." The shop owner comes over. "That'll be three euro," she informs me hesitantly. I stop short. "Three euro? Isn't that around five dollars?" I ask incredulously. Mom and I buy at least six bottles of perfume each, congratulating ourselves on saving gobs of money. The owner's so thrilled with her big sale she gives us scarves to take home. Matthew finally buys his Turkish rug in the Old City, although he's appalled at the exchange rate. I can't even read the receipt since it's in Greek. He could have paid eleventy million euros for all I care — I have enough perfume for my whole life!

- The Rhodes synagogue has stood for over five hundred years. There are only thirty Jews left on Rhodes after most were murdered or deported in World War II. These thirty survived and vowed to restore the synagogue, which they did with funding from American Express. They can only perform certain services with ten men or more, so our tour makes up the additional men needed for them to say these prayers. Dad and Matthew are moved to be part of the services. Mom and I buy wraparound pants from a vendor passing by outside. "I'll take the orange ones for me, and black for Glynis," I decide. Mom buys Tía Lupe some black ones too. They're both tall and thin and will look amazing in these pants.

- Back on the ship, we find we've missed lunch and have to go to the Captain's Club for a restricted menu. The waitress tells us what four items are available. Mom: "I don't want any of those things. Can I see the menu?" The waitress repeats, "There is no menu," three times before Mom sulkily orders a grilled cheese sandwich. I point out she's lucky they have food at all since we missed lunch. She retorts, "We're paying for the cruise. They have to feed us."

- Back in our twin bed cabin, I try to figure out the Rubik's Cube of my new orange wraparound pants. After almost strangling myself, I finally get them tied on. My new belly dancing scarves from Turkey look great over them!

Cyprus

- Getting off the ship at the Cyprus port, we're directed to get on the #30 bus to get into town. Unfortunately, the #30 bus teems with our fellow passengers, who are arguing with the bus driver over why he can't make change for a twenty for the whole crowd (even though the sign says, "Exact change"). "Let's get a cab," Matthew suggests wearily and Dad agrees. The cab ride traumatizes me. They drive on the opposite side of the road here, like England. "I feel like I'm in a car chase scene!" I complain. The cabbie lets us out in the shopping area and on impulse I buy a gold and scarlet leather hassock. Matthew points out, "We don't need that," about a hundred times before I remind him of his eleventy million euro rug. He shuts it. Besides, we're on our third currency, Cypriot pounds, and I can't even pretend to have a clue how much anything costs.

- We elect to take another white-knuckle cab ride to Dassoudi Beach on the Mediterranean. Dad pays $20 for four lounge chairs and two umbrellas, a steal! Mom sits bolt upright. "Why aren't those women wearing tops?" she questions sternly, pointing at the least-attractive women on the beach. Their floppy boobs droop all over the place. Matthew winces. "Vicki, it's not as though we want to be looking at their boobs. But the Mediterranean has a lot freer of a culture than the States." Somehow Dad still gets in trouble for coming here, even though Mom was the one who heard about it on the ship and insisted on coming here.

- I love a beach where they bring your beers right to you! Plus, you can order milkshakes and fries as well! I lay happily on my lounge chair, drinking my chocolate milkshake. "This is the life," I announce. I would take my top off too, but not in front of my dad. Matthew and I discuss parasailing but decide against it. "Sharks could see us for miles around," I warn Matthew.

- Mom says she'll be right back; she's just going across the street. She returns two hours later in a new disguise hat and muumuu. Meanwhile, we all have been cultivating ulcers since she left and we realized we might not make it back to the ship in time. We barely make it, since Mom, despite hearing the ship's horn honking, fools around in the gift shop at the dock till I physically drag her out. "I swear Vicki, if you miss the ship, I'm not coming back to get you," Dad warns. Mom retorts, "Why not? So you could go back to that pervert beach?"

- Matthew and I pack that night. Mom warns us not to put our bags out too early because "pranksters and hooligans" may do something to them. We try not to crack up right in front of her, but it's beyond my ability to hold it in. "Even with these extra duffel bags we bought, we barely have enough room," Matthew tells me, straining to zip his bag. The rug takes up ninety percent of the room.

Return to Haifa

- All the crew did with our bags was pile them up at the end of the hall and block the stairwell. "Typical," sighs Matthew, scrambling over the luggage blockade to get back in later that night. Housekeeping keys in at 6:30am to wake us up. Matthew grabs at the covers and yells, "It says Privacy Please for a reason!" but she doesn't speak any English. Mayhem at breakfast. The sign on the door says Closed, but someone decides he wants to go in anyway. He opens the door, and the bouncer, purple with rage, pushes him out into the hall. There are no pancakes or croissants left when we get inside. Or plates.

- Upon entering the debarkation terminal, we hear a man flipping out. Not your normal I-want-my-way-and-I want-it now yelling so common to these parts, but **seriously** yelling...until he gets spirited away by Security. There are three people working passport control for four hundred passengers, who—surprise surprise—start yelling and complaining. Complaining needs no translation. A police officer comes in and announces: "If you are unhappy with the service you are receiving, contact the Ministry of Tourism to complain." He follows up with a "What am I supposed to do?" shrug and head shaking. He leaves quickly. Matthew and I get stopped at all three security checkpoints again.

- Cruising with my parents has been a good way to see some of the surrounding countries and experience new cultures firsthand. As my dad points out, "Some cultures are crap," and despite being brainwashed to be politically correct, Matthew and I wholeheartedly agree. Wild boars indeed! My mom just smiles her "I got out of the house for four days, yippee for me!" smile and says nothing. She'd face worse than wild boars to have a little fun these days. We drive back to Netanya with Mom and Dad to be close to the airport for our early flight tomorrow.

• Dad complains about all the other drivers while making unsafe lane changes, tailgating cars ahead of us, and slamming on his brakes for people tailgating us.

• Mom fills the drive time by asking questions that we don't know the answer to:
  • "Why is the road wet here?'
  • "What are those people doing?"
  • "Where is the next restaurant?"
  • "Why don't the police stop him?"

• Dad tries to parallel park in a tight space. A French woman comes by and says, "You can't park there." I wonder what new sign Dad is ignoring, and he asks suspiciously, "Why not? There's no sign!" She looks perplexed. "Because your car won't fit." She gives us her space, but Mom worries she tricked us into parking in a tow away zone because the French are anti-Semitic. We point out the anti-Semitic French people aren't the ones coming to Israel — they're the French Jews fleeing anti-Semitic France.

• My parents force Matthew and I to swap hotel rooms because their room, a comfortable temperature, is "too hot. It's like an oven. Or the park." I'm freezing cold in our room, so we go with the swap. In the morning, Mom snips, "Well, thanks a lot for giving us the bad room." Somehow, it's our fault their AC died, their bed was lumpy, and the view was bad. I mention how much we appreciated the improved view *while we were asleep*, but irony is lost on everyone but Matthew. "I got it," he whispers, squeezing my hand sympathetically.

- We go down for breakfast at 7 a.m., since the sign by the desk said Breakfast 7-9. The clerk laughs and says, "That sign is four years out of date. Breakfast is at 8." My parents throw a fit and they open the dining room early for us. Despite the fact they have already pushed it, my mom begins asking the kitchen staff, who is still setting up for the 8 a.m. breakfast, for things like coffee and jam. "Not ready yet!" the waitress protests. Dad raises his eyebrows. "You best get it ready!"

- Drive to the airport. The commentary track from Mom:
  - "Watch it, Sam....WATCH IT! You almost hit another car!"
  - "I can't just pretend to be happy if I'm not happy. You're leaving; of course I'm not happy."
  - "I don't remember having all of those fights before your wedding, Melissa. I think you must be exaggerating." (!!!!)
  - "Are you turning left, Sam? I can't tell which way you're turning, because you're looking ahead. Don't look ahead if you're going to turn."
  - "Where is the restroom in this parking lot?" (No, there are no restrooms in parking lots there either.)

- Dad finally tells her to zip it. I can't believe he only said zip it. I'm sure he's thinking bad words to himself. Undeterred, she announces that if she didn't "help him drive," he'd get into accidents all the time. I point out that my dad has never actually had a car accident, ever. She blithely replies, "Because of my help."

- Happily, at the airport we get moved to a special line for people who'll be late for their flight to JFK. Sadly, I realize I have left my toiletry bag, containing my Pills, in the car. Matthew refuses to let me signal my parents. That's the last bit of drama we need—my parents getting hauled off by Security as we flee the country. "It obviously hasn't hit you that you'll be wearing condoms for a month, right?" I demand as we board the plane. The stunned look on his face tells me he didn't think of that. Perhaps my parents can FedEx the Pills? "Or maybe in two weeks the Pill will be out of my system, like Courtney said?" Matthew looks stunned for the second time in two minutes. "The peace and quiet bothers you that much?" Matthew asks, obviously not missing my nephews as much as I do. Then he looks at me. "We're not ready for kids yet. You know that, right?" Yeah, yeah, I know. Not yet. But soon...

Nowhere to Eat at Pike's Market

Seattle, WA
January 2005

Liz has somehow convinced her entire family to move to Washington to be near her. Hmm, that must be nice to have a family that doesn't completely abandon you and move to another country. How novel. The more time we spend with the Finnertys, the more attractive having a close-knit family looks.

Suggested Soundtrack: "Coconut"-Harry Nilsson, "Let's Stay Together"-Al Green, anything by The Wiggles

- Announcement at the airport: "Will the driver of a tan Toyota Camry, with three small children inside, please return to your vehicle? It is in the process of being cited and towed. We need you to remove your children." We hear the announcement repeated five times, indicating the parents WANT the children to be towed away.

- As we make our way to the terminal, Matthew realizes he has to run back to the car and leave his pocketknife, which will never pass security. I give a loud sigh of despair when we see the long security line, and head to the electronic ticket counter. "Excuse me, but I keep getting an error message telling me to see the ticket agent," I announce. Dan the ticket agent takes our IDs and says, "I have your reservation here, but since *you're both on the FCC Security List*, I have to go make a phone call..." Matthew resigns himself to missing our first flight ever and we determine that neither of us knows what happens if you miss your flight. Do you just get another one? Or do they take your money and run? Eventually, Dan comes back and we are allowed to get boarding passes, leaving me to wonder how he convinced them over the phone that we didn't seem threatening. How many Johnsons are on that list, anyway? I figure I'll use my 10% off coupon another time. We sprint to the gate, panting as we near the gate agent, who sneers, "Johnson?" even though we have *eight* minutes before we depart. She reprimands us for holding up the whole plane anyway, and makes us check our bags at the gate with hot pink tickets. "They may as well say 'Busted!' on them," I whisper indignantly to Matthew as we board.

• The tiny Holly Hobby plane has only two seats on each side and an aisle not wide enough for our bags. Are the other passengers all carrying Snoopy kids' luggage? Across the aisle, a woman needlepoints a *Winnie the Pooh* sampler. We're a security risk, but they let her on with a giant needle? Her adorable daughter tugs on her arm and says, "I want shampoo! Shampoo!" We hope she isn't carrying head lice. She shoves a Shamu stuffed toy at the little girl to shut her up.

• Colin picks us up at the airport with surprises: four bottles of kosher wine (the good stuff!), two challah bread loaves, and packages of kosher turkey and pastrami from the deli! Matthew feels cheated that there is no pastrami at *our* grocery store back home. I can tell he's trying to think of a nice way to tell me he's not sharing the pastrami with me. "Don't worry," I assure him, "I have no interest in that pastrami." His face lights up. "I love you so much!" he tells me gratefully.

• We end up at lunch at Red Robin. I ask the waitress, "Which is better, the Gardenburger or Boca Burger patty?" She replies, "I don't know, I don't eat pretend hamburgers." I opt for the Boca Burger. I feel like calling her snapperhead like Surly Jason.

- "We're home!" Colin announces, and Jordan comes running to give Daddy hugs. At age four, Jordan won't hug us as he's too big for that, but gives us high-fives instead. We'll take them.

- Liz and Jordan get into a tussle of nose blowing vs. nose picking. Jordan insists that picking "gets the bugs out." He's not wrong, but we do see Liz's point. In the struggle, Jordan hits Liz and gets a time-out in the Room of Punishment (the laundry room). He eventually apologizes. Liz says, "Are you sorry for hitting Mommy?" Jordan shouts back, "No, for picking my nose." An apology is an apology, even if it's for the wrong thing, and he bounds to freedom.

- I go up to take a shower and break the towel rack. I can't fix it with any available implements in the bathroom. Why do things like this always happen to me? At least it's not the medicine cabinet. I don't go poking around those any more. Inexplicably, a jar of jellybeans sits on the bathroom counter, possibly for snacks? Jordan solves the mystery for me when he goes to the potty. "How many jellybeans do I get for number two?"

- Jordan gets very excited about eating the challah bread with the honey, and exclaims, "Isn't it funny how a bear likes honey?" Liz asks Jordan what he wants for dinner. "Doughnuts." No. "Ok, honey then." We break open the first bottle of wine at dinner, and Matthew tells Colin we have a one-glass <u>minimum</u> for Sabbath. Colin considers converting to Judaism for the wine, and Jordan will convert to **any** religion encouraging the eating of honey, because "Isn't it funny how a bear likes honey?" Jordan also makes himself a "harmonica"/yarmulke, out of a bread crust. All the crumbs left in his hair do not amuse Liz. She's consoled there was no honey on that piece, as Jordan doesn't actually eat the bread. He's only licking the honey off.

- After dinner, Jordan tells Colin he needs a new tummy, and he can screw one in as soon as he gets his tool set out. When asked where he will buy the new tummy, he answers, "Old Navy!" Colin shoots Liz a look that says, "This boy spends too much time at the mall." Matthew violates the laws of Sabbath by getting sucked into Jordan's Home Depot toy tool set, and turns on a play sander. I'm not sure Matthew actually knows what a real life sander *does*, but he seems entertained by the play one. Jordan performs an after-dinner concert of "Let's Stay Together'" from *Pulp Fiction*. He encores with "Coconut." Matthew wants Jordan to go backwards up the stairs and sing "So Long, Farewell" like Gretl in *The Sound of Music*, but he does not exist solely for our entertainment.

- We awaken the next morning to Jordan and Colin yelling, "Yee-ha!" in the upstairs bathroom as Jordan gets blown dry from his bath. Liz comes down with Jordan to feed him breakfast. "Doughnuts?" he requests hopefully, but Liz holds firm on the healthy-food front. Colin gets Lucky Charms, "the cereal of my people," and Jordan asks for "Daddy Cheerios." (Also known as Lucky Charms). Colin tries to trick him with *actual* Cheerios, and Jordan shakes his head and says, "Not those! **DADDY** Cheerios." He shakes the box for emphasis. Liz crosses her arms, wondering how Colin will explain this apparent hypocrisy. Colin says, "Mommy will tell you when you're old enough for Daddy Cheerios," and escapes.

- Colin, Matt, Jordan and I hike a trail near their house, Jordan wearing cowboy boots despite the snowy path. Yee-ha! We end up at the playground by their house and Jordan plays on the jungle gym. Matthew attempts to test drive a small rocking elephant. I hear him say worriedly, "Hey, this spring is pretty loose...GAH!" Colin falls to the ground laughing, right by where Matthew flipped headfirst over the elephant and landed on his back in a pile of woodchips, the elephant bobbing maniacally back and forth. Colin and I crack up at random the rest of the day, remembering how funny and startled Matthew looked as he was doing a flip.

- Jordan stages a sit-in protest against going home, using Ghandi as his model. Colin lures Jordan with (false) promises of "hot cocoa...*and* we'll play Candyland!" The rest of us take naps when we get home, and then Liz takes Jordan to the library. Colin sifts through the book choices.

  - "What's that one, Jordan?"
  - "'Book Book', Daddy."
  - "No, it's called—hey, it **is** called 'Book Book'! What's this one? 'I Want a Pet'? What's Mommy doing getting dirty books like this one! No pets!"

- The nose picking/no picking lobbyists continue to disagree. Liz, idealistic: "Jordan, get a tissue and blow your nose." Colin, realistic: "Jordan, pick your nose in your own room, not in front of everyone." Liz's sister, Janet, and her husband, Jeremy, weigh in when they come over to baby-sit Jordan while we all go out to dinner and a movie. "Picking your nose is gross, Jordan," Janet tells him definitely. We have dinner at Frankie's, an Italian place near the house.

- Liz and I insist on seeing *The Phantom of the Opera* (according to Matthew and Colin, "The *Ishtar* of our time.") Highlights:

  - The Phantom actor cannot sing. Not at all. He's almost as bad as Jacob, my choir camp boyfriend. The mask he wears covers a face like road kill, Fraggle Rock puppet hair, and a glue-on mustache doubling as an eyebrow.

  - We see the Phantom's lair—what a dump. Like The Grotto. Liz whispers, "He brings one guest down here, **ever**, and doesn't even bother to clean up?" Matthew wants to know how he got the Pottery Barn catalog down there, and where he had them deliver the furniture.

  - Raoul tries to run after Christine when she gets kidnapped, but looks discouraged upon seeing eleventy million spiral stairs he has to go down to find her. "Where's the elevator?" I whisper to Liz, and then burst out laughing as he falls through a trap door conveniently located in the **solid stone** stairs. "Oh, here it is," Liz snickers.

- A mesh grate begins to magically lower itself onto Raoul. "The Phantom's Erector Set came with a remote?" Matthew asks scathingly. He's already totting up all the bad movies I owe him for this one, and mutters, "Joel Schumacher totally ripped this off from the trash compacter scene in *Star Wars*." He considers, and then adds, "I would rather be compacted in trash than swim in the Paris sewer system."

- Back at home, Janet asks Liz, "Where did these stains in the carpet come from?" Liz and Jeremy accuse Colin of gesturing while intoxicated and spilling drinks on the rug. Janet points out that Colin did the same thing at her wedding. Colin retorts, "That was *less* traumatic than when I knocked over a whole tray of glasses at Melissa and Matt's wedding!" (while gesturing with a drink in his hand). Matthew and I in unison: "You did what!?!" Janet also mentions that Jordan cheated at Candyland and just went as many spaces as he felt like. Colin: "I'm glad we didn't play with him earlier, if he was going to cheat." Liz begins cleaning Colin's wine stains off the carpet. Matthew questions why *some* adults, like Colin and I, don't use sippy cups instead open glasses.

- Before falling asleep, Matthew wishes for a black cape to flourish dramatically in meetings, along with his own theme music which could somehow be wired into the cape. "But not organ music, like the stupid Phantom." Does everyone talk about these things in bed or only my husband?

- We hit Denny's for breakfast again. "We only come here with you guys," Liz says innocently, unaware that she associates us with tacky Denny's. Jordan uses his pancakes as a vehicle to deliver whipped cream and cherries to his mouth, but not much else. Jordan and Liz go home for naptime, while Colin, Matthew and I go to Snoqualmie Falls. The Falls are beautiful and impressive. We hike around all afternoon and play in the snow. "Let's get drinks in Salish Lodge," I suggest, and Colin seconds. Matthew points out, "We are going to Liz's parents' house for dinner soon. Maybe don't drink, say, **four** Captain and Cokes before we go." Colin and I look startled and begin counting our empty glasses. "Fine, No-Fun Boy!" I slur, finishing Captain and Coke #3 defiantly. Matthew notices a bar on the way home with a sign reading, "Welcome Hunters!" "Do the hunters drink <u>before</u> they go out hunting, resulting in lots of accidental shootings? Or after?"

• At dinner, Janet brings up the Oprah episode she saw that day about women with gay husbands. Matthew tells the story of how one of his shipmates in the Navy found videotape **in the camera** of her husband and his male best friend having sex while they were supposed to be babysitting the kids. It wins as Best Story. Dinner with Liz's family—her parents, both sisters and their husbands, and all of us makes me really miss my own family. Not that dinner with my family is always this relaxing, but I miss being part of the day to day life of my own parents and sister. I wonder if I'll ever stop missing them and wondering if it would be better to move to Israel.

• Back home, things are very quiet. Matthew revels in it, but I miss the sound of Jordan's chatter and funny comments and little songs. I miss my own nephews and the same things. Is it really time? Maybe I'm ready for some family of my own. "It's not that you're not enough for me," I assure Matthew as we get ready for bed one night. "It's just that I think I'm ready for more." He asks plaintively, "Can we just do a few more things first?" The List of Things to do Before Kids gets started that night.

Brendan is Your Friendan to the Endan

Lake Tahoe
January 2005
Over the past two years, since meeting up with them in San Francisco, Matthew and I have become good friends with Brendan and Leah. They invite us on a ski trip right before my 32ⁿᵈ birthday, and we have a great time...other than the whole skiing part.

Suggested Soundtrack: "The Reason"-Hoobastank, anything by U2, "So I Married an Axe Murderer"-soundtrack

- I pull us into the magic long-term parking lot discovered on last our trip out of San Diego. "It doesn't look so good in the daylight," I mention, noticing we access the lot by a service road and pass by a row of burnt-out Border Patrol bunkers. Matthew thinks we're in Watts.

- Once past Security, we scope out our food options. "If I eat pizza, I'll feel like throwing up the whole flight," I debate, "but pizza always sounds so good." Matthew, claiming he'll scout for food, returns with a mini pizza for himself and nothing for me, saying, "I didn't know what you wanted." I stare ominously at him. "But you knew I wanted *something*, right? So how could you come back here with nothing for me?" He shrugs, shoveling cheese into his mouth. I feel like smacking him as I get up to procure my own pizza. Serve him right if I throw up on him! We doubt we'll get seats together as the flight looks full, but Matthew tries to look on the bright side: "Someone will probably switch because no one would want to sit by either of us." He's right—we are undesirable seatmates, what with our giant coats and stinky pizza smell.

- Brendan greets us at the airport and we drive over to Avis. "Can you only get a job here if you're Sikh?" I wonder aloud. Clearly there's some nepotism in the staffing. Matthew winces as Brendan asks me to remove a cone so he can park directly in front of the door. Matthew assumes the cone was there for a reason and the police will cite us for illegal cone movement. Sikh #12 at the rental counter keeps asking if I am going to be driving, to which Matthew resoundingly says, "No. She will not be driving any large vehicles in snow." I scowl at him, then peer at his driver's license. "That's from four addresses ago," I accuse him. He looks embarrassed. "I know, but I like the picture."

- 750,000 Explorers, our rental car of choice, have been recalled due to faulty cruise control switches catching on fire, which alarms no one but me. Brendan and Matthew reason, "If we don't use the cruise control, it won't catch on fire," but I conjecture the switch is connected to other things that might be flammable as well. Brendan reflects on this. "Well, definitely don't mention that to Leah," he warns me. Brendan leads us from the airport to his house like a scene out of *Mission: Impossible*. Matthew struggles to keep up in the behemoth vehicle, but clearly loves the height of the SUV.

- We go out to a Chinese restaurant for dinner, where Brendan speaks Chinese to the staff and we have no idea what he's ordering us. "Don't get me noodles," Matthew pleads. "I hate noodles." While waiting for our food, they describe their recent trip to Japan:

  - In Japan where they stayed, the owner of the place had them remove their shoes upon entering and gave them house slippers to wear. Additionally, you get WC (water closet) slippers that you wear when you use the toilet, because obviously you need special footwear for that. The potty slippers have a picture of a man peeing on them, so they can distinguish themselves from the other slippers. "If you do not choose to wear your potty slippers and leave them outside the door, the owner will twirl out and bang on the door while you're in there, as though at that point you would open the door and change shoes," Brendan reminisces.

- Leah tells us disgustedly, "The owner didn't give us new slippers either, but ones other people had worn already. Oh, and we also had to shower before taking your bath, because everyone used the same boiling hot bath water. If you miss your half-hour window of bath time, the owner would twirl out about that too."

- I refrain from asking the obvious question: "What if someone peed in the communal bath, either wearing the WC slippers or not?"

- I go to the bathroom and Brendan starts banging on the door, even going so far as to pop the lock with his keychain, being possibly as obnoxious as the owner of the Japanese hotel. I'm already washing my hands though, and making mental notes to avoid Japan. As I return to the table I hear Matthew asking, "Why do the plates have pictures of dragons, rising suns and then randomly, ice cream cones on them?" Brendan checks and says, "Those are clouds, not ice cream cones." Matthew now wants to know why we can't have a lazy Susan on our table at home to relieve the unnecessary burden of handing things to each other, until Brendan spins it around and it clips water glasses and teacups, spilling them over. "That's why," I tell him unnecessarily, mopping up my water. "But I wouldn't spin it around that fast," Matthew empty-promises. Leah laughs. "Yeah, Brendan would promise that too, but it would be a lie."

- Other dinner stories:

  - Leah went scuba diving at night with only a flashlight, giving her two feet of visibility. Matthew: "How does it feel when the last thing you see is a giant set of jaws two feet away? Sharks could be anywhere, you know!"

- Brendan, while in Fiji, drank hallucinogenic beverages with natives, and then decided to go out on a boat with a couple of guys going spear fishing. He dove into the water to swim with the fish, conveniently forgetting that *men with spears* were aiming them into the water right around him. He surfaced and found the fishermen were suddenly nowhere to be seen, a la *Open Water*. So he swam to shore where the fishermen greeted him with, "Did you see the size of that **shark** out there?"

- Brendan recommends befriending a Sikh family while in India, because they carry swords and will protect you from the Indian mafia. I regret not being friendlier back at Avis.

- Guides will try to dissuade you from touching, say, a giant poisonous caterpillar, but Brendan "does not put much store" in those kinds of warnings and pets the caterpillar anyway. I ask faintly, "Why would you feel compelled to touch anything that *might* be poisonous?"

- Matthew accuses me of "limiting his adventures" by forbidding him from going on the Great White Shark Adventure Boat off the Farillon Islands. I remind him, "I don't want to be married to someone with hook hands or a peg leg when it gets eaten by Jaws leaping out of the chum water. Besides, you get seasick."

- After some debate, we decide to leave for Tahoe at 7 a.m. "Let's get Dan to buy the chains," Leah suggests. "That'll save us one stop, since we don't know how long the drive will be." Brendan scoffs optimistically, "It shouldn't take any longer than four hours." Leah is a realist: "There could be traffic, it could be snowing, we might still have to stop for chains, there could be an accident, we have to eat, and we have to pee..." Brendan raises his hand to stop her. "So you're thinking four and a half hours then?" She rolls her eyes as she walks out of the room to make us bedtime tea.

- I'm so excited when I wake up that I roll over and wake Matthew up, too. "Come on, let's get in the shower," I whisper. It's still quiet and dark out. Matthew staggers into the bathroom with me before asking to look at my watch. "It's 4:30 a.m.! Not 5:30! Why did you wake me up?" Guiltily, I back out of the bathroom. "It *looked* like my watch said 5:30..." Back in bed, Matthew seethes. "How can you be 31 and not be able to tell time? How did you ever get out of 3rd grade?"

- I draw in breath to tell him, but he says sharply, "No talking! No talking! You go to sleep **now**!" as though he commands a Japanese prison camp. Not that I was offered any WC slippers. Now I can't sleep as I have several burning questions I want to ask:

  - Did all three of the Apollo 13 astronauts get out on the moon? If not, isn't that like taking someone to Disneyland and then leaving them in the car?
  - Does he think the Fossil people will let me exchange my watch for one with numbers? That should help a lot!
  - What should I wear tomorrow? Rather, later today.
  - Does he like pineapple? I can never remember...

- I take the first shower and, as I return, Matthew asks wryly, "Did you leave me a towel or do I just get a washcloth to dry off with?" He will never understand why women need two towels, although I have repeatedly explained the hair-drying process. We're all ready to go at 7:30, a vacation miracle. Dan has not even packed when Brendan calls him at 8 a.m., **and** he can't commit to getting chains, earning one strike from Leah and me. "He's already become a potential liability," I warn, and Leah nods vigorously, her blonde hair bouncing against her shoulders.

- The windows fog up and Matthew demands I clean them. "With what? My hands? The Sikhs didn't leave us paper towels," I retort. He suggests licking, but my prehensile giraffe tongue will not reach the back windows and he subsides.

- When Leah gets carsick, Brendan courteously offers her a hat to throw up in. This leads into a story of Brendan drinking a whole pitcher of margaritas, and then refilling the empty pitcher to the rim with his own vomit. Leah gets sicker than ever.

- We successfully pick up Dan, who's zipping his bag as we pull in. Dan towers over both Brendan and Matthew, but Brendan insists on his turn to drive, and Matthew calls shotgun. Dan crams himself in the back next to Leah and I. In the car, somehow we begin talking about pets. "My family had parakeets that liked anal sex, and if you looked at them afterward, their anuses would be pulsating," he describes graphically. Leah remembers she witnessed a duck rape in Australia. "Or maybe the ducks just like it rough," she concludes. Brendan's father kept a pack of large dogs, and Dan asks, "Was he going to race the Iditarod with them?" Dan's strike gets removed for the usage of the word "Iditarod."

- After breakfast at Cracker Barrel, where Dan describes Mr. Pibb as "Dr. Pepper—without the MD," we speculate about how the woman we saw there with two broken arms managed to break them both at the same time. As we begin ascending into the mountains, we notice everyone has pulled off to put on chains. It turns out we're not actually required to put on chains, as we discover when the chain guy allows us to pass. "Oh, look, we're safe, the random guy in the knit cap waved us by," Dan says skeptically, tousling his short brown hair after removing his own knit cap.

- Our cabin totally rocks! I originally volunteered to research and rent the cabin, but Brendan, disgusted with the affordable but utilitarian cabins I chose, opted to take over and book a swanky, expensive cabin instead. The owners of our swanky cabin are obsessed with wolves. Judging from the décor, no cabin is complete without a wolf end table, two wolf lamps, wolf pictures in every room (some of them rather menacing) and just for fun, deer nightlights looking skittishly at all the wolves.

- Leah begins a standard grocery list, but I insist, "No grocery list is complete without a bottle of vanilla vodka and diet Vanilla Coke to make Skinny Bitches with!" After writing my requests on the communal grocery list, I carefully pull out the sparkly drinking straw I pilfered from Jonathan's house. I predict it will get some hard use this trip.

- Dan reads from a guest journal on the wolf coffee table: "I lick this kaben. I took sky lessons. It is so cold here. My mother is a reptile, because she is cold blooded." He immediately begins planning the obscene entry he'll write later. He looks innocent enough, but I suspect he, Brendan and Evan are the sort of guys who egg each other on to folly. Brendan and Dan leave to pick up their friend Evan, who grudgingly leaves the casino where the bus dropped him from the Reno airport. Together, the three of them are a menace as they begin sharing stories from college back at the wolf cabin. Or kaben, if you prefer. Evan begins misquoting from *Silence of the Lambs*: "It makes me a drink, or it gets the hose again!" He's a very sarcastic Filipino in great shape from years in the Navy.

- Leah tries a sip of my drink out of the Official Drinking Straw, probably sending her into a sugar coma. "Wow, that's strong," she gasps, covering her mouth. Brendan tries it too, but sips directly from the glass, risking oral herpes from whoever was here before. "Mmmm..." Leah clearly is the impetus for their healthy eating habits. I'm on vacation, so whatever.

- After several drinks (except for Leah), we all start trickling into the hot tub on the deck. Matthew and Brendan find out they are twinsies—they have essentially the same swim trunks. No one knows what to say about that. "We'll just all pretend that didn't happen," Evan decides, and we all cheers on it.

- In the hot tub, I give Leah a friendly slap on the ass as she gets in, because really, why not? Also, I've had five drinks at this point. She looks startled but bemused. I cheers her with my Skinny Bitch, the straw sparkling in the moonlight. Evan, in either a drunken frenzy or an astonishing display of laziness, tries to open his beer by banging the cap against the wood railing, breaking off a chunk and losing us the security deposit. Brendan looks immediately pissed, but there's no point in ruining the evening over it. What's done is done. Evan also harasses Brendan to get out and turn the jets on. "It turns on the jets or it gets the hose again." Dan leans over to me. "He's super wasted." Yeah, you think?

- Brendan brought slippers outside with him, but they are not WC slippers, just regular ones. "Those will freeze to the deck," Leah predicts as she gets out and goes in the house. Out of stubbornness or just forgetfulness, Brendan leaves them there overnight where they do, in fact, freeze to the deck. I get out to lure Leah back, but get a nosebleed (from the Jacuzzi, altitude and liquor), and drip blood all over the bathroom. She flees up the stairs away from the bleeding girl who spanked her. I think I do an excellent job of cleaning up the blood, but I actually do about as well as Evan when he once threw up into some girl's couch cushions and then just left, telling no one. Once the bleeding stops, I refresh my drink and get back in the hot tub, turning on the jets again so Brendan won't have to. What a Good Samaritan I am!

- Getting up to go skiing turns out to be rough. Plus, we have to create a logistic chain rivaling the building of the railroads to get all people and equipment to the lodge (where you can't find parking). It's like one of those word problems where you have goats, wolves, and bales of hay on the bank of a river and you have to get them all across. I hate math. Dan and Evan are smart and get dropped off at the lodge, watching the gear. They are the tallest, so it will be easiest to spot them.

- We walk down to the lifts, and are 90% there when Brendan realizes he forgot his goggles. Leah says he should *sprint* back to get them. She is The Punisher! Matthew feels bad for Brendan to walk back alone, so we all guilt Leah into walking back with us. I remembered my goggles, but no one mentions I have them on my head upside-down. When I see the photos, I feel like such a dork.

- Matthew and I decide to start at the beginner runs, since we haven't skied in ten years. The poorly planned run bottlenecks immediately and a giant pile of fallen bodies block the path. I realize quickly I do not have the skill to maneuver around people who are as uncoordinated as I am, and unlike driving, I cannot just honk my horn and pass. I ram into a large Japanese man lying in the snow and fall onto the shoulder I hurt a week ago, when I fell down on slippery concrete, ironically, in front of my doctor's office. I can't push myself up. Matthew rescues me, and we do better on the intermediate runs since there are fewer obstacles. My skiing skills have not magically improved since Jonathan <u>didn't</u> teach me how to ski ten years ago. But on the positive side, he's not here to yell at me in disgust either.

- We take the lift to the run that will lead to our lunch meeting spot, which to me looks as steep as the Cliffs of Insanity from *The Princess Bride*. We arrive late for lunch; I am too afraid of falling and being stuck, like the little boy in *A Christmas Story*. My pride and shoulder are wounded. Matthew says my warranty expired the day we got married, and I should have had a sign reading "As Is" around my neck.

- In line to get food, Brendan asks, "Will you hold my beer? I want Dan and Evan to order me hot chocolate." I consider taking a sip, but decide no—he drank out of that unknown cup yesterday, and with all my other problems I can't afford to catch oral herpes. Dan and Evan apparently race the Iditarod and back to get hot chocolates. Lunch comes out to be $32 a couple for two veggie burgers, and suddenly everyone hurts right in the ass where the food people did not use lube. We all feel like Dan's parakeets, pulsating from our lunch ass rape.

- Leah, figuring she ought to do some community service, offers, "Melissa, I'll ski with you after lunch and give you some pointers." I gratefully accept after she assures me she doesn't want to ski with Brendan anymore anyway. Matthew decides to go with Brendan. "So you guys are swapping?" Dan inquires suggestively, glancing at Leah and I. Leah is no longer The Punisher—she's Annie Sullivan the Miracle Worker! I only fall twice, thanks to Leah's mad skills. Unfortunately, both falls are directly in front of the lift, where everyone points and laughs. Leah assures me she fell too, but I think she took a pity fall. She's a much better teacher than Jonathan was, or else I'm paying more attention to skiing and not having to listen to someone living a lie.

- Back at the kaben, we discuss dinner plans. Evan insists we go to a steakhouse, then a topless bar, instructing, "It does what it's told. It doesn't make excuses." Evan's wife probably appreciates Dan talking him down to Cecil's Steaks and Seafood. Evan makes a squeezed-in reservation at 8 p.m. Matthew gloats quietly in victory. I harped on him last night when I found out it took Evan eight months to propose and it took Matthew three years. He whispers, "See? He proposed quickly, but he didn't invite his wife on this trip and he wants to go to topless bars. You better zip it about the proposing. I am clearly the best husband here!"

- Dan and I run in to Raley's market to get money and beer for later. Meanwhile, in the car a debate rages over the best place to park. Leah, as the driver, should be allowed to choose, but Brendan wants to park at Raley's and walk to the restaurant in the cold. Brendan sits in the time-out seat in the back as we drive around and carps, "If we had parked at Raley's, we would be there by now," about a hundred times. My temper flares and I shout, "Brendan, you are so annoying right now, and if **I** were driving, I would have driven us straight into a flagpole at top speed to shut you up!" He's quiet for about two minutes. Leah has the patience of Job and doesn't seem irritated, even when he resumes bitching about how long it took to eventually park at Raley's, where we started from.

• Evan, who insisted upon going to a steak place, orders. "I think I'll have the Thai chicken pizza." Dan stares at him in disbelief. "You made us come to a steakhouse and you don't even get steak?" Leah realizes, "We could have ordered in pizza and beer from Shakey's, but instead we're spending tons of money at Cecil's." Evan admits, "I only wanted steak if we were going to a topless bar, but now I don't care." He doesn't seem to feel guilty; perhaps in the Navy they train guilt out of you. Our waitress, who looks "ridden hard and put away wet," as Matthew describes, tells us she'll "take our order and not put it in for a while, since the kitchen is really backed up." There's another waitress with a tattoo on the back of her neck, but she seems nicer than ours.

• Brendan, hungry, yells, "Hey, where's our high-strung spastic waitress?" From directly behind him she says, "Is everything OK?" Matthew proclaims Brendan the id of the group, and wants to use him to do things that Matthew himself would not, such as lifting the ponytail of the waitress with the neck tattoo to see conclusively what the design is. Dan shows good taste for not hitting on the neck tattoo waitress. "I agree," I say approvingly. "Her tattoo looks like a giant pot leaf." He turns his blue eyes on me in a grateful smile. I suspect Brendan and Evan harass him more than he'd like.

• Evan comes up with the slogan, "Brendan is your friendan to the endan," in case Brendan ever runs for office (in Munchkinland, where the slogan might work). Then, bored,

Evan and Brendan plot to set Dan up with a sexy librarian girl who looks like she might be waiting for someone. They enlist the help of our waitress, who now has red bloodshot eyes after her fix in the bathroom and a newly cheerful disposition. Her advice? "The one who waits masturbates." No one can believe she just said that, but she continues, encouraging Dan to drink more beer and have "liquid courage." We flee Cecil's, Brendan and Evan chiding Dan about not "taking the bull by the horns."

- Back in the hot tub, Evan waxes philosophical, and tells us, "You don't want to be the 'glass is half empty' guy or the 'glass is half full' guy. You want to be the 'Who drank my f-ing water?' guy." Leah whispers, "Or the 'You broke the hot tub and lost us our deposit' guy."

- I wake up Matthew at 4:30 a.m. again, because I'm awake and bored. He asks threateningly, "Do you want another nosebleed?" I look scornfully at him. He immediately backpedals, "Forget it; you would kill me in my sleep, like *The Burning Bed.*" Yes, at 4:30 a.m., when I seem to be all *sorts* of awake.

- In the real morning, Brendan asks, "Does anyone want raw milk?" then opens the cap and sniffs. "Ew, I mean yogurt." Dan, Evan and I plot how to get pancakes instead. Dan begins crooning, "It wants pancakes from Heidi's..." towards the kitchen. Brendan, heartless in his all-black cat burglar/ninja pajamas, won't take us for pancakes. "Brendan is your friendan to the endan," Evan cajoles, but to no avail.

- I pull out my drawer to get a sweater and the whole drawer face comes off. Damn those Swedes and their wooden pegs! I jam the drawer back together and hope it doesn't come out of our deposit, too. Over a not-as-good-as-pancakes breakfast, Evan and Dan reminisce about the snowboard park area. Evan calls one jump, "Highway to Paralysis" and Dan calls another "The I Don't Want to Be Able to Have Kids Anymore." Matthew and Brendan both laugh uncannily like Tom Hulse in *Amadeus* when they really get going. Twinsies again. Evan hugs us all around before he heads back home. Leah wonders, "What's taking Brendan and Dan so long to drop off Evan? The shuttle picks up right by Raley's." I psychically predict, "They went to get coffee—or to a topless bar." It's too bad there are no prizes for being right, as Brendan and Dan eventually return with Starbucks cups.

- While skiing that day, I don't fall at all, probably because every time I get to a lift I say, "Please, God, do not let me fall in front of all these hot Australian guys," and my prayers are answered.

- Being new to the etiquette of leaving people in your group behind if you can't find them, I insist Matthew go back to look for Dan, and he makes me swear I won't go wandering off and he'll be right back. Matthew accidentally takes the wrong run and skis down the whole mountain, arriving at the lodge where Dan is already waiting. Meanwhile, I wait by the lift for forty minutes in a blizzard that threatens to whisk me away to Oz, wondering when the medics will come tell me I'm a widow.

- A hot Australian snowboard instructor, on his third time passing me off the lift, asks, "You waitin' for someone?" What do I say? Maybe God answered my prayers too much? "My husband," I answer slowly, "but I might be a widow as we speak." He laughs and says, "Well, if you don't find him, we're having a party at my house tonight, just ask instructors for directions," and boards away.

- Maybe Matthew has broken everything and can only blink his eyes and no one understands him? A group of snowboarders come off the lift, and one calls to another, "Dude, the babe factor up here is seriously lacking!" As I can see his ass crack peeking out above the waistband of his dirty long johns, I might say the same to him. The lift operator comes out of her little booth. "Are you Matthew

Johnson's wife?" I nod, waiting for the bad news. "He's down at the lodge eating lunch and says to come down right away." I yell back, "Are you f-ing kidding me?" I have never skied faster or better. Maybe rage improves performance?

- Arriving at the lodge, I am interested to hear what happened. "Good story? Long story?" Everyone thinks I'm the idiot for essentially not having the common sense to come in out of the rain. We settle in to eat lunch, do a couple more runs and then come back to the lodge for hot chocolate. We meet Dan there, lusting after a Peruvian barista named Sofia. I forgot how hot ski resort employees are! I wonder if that bartender from my Mammoth trip has been promoted up here...

- Leah strolls in, remarking, "Despite the fact that the lifts are closing, Brendan went up to do one last run." He finally shows up, peeved that his last run wasn't good. Leah tries to appease him with hot chocolate. Brendan's ski gloves have plastic brass knuckles in them, which apparently come in handy with his bad temper. Brendan: "This guy cut in front of us, on purpose, and I was like, What the f-k, motherf-k-r, and he was like, Sorry, and I was like, F-k-g right, you should be, and I was ready to kick his ass..." Leah: "He cut because three kids in front of us didn't move so he thought we were waiting with them. It was no big deal." Dan volunteers: "I helped a little kid who fell...but not in a Michael Jackson sort of way." As we get ready for dinner, Matthew remarks, "I think Dan has a crush on you." I scoff. "Please! I'm old and headed for the glue factory! No one would bother having a crush on me." He says softly, "I do...even if you can't tell time and threaten to kill me." I kiss him appreciatively.

- We go to an Italian place for dinner. The calendar at the restaurant has wolves on it, and Dan tells me, "I suspect they stole it from our cabin. I mean, kaben." Matthew wants to repeat the cute décor and create a Geppetto's Village breakfast nook in our house, complete with piped-in yodeling. I don't know what we'll wear in our nook. Brendan says lederhosen cost like $1000 in Germany.

- Brendan blows his nose. "Is that a cloth napkin? You know other people will have to use that," I reprimand him. He replies cavalierly, "They wash them first. I'm too full to get up." He tells the waiter "This fettuccini Alfredo is so good, I want my children baptized in it!" We overtip for the good Alfredo sauce.

- After dinner, back at the kaben with drinks, we share relationship stories:

  - Leah starts her story, "This guy I was doing..." which seems totally out of character for her. It gets even better when it's revealed his goal in life was to become an elevator repairman, and he called everyone in the phone book with her name to find her. "Loser!" Brendan yells and kisses her.

  - Matthew somehow went from having relationships with pliant virgins to marrying the most demanding person he has ever met. He still seems stunned. "You just got lucky," I assure him, adjusting my feet in his lap.

  - Brendan still doesn't get why Leah was upset that, days before he moved up north to be with her, he ended a 6-month relationship she didn't know about. "Why shouldn't I date until I moved?" he demands.

  - I ask Leah how many boyfriends she had before she met Brendan. She replies, "None before, but a few after." OK...

- The conversation turns to ghosts. Brendan tells about a friend who saw a man walk to his bedroom closet, but when he opened the closet *there was no one there.* I will have to wear what I'm wearing for the rest of my life because I will never open a closet door again. My underwear is in a drawer, and no stories about drawer ghosts come out, so I'm safe there. He tells more ghost stories, this time about his own house. "Where did you live? The Haunted Mansion at Disneyland?" I ask uneasily.

- The next morning, Brendan declares, "If we get charged for opening beers on the deck railing, I'm charging Evan." By chance, he finds the deck piece and wedges it back in, saving Evan hundreds.

- Dan skirts the wolf end table but Brendan rolls it around and makes it follow him and talk to him. "Dan, stay here with me and put beers on my head...Daaaannn!" Dan cooperates only when Brendan agrees to take us for pancakes at Heidi's. "Brendan *is* our friendan to the endan."

- At Heidi's, we finally get pancakes. Matthew and Brendan find they are simpatico on possible boy baby names:
  - Magnus Johnson for us
  - Maximum Monahan for them
  - (Eye rolling from Leah and I. Dan just quietly eats his pancakes.)

- Sad rite of passage: Having to return extra beer to Raley's because in our heyday, there would have been no extra, and we would already be drinking road sodas.

- In the car, talk turns to our weddings. I describe the permanent scar I have from the corset I wore under my gown. Leah confesses she was boiling, so she didn't wear anything under her gown. Brendan tells us about the dance lessons he had to take and Leah mimics him, demonstrating his spastic hip movements and wild arm shaking for us. I don't remember him dancing badly in Mexico, but I was drunk...

- We drop Dan off in Sacramento, and then drop Brendan and Leah off. Brendan reminds us he will send us the giant bill for the very expensive cabin. "Did anyone see what Evan wrote in the journal before we left?" Brendan pauses, setting his bag on the ground. "It was something about the Jacuzzi...and foam," I answer. We both grin, remembering Mario and Vera in the Jacuzzi in Mexico. Oh wait, that was gross, not funny.

- Matthew and I drive back to Avis to drop off the car. Sikh #27 directs us to park the car. I smile and act friendly, remembering Brendan's advice to befriend them. Sikh #26 looks admiringly at the filthy Explorer, which miraculously did not catch fire all weekend. "Now **that's** the way to return a rental."

The Goat Tent

Yosemite, CA
October 2005

Having decided that we want to start a family next year, Matthew and I are panicking, making sure we do absolutely everything we want to do before we have kids. Everyone says you never have any money again, nor any time, so we want to pack in the experiences before we sit home every night, mourning our lost youth. Brendan and Leah invite us camping. Camping! A camping trip with friends! We must do this before we have kids, so off we go!

Suggested Soundtrack: "I Drove All Night"-Cyndi Lauper, Moulin Rouge soundtrack.

- While packing for our camping trip to Yosemite, our Russian stacking doll method of suitcase storage backfires as Matthew trips over the minefield of baggage and almost cracks his head open on the coffee table. He narrowly avoids a visit to the emergency room—and having to call the ranger station to tell Brendan and Leah we aren't coming.

- Finally, after getting gas and buying coffee from Trailer Trash Barbie at the Circle K, we get on the road at 10:45 p.m. and look at the directions. Matthew eyes the directions suspiciously and announces, "The 71 can't be a real freeway." When I claim, "It must be—otherwise it wouldn't be on Mapquest!" he Scrabble challenges with, "In thirty years of living in California, have you ever seen it or driven on it?" We elect to skirt the fake 71 pseudo-freeway.

- "Yuck, there's World Buffet. I hate that place," I grimace as we drive through Fullerton. We speculate on whether *any* cook can really be an expert in *every* world cuisine. "The Iron Chef..." Matthew begins, but I cut him off with,

"Doesn't World Buffet remind you of Henry VIII's Prime Rib 'n' Sushi in San Francisco?" It had the worst prime rib ever. The sushi bar area, separated from the prime rib area by a giant aquarium (so the fish could watch the sushi carnage and live in fear), smelled like Sea World at the end of the day.

- At 3 a.m., Matthew pulls over for gas at an AM/PM. Sitting in the doorway, with her arm draped loosely around a bin of Halloween candy, an old woman (who looks just like Winona Ryder at the end of *Edward Scissorhands*) adjusts her giant, scraggly white bun. Fragile and cobweb delicate, her bun is the most vital thing about her. "Is she a customer or a Halloween decoration?" Matthew murmurs as we choose our candy bars and head for the coffee maker. Back outside, Matthew hastily departs. "It smells like they hose down the asphalt with vomit instead of water," he remarks in disgust, closing the vents in the car. Thirteen miles into the 41 freeway, it abruptly ends and becomes Dead Man's Curve. The road starts veering all over, like the New Orleans DUI test area from years ago.

- At 4:44 a.m., we pass an exodus of vehicle caravans out of Yosemite. We get trapped behind a giant truck making an 80-point turn. Once the truck finishes and disappears, I cry, "God is punishing me! Why else would a steamroller be ahead of us?" The steamroller's maximum speed, according to our speedometer, is 3 miles an hour. I begin searching for some sort of cord with which to hang myself unless we pass him. "Stop thrashing around! I can't pass a steamroller!" Matthew warns me, fishing in the candy bag to try and appease me with Kit Kats. The steamroller finally pulls off with the rest of the tar gnomes who are "fixing" the road. Matthew reluctantly passes a gas station. "Even though we have half a tank, who knows where the next one will be?" Guess who's getting a gas can for Chanukah? "Just drive away from that light-up scarecrow...oh, wait, it's a creepy clown doll!" I keep watch behind us in case the clown from *It* shambles after us with its bloody toy pitchfork.

- Once we get into Yosemite at 5:45 a.m., we have no idea where to go—are we going to the valley? A village? I spot a pair of guys getting out of their car with ropes. "Do you know how to get to the campground?" I call out the window. They do! They direct us and wave us on our way. "I guess they got stuck behind the steamroller too," I tell Matthew as we drive away. "Why do you think so?" he asks curiously. "Well, they have those ropes out to hang themselves," I point out. Matthew sighs and says, "They're rock climbing." At 5:45 a.m.? I would hang myself on accident at that hour. Suddenly, I yell, "A bear!" and point...to a lifelike <u>sign</u> of a bear ripping open a car door where the people left raw meat on the seat or something. Matthew gives me a foul look; he nearly drove into a tree because of my shouting.

- The beacon of Brendan's personalized license plate lets us know we've found the campsite, and we pass out in the car at 7 a.m., throwing our sleeping bags over us. I awaken at 8 a.m. to see Leah in our rearview mirror, wondering who parked the dirty car and blocked them in. We get out and hug them, and spot coffee brewing on the table. "This is the noisiest campsite ever," Brendan informs us, handing us cups of coffee. I look around. There are already troops of children running and screaming at 8 a.m. Not a good sign. "I just hope the people who played Led Zeppelin until 11 p.m. last night check out soon," he adds, shoving his hands into the pockets of his gray jacket. It's also chilly.

- Matthew begins rummaging through the car and unpacking our stuff. "Where are my gloves? Where's my hat? Did we forget them?" he panics, blowing through his cupped palms to keep them warm. He realizes "we" have forgotten gloves for Matthew, a warm hat for Matthew, hiking socks for Matthew...seeing a trend here? "We" have also forgotten our folding chairs, which were buried under piles of things to give to Goodwill in my car trunk, and our long johns. "This happens when one person *assumes* the other person will pack for himself, but instead he's wandering around the kitchen eating peanut butter out of the jar, humming a little tune," I accuse Matthew. Leah gives me a sympathetic look. I know she has knuckled and just begun packing for both of them.

- The breakfast oatmeal, pre-flavored apples and cinnamon, turns out good. Leah was given strict instructions to avoid unflavored oatmeal at all costs, with Matthew threatening to boycott the trip. Leah tends to be the healthiest eater of our group, so she sometimes inflicts her Spartan food on the rest of us. However, also being the most organized, she ends up doing all the shopping so we get whatever she brings.

- Despite only having one hour of sleep, Matthew and I elect to rally and go on a hike to Vernal Falls. "On the map, the hike says Easy/Strenuous, and there are 'some stairs.'" Leah reads doubtfully, peering up at the Falls. In real life, the hike becomes Easy/Write Your Will, as there are over *six hundred* steep, slippery stone stairs. I begin making up lies to tell my physical therapist and chiropractor and muttering, "Ow!" under my breath as my knees begin clicking at each torturous step.

Our friends on the trail:

- An 80-year-old Asian woman cranking through the hike and making me feel like I should be shot and given to the glue factory. She carries a bamboo walking pole, not unlike the woman Matthew hoped would stick fight on the plane to Seattle.

- Loud Italian guy in a pink sweater with horrific teeth gaps. Loud Italian guy travels with Loud Friend and Loud Friend's girlfriend, who they insist should pose on a precariously placed rock, where she will fall off and be killed. I offer to take the photo of all three of them on Suicide Rock. At least she can take them with her when she flips off to her doom.

- New Parents, who are hiking with their baby. The husband carries her in a Snugli. Matthew: "That's great! When we have kids, I'll carry them in the backpack and we'll hike around with them!"

- Dolphin Shorts, a clearly European man wearing black socks, white tennis shoes and dolphin shorts. At 6'3" he's much too tall for his shorts. Leah remembers being in the library in college when a man in too-short shorts sat opposite her and she could see up them "and it was all maroon and repulsive..."

- Finally, we stagger to the top of the Stairway to Heaven, Matthew complaining that his leg hurts, and if we had a baby, "we'd have to leave it at the base of the stairs and hope no one took it." Matthew and Brendan wander over to the river and perch on rocks in the water. They both immediately strip off shoes and socks and dunk their feet in the freezing cold water. Brendan notes the scene looks like the picture on the Arrowhead water bottles, "except for the sweaty feet in the water." We eat a lovely picnic lunch Leah packed and linger about.

- Hiking back down the stairs is not, contrary to popular belief and Matthew's optimistic attitude, "much easier." I'm pretty sure they removed the easy hikes Courtney and I did in 8th grade. Were they really easy or do I just remember them differently? Brendan reminisces, "The stairs remind me of hiking in Nepal with this Sherpa guide who wore flip flops. He stayed right on the edge of the mountain while carrying all my stuff. But I couldn't even complain, because he had all my stuff and could have chucked it at any time." Leah asks, "Was that the guide who kept smiling at you and trying to hold your hand?" Aside, to us: "He loves telling THAT story!"

- Snack time back at the camp—Cadbury chocolate, cheese, soy pepperoni and wine! As poor Leah did all the grocery shopping for this trip, I emailed her long lists of products that are kosher, little pictures of the markings demonstrating a product was kosher, and ingredients that are definitely not kosher. She had to be Whole Foods sleuth, and has come up with fabulous treats! Even the oatmeal was good.

- Matthew finally gives up on inflating our air mattresses with the pump that plugs into the lighter, and just blows them up. Feeling lightheaded, he finally staggers off to take a nap in our tiny tent, the limited sleep catching up with him at last. "My cabin on my 8th grade trip looked like the Hilton compared to that tent," I remark, breaking off another piece of Cadbury. Brendan takes photos so I can send them to Courtney. She'll be horrified. I take some additional photos of the Yosemite Valley. It seems much bigger than I remember, too. Did I just forget everything in the trauma of seeing Jonathan and Courtney kiss back then?

- Leah takes charge and gets dinner ready for everyone. Compared to Leah, the rest of us seem both lazy and incompetent. Brendan builds the campfire and shoos Leah away after she tosses some wood onto it, complaining she has "no strategy, no placement, you're just tossing it in..." One of the neighbors wanders around for a while, yelling, "Elmo!" but it also sounds like it could be Elmer or Wilbur or something. I think he's lost his pet, but Matthew thinks he's playing a Sesame Street version of Marco Polo.

- "Brendan, are you competing in a marshmallow-eating contest by yourself?" Leah asks incredulously. "Just hook up a conveyer belt to your mouth." Brendan settles into his chair and lines up more marshmallows on his skewer.

- Matthew adjusts his hat flaps so he looks like he's auditioning for the Colonel Kurtz role in *Apocalypse Now*. It's not a warm hat, but he stubbornly insists, "Any hat will keep you warm; it's all a matter of heat not escaping through your head." Yeah, that's why we see so many people in winter wearing straw beach hats—because they're so warm and snuggly. I finally get tired and Matthew and I go off to our tent to bed.

- Matthew discovers he rested his feet too close to the fire and the glue from his boot sole has melted, leaving part of the sole flapping about. "These boots are basically ruined," he says mournfully, flapping the sole at me. "So now you have no gloves, no hat, no long underwear and no shoes," I retort, adding a sweatshirt and my own hat and gloves to my sleeping ensemble. I wish there were such things as nose muffs, and that I had one. I am so freezing cold.

- In the morning, Matthew makes his oatmeal all wet and creamy, like a bowl of throw-up. Mine has the consistency of library paste by comparison. We all drink Thin Mints, hot cocoa with peppermint schnapps in it, mmmmm. "Let's do an Easy hike to Mirror Lake this morning," I suggest, stretching my legs and feeling the muscles protest. Everyone nods agreement. It starts raining, so Brendan wanders off to put on his waterproof pants. Leah takes one look at him and insists, "Those are my pants. Take them off!" He retorts that they're *his* pants and starts trying to look at the tag in them, an impossible task. I burst out laughing. "You look like a dog chasing its own tail...except wearing skintight pants!" Leah posits that Irish people are very stubborn, or maybe just Brendan.

- The Mirror Lake trail, aka the Horse Poo Trail, leads us on a beautiful path. Brendan minces along in Leah's pants. She snickers every so often when he tries to remove the wedgie the pants naturally give him. I'm just happy I'm not having my period nor wearing glasses, both of which made my previous trip a nightmare. I'm also in love, which makes every trip so much better.

- We arrive at a completely dry sandy rocky area and pass it by, assuming the lake must be further down the trail. Five minutes, we return. "Mirror Lake should be right here," Leah proclaims, pointing to a spot on the map. "It's missing." We peer at the dry lake bed where all the water should be. I can't believe the whole lake dried up. Maybe they should release the Hetch Hetchy Dam and let the water flow free! Or maybe I still have no idea what a dam does or the repercussions of dismantling it. Another camper assures us, "It's October now. It'll come back in the spring."

- It begins to rain (again), which in the sunshine looks amazing, like little drops of sunlight falling onto us. The downside: my hair becomes an Afro. Matthew and I did remember our cheap plastic rain ponchos in our haphazard packing, but feel grungy compared to Brendan and Leah's nice rain jackets and matching waterproof pants, which in retrospect might have been a mistake.

- Another hiker is making sand angels, but she may live to regret it; her hair gets all sandy. Still, she seems exuberant and enjoys her sand angels.

- We all plunk down on the lake bed, in the sand, in the rain, and eat cheese sandwiches Leah made us for lunch. During lunch, Brendan tries to convince Leah to detour on their way home. "I want to see my family's old vacation house." Leah refutes this plan—she will not go hours out of her way to see a rickety old house. Brendan pleads, "It's only forty five minutes out of the way," but she clearly thinks he's underestimating. "Like it only took four hours to get to Tahoe?" Matthew would totally go with him, being a sentimental soul himself, but he's not invited.

- Back at camp, Leah and Brendan decide to go use the showers. Matthew and I opt for naptime since it's still Sabbath and we won't drive to the shower area with them. We feel grateful that we did **not** go after hearing their shower war stories. Brendan: "It was like taking a shower in prison!" (His was in a portable trailer, like the one I had for science in 10th grade). Leah describes the women's shower: "You had to get undressed in this freezing, dirty tile room, and I forgot my flip flops, and then you had to go down this long, cold hallway, naked, and the water was either scalding hot or ice cold, and there were clumps of hair all over the floor..." Again, like 8th grade.

- Brendan builds up the fire, shivering in the chilly night air, and we roast more marshmallows. Leah makes us dinner again, and I get a grilled cheese sandwich. "Whenever I make them, the bread turns black but the cheese stays solid. What am I doing wrong?" I ask Leah plaintively.

- I flirt with danger, putting the metal marshmallow fork directly in my mouth, until I get careless and accidentally cauterize the inside of my mouth and burn my lower lip. "I told you to take the marshmallow off the fork first," Matthew lectures, leaning over to see what happened. He brushes his boiling hot marshmallow into my nose, which finally warms it up. "Ouch!" I scream. Brendan almost cracks his head open on the bear locker, trying to see why I'm screaming, and then almost breaks both legs falling over the picnic bench. Leah looks horrified at his shin bruises. I try to back my folding chair away from the fire to tend my nose, but it folds up on itself and I flip over backwards in the chair and fall directly onto my back. Matthew jumps up, positive I have finally speared myself with the marshmallow fork, but I managed to avoid a puncture wound and have not even spilled my beer! The last five minutes have shaken us all, and I take a big swig of my beer and put down the marshmallow fork for good.

- Around the campfire, Brendan tells us about how he got roped into forced labor picking grapes at a winery in Taiwan, and how they offered him a tatami mat with candy and ants all over it. Matthew wonders about the advisability of making "friends" when you travel if they sell you into slavery. "Well, I was trying to hook up with her, and she invited me to her family's winery to pick grapes. I thought it would be all romantic. I definitely didn't know I was going to be a day laborer!" Brendan clarifies.

- As we head into our tent, Matthew remarks, "Does it smell a little goaty in here, or is it me?" I'm grateful I have tiny underdeveloped sinuses and can't smell our petting zoo tent. I bet there are wavy Pig Pen stink lines wafting from our sleeping bags. He opens the little side flap windows, but it's still pretty close quarters. Freezing cold that night, I put on <u>all</u> the clothes I brought on the trip to layer. Later, I learn I should have taken **off** all my clothes, which seems not only counter-intuitive but dangerous. What if a bear came and I had to run outside naked? This same logic forced me to stop tanning; I worried there would be an earthquake and I would either have to run outside naked or the tanning bed would get stuck and I would burn to a crisp. I roll over and notice Matthew's bare chest. He has thrown his fleecy pants out of his sleeping bag, where they lie in an enticing fleece puddle. Did I somehow get the heat-repellant sleeping bag? How does he not need a shirt?

- In the morning, we decide to pack up and do one last small hike before noon. Matthew tries to bar me from packing the leftover salami in our car, but I swear, "I'll eat it on the way home." Leah looks pleased to avoid driving home with the salami herself. "I don't want to take any of the food I don't want Brendan to eat," she confides, slipping me the extra chocolate and marshmallows as well.

- Matthew tries to jam my sleeping bag into a tiny sack, violating the laws of physics to do so. Eventually he gives up and throws it in the trunk, where he discovers the actual bag it came with.

- We eat breakfast, noting our new oatmeal packages have Dino "Facts" on them. "Realize when I say 'facts' here, I mean random lies people just made up and how do you get that job?" I announce. "You've been hostile about science ever since you and Courtney got kicked out of AP Bio in your freshman year," Matthew accuses me. "I just don't believe everything I read," I reply loftily, finishing the last of my Thin Mint.

- We park at Yosemite Village and begin our hike to Lower Yosemite Falls. Yosemite Falls are also missing. We see a tiny stream of water high in the distance. "October doesn't seem like the ideal time to come here," Leah points out. We're still glad to have done the hike, even if the Falls have gone the way of Mirror Lake.

- We try to eat lunch at Yosemite Lodge, aka The Overlook Hotel in *The Shining*. Matthew teases me, "Where are the little girls who 'want you to stay with them forever ever ever ever'?" I shudder and head back to the car. "The food here costs $32 a person for brunch, and all the food has ham and bacon," Leah wrinkles her nose and turns to leave. Back at Yosemite Village, everyone else gets fries and veggie burgers. I go to buy souvenirs instead, selecting a package of beer glasses and a coffee mug.

- Brendan becomes obsessed with having beer glasses, too. Leah tells him, "You have three hundred cups already cluttering up the garage. We have no need for beer glasses." In despair, he argues the importance of owning Yosemite glasses on the drive all the way out of the valley. Then he switches to wanting to see the old vacation house. Leah needs a limo divider she can put up, soundproofing her side of the car.

- Our car reeks of salami and goat the whole way home, like we bought a salami and goat air freshener on purpose. "I'm going to have to sell this car," Matthew yells over the wind rushing in from all the open windows. Despite the lingering stench, we have crossed one thing off our Things to Do Before Kids list: go camping together, and Matthew gets a twofer—he's never been to Yosemite.

- "So how was Yosemite?" Courtney asks me on the phone. I hear her daughter, Samantha, crying in the background. "We had a great time, but I missed you a lot," I tell her honestly. "I kept thinking about being there with you and Jonathan. Although at least now I could buy my own

Swatch, if I wanted to." In a surprising burst of candor, she confesses, "I don't know if I'd want to go back. I like the memories I have." I do too, but I also like to keep making more memories. "Give Samantha a kiss from Auntie Mel," I say, making kissing noises. "Thanks for calling. I miss you too," Courtney says softly before hanging up the phone.

The Gang's All Here

Huntington Beach, CA
February 2006

At Jeanine's wedding, I realize all my friends who are likely to get married are married. I'm married, for which I am forever thankful. Jeanine's wedding ensures that, at age 32, we can fulfill our high school fantasy of the Waterfront Hilton wedding!

- Matthew and I meet Jonathan, who, as Wedding Bitch, scurries to pick up food for Kelly and Jeanine. "When did Kelly fly in from New York? Does she like it there?" I ask as Matthew checks us in. "She *loves* it," he answers, looking nervously at his watch. "Meet me at the restaurant when you're done—I have to go right now!" he calls, rushing off before any frantic brides can call and complain.

- Meanwhile, Matthew tries to explain to the front desk person that we need to be able to stay in our room, charge food and drinks, and then check out, all without signing for anything, because it's the Sabbath. She seems suspicious but unwilling to be religiously discriminatory. We also get upgraded to a suite, while Kelly, Chad, Jonathan, and Jonathan's roommate Angie, get stuck in a tiny midget room as usual. Chad will flip out later, if he's sober enough to notice. We have the luck of the Irish when it comes to hotels! Or the Luck of the Jewish.

- Jonathan, released from bondage "for now", goes to lunch with us at what is essentially the Tiki Room from Disneyland, called Surfer Joe's or something. Matthew and I both have sinus infections and Matthew has bronchitis, but he announces, "Beer will mix fine with our cornucopia of medications." We all cheers each other. Jonathan looks really good, having lost a lot of weight on Weight Watchers. We throw our points to the wind and eat fries.

- Jonathan fills us in on the drama of the day: "So Jeanine and Kelly have been madwomen today. I keep telling myself it's the pregnancy hormones making Jeanine crazy." I swig my beer. "How does her dress look?" Matthew develops a glazed look, either from boredom or meds. "Her boobs look fantastic!" Jonathan enthuses, signaling the waitress for more beers. As we snack on fries, we watch them putting out the chairs for the ceremony overlooking the beach. "That chuppah is the size of a beach towel," I remark, wondering how everyone will fit under it, since Jeanine has the biggest wedding party of us all. Jonathan grumbles, "At least it doesn't weigh four hundred pounds and have to be hand-carried for forty five minutes, like at **your** wedding."

- He breaks off his grousing to answer Angie's call. "I'm five miles from our house after forty minutes on the road, which does not bode well for an on-time arrival! I'm definitely going to be late, and I have a bladder infection!" she cries, honking the horn. Jonathan agrees to leave a room key for her at the concierge desk, forgetting that he's drunk and will probably botch this mission. We pay and go get ready.

- I shove Matthew in the bathroom to get ready, where he realizes he has brought a cufflink shirt and no cufflinks, no belt, and barely remembered his shoes, which are dusty and need polish. "Great! I can't take my jacket off all night! Everyone will think I'm white trash," he moans bitterly, casting me evil glances. "Don't look at me! It's Yosemite all over again! I can't be responsible for all your clothes too!" I snatch my evening purse up and lead the way out, fuming that he hasn't even complimented me.

- Jonathan and Chad's room looks chaotic, mostly due to Chad steaming up the whole room with his lengthy shower. Chad cuts himself shaving and bleeds all over his shirt collar. "Jonathan! Turn up that radio! The guy I met last night is on and he's going to shout out to me!" he demands from the steamy bathroom. The interview ends without a mention of Chad. Jonathan gets forced back into bondage to get the blood out of Chad's shirt, while Chad flails around yelling, "I don't know what to do! How could Jerry forget about me like that?" Rifling through Chad's bag, Jonathan wants to know, "Why do you have dirty coffee filters in here?" Chad doesn't deign to respond, continuing to complain bitterly.

- Jonathan ingeniously gets the blood out with vodka. Ironically, Chad accuses him of "wasting vodka for no good reason." It's not our vodka, so we don't get involved. Jonathan makes potently strong Skinny Bitches out of the remaining vodka and diet vanilla Coke. These calm us. Matthew's eyes begin to glaze over again. Finally, Chad finishes making phone calls for work, all of which end with, "Call me back, but after 9 I'll be hammered." We hustle him out of the room to avoid being late. Outside by the wedding, we find ourselves directly *behind* Jeanine and the bridal party. We stealthily dodge behind planters so she won't see we're late, thanks to Jonathan, who read the invitation wrong. "I swear it said 6," he mutters, fishing for the card in his jacket. "Angie's going to miss the whole thing."

- The sun sets on the beach, and the photos will come out absolutely beautiful. Jonathan sits on the end to take pictures while the rest of us huddle by the heaters. "It's gorgeous, but I'm freezing," Chad whispers, pulling his jacket around himself. Matthew offers me his jacket, but then remembers he can't take it off or everyone will see he is white trash with no cufflinks. Chad whispers that the groomsmen all look like bouncers. They're all very big and burly, and Chad eyes them lasciviously. It's like the gay bar in Boston all over again.

- Jeanine looks fantastic, her pregnancy mostly visible in her breasts, which are **huge** and spill over the top of her strapless gown. I fear a wardrobe malfunction under the tiny chuppah. "I told you, her boobs are amazing," Jonathan says a little too loudly. Some family members turn around and he glares at them.

- Rabbi Barry wears what appears to be a graduation robe as he welcomes us. Friendly and jovial, and to his credit, not ogling Jeanine's breasts, he's a great officiant. He invites the mothers to light the unity candle with Jeanine and Allen, her fiancé. Matthew and I are puzzled, as Jewish weddings don't have unity candles. Jonathan advises us to "be breezy" and "just go with it", as we have limited experience at interfaith weddings. Rabbi Barry also has Jeanine and Allen put their hands over each others' hearts, but Allen cannot avoid Jeanine's cleavage, and appears to be feeling her up. Jonathan snaps a photo.

- We come to the part of the ceremony where Allen breaks the glass. Allen stamps on what appears to be a large martini glass, which could slice off his ankle. They kiss and are married! The baby will be born in wedlock, like Jeanine has always dreamed!

- At the cocktail hour, Jonathan plies us with liquor. "Drink as much as you can during the free-bar period," he advises us. No wonder our wedding bar bill was so high. We eat little bread/cream cheese things, which Jonathan hates and shouts loudly, "That tastes like my asshole!" More family members look around. "Here, eat a cheese pastry," Matthew encourages, shutting Jonathan up quickly before he offends anyone else. Rabbi Barry wanders by in his robe and cheerses us with his apple martini. "Mazal tov!" he shouts, clearly enjoying the free bar as well. He sidles up to Matthew. "Were you cold out there? My nipples were like rocks throughout the ceremony! Brrr!" He raises his glass to us again and meanders off. We are all speechless.

- Chad, a picky eater at best, pounces on the chicken skewers but has to spit out water chestnuts disguised as chicken bits. I accost every waiter passing by, greedily scooping up anything with cheese in it. Pastry flakes fall down my cleavage. Jonathan rushes up to us. "Let's go outside. I've offended Aunt Enid, and she's in the Jewish Mafia! She might put a hit on me!" We flank him and sidle outside. Chad lights a cigarette. "How can you smoke? You know how bad they are for you," I admonish him. He exhales, "I won't get cancer from smoking because I don't inhale." Jonathan and Matthew scoff at this logic, having quit smoking themselves. Kelly comes over after the pictures are taken. "You look good in your bridesmaid dress," Matthew offers sincerely. She laughs derisively. "No one looks good in a bridesmaid dress." She can just shut it, never having had to publicly appear at a wedding in a Renaissance tapestry, a yellow linebacker gown, pink taffeta ruffles, mint green water wings, or mauve handkerchief skirts, like I have.

• Angie finally arrives after a tussle with the concierge. Jonathan did leave a key with a note that read "Rock Star Angie!" However, since hotels no longer put room numbers on the keys, she had no idea which door it opened. Eventually someone illegally gave her the room number, and when she opened the door she thought wild boars had been set free in the room and destroyed it. "So what's new?" Kelly asks her, sipping the last of the free liquor. Angie tells us about making out with a sexy stranger on a plane to Brazil recently, but won't confirm Jonathan's report that she joined the mile high club. "That's over now, and I have a new guy, Tommy. Jonathan flirted with Tommy when I brought him to the house." Jonathan smirks. Chad tells Jonathan he's a "troll under a bridge" for flirting with Tommy. "Please. If Tommy's gay, we should find out early on," Jonathan answers dismissively. "Let's go see where we're sitting now that the bar's closed."

• Jonathan gets our table cards and we feel sorry for the two random people that have to be seated with us. At the reception, Chad complains, "Jonathan got me a vodka tonic, instead of vodka and Sierra Mist!" Matthew wrinkles his nose. "Who drinks vodka and Sierra Mist? That sounds **so** repulsive." Chad narrows his eyes. "Shut it, White Trash!" Jonathan snarls, "The drinks are $75 each—you'll drink it and like it." I swap Chad my screwdriver, which he spits out and declares, "The orange juice tastes rotten!" All the ketchup over the years has ruined his taste buds; the juice tastes fine. Matthew and Angie, the bar ambassadors, are sent to the bar to exchange the rotten orange juice and tonic drinks.

- The bridal party gets up to dance with each other, and then other people can cut in. Although Jonathan promised Kelly he would cut in and save her, he cavalierly sips his drink and says, "She'll be fine...I wish Courtney and Charlie and Glynis could have come. It would have been fun to see them." He's obviously had a few too many, because Jeanine was never all that close with Glynis or Courtney, and she hasn't spoken to Charlie since they broke up for good. But we would have had fun if they had been there, so we cheers them with the last of the pre-dinner drinks. Jeanine's dad, a former minister, offers a blessing and prayer before dinner. "I wonder what he thought of the Jewish wedding ceremony and Rabbi Barry," Angie muses.

- Two of the guests wander around offering people bites of their meat, which they are carrying around on forks like meat popsicles. Chad sprints away from the table when they serve lobster bisque. He only returns when he receives a salad and meat to chase the lobster smell away.

- I notice a magician at the table behind us. Oh, no, not a magician! I pray that he does not approach our table. Angie's the only person possibly nice enough to humor him. No, instead he heads for the front of the room, where he proceeds to "entertain" us with questionable humor and children's magic tricks for the next thirty minutes. Chad and Kelly go back to the room, retrieving flasks to cut the bar bill, leaving Matthew, Angie and I to pretend to be entertained by Gonzo the Magician.

- Jonathan dashes out of the room entirely. He hates magicians and clowns even more than I do. Jeanine joins him, washing her hands of any responsibility. "Please, would **I** hire a magician for my wedding?" She explains the magician was Allen's idea. She argued their wedding would seem like a 5-year-old's birthday party, but it's some family member and he's giving his performance as their wedding gift. I know what Roger would say: "Can I have the gift receipt for that?" Jonathan and Jeanine re-enter the room, where Jonathan bursts out laughing in the dead silence, then claps both his hands over his mouth like he's in a silent film, drawing even more attention to himself.

- Dancing begins, and Matthew gamely tries to dance. He almost passes out from depleted oxygen levels and sprawls drunkenly in a chair for the rest of the night. Jonathan unties his tie, preparatory to tying it around his head. The DJ plays Hava Nagilah, which no one knows how to do. Everyone just runs in a circle, until I yell, "Grapevine! Grapevine!" Jonathan snaps to immediately and together we get the group on track. Allen's groomsmen hoist him aloft in a chair. He looks wasted and a little like he might be sick. Jonathan tries to get Jeanine airborne, but she yells, "No, Jonathan! My baby!" We all start laughing. "Only Jeanine would scream that at her own wedding," Chad shouts approvingly. At this moment, I notice a chocolate fountain and rows of marshmallows and Rice Krispy treats to dunk in it. We've arrived in Candyland! Jonathan runs faster than he has since 8th grade to the fountain. Workers beat him back and yell, "It's not ready! No chocolate yet!"

- Kelly talks to some guy she's had a crush on for hours, ignoring his wife's irritated glances. She finally loses her temper on Jonathan, who hates being ignored and is literally plucking at her skirt. Kelly screams at him, "I am having a conversation! Get away!" Jonathan screams back, "Well, maybe you should have a conversation with someone who's not married! Get over him, Kelly!" Interrupting the debacle, Jeanine and Allen do the bouquet toss and the garter toss, whereupon Jonathan begins slamming his fist on the table and demanding, "What about the gays!! What is there for the gays here??" Chad, wiping his sweaty face off on the tablecloth, sighs resignedly, "He's going to get us gay bashed—again."

• A conga line appears from nowhere, and Jonathan and I try to get Jeanine in it, but I succeed only in stepping on her dress and ripping it, luckily not pulling it down and exposing her bosom. The conga line morphs into a limbo contest where I'm basically molesting Jeanine's dad, so I return to my table. Matthew can still barely breathe from his last foray onto the dance floor. "If you die tonight, how much life insurance do you have?" I ask pragmatically. He gives me a dirty look and continues wheezing and sipping his drink, ignoring the drama. Drunken recriminations are being shouted at our table—notably Kelly yelling, "At least I try to meet people, Jonathan! What about you?" Jonathan lashes back that he doesn't hit on married men, and Kelly storms off.

• Poor Angie, desperately trying to recover from a painful bladder infection walks Matthew and I back to the room (we can't use the electronic key during Sabbath). "Everyone else wants to stay till midnight, and then go to the party in Jeanine and Allen's suite. I want to sleep for the rest of my life. Good night."

• We find out the next day Jeanine put the kibosh on Allen's after-party, so Jonathan, Chad and Kelly walked two miles to Perq's, which used to be a scary biker bar when we lived here, but now has cover bands. Jonathan, who literally kicked off his shoes on the dance floor, narrowly missing clocking someone in the head, develops blisters from the walk and complains the whole time they drink at Perq's. Kelly gets them a cab back to the hotel, where they burst in screaming at 3 a.m., waking Angie from her sound and much-needed sleep. Room service cheeseburgers at 4 a.m. seem like a bargain when you're wasted and starving and

IHOP is closed. "I can't believe IHOP isn't 24 hour," Chad marvels, biting into his cheeseburger. "This isn't West Hollywood. IHOP isn't a meat market in Orange County," Jonathan reminds him.

- In the morning, I go out on our balcony to peer into their room and see if they're up. I'm greeted by a *completely naked man* opening the curtains in the room above them. He seems unaware the whole resort can see full frontal nudity. I see Kelly moving around in their room, so we get ready and go down there. There are room service trays with leftover food all over the room. Matthew makes barfing noises. "It stinks like rotten moldy cheese in here. How can you stand it?" Jonathan flips out when he discovers Chad has used Jonathan's luggage as a trash can for dirty napkins and empty cups. Angie just moans and rolls over.

- We decide to go back to Surfer Joe's for lunch and get seated outside immediately. Meanwhile, Kelly wants to know why Chad hasn't sold her car for her yet, and they get into an involved discussion, ending with Chad shouting, "Sell it yourself, then, if you think I'm slacking."

- Jonathan predicts he, Chad and Kelly will end up as old women in Palm Springs, bickering and wearing muumuus. We all agree this is their only possible future. This leads to recalling the Renaissance muumuu I wore to be in Glynis' wedding, while Chad contends having to wear tights to a wedding was much worse, driving us to drink at Taco Mac in Georgia at every opportunity. Reminiscing about Taco Mac leads Chad to remember the horrible bar in Buena Park that they walked to after my wedding, where Chad stole a woman's bicycle parked outside and rode it around inside the bar. We laugh till we can't breathe. So many funny stories.

- We run into Allen and Jeanine at lunch. Allen has the worst hangover ever. They're quietly eating, and then plan to go home and hang out the rest of the day, opening presents and reliving the night. Maybe they'll do a honeymoon sometime later. Matthew and I stay after everyone else has left. We had a great time drinking and partying with everyone last night...but we're just as happy to be sitting here together, talking and watching the sunset. We have a balance. It's a nice place to be. Especially when compared to being in the car with Kelly, Chad and Jonathan, bickering the whole way back to Los Angeles.

• I call Courtney later to fill her in on the night. "Even though it doesn't happen often, when we all get together, it's the best," I remind Courtney, who hasn't been back since my wedding. "I know. It's good to sometimes look back and see where we've been, but it's even better seeing where we are," she answers. Samantha laughs in the background, and she laughs too. "Have things turned out better than you thought they would?" she asks me seriously. "Oh yeah," I smile, ruffling Matthew's hair as he naps in my lap. "I thought I was doomed to a life of booty calls." She sighs. "Mel, there were days where we wouldn't even qualify for booty calls. In fourth grade, with those granny glasses, we could have joined a convent." She considers. "Except you, being Jewish."

• I reflect how lucky I am to have found Matthew. To have all my old friends. To have so many new friends. And hopefully next year...a new baby. "Good night, Court. Give Samantha and Damon my love."

• "Goodnight, Mel. Say hi to Matthew for us." I will. He's right here where he belongs.

Thank you is not nearly vast enough for what I want to say to:

Matthew, who is everything I ever wanted and much much more

My wonderful crazy family- Mom, Dad, Rachel and Co., you are pure comedy without even trying and I love and miss you all so much

My stateside family- Bob, Cheryl, Kris, Jeff, Noah and Shane- you guys are rocks for me. Thank you so much for welcoming me into the Johnson clan

Misha, Greg, Glynis, Chad, Jeanine, Kristy, Chase and Penelope- that reads like a program from junior year. I love that while we've all grown up a little at a time, we haven't left each other behind. Thank you so much for still being a part of my life 20 years later! If I get rich, I'll take you somewhere good.

Tim, Marika, Brendan, Leah, Sue, Chip, Renee, Ryan, Doug, Kathleen, Trey, Lauren, Brady, Allen, Chris and Lisa- thank you for all the good times you let me chronicle and many more to come!

David, Andy, Vinay, Michelle, Andrea, Meghan, Scott, Susie and everyone else who read these and said they were funny. I appreciate all your support and encouragement!

Made in the USA